CALIFORNIA TRAILS
CENTRAL MOUNTAINS REGION

Warning: While every effort has been made to make the 4WD trail descriptions in this book as accurate as possible, some discrepancies may exist between the text and the actual trail. Hazards may have changed since the research and publication of this edition. Adler Publishing Company, Inc., and the authors accept no responsibility for the safety of users of this guide. Individuals are liable for all costs incurred if rescue is necessary.

Printed in the United States of America

Cover photos
Clockwise from bottom left: Frazier Mountain Trail, Burro Schmidt Tunnel Trail, Pozo Road

Rear cover photos
From left: Potrero Seco Trail, Movie Flat Trail

CALIFORNIA TRAILS
CENTRAL MOUNTAINS REGION

PETER MASSEY
JEANNE WILSON
ANGELA TITUS

ADLER
PUBLISHING

Acknowledgements

Many people and organizations have made significant contributions to the research and production of this book.

Cover Design Concept: **Rudy Ramos**
Text Design and Maps: **Deborah Rust Design**
Layout: **Bob Schram**
Copyediting and Proofreading: **Sallie Greenwood, Robin Loveman**

We would also like to thank the staff at many offices of the National Forest Service who provided us with valuable assistance.

Publisher's Note: Every effort has been taken to ensure that the information in this book is accurate at press time. Please visit our website to advise us of any changes or corrections you find. We also welcome recommendations for new 4WD trails or other suggestions to improve the information in this book.

Adler Publishing Company, Inc.
1601 Pacific Coast Highway, Suite 290
Hermosa Beach, CA 90254
Phone: 800-660-5107
Fax: 310-698-0709
4WDbooks.com

ADLER
PUBLISHING

Contents

Before You Go

Why a 4WD Does It Better

The design and engineering of 4WD vehicles provide them with many advantages over normal cars when you head off the paved road:

■ improved distribution of power to all four wheels;

■ a transmission transfer case, which provides low-range gear selection for greater pulling power and for crawling over difficult terrain;

■ high ground clearance;

■ less overhang of the vehicle's body past the wheels, which provides better front- and rear-clearance when crossing gullies and ridges;

■ large-lug, wide-tread tires;

■ rugged construction (including underbody skid plates on many models).

If you plan to do off-highway touring, all of these considerations are important whether you are evaluating the capabilities of your current 4WD or are looking to buy one; each is considered in detail in this chapter.

To explore the most difficult trails described in this book, you will need a 4WD vehicle that is well rated in each of the above features. If you own a 2WD sport utility vehicle, a lighter car-type SUV, or a pickup truck, your ability to explore the more difficult trails will depend on conditions and your level of experience.

A word of caution: Whatever type of 4WD vehicle you drive, understand that it is not invincible or indestructible. Nor can it go everywhere. A 4WD has a much higher center of gravity and weighs more than a car, and so has its own consequent limitations.

Experience is the only way to learn what your vehicle can and cannot do. Therefore, if you are inexperienced, we strongly recommend that you start with trails that have lower difficulty ratings. As you develop an understanding of your vehicle and of your own taste for adventure, you can safely tackle the more challenging trails.

One way to beef up your knowledge quickly, while avoiding the costly and sometimes dangerous lessons learned from on-the-road mistakes, is to undertake a 4WD course taught by a professional. Look in the Yellow Pages for courses in your area.

Using This Book

Route Planning

The regional map on pages 24 and 25 provide a convenient overview of the trails in the Central Mountains Region of California. Each 4WD trail is shown, as are major highways and towns, to help you plan various routes by connecting a series of 4WD trails and paved roads.

As you plan your overall route, you will probably want to utilize as many 4WD trails as possible. However, check the difficulty rating and time required for each trail before finalizing your plans. You don't want to be stuck 50 miles from the highway—at sunset and without camping gear, since your trip was supposed to be over hours ago—when you discover that your vehicle can't handle a certain difficult passage.

Difficulty Ratings

We use a point system to rate the difficulty of each trail. Any such system is subjective, and your experience of the trails will vary depending on your skill and the road conditions at the time. Indeed, any amount of rain may make the trails much more difficult, if not completely impassable.

We have rated the 4WD trails on a scale of 1 to 10—1 being passable for a normal passenger vehicle in good conditions and 10 requiring a heavily modified vehicle and an experienced driver who expects to encounter vehicle damage. Because this book is designed for owners of unmodified 4WD vehicles—who we assume do not want to damage their vehicles—most of the trails are rated 5 or lower. A few trails are included that rate as high as 7, while those rated 8 to 10 are beyond the scope of this book.

This is not to say that the moderate-rated trails are easy. We strongly recommend that inexperienced drivers not tackle trails rated at 4 or higher until they have undertaken a number of the lower-rated ones, so that they can gauge their skill level and prepare for the difficulty of the higher-rated trails.

In assessing the trails, we have always assumed good road conditions (dry road surface, good visibility, and so on). The factors influencing our ratings are as follows:

■ obstacles such as rocks, mud, ruts, sand, slickrock, and stream crossings;

■ the stability of the road surface;

■ the width of the road and the vehicle clearance between trees or rocks;

■ the steepness of the road;

■ the margin for driver error (for example, a very high, open shelf road would be rated more difficult even if it was not very steep and had a stable surface).

The following is a guide to the ratings.

Rating 1: The trail is graded dirt but suitable for a normal passenger vehicle. It usually has gentle grades, is fairly wide, and has very shallow water crossings (if any).

Rating 2: High-clearance vehicles are preferred but not necessary. These trails are dirt roads, but they may have rocks, grades, water crossings, or ruts that make clearance a concern in a normal passenger vehicle. The trails are fairly wide, making passing possible at almost any point along the trail. Mud is not a concern under normal weather conditions.

Rating 3: High-clearance 4WDs are preferred, but any high-clearance vehicle is acceptable. Expect a rough road surface; mud and sand are possible but will be easily passable. You may encounter rocks up to 6 inches in diameter, a loose road surface, and shelf roads, though these will be wide enough for passing or will have adequate pull-offs.

Rating 4: High-clearance 4WDs are recommended, though most stock SUVs are acceptable. Expect a rough road surface with rocks larger than 6 inches, but there will be a reasonable driving line available. Patches of mud are possible but can be readily negotiated; sand may be deep and require lower tire pressures. There may be stream crossings up to 12 inches deep, substantial sections of single-lane shelf road, moderate grades, and sections of moderately loose road surface.

Rating 5: High-clearance 4WDs are required. These trails have either a rough, rutted surface, rocks up to 9 inches, mud and deep sand that may be impassable for inexperienced drivers, or stream crossings up to 18 inches deep. Certain sections may be steep enough to cause traction problems, and you may encounter very narrow shelf roads with steep drop-offs and tight clearance between rocks or trees.

Rating 6: These trails are for experienced four-wheel drivers only. They are potentially dangerous, with large rocks, ruts, or terraces that may need to be negotiated. They may also have stream crossings at least 18 inches deep, involve rapid currents, unstable stream bottoms, or difficult access; steep slopes, loose surfaces, and narrow clearances; or very narrow sections of shelf road with steep drop-offs and possibly challenging road surfaces.

Rating 7: Skilled, experienced four-wheel drivers only. These trails include very challenging sections with extremely steep grades, loose surfaces, large rocks, deep ruts, and/or tight clearances. Mud or sand may necessitate winching.

Rating 8 and above: Stock vehicles are likely to be damaged, and drivers may find the trail impassable. Highly skilled, experienced four-wheel drivers only.

Scenic Ratings

If rating the degree of difficulty is subjective, rating scenic beauty is guaranteed to lead to arguments. Southern California's Central Mountains contains a spectacular variety of scenery—from its Pacific Ocean panoramas to its desert wilderness. Despite the subjectivity of attempting a comparative rating of diverse scenery, we have tried to provide a guide to the relative scenic quality of the various trails. The ratings are based on a scale of 1 to 10, with 10 being the most attractive.

Remoteness Ratings

Many trails in the Central Mountains Region are in remote mountain or desert country; sometimes the trails are seldom traveled, and the likelihood is low that another vehicle will appear within a reasonable time to assist you if you get stuck or break down. We have included a ranking for remoteness of +0 through +2. Extreme summer temperatures can make a breakdown in the more remote areas a life-threatening experience. Prepare carefully before tackling the higher-rated, more remote trails (see Special Preparations for Remote Travel, page 11). For trails with a high remoteness rating, consider traveling with a second vehicle.

Estimated Driving Times

In calculating driving times, we have not allowed for stops. Your actual driving time may be considerably longer depending on the number and duration of the stops you make. Add more time if you prefer to drive more slowly than good conditions allow.

Current Road Information

All the 4WD trails described in this book may become impassable in poor weather conditions. Storms can alter roads, remove tracks, and create impassable washes. Most of the trails described, even easy 2WD trails, can quickly become impassable even to 4WD vehicles after only a small amount of rain. For each trail, we have provided a phone number for obtaining current information about conditions.

Abbreviations

The route directions for the 4WD trails use a series of abbreviations as follows:

SO	CONTINUE STRAIGHT ON
TL	TURN LEFT
TR	TURN RIGHT
BL	BEAR LEFT
BR	BEAR RIGHT
UT	U-TURN

Using Route Directions

For every trail, we describe and pinpoint (by odometer reading) nearly every significant feature along the route—such as intersections, streams, washes, gates, cattle guards, and so

on—and provide directions from these landmarks. Odometer readings will vary from vehicle to vehicle, so you should allow for slight variations. Be aware that trails can quickly change in the desert. A new trail may be cut around a washout, a faint trail can be graded by the county, or a well-used trail may fall into disuse. All these factors will affect the accuracy of the given directions.

If you diverge from the route, zero your trip meter upon your return and continue along the route, making the necessary adjustment to the point-to-point odometer readings. In the directions, we regularly reset the odometer readings—at significant landmarks or popular lookouts and spur trails—so that you won't have to recalculate for too long.

Most of the trails can be started from either end, and the route directions include both directions of travel; reverse directions are printed in blue below the main directions. When traveling in reverse, read from the bottom of the table and work up.

Route directions include cross-references whenever two 4WD trails included in this book connect; these cross-references allow for an easy change of route or destination.

Each trail includes periodic latitude and longitude readings to facilitate using a global positioning system (GPS) receiver. These readings may also assist you in finding your location on the maps. The GPS coordinates are given in the format dd°mm.mm'. To save time when loading coordinates into your GPS receiver, you may wish to include only one decimal place, since in Southern California, the first decimal place equals about 165 yards and the second only about 16 yards.

Map References

We recommend that you supplement the information in this book with more-detailed maps. For each trail, we list the sheet maps and road atlases that provide the best detail for the area. Typically, the following references are given:

■ Bureau of Land Management Maps
■ U.S. Forest Service Maps
■ *California Road & Recreation Atlas*, 2nd ed. (Medford, Oregon: Benchmark Maps, 2000)—Scale 1:300,000

■ *Southern & Central California Atlas & Gazetteer,* 5th ed. (Yarmouth, Maine: DeLorme Mapping, 2000)—Scale 1:150,000

■ Maptech-Terrain Navigator Topo Maps—Scale 1:100,000 and 1:24,000

■ *Trails Illustrated* Topo Maps; National Geographic Maps—Various scales, but all contain good detail

We recommend the *Trails Illustrated* series of maps as the best for navigating these trails. They are reliable, easy to read, and printed on nearly indestructible plastic paper. However, this series covers only a few of the 4WD trails described in this book.

The DeLorme Atlas the advantage of providing you with maps of the state at a reasonable price. Although its 4WD trail information doesn't go beyond what we provide, it is useful if you wish to explore the hundreds of side roads.

U.S. Forest Service maps lack the topographic detail of the other sheet maps and, in our experience, are occasionally out of date. They have the advantage of covering a broad area and are useful in identifying land use and travel restrictions. These maps are most useful for the longer trails.

In our opinion, the best single option by far is the Terrain Navigator series of maps published on CD-ROM by Maptech. These CD-ROMs contain an amazing level of detail because they include the entire set of 1,941 U.S. Geological Survey topographical maps of California at the 1:24,000 scale and all 71 maps at the 1:100,000 scale. These maps offer many advantages over normal maps:

■ GPS coordinates for any location can be found and loaded into your GPS receiver. Conversely, if you have your GPS coordinates, your location on the map can be pinpointed instantly.

■ Towns, rivers, passes, mountains, and many other sites are indexed by name so that they can be located quickly.

■ 4WD trails can be marked and profiled for elevation changes and distances from point to point.

■ Customized maps can be printed out.

Maptech uses 14 CD-ROMs to cover the entire state of California; they can be purchased individually or as part of a two-state package at a heavily discounted price. The CD-ROMs can be used with a laptop computer and a GPS receiver in your vehicle to monitor your location on the map and navigate directly from the display.

All these maps should be available through good map stores. The Maptech CD-ROMs are available directly from the company (800-627-7236, or on the internet at www.maptech.com).

Backcountry Driving Rules and Permits

Four-wheel driving involves special driving techniques and road rules. This section is an introduction for 4WD beginners.

4WD Road Rules

To help ensure that these trails remain open and available for all four-wheel drivers to enjoy, it is important to minimize your impact on the environment and not be a safety risk to yourself or anyone else. Remember that the 4WD clubs in California fight a constant battle with the government and various lobby groups to retain the access that currently exists.

The fundamental rule when traversing the 4WD trails described in this book is to use common sense. In addition, special road rules for 4WD trails apply:

■ Vehicles traveling uphill have the right of way.

■ If you are moving more slowly than the vehicle behind you, pull over to let the other vehicle by.

■ Park out of the way in a safe place. Blocking a track may restrict access for emergency vehicles as well as for other recreationalists. Set the parking brake—don't rely on leaving the transmission in park. Manual transmissions should be left in the lowest gear.

Tread Lightly!

Remember the rules of the Tread Lightly!® program:

- Be informed. Obtain maps, regulations, and other information from the forest service or from other public land agencies. Learn the rules and follow them.

- Resist the urge to pioneer a new road or trail or to cut across a switchback. Stay on constructed tracks and avoid running over young trees, shrubs, and grasses, damaging or killing them. Don't drive across alpine tundra; this fragile environment can take years to recover.

- Stay off soft, wet roads and 4WD trails readily torn up by vehicles. Repairing the damage is expensive, and quite often authorities find it easier to close the road rather than repair it.

- Travel around meadows, steep hillsides, stream banks, and lake shores that are easily scarred by churning wheels.

- Stay away from wild animals that are rearing young or suffering from a food shortage. Do not camp close to the water sources of domestic or wild animals.

- Obey gate closures and regulatory signs.

- Preserve America's heritage by not disturbing old mining camps, ghost towns, or other historical features. Leave historic sites, Native American rock art, ruins, and artifacts in place and untouched.

- Carry out all your trash, and even that of others.

- Stay out of designated wilderness areas. They are closed to all vehicles. It is your responsibility to know where the boundaries are.

- Get permission to cross private land. Leave livestock alone. Respect landowners' rights.

Report violations of these rules to help keep these 4WD trails open and to ensure that others will have the opportunity to visit these backcountry sites. Many groups are actively seeking to close these public lands to vehicles, thereby denying access to those who are unable, or perhaps merely unwilling, to hike long distances. This magnificent countryside is owned by, and should be available to, all Americans.

Special Preparations for Remote Travel

Due to the remoteness of some areas in California and the very high summer temperatures, you should take some special precautions to ensure that you don't end up in a life-threatening situation:

- When planning a trip into the desert, always inform someone as to where you are going, your route, and when you expect to return. Stick to your plan.

- Carry and drink at least one gallon of water per person per day of your trip. (Plastic gallon jugs are handy and portable.)

- Be sure your vehicle is in good condition with a sound battery, good hoses, spare tire, spare fan belts, necessary tools, and reserve gasoline and oil. Other spare parts and extra radiator water are also valuable. If traveling in pairs, share the common spares and carry a greater variety.

- Keep an eye on the sky. Flash floods can occur in a wash any time you see thunderheads—even when it's not raining a drop where you are.

- If you are caught in a dust storm while driving, get off the road and turn off your lights. Turn on the emergency flashers and back into the wind to reduce windshield pitting by sand particles.

- Test trails on foot before driving through washes and sandy areas. One minute of walking may save hours of hard work getting your vehicle unstuck.

- If your vehicle breaks down, stay near it. Your emergency supplies are there. Your car has many other items useful in an emergency. Raise your hood and trunk lid to denote "help needed." Remember, a vehicle can be seen for miles, but a person on foot is very difficult to spot from a distance.

- When you're not moving, use available shade or erect shade from tarps, blankets, or seat covers—anything to reduce the direct rays of the sun.

- Do not sit or lie directly on the ground. It may be 30 degrees hotter than the air.

- Leave a disabled vehicle only if you are positive of the route and the distance to help. Leave a note for rescuers that gives the time you left and the direction you are taking.

■ If you must walk, rest for at least 10 minutes out of each hour. If you are not normally physically active, rest up to 30 minutes out of each hour. Find shade, sit down, and prop up your feet. Adjust your shoes and socks, but do not remove your shoes—you may not be able to get them back on swollen feet.

■ If you have water, drink it. Do not ration it.

■ If water is limited, keep your mouth closed. Do not talk, eat, smoke, drink alcohol, or take salt.

■ Keep your clothing on despite the heat. It helps to keep your body temperature down and reduces your body's dehydration rate. Cover your head. If you don't have a hat, improvise a head covering.

■ If you are stalled or lost, set signal fires. Set smoky fires in the daytime and bright ones at night. Three fires in a triangle denote "help needed."

■ A roadway is a sign of civilization. If you find a road, stay on it.

■ When hiking in the desert, equip each person, especially children, with a police-type whistle. It makes a distinctive noise with little effort. Three blasts denote "help needed."

■ To avoid poisonous creatures, put your hands or feet only where your eyes can see. One insect to be aware of in Southern California is the Africanized honeybee. Though indistinguishable from its European counterpart, these bees are far more aggressive and can be a threat. They have been known to give chase of up to a mile and even wait for people who have escaped into the water to come up for air. The best thing to do if attacked is to cover your face and head with clothing and run to the nearest enclosed shelter. Keep an eye on your pet if you notice a number of bees in the area, as many have been killed by Africanized honeybees.

■ Avoid unnecessary contact with wildlife. Some mice in California carry the deadly hantavirus, a pulmonary syndrome fatal in 60 to 70 percent of human cases. Fortunately the disease is very rare—by February 2006, only 43 cases had been reported in California and 438 nation-wide—but caution is still advised. Other rodents may transmit bubonic plague, the same epidemic that killed one-third of Europe's population in the 1300s. Be especially wary near sick animals and keep pets, especially cats, away from wildlife and their fleas. Another creature to watch for is the western black-legged tick, the carrier of Lyme disease. Wearing clothing that covers legs and arms, tucking pants into boots, and using insect repellent are good ways to avoid fleas and ticks.

Obtaining Permits

Backcountry permits, which usually cost a fee, are required for certain activities on public lands in California, whether the area is a national park, state park, national monument, Indian reservation, or BLM land.

Restrictions may require a permit for all overnight stays, which can include backpacking and 4WD or bicycle camping. Permits may also be required for day use by vehicles, horses, hikers, or bikes in some areas.

When possible, we include information about fees and permit requirements and where permits may be obtained, but these regulations change constantly. If in doubt, check with the most likely governing agency.

Assessing Your Vehicle's Off-Road Ability

Many issues come into play when evaluating your 4WD vehicle, although most of the 4WDs on the market are suitable for even the roughest trails described in this book. Engine power will be adequate in even the least-powerful modern vehicle. However, some vehicles are less suited to off-highway driving than others, and some of the newest, carlike sport utility vehicles simply are not designed for off-highway touring. The following information should enable you to identify the good, the bad, and the ugly.

Differing 4WD Systems

All 4WD systems have one thing in common: The engine provides power to all four wheels rather than to only two, as is typical in most standard cars. However, there are a number of differences in the way power is applied to the wheels.

The other feature that distinguishes nearly all 4WDs from normal passenger vehicles is that the gearboxes have high and low ratios that effectively double the number of gears. The high range is comparable to the range on a passenger car. The low range provides lower speed and more power, which is useful when towing heavy loads, driving up steep hills, or crawling over rocks. When driving downhill, the 4WD's low range increases engine braking.

Various makes and models of SUVs offer different drive systems, but these differences center on two issues: the way power is applied to the other wheels if one or more wheels slip, and the ability to select between 2WD and 4WD.

Normal driving requires that all four wheels be able to turn at different speeds; this allows the vehicle to turn without scrubbing its tires. In a 2WD vehicle, the front wheels (or rear wheels in a front-wheel-drive vehicle) are not powered by the engine and thus are free to turn individually at any speed. The rear wheels, powered by the engine, are only able to turn at different speeds because of the differential, which applies power to the faster-turning wheel.

This standard method of applying traction has certain weaknesses. First, when power is applied to only one set of wheels, the other set cannot help the vehicle gain traction. Second, when one powered wheel loses traction, it spins, but the other powered wheel doesn't turn. This happens because the differential applies all the engine power to the faster-turning wheel and no power to the other wheels, which still have traction. All 4WD systems are designed to overcome these two weaknesses. However, different 4WDs address this common objective in different ways.

Full-Time 4WD. For a vehicle to remain in 4WD all the time without scrubbing the tires, all the wheels must be able to rotate at different speeds. A full-time 4WD system allows this to happen by using three differentials. One is located between the rear wheels, as in a normal passenger car, to allow the rear wheels to rotate at different speeds. The second is located between the front wheels in exactly the same way. The third differential is located between the front and rear wheels to allow different rotational speeds between the front and rear sets of wheels. In nearly all vehicles with full-time 4WD, the center differential operates only in high range. In low range, it is completely locked. This is not a disadvantage because when using low range the additional traction is normally desired and the deterioration of steering response will be less noticeable due to the vehicle traveling at a slower speed.

Part-Time 4WD. A part-time 4WD system does not have the center differential located between the front and rear wheels. Consequently, the front and rear drive shafts are both driven at the same speed and with the same power at all times when in 4WD.

This system provides improved traction because when one or both of the front or rear wheels slips, the engine continues to provide power to the other set. However, because such a system doesn't allow a difference in speed between the front and rear sets of wheels, the tires scrub when turning, placing additional strain on the whole drive system. Therefore, such a system can be used only in slippery conditions; otherwise, the ability to steer the vehicle will deteriorate and the tires will quickly wear out.

Some vehicles, such as Jeeps with Selectrac and Mitsubishi Monteros with Active Trac 4WD, offer both full-time and part-time 4WD in high range.

Manual Systems to Switch Between 2WD and 4WD. There are three manual systems for switching between 2WD and 4WD. The most basic requires stopping and getting out of the vehicle to lock the front hubs manually before selecting 4WD. The second requires you to stop, but you change to 4WD by merely throwing a lever inside the vehicle (the hubs lock automatically). The third allows shifting between 2WD and 4WD high range while the vehicle is moving. Any 4WD that does not offer the option of driving in 2WD must have a full-time 4WD system.

Automated Switching Between 2WD and 4WD. Advances in technology are leading to greater automation in the selection of two- or four-wheel drive. When operating in high range, these high-tech systems use sensors to monitor the rotation of each wheel. When any slippage is detected, the vehicle switches the proportion of power from the wheel(s) that is slipping to the wheels that retain grip. The proportion of power supplied to each wheel is therefore infinitely variable as opposed to the original systems where the vehicle was either in two-wheel drive or four-wheel drive.

In recent years, this process has been spurred on by many of the manufacturers of luxury vehicles entering the SUV market—Mercedes, BMW, Cadillac, Lincoln, and Lexus have joined Range Rover in this segment.

Manufacturers of these higher-priced vehicles have led the way in introducing sophisticated computer-controlled 4WD systems. Although each of the manufacturers has its own approach to this issue, all the systems automatically vary the allocation of power between the wheels within milliseconds of the sensors' detecting wheel slippage.

Limiting Wheel Slippage

All 4WDs employ various systems to limit wheel slippage and transfer power to the wheels that still have traction. These systems may completely lock the differentials or they may allow limited slippage before transferring power back to the wheels that retain traction.

Lockers completely eliminate the operation of one or more differentials. A locker on the center differential switches between full-time and part-time 4WD. Lockers on the front or rear differentials ensure that power remains equally applied to each set of wheels regardless of whether both have traction. Lockers may be controlled manually, by a switch or a lever in the vehicle, or they may be automatic.

The Toyota Land Cruiser offers the option of having manual lockers on all three differentials, while other brands such as the Mitsubishi Montero offer manual lockers on the center and rear differential. Manual lockers are the most controllable and effective devices for ensuring that power is provided to the wheels with traction. However, because they allow absolutely no slippage, they must be used only on slippery surfaces.

An alternative method for getting power to the wheels that have traction is to allow limited wheel slippage. Systems that work this way may be called limited-slip differentials, posi-traction systems, or in the center differential, viscous couplings. The advantage of these systems is that the limited difference they allow in rotational speed between wheels enables such systems to be used when driving on a dry surface. All full-time 4WD systems allow limited slippage in the center differential.

For off-highway use, a manually locking differential is the best of the above systems, but it is the most expensive. Limited-slip differentials are the cheapest but also the least satisfactory, as they require one wheel to be slipping at 2 to 3 mph before power is transferred to the other wheel. For the center differential, the best system combines a locking differential and, to enable full-time use, a viscous coupling.

Tires

The tires that came with your 4WD vehicle may be satisfactory, but many 4WDs are fitted with passenger-car tires. These are unlikely to be the best choice because they are less rugged and more likely to puncture on rocky trails. They are particularly prone to sidewall damage as well. Passenger vehicle tires also have a less aggressive tread pattern than specialized 4WD tires, and provide less traction in mud.

For information on purchasing tires better suited to off-highway conditions, see Special 4WD Equipment, page 20.

Clearance

Road clearances vary considerably among different 4WD vehicles—from less than 7 inches to more than 10 inches. Special vehicles may have far greater clearance. For instance, the Hummer has a 16-inch ground clearance. High ground clearance is particularly advantageous on the rockier or more rutted 4WD trails in this book.

When evaluating the ground clearance of your vehicle, you need to take into account the clearance of the bodywork between the wheels on each side of the vehicle. This is particularly relevant for crawling over larger rocks. Vehicles with sidesteps have significantly lower clearance than those without.

Another factor affecting clearance is the approach and departure angles of your vehicle—that is, the maximum angle the ground can slope without the front of the vehicle hitting the ridge on approach or the rear of the vehicle hitting on departure. Mounting a winch or tow hitch to your vehicle is likely to reduce your angle of approach or departure.

If you do a lot of driving on rocky trails, you will inevitably hit the bottom of the vehicle sooner or later. When this happens, you will be far less likely to damage vulnerable areas such as the oil pan and gas tank if your vehicle is fitted with skid plates. Most manufacturers offer skid plates as an option. They are worth every penny.

Maneuverability

When you tackle tight switchbacks, you will quickly appreciate that maneuverability is an important criterion when assessing 4WD vehicles. Where a full-size vehicle may be forced to go back and forth a number of times to get around a sharp turn, a small 4WD might go straight around. This is not only easier, it's safer.

If you have a full-size vehicle, all is not lost. We have traveled many of the trails in this book in a Suburban. That is not to say that some of these trails wouldn't have been easier to negotiate in a smaller vehicle! We have noted in the route descriptions if a trail is not suitable for larger vehicles.

In Summary

Using the criteria above, you can evaluate how well your 4WD will handle off-road touring, and if you haven't yet purchased your vehicle, you can use these criteria to help select one. Choosing the best 4WD system is, at least partly, subjective. It is also a matter of your budget. However, for the type of off-highway driving covered in this book, we make the following recommendations:

■ Select a 4WD system that offers low range and, at a minimum, has some form of limited slip differential on the rear axle.

■ Use light truck, all-terrain tires as the standard tires on your vehicle. For sand and slickrock, these will be the ideal choice. If conditions are likely to be muddy, or if traction will be improved by a tread pattern that will give more bite, consider an additional set of mud tires.

■ For maximum clearance, select a vehicle with 16-inch wheels or at least choose the tallest tires that your vehicle can accommodate. Note that if you install tires with a diameter greater than standard, the odometer will under calculate the distance you have traveled. Your engine braking and gear ratios will also be affected.

■ If you are going to try the rockier 4WD trails, don't install a sidestep or low-hanging front bar. If you have the option, have underbody skid plates mounted.

■ Remember that many of the obstacles you encounter on backcountry trails are more difficult to navigate in a full-size vehicle than in a compact 4WD.

Four-Wheel Driving Techniques

Safe four-wheel driving requires that you observe certain golden rules:

■ Size up the situation in advance.

■ Be careful and take your time.

■ Maintain smooth, steady power and momentum.

■ Engage 4WD and low-range gears before you get into a tight situation.

■ Steer toward high spots, trying to put the wheel over large rocks.

■ Straddle ruts.

■ Use gears and not just the brakes to hold the vehicle when driving downhill. On very steep slopes, chock the wheels if you park your vehicle.

■ Watch for logging and mining trucks and smaller recreational vehicles, such as all-terrain vehicles (ATVs).

■ Wear your seat belt and secure all luggage, especially heavy items such as tool boxes or coolers. Heavy items should be secured by ratchet tie-down straps rather than elastic-type straps, which are not strong enough to hold heavy items if the vehicle rolls.

California's 4WD trails have a number of common obstacles, and the following provides an introduction to the techniques required to surmount them.

Rocks. Tire selection is important in negotiating rocks. Select a multiple-ply, tough sidewall, light-truck tire with a large-lug tread.

As you approach a rocky stretch, get into 4WD low range to give yourself maximum slow-speed control. Speed is rarely necessary, because traction on a rocky surface is usually good. Plan ahead and select the line you wish to take. If a rock appears to be larger than the clearance of your vehicle, don't try to straddle it. Check to see that it is not higher than the frame of your vehicle once you get a wheel over it. Put a wheel up on the rock and slowly climb it, then gently drop over the other side using the brake to ensure a smooth landing. Bouncing the car over rocks increases the likelihood of damage, as the body's clearance is reduced by the suspension compressing. Running boards also significantly reduce your clearance in this respect. It is often helpful to use a "spotter" outside the vehicle to assist you with the best wheel placement.

Steep Uphill Grades. Consider walking the trail to ensure that the steep hill before you is passable, especially if it is clear that backtracking is going to be a problem.

Select 4WD low range to ensure that you have adequate power to pull up the hill. If the wheels begin to lose traction, turn the steering wheel gently from side to side to give the wheels a chance to regain traction.

If you lose momentum, but the car is not in danger of sliding, use the foot brake, switch off the ignition, leave the vehicle in gear (if manual transmission) or park (if automatic), engage the parking brake, and get out to examine the situation. See if you can remove any obstacles, and figure out the line you need to take. Reversing a couple of yards and starting again may allow you to get better traction and momentum.

If halfway up, you decide a stretch of road is impassably steep, back down the trail. Trying to turn the vehicle around on a steep hill is extremely dangerous; you will very likely cause it to roll over.

Steep Downhill Grades. Again, consider walking the trail to ensure that a steep downhill is passable, especially if it is clear that backtracking uphill is going to be a problem.

Select 4WD low range and use first gear to maximize braking assistance from the engine. If the surface is loose and you are losing traction, change up to second or third gear. Do not use the brakes if you can avoid it, but don't let the vehicle's speed get out of control. Feather (lightly pump) the brakes if you slip under braking. For vehicles fitted with an anti-lock braking system, apply even pressure if you start to slip; the ABS helps keep vehicles on line.

Travel very slowly over rock ledges or ruts. Attempt to tackle these diagonally, letting one wheel down at a time.

If the back of the vehicle begins to slide around, gently apply the throttle and correct the steering. If the rear of the vehicle starts to slide sideways, do not apply the brakes.

Sand. As with most off-highway situations, your tires are the key to your ability to cross sand. It is difficult to tell how well a particular tire will handle in sand just by looking at it, so be guided by the manufacturer and your dealer.

The key to driving in soft sand is floatation, which is achieved by a combination of low tire pressure and momentum. Before crossing a stretch of sand, reduce your tire pressure to between 15 and 20 pounds. If necessary, you can safely go to as low as 12 pounds. As you cross, maintain momentum so that your vehicle rides on the top of the soft sand without digging in or stalling. This may require plenty of engine power. Avoid using the brakes if possible; removing your foot from the accelerator alone is normally enough to slow or stop. Using the brakes digs the vehicle deep in the sand.

Pump the tires back up as soon as you are out of the sand to avoid damage to the tires and the rims. Pumping back up requires a high-quality air compressor. Even then, it is a slow process.

In the backcountry of Southern California, sandy conditions are commonplace. You will therefore find a good compressor most useful.

Slickrock. When you encounter slickrock, first assess the correct direction of the trail. It is easy to lose sight of the trail on slickrock, because there are seldom any developed edges. Often the way is marked with small cairns, which are simply rocks stacked high enough to make a landmark.

All-terrain tires with tighter tread are more suited to slickrock than the more open, luggier type tires. As with rocks, a multiple-ply sidewall is important. In dry conditions, slickrock offers pavement-type grip. In rain or snow, you will soon learn how it got its name. Even the best tires may not get an adequate grip. Walk steep sections first; if you are slipping on foot, chances are your vehicle will slip, too.

Slickrock is characterized by ledges and long sections of "pavement." Follow the guidelines for travel over rocks. Refrain from speeding over flat-looking sections, because you may hit an unexpected crevice or water pocket, and vehicles bend easier than slickrock! Turns and ledges can be tight, and vehicles with smaller overhangs and better maneuverability are at a distinct advantage—hence the popularity of the compacts in the slickrock mecca of Moab, Utah.

On the steepest sections, engage low range and pick a straight line up or down the slope. Do not attempt to traverse a steep slope sideways.

Mud. Muddy trails are easily damaged, so they should be avoided if possible. But if you must traverse a section of mud, your success will depend heavily on whether you have open-lugged mud tires or chains. Thick mud fills the tighter tread on normal tires, leaving the tire with no more grip than if it were bald. If the muddy stretch is only a few yards long, the momentum of your vehicle may allow you to get through regardless.

If the muddy track is very steep, uphill or downhill, or off camber, do not attempt it. Your vehicle is likely to skid in such conditions, and you may roll or slip off the edge of the road. Also, check to see that the mud has a reasonably firm base. Tackling deep mud is definitely not recommended unless you have a vehicle-mounted winch—and even then—be cautious, because the winch may not get you out. Finally, check to see that no ruts are too deep for the ground clearance of your vehicle.

When you decide you can get through and have selected the best route, use the following techniques to cross through the mud:

■ Avoid making detours off existing tracks to minimize environmental damage.

■ Select 4WD low range and a suitable gear; momentum is the key to success, so use a high enough gear to build up sufficient speed.

■ Avoid accelerating heavily, so as to minimize wheel spinning and to provide maximum traction.

■ Follow existing wheel ruts, unless they are too deep for the clearance of your vehicle.

■ To correct slides, turn the steering wheel in the direction that the rear wheels are skidding, but don't be too aggressive or you'll overcorrect and lose control again.

■ If the vehicle comes to a stop, don't continue to accelerate, as you will only spin your wheels and dig yourself into a rut. Try backing out and having another go.

■ Be prepared to turn back before reaching the point of no return.

Stream Crossings. By crossing a stream that is too deep, drivers risk far more than water flowing in and ruining the interior of their vehicles. Water sucked into the engine's air intake will seriously damage the engine. Likewise, water that seeps into the air vent on the transmission or differential will mix with the lubricant and may lead to serious problems in due course.

Even worse, if the water is deep or fast flowing, it could easily carry your vehicle downstream, endangering the lives of everyone in the vehicle.

Some 4WD manuals tell you what fording depth the vehicle can negotiate safely. If your vehicle's owner's manual does not include this information, your local dealer may be able to assist. If you don't know, then avoid crossing through water that is more than a foot or so deep.

The first rule for crossing a stream is to know what you are getting into. You need to ascertain how deep the water is, whether there are any large rocks or holes, if the bottom is solid enough to avoid bogging down the vehicle, and whether the entry and exit points are negotiable. This may take some time and involve getting wet, but you take a great risk by crossing a stream without first properly assessing the situation.

The secret to water crossings is to keep moving, but not too fast. If you go too fast, you may drown the electrics, causing the vehicle to stall midstream. In shallow water (where the surface of the water is below the bumper), your primary concern is to safely negotiate the bottom of the stream, to avoid any rock damage and to maintain momentum if there is a danger of getting stuck or of slipping on the exit.

In deeper water (between 18 and 30 inches), the objective is to create a small bow wave in front of the moving vehicle. This requires a speed that is approximately walking pace. The bow wave reduces the depth of the water around the engine compartment. If the water's surface reaches your tailpipe, select a gear that will maintain moderate engine revs to avoid water backing up into the exhaust; and do not change gears midstream.

Crossing water deeper than 25 to 30 inches requires more extensive preparation of the vehicle and should be attempted only by experienced drivers.

Snow. The trails in this book that receive heavy snowfall are closed in winter. Therefore, the snow conditions that you are most likely to encounter are an occasional snowdrift that has not yet melted or fresh snow from an unexpected storm. Getting through such conditions depends on the depth of the snow, its consistency, the stability of the underlying surface, and your vehicle.

If the snow is no deeper than about 9 inches and there is solid ground beneath it, crossing the snow should not be a problem. In deeper snow that seems solid enough to support your vehicle, be extremely cautious: If you break through a drift, you are likely to be stuck, and if conditions are bad, you may have a long wait.

The tires you use for off-highway driving, with a wide tread pattern, are probably suitable for these snow conditions. Nonetheless, it is wise to carry chains (preferably for all four wheels), and if you have a vehicle-mounted winch, even better.

Vehicle Recovery Methods

If you do enough four-wheel driving, you are sure to get stuck sooner or later. The following techniques will help you get back on the go. The most suitable method will depend on the equipment available and the situation you are in—whether you are stuck in sand, mud, or snow, or are high-centered or unable to negotiate a hill.

Towing. Use a nylon yank strap of the type discussed in the Special 4WD Equipment section, page 20. This type of strap will stretch 15 to 25 percent, and the elasticity will assist in extracting the vehicle.

Attach the strap only to a frame-mounted tow point. Ensure that the driver of the stuck vehicle is ready, take up all but about 6 feet of slack, then move the towing vehicle away at a moderate speed (in most circumstances this means using 4WD low range in second gear) so that the elasticity of the strap is employed in the way it is meant to be. Don't take off like a bat out of hell or you risk breaking the strap or damaging a vehicle.

Never join two yank straps together with a shackle. If one strap breaks, the shackle will become a lethal missile aimed at one of the vehicles (and anyone inside). For the same reason, never attach a yank strap to the tow ball on either vehicle.

Jacking. Jacking the vehicle allows you to

pack rocks, dirt, or logs under the wheel or to use your shovel to remove an obstacle. However, the standard vehicle jack is unlikely to be of as much assistance as a high-lift jack. We highly recommend purchasing a good high-lift jack as a basic accessory if you decide that you are going to do a lot of serious, off-highway four-wheel driving. Remember a high-lift jack is of limited use if your vehicle does not have an appropriate jacking point. Some brush bars have two built-in forward jacking points.

Tire Chains. Tire chains can be of assistance in both mud and snow. Cable-type chains provide much less grip than link-type chains. There are also dedicated mud chains with larger, heavier links than on normal snow chains. It is best to have chains fitted to all four wheels.

Once you are bogged down is not the best time to try to fit the chains; if at all possible, try to predict their need and have them on the tires before trouble arises. An easy way to affix chains is to place two small cubes of wood under the center of the stretched-out chain. When you drive your tires up on the blocks of wood, it is easier to stretch the chains over the tires because the pressure is off of them.

Winching. Most recreational four-wheel drivers do not have a winch. But if you get serious about four-wheel driving, this is probably the first major accessory you should consider buying.

Under normal circumstances, a winch would be warranted only for the more difficult 4WD trails in this book. Having a winch is certainly comforting when you see a difficult section of road ahead and have to decide whether to risk it or turn back. Also, major obstacles can appear when you least expect them, even on trails that are otherwise easy.

Owning a winch is not a panacea to all your recovery problems. Winching depends on the availability of a good anchor point, and electric winches may not work if they are submerged in a stream. Despite these constraints, no accessory is more useful than a high-quality, powerful winch when you get into a difficult situation.

If you acquire a winch, learn to use it properly; take the time to study your owner's manual. Incorrect operation can be extremely dangerous and may cause damage to the winch or to your anchor points, which are usually trees.

Navigation by the Global Positioning System (GPS)

Although this book is designed so that each trail can be navigated simply by following the detailed directions provided, nothing makes navigation easier than a GPS receiver.

The global positioning system (GPS) consists of a network of 24 satellites, nearly 13,000 miles in space, in six different orbital paths. The satellites are constantly moving at about 8,500 miles per hour and make two complete orbits around the earth every 24 hours.

Each satellite is constantly transmitting data, including its identification number, its operational health, and the date and time. It also transmits its location and the location of every other satellite in the network.

By comparing the time the signal was transmitted to the time it is received, a GPS receiver calculates how far away each satellite is. With a sufficient number of signals, the receiver can then triangulate its location. With three or more satellites, the receiver can determine latitude and longitude coordinates. With four or more, it can calculate elevation. By constantly making these calculations, it can determine speed and direction. To facilitate these calculations, the time data broadcast by GPS is accurate to within 40 billionths of a second.

The U.S. military uses the system to provide positions accurate to within half an inch. When the system was first established, civilian receivers were deliberately fed slightly erroneous information in order to effectively deny military applications to hostile countries or terrorists—a practice called selective availability (SA). However on May 1, 2000, in response to the growing importance of the system for civilian applications, the U.S. government stopped intentionally downgrading GPS data. The military gave its support to this change once new technology made it possible to selectively degrade the system within any defined geographical area on demand. This new feature of the system has made it safe to have higher-quality signals available for civilian use. Now, instead of the civilian-use signal having a margin of error between 20 and 70 yards, it is only about one-tenth of that.

A GPS receiver offers the four-wheeler numerous benefits:

■ You can track to any point for which you know the longitude and latitude coordinates with no chance of heading in the wrong direction or getting lost. Most receivers provide an extremely easy-to-understand graphic display to keep you on track.

■ It works in all weather conditions.

■ It automatically records your route for easy backtracking.

■ You can record and name any location, so that you can relocate it with ease. This may include your campsite, a fishing spot, or even a silver mine you discover!

■ It displays your position, enabling you to pinpoint your location on a map.

■ By interfacing the GPS receiver directly to a portable computer, you can monitor and record your location as you travel (using the appropriate map software) or print the route you took.

However, remember that GPS units can fail, batteries can go flat, and tree cover and tight canyons can block the signals. Never rely entirely on GPS for navigation. Always carry a compass for backup.

Special 4WD Equipment

Tires

When 4WD touring, you will likely encounter a variety of terrain: rocks, mud, talus, slickrock, sand, gravel, dirt, and bitumen. The immense array of tires on the market includes many specifically targeted at one or another of these types of terrain, as well as tires designed to adequately handle a range of terrain.

Every four-wheel driver seems to have a preference when it comes to tire selection, but most people undertaking the 4WD trails in this book will need tires that can handle all of the above types of terrain adequately.

The first requirement is to select rugged, light-truck tires rather than passenger-vehicle tires. Check the size data on the sidewall: it should have "LT" rather than "P" before the number. Among light-truck tires, you must choose between tires that are designated "all-terrain" and more-aggressive, wider-tread mud tires. Either type will be adequate, especially on rocks, gravel, talus, or dirt. Although mud tires have an advantage in muddy conditions and soft snow, all-terrain tires perform better on slickrock, in sand, and particularly on ice and paved roads.

When selecting tires, remember that they affect not just traction but also cornering ability, braking distances, fuel consumption, and noise levels. It pays to get good advice before making your decision.

Global Positioning System Receivers

GPS receivers have come down in price considerably in the past few years and are rapidly becoming indispensable navigational tools. Many higher-priced cars now offer integrated GPS receivers, and within the next few years, receivers will become available on most models.

Battery-powered, hand-held units that meet the needs of off-highway driving currently range from less than $100 to a little over $300 and continue to come down in price. Some high-end units feature maps that are incorporated in the display, either from a built-in database or from interchangeable memory cards. Currently, only a few of these maps include 4WD trails.

If you are considering purchasing a GPS unit, keep the following in mind:

■ Price. The very cheapest units are likely outdated and very limited in their display features. Expect to pay from $125 to $300.

■ The display. Compare the graphic display of one unit with another. Some are much easier to decipher or offer more alternative displays.

■ The controls. GPS receivers have many functions, and they need to have good, simple controls.

■ Vehicle mounting. To be useful, the unit needs to be placed where it can be read easily by both the driver and the navigator. Check that the unit can be conveniently located in your vehicle. Different units have different shapes and different mounting systems.

■ Map data. More and more units have map data built in. Some have the ability to download maps from a computer. Such maps are normally sold on a CD-ROM. GPS units have a finite storage capacity and having the ability to download maps covering a narrower geographical region means that the amount of data relating to that specific region can be greater.

■ The number of routes and the number of sites (or "waypoints") per route that can be stored in memory. For off-highway use, it is important to be able to store plenty of waypoints so that you do not have to load coordinates into the machine as frequently. Having plenty of memory also ensures that you can automatically store your present location without fear that the memory is full.

■ Waypoint storage. The better units store up to 500 waypoints and 20 reversible routes of up to 30 waypoints each. Also consider the number of characters a GPS receiver allows you to use to name waypoints. When you try to recall a waypoint, you may have difficulty recognizing names restricted to only a few characters.

■ Automatic route storing. Most units automatically store your route as you go along and enable you to display it in reverse to make backtracking easy.

After you have selected a unit, a number of optional extras are also worth considering:

■ A cigarette lighter electrical adapter. Despite GPS units becoming more power efficient, protracted in-vehicle use still makes this accessory a necessity.

■ A vehicle-mounted antenna, which will improve reception under difficult conditions. (The GPS unit can only "see" through the windows of your vehicle; it cannot monitor satellites through a metal roof.) Having a vehicle-mounted antenna also means that you do not have to consider reception when locating the receiver in your vehicle.

■ An in-car mounting system. If you are going to do a lot of touring using the GPS, consider attaching a bracket on the dash rather than relying on a Velcro mount.

■ A computer-link cable and digital maps. Data from your GPS receiver can be downloaded to your PC; maps and waypoints can be downloaded from your PC; or if you have a laptop computer, you can monitor your route as you go along, using one of a number of inexpensive map software products on the market.

Yank Straps

Yank straps are industrial-strength versions of the flimsy tow straps carried by the local discount store. They are 20 to 30 feet long and 2 to 3 inches wide, made of heavy nylon, rated to at least 20,000 pounds, and have looped ends.

Do not use tow straps with metal hooks in the ends (the hooks can become missiles in the event the strap breaks free). Likewise, never join two yank straps together using a shackle.

CB Radios

If you are stuck, injured, or just want to know the conditions up ahead, a citizen's band (CB) radio can be invaluable. CB radios are relatively inexpensive and do not require an Federal Communications Commission license. Their range is limited, especially in very hilly country, as their transmission patterns basically follow lines of sight. Range can be improved using single sideband (SSB) transmission, an option on more expensive units. Range is even better on vehicle-mounted units that have been professionally fitted to ensure that the antenna and cabling are matched appropriately.

Winches

There are three main options when it comes to winches: manual winches, removable electric winches, and vehicle-mounted electric winches.

If you have a full-size 4WD vehicle—

which can weigh in excess of 7,000 pounds when loaded—a manual winch is of limited use without a lot of effort and considerable time. However, a manual winch is a very handy and inexpensive accessory if you have a small 4WD. Typically, manual winches are rated to pull about 5,500 pounds.

An electric winch can be mounted to your vehicle's trailer hitch to enable it to be removed, relocated to the front of your vehicle (if you have a hitch installed), or moved to another vehicle. Although this is a very useful feature, a winch is heavy, so relocating one can be a two-person job. Consider that 5,000-pound-rated winches weigh only about 55 pounds, while 12,000-pound-rated models weigh around 140 pounds. Therefore, the larger models are best permanently front-mounted. Unfortunately, this position limits their ability to winch the vehicle backward.

When choosing among electric winches, be aware that they are rated for their maximum capacity on the first wind of the cable around the drum. As layers of cable wind onto the drum, they increase its diameter and thus decrease the maximum load the winch can handle. This decrease is significant: A winch rated to pull 8,000 pounds on a bare drum may only handle 6,500 pounds on the second layer, 5,750 pounds on the third layer, and 5,000 pounds on the fourth. Electric winches also draw a high level of current and may necessitate upgrading the battery in your 4WD or adding a second battery.

There is a wide range of mounting options—from a simple, body-mounted frame that holds the winch to heavy-duty winch bars that replace the original bumper and incorporate brush bars and mounts for auxiliary lights.

If you buy a winch, either electric or manual, you will also need quite a range of additional equipment so that you can operate it correctly:

- at least one choker chain with hooks on each end,
- winch extension straps or cables,
- shackles,
- a receiver shackle,
- a snatch block,
- a tree protector,
- gloves.

Grill/Brush Bars and Winch Bars

Brush bars protect the front of the vehicle from scratches and minor bumps; they also provide a solid mount for auxiliary lights and often high-lift jacking points. The level of protection they provide depends on how solid they are and whether they are securely mounted onto the frame of the vehicle. Lighter models attach in front of the standard bumper, but the more substantial units replace the bumper. Prices range from about $150 to $450.

Winch bars replace the bumper and usually integrate a solid brush bar with a heavy-duty winch mount. Some have the brush bar as an optional extra to the winch bar component. Manufacturers such as Warn, ARB, and TJM offer a wide range of integrated winch bars. These are significantly more expensive, starting at about $650.

Remember that installing heavy equipment on the front of the vehicle may necessitate increasing the front suspension rating to cope with the additional weight.

Portable Air Compressors

Most portable air compressors on the market are flimsy models that plug into the cigarette lighter and are sold at the local discount store. These are of very limited use for four-wheel driving. They are very slow to inflate the large tires of a 4WD vehicle; for instance, to reinflate from 15 to 35 pounds typically takes about 10 minutes for each tire. They are also unlikely to be rated for continuous use, which means that they will overheat and cut off before completing the job. If you're lucky, they will start up again when they have cooled down, but this means that you are unlikely to reinflate your tires in less than an hour.

The easiest way to identify a useful air compressor is by the price—good ones cost $200 or more. Many of the quality units feature a Thomas-brand pump and are built to last. Another good unit is sold by ARB. All these pumps draw between 15 and 20 amps and thus should not be plugged into the cigarette lighter socket but attached to the vehicle's battery with clips. The ARB unit can be permanently mounted under the hood. Quick-Air makes a range of units including a 10-amp compressor that can be plugged into the cigarette lighter socket and performs well.

Auxiliary Driving Lights

There is a vast array of auxiliary lights on the market today and selecting the best lights for your purpose can be a confusing process.

Auxiliary lights greatly improve visibility in adverse weather conditions. Driving lights provide a strong, moderately wide beam to supplement headlamp high beams, giving improved lighting in the distance and to the sides of the main beam. Fog lamps throw a wide-dispersion, flat beam; and spots provide a high-power, narrow beam to improve lighting range directly in front of the vehicle. Rear-mounted auxiliary lights provide greatly improved visibility for backing up.

For off-highway use, you will need quality lights with strong mounting brackets. Some high-powered off-highway lights are not approved by the Department of Transportation for use on public roads.

Roof Racks

Roof racks can be excellent for storing gear, as well as providing easy access for certain weatherproof items. However, they raise the center of gravity on the vehicle, which can substantially alter the rollover angle. A roof rack is best used for lightweight objects that are well-strapped down. Heavy recovery gear and other bulky items should be packed low in the vehicle's interior to lower the center of gravity and stabilize the vehicle.

A roof rack should allow for safe and secure packing of items and be sturdy enough to withstand knocks.

Packing Checklist

Before embarking on any 4WD adventure, whether a lazy Sunday drive on an easy trail or a challenging climb over rugged terrain, be prepared. The following checklist will help you gather the items you need.

Essential

- ❐ Rain gear
- ❐ Small shovel or multipurpose ax, pick, shovel, and sledgehammer
- ❐ Heavy-duty yank strap
- ❐ Spare tire that matches the other tires on the vehicle
- ❐ Working jack and base plate for soft ground
- ❐ Maps
- ❐ Emergency medical kit, including sun protection and insect repellent
- ❐ Bottled water
- ❐ Blankets or space blankets
- ❐ Parka, gloves, and boots
- ❐ Spare vehicle key
- ❐ Jumper leads
- ❐ Heavy-duty flashlight
- ❐ Multipurpose tool, such as a Leatherman
- ❐ Emergency food—high-energy bars or similar

Worth Considering

- ❐ Global Positioning System (GPS) receiver
- ❐ Cell phone
- ❐ A set of light-truck, off-highway tires and matching spare
- ❐ High-lift jack
- ❐ Additional tool kit
- ❐ CB radio
- ❐ Portable air compressor
- ❐ Tire gauge
- ❐ Tire-sealing kit
- ❐ Tire chains
- ❐ Handsaw
- ❐ Binoculars
- ❐ Firearms
- ❐ Whistle
- ❐ Flares
- ❐ Vehicle fire extinguisher
- ❐ Gasoline, engine oil, and other vehicle fluids
- ❐ Portable hand winch
- ❐ Electric cooler

If Your Credit Cards Aren't Maxed Out

- ❐ Electric, vehicle-mounted winch and associated recovery straps, shackles, and snatch blocks
- ❐ Auxiliary lights
- ❐ Locking differential(s)

Trails in the Central Mountains Region

Movie Flat Trail

STARTING POINT US 395 at the intersection with Moffat Ranch Road, 6 miles north of Lone Pine

FINISHING POINT US 395 at Lone Pine

TOTAL MILEAGE 11.7 miles, plus 1.5-mile spur to Old Abe Mine

UNPAVED MILEAGE 8.5 miles, 1.5-mile spur

DRIVING TIME 1 hour

ELEVATION RANGE 3,800–5,000 feet

USUALLY OPEN Year-round

BEST TIME TO TRAVEL Fall to spring in dry weather

DIFFICULTY RATING 1

SCENIC RATING 9

REMOTENESS RATING +0

Special Attractions

- Scenic drive through the picturesque Alabama Hills.
- Road passes the locations where many movies were filmed.
- Views of Mount Whitney and the Sierra Nevada.

History

The low granite Alabama Hills were formed around 100 million years ago, roughly the same time as the formation of the neighboring High Sierra. Their striking shapes and outcroppings are the result of weathering and erosion from summer heat and winter snows.

In the early 1860s, conflict between the native Paiute and settlers came to a head. The Paiute found the settlers' cattle to be a convenient food source during the harsh winter months. The settlers retaliated by attacking and killing several of the Indians, who reciprocated by killing several settlers. The Owens Valley Indian wars ended in the winter of 1862 in the Alabama Hills, when settlers destroyed the Paiute's food reserves. In the spring of 1863, the Paiute were relocated south to Fort Tejon in the Tehachapi Mountains.

Passing through the boulder outcrops on Movie Flat Trail evokes the feel of many Western movie settings

Headframe, engine, and dangerous, deep open mine shaft—not a movie set, but a reminder of busier times on the trail

The Alabama Hills were named after mines in the region that, in turn, were named by southern sympathizers after the Confederate battleship *Alabama,* which was a scourge to northern shipping during the Civil War. The Yankee battleship *Kearsarge* sank the *Alabama* in 1864 off the coast of Normandy. Local northern sympathizers made their feelings clear by naming a new mining settlement Kearsarge after their battleship. Kearsarge can be found east of Independence.

Today the Alabama Hills are most renowned for their continued use as the setting for a number of movies. Since the 1920s, hundreds of movies, TV series, and commercials have been filmed in the Alabama Hills, including *The Lone Ranger, Gunga Din, Tremors, Joshua Tree,* and a number of other Westerns. A plaque at the start of the dirt road commemorates the feature films. It was dedicated by Roy Rogers, who made his first starring feature here in 1938.

Located at the end of the trail, the town of Lone Pine was named after a solitary pine tree that grew beside the creek. In the 1870s, the town was a supply point for mining towns to the east such as Kearsarge, Cerro Gordo, and Darwin.

In 1969, the Bureau of Land Management created the Alabama Hills Recreation Area in an effort to preserve the natural and cultural significance of the hills for future generations.

Description

This extremely popular road runs through the Alabama Hills Recreation Area, along a low range of hills on the west side of the Owens Valley. The road's popularity stems from the rocky, boulder-strewn hillsides that have served as the setting for movies and TV series.

The trail is an easy graded road, suitable for a passenger car in dry weather. However, the large jumbled boulders of the Alabama Hills are anything but ordinary. The trail follows the graded Moffat Ranch Road before climbing to Movie Flat, where many Westerns have been filmed. A number of side trails invite further exploration and a closer look at the landscape. Most of these are more suitable for high-clearance vehicles. Typically, these side trails either loop back to join the main trail or dead-end after a short distance.

One 3-rated spur goes 1.5 miles past the remains of a mine, where there is a substantial loading hopper, headframe, adits, and shafts. It eventually ends at the Old Abe Mine, high above Owens Valley. Care should be taken in this region—the shafts are deep and unmarked. In addition, the final section of trail to the Old Abe Mine is narrow and very off-camber. In some places it will tilt vehicles toward the drop.

The main Movie Flat Trail joins Whitney Portal Road, which is the major paved road that offers hiking access to Mount Whitney, the highest point in the contiguous United States (14,496 feet). Hiking permits are required for day and overnight hikes; advance permit reservations are essential.

Current Road Information

BLM Bishop Field Office
351 Pacu Lane, Suite 100
Bishop, CA 93514
(760) 872-5000

Map References

BLM   Mt. Whitney
USFS   Inyo National Forest
USGS   1:24,000   Manzanar, Union Wash,
       Lone Pine
       1:100,000 Mt. Whitney
Maptech CD-ROM: Kings Canyon/
       Death Valley
Southern & Central California Atlas & Gazetteer, p. 27
California Road & Recreation Atlas, p. 87

Route Directions

▼ 0.0   From US 395, 6 miles north of Lone Pine, zero trip meter and turn southwest on paved Moffat Ranch Road at the sign. Cross over cattle guard; then track on left and track on right.

2.8 ▲   Trail ends at T-intersection with US 395. Turn right for Lone Pine; turn left for Independence.
           GPS: N36°41.02′ W118°06.35′

LONE PINE

The Inyo County town of Lone Pine was settled in the 1860s as a supply point for local miners. The first cabin was constructed in the area in 1862, and a post office was established in 1870. When mining slowed at Cerro Gordo and Darwin, Lone Pine evolved to cater to farmers and ranchers. An adobe wall behind the La Florista flower shop is a remnant of an 1860s building. Lone Pine got its name because of a pine tree that stood alone

Lone Pine

at the entrance to Lone Pine Canyon. Unfortunately, a flood destroyed the lonely tree was destroyed many years ago.

The beautiful Alabama Hills are near town and were discovered by Hollywood in the 1920s. Many Westerns and war movies have been set against this backdrop. TV shows, feature films, and commercials continue to be filmed in the area. It is not uncommon to see camera crews in Lone Pine capturing the ambience of a typical western town. An annual film festival pays homage to the movie industry's history in the area.

Still, Lone Pine's biggest attraction is the surrounding backcountry. Within two hours of the settlement one can visit the highest point in the continental United States, Mount Whitney (14,496 feet above sea level), or the lowest point, Badwater Basin (246 feet below sea level). A 100-mile bike race held every March requires participants to complete a two-day ride from Stovepipe Wells in Death Valley to the Mount Whitney trailhead. The overnight stop is in Lone Pine. The hundreds of dirt roads through Owens Valley make the area perfect for backcountry driving. Mountain bikers also enjoy the region, which is also well known for its trout fishing, some of the best in the eastern Sierra. Fishing season begins the first Saturday in March, earlier than in most areas.

Lone Pine has no municipal government, but the town's Chamber of Commerce organizes many community events and promotes the surrounding area. The chamber occupies a historic building in town—the old Lone Pine Hotel, completed in 1918. The hotel used to house movie stars when many Westerns were being filmed in the area. At the time of the last census, Lone Pine had a population of 2,257.

▼ 0.2 TL Cross over Los Angeles Aqueduct; then immediately turn left, remaining on Moffat Ranch Road, and cross cattle guard. Road is now graded dirt.

2.6 ▲ TR T-intersection. Cross cattle guard and turn right onto paved road. Immediately cross over Los Angeles Aqueduct.
GPS: N36°41.05' W118°06.58'

▼ 0.4 SO Track on right and track on left; then cross over Hogback Creek. Two tracks on left. Remain on main graded road.

2.4 ▲ SO Two tracks on right. Cross over Hogback Creek; then track on right and track on left.

▼ 1.1 SO Track on left.
1.7 ▲ SO Track on right.

▼ 2.2 SO Track on right crosses through Hogback Creek.
0.6 ▲ SO Track on left crosses through Hogback Creek.
GPS: N36°40.01' W118°08.22'

▼ 2.8 BL Bear left onto graded dirt road marked Moffat Ranch Road and zero trip meter.

Main graded road continues on right.
0.0 ▲ Continue to the north.
GPS: N36°39.49' W118°08.34'

▼ 0.0 Continue to the south.
0.9 ▲ SO Main graded dirt road enters on left. Remain on Moffat Ranch Road and zero trip meter.

▼ 0.4 SO Track on left; then track on right.
0.5 ▲ SO Track on left; then track on right.
GPS: N36°39.14' W118°08.23'

▼ 0.5 SO Track on right.
0.4 ▲ SO Track on left.

▼ 0.7 SO Track on right; then track on left.
0.2 ▲ SO Track on right; then track on left.

▼ 0.9 BR Small track on left up hill. Zero trip meter at second track on left, which runs along shallow valley and is the start of 3-rated spur to Old Abe Mine. Continue along main trail.

0.0 ▲ Continue to the northwest and pass second track on right, which climbs up hill.
GPS: N36°38.94' W118°07.82'

Green vegetation at a creek crossing stands out against the otherwise arid landscape along Movie Flat Trail

CENTRAL MOUNTAINS #1: MOVIE FLAT TRAIL

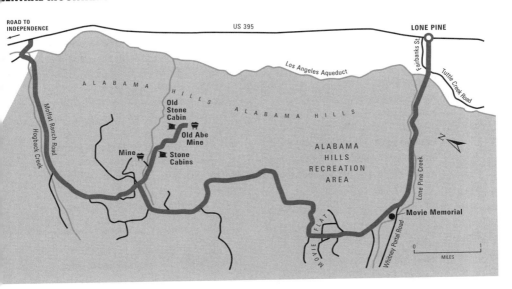

Spur to Old Abe Mine

▼ 0.0   Start of spur.

▼ 0.1   BL   Track on right.

▼ 0.2   SO   Track on left across wash goes to mine visible on hillside to the left.

▼ 0.6   SO   Track on right goes to old stone walls and remains of stone cabins alongside creek.
GPS: N36°38.94' W118°07.21'

▼ 1.3   SO   Remains of old stone cabin and mining shafts on left. From here, trail is extremely narrow.
GPS: N36°38.77' W118°06.76'

▼ 1.5   UT   Trail ends at Old Abe Mine. Room for only one vehicle to turn at end.
GPS: N36°38.67' W118°06.63'

Continuation of Main Trail

▼ 0.0   Continue to the southwest past small track on right.

5.4 ▲   BL   Small track on left; then track right, which runs along shallow valley and is start of 3-rated spur to Old Abe Mine. Zero trip meter and continue along main trail.

GPS: N36°38.94' W118°07.82'

▼ 0.2   SO   Track on left.

5.2 ▲   SO   Track on right.

▼ 0.4   TL   Join wide graded dirt road, which continues on right.

5.0 ▲   TR   Join graded dirt road, leaving main dirt road on left.
GPS: N36°38.66' W118°08.12'

▼ 0.5   SO   Cross through wash.

4.9 ▲   SO   Cross through wash.

▼ 0.7   SO   Track on left.

4.7 ▲   SO   Track on right.

▼ 1.1   SO   Track on right.

4.3 ▲   SO   Track on left.

▼ 1.9   SO   Track on right.

3.5 ▲   SO   Track on left.

▼ 2.5   SO   Cross through wash.

2.9 ▲   SO   Cross through wash.

▼ 2.6   SO   Track on left.

2.8 ▲   SO   Track on right.

▼ 3.0   SO   Track on left.

2.4 ▲   SO   Track on right.

▼ 3.2   SO   Two tracks on left and track on right.

2.2 ▲   SO   Two tracks on right and track on left.

▼ 3.6   SO   Track on right and track on left.

1.8 ▲   SO   Track on right and track on left.

▼ 3.9   BL   Track on left; then bear left, remaining

		on major graded dirt road. Graded dirt road also goes straight ahead.
1.5 ▲	BR	Bear right past graded dirt road on left; then track on right.

GPS: N36°36.66' W118°07.48'

▼ 4.0	SO	Track on left.
1.4 ▲	SO	Track on right.
▼ 4.1	SO	Track on left.
1.3 ▲	SO	Track on right.
▼ 4.2	SO	Track on right.
1.2 ▲	SO	Track on left.
▼ 4.3	SO	Track on right.
1.1 ▲	SO	Track on left.
▼ 4.4	SO	Two tracks on right and two tracks on left.
1.0 ▲	SO	Two tracks on right and two tracks on left.
▼ 4.5	SO	Track on left.
0.9 ▲	SO	Track on right.
▼ 4.6	SO	Track on right and track on left.
0.8 ▲	SO	Track on right and track on left.
▼ 4.8	SO	Two tracks on right. Road is now paved. Remain on major road. Many tracks on left and right.
0.6 ▲	SO	Two tracks on left. Road is now graded dirt.

GPS: N36°35.95' W118°07.01'

▼ 4.9	SO	Two tracks on left.
0.5 ▲	SO	Two tracks on right.
▼ 5.2	SO	Road is now graded dirt.
0.2 ▲	SO	Road is now paved. Remain on major road. Many tracks on left and right.
▼ 5.4	TL	T-intersection with paved Whitney Portal Road. Turn left toward Lone Pine. There is a movie memorial at the intersection. Zero trip meter.
0.0 ▲		Continue to the north.

GPS: N36°35.75' W118°06.48'

▼ 0.0		Continue to the east.
2.6 ▲	TR	Turn right onto graded dirt Movie Road at signpost. There is a movie memorial at the intersection. Zero trip meter.
▼ 2.0	SO	Leaving Alabama Hills Recreation Area; then cross over Los Angeles Aqueduct.
0.6 ▲	SO	Cross over Los Angeles Aqueduct; then enter Alabama Hills Recreation Area.
▼ 2.1	SO	Tuttle Creek Road on right and Fairbanks Street on left. Entering edge of Lone Pine. Remain on major paved road.
0.5 ▲	SO	Leaving Lone Pine. Tuttle Creek Road on left and Fairbanks Street on right. Remain on major paved road.
▼ 2.6		Trail ends in Lone Pine at stoplight on US 395.
0.0 ▲		From Lone Pine on US 395, zero trip meter and turn southwest on paved Whitney Portal Road at stoplight. Remain on paved road, ignoring turns on left and right.

GPS: N36°36.30' W118°03.71'

CENTRAL MOUNTAINS #2

Delilah Fire Lookout Trail

STARTING POINT Kings Canyon Road (California 180), 4.8 miles west of Sequoia Lake settlement
FINISHING POINT Delilah Fire Lookout
TOTAL MILEAGE 7.5 miles (one-way)
UNPAVED MILEAGE: 6 miles
DRIVING TIME 45 minutes (one-way)
ELEVATION RANGE 4,300–5,200 feet
USUALLY OPEN Year-round
BEST TIME TO TRAVEL Year-round
DIFFICULTY RATING 2
SCENIC RATING 8
REMOTENESS RATING +0

Special Attractions
- Delilah Fire Lookout.
- Panoramic views from a narrow ridge trail.

Description
This short trail leads up a well-formed road to the Delilah Fire Lookout. From the lookout there are panoramic views over the Kings River Valley to Patterson Bluffs and over the forest toward Fresno. In dry weather, this trail is generally suitable for a high-clearance 2WD vehicle.

One of the highlights is the section of trail that runs through oaks and manzanitas along the narrow Pine Ridge, offering spectacular views to the east and west. The early stages of the trail pass through private property. Re-

Delilah Fire Lookout Trail runs along the narrow Pine Ridge with views to the west and east

main on the main trail and take it slow to keep dust to a minimum. The trail follows a small, formed road past some cabins.

The trail ends at the Delilah Lookout Tower at 5,176 feet. The steel and timber tower is not gated at the bottom and it is normally possible to climb up most of the way. The views are well worth the effort.

Current Road Information

Sequoia National Forest
Hume Lake Ranger District
35860 East Kings Canyon Road
Dunlap, CA 93621
(559) 338-2251

Map References

BLM   Fresno
USFS Sequoia National Forest
USGS 1:24,000 Miramonte, Verplank
       Ridge
       1:100,000 Fresno
Maptech CD-ROM: Central Coast/Fresno
Southern & Central California Atlas & Gazetteer, p. 25
California Road & Recreation Atlas, p. 78

Route Directions

▼ 0.0   From Kings Canyon Road (California 180), 4.8 miles west of Sequoia Lake, zero trip meter and turn west on small paved road, following sign to Delilah Lookout. Remain on main paved road.
GPS: N36°44.86' W119°03.04'

▼ 0.2   SO McKenzie Helipad on left.
▼ 1.0   BL Paved road on right is 13S97 to Millwood.
GPS: N36°45.27' W119°03.28'

▼ 1.2   SO Cattle guard.
▼ 1.5   BR Bear right onto graded dirt road, following sign for Delilah Lookout and Kings River.
GPS: N36°45.55' W119°03.50'

▼ 1.8   BL Track on right through gate.
▼ 2.1   SO Track on right is private.
▼ 2.6   SO Two tracks on right.
▼ 2.7   BL Track on right is Central Mountains #3: Davis Flat Trail (12S01). Also small track on right. Zero trip meter.

Delilah Fire Lookout is still used and has excellent 360-degree views

CENTRAL MOUNTAINS #2: DELILAH FIRE LOOKOUT TRAIL

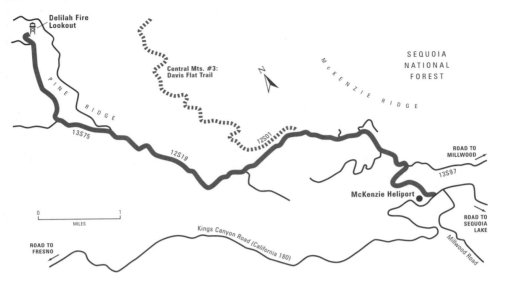

GPS: N36°46.09' W119°04.39'

▼ 0.0   Continue to the northwest.

▼ 0.8   BR   Track on right; then cattle guard.
              Entering private property; then track
              on left. Remain on main graded road
              through private property for next mile.
              GPS: N36°45.94' W119°05.25'

▼ 1.9   SO   Cattle guard; then closure gate. Exiting
              private property.
              GPS: N36°46.42' W119°06.05'

▼ 2.8   BL   Bear left onto 13S75. Trail starts to
              climb toward lookout.
              GPS: N36°46.93' W119°06.58'

▼ 3.5   SO   Track on left.

▼ 4.6   BR   Continue to Delilah Fire Lookout. Road
              is now marked 13S75A. Small track
              on left.
              GPS: N36°48.12' W119°07.00'

▼ 4.8   Trail ends at the Delilah Fire Lookout.
         GPS: N36°48.27' W119°06.99'

The still-active Delilah fire lookout on Pine Ridge

Davis Flat Trail

STARTING POINT Trimmer Springs Road, 1.6
   miles east of Kirch Flat USFS Campground
FINISHING POINT Central Mountains #2:
   Delilah Fire Lookout Trail, 2.7 miles
   north of California 180
TOTAL MILEAGE 16.1 miles
UNPAVED MILEAGE: 16.1 miles
DRIVING TIME 1.5 hours
ELEVATION RANGE 1,000–4,400 feet
USUALLY OPEN April to December
BEST TIME TO TRAVEL April to December
DIFFICULTY RATING 2
SCENIC RATING 9
REMOTENESS RATING +1

Special Attractions

- Boating and fishing at Pine Flat Reservoir.
- Excellent choice of campsites along the Kings River.
- Whitewater rafting and kayaking on the Kings River.
- Long, winding trail through Sequoia National Forest.

History

Mill Flat Camp was a junction point on a remarkable flume that transported lumber from McKenzie Ridge down to Sanger. This feat of engineering belonged to the Sanger Lumber Company, which constructed a sawmill at what is now the site of Millwood (located east of the southern end of this trail). Millwood was the first major logging camp in the region, and it expanded to include houses and a variety of businesses, including a red light district a mile down the road from the main camp. Millwood became a popular summer getaway spot for people from the hotter Central Valley. The accommodation houses were upgraded to cater to the tastes of these vacationers. A stagecoach would leave from Sanger shortly after dawn and travel east to Dunlap for a change of horses before making the long, steep climb to Millwood.

The lumber industry was growing hand in hand with the gold mining industry in Northern California and investors were eager to claim the abundant timber. Loggers cut down pines, firs, and giant sequoias. Narrow gauge railroads and beasts of burden delivered the fallen giants to the blades of the sawmill.

Sequoia Lake was established above the mill in 1889 with the construction of a dam. Lake water provided the flume with the momentum to float rough-sawn lumber down to the Kings River. The 62-mile-long flume followed alongside Mill Flat Creek for much of the descent and was reported to be the longest of its kind in the world. The flume joined the Kings River at Mill Flat. From there, the lumber continued its journey downriver to the Sanger Company's finishing mill in the flat San Joaquin Valley.

The lumber company expanded, developing additional sawmills, settlements, and reservoirs. Converse Basin, near Long Meadow, was one region that supplied the mills with more timber. In the early 1900s, the Hume Bennett Lumber Company created Hume Lake (located to the east of this trail) in only four months, using reinforced concrete for the dam. This lake was large enough to act as a storage pond for the massive logs, something that was not practical at the Millwood site.

The flume was extended and more railroads were built to bring in timber from farther afield. However, dwindling returns and increased expenses meant that by 1910, the big timber-cutting days were on the wane. Fires, World War I, and labor problems hastened the industry's decline. Some sections of the flume were burned down; other sections were dismantled. When the sawmill was no longer viable, it closed. With its closure, Millwood dwindled and eventually disappeared.

Crabtree, another site found along this trail, got its name from John F. Crabtree. He settled here in 1911, working a total of 157 acres around the junction of Davis and Mill Flat Creeks.

The Kings River has a simple Spanish explanation behind its name. The river was called Río de los Santos Reyes (Spanish for Holy Kings River). It was named after the

Bridge over the wide Kings River at the northern end of Davis Flat Trail

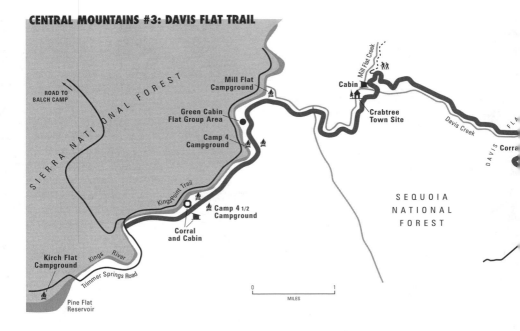

three kings from Christian religion who brought gifts to the newborn Jesus.

Description

This long trail begins near Pine Flat Reservoir, a beautiful convoluted reservoir with many arms. The man-made lake is set in a deep valley along the boundary between the Sierra and Sequoia National Forests. The reservoir has a marina, which is popular for water skiing, boating, and fishing. There are semi-developed campgrounds along the lakeshore that are open for part of the year. The river is also popular with whitewater rafters and kayakers who ride the rough stretch of water from Garnet Dike to Kirch Flat. The rapids are rated as class III to IV, and the best conditions are normally found in late May and early June.

The trail starts near the eastern end of the reservoir, leading east on the south bank of the Kings River along a well-used but unmarked dirt road. Initially it travels above the river, but by the time it reaches Camp 4 ½ it is traveling alongside it. The river is wide and is a designated Wild and Scenic River. It is managed for wild trout, and there are many places to cast a line.

There are also many places for a quiet camp along the riverbank. Surprisingly, this trail is seldom used. It passes other camping spots, both national forest campgrounds and informal sites before it moves away from the Kings River and follows the tight valley along Mill Creek.

Looking to the north as the trail climbs reveals striking views over the Kings River Valley, Sierra National Forest, and gray Patterson Bluffs. The vegetation is a mixture of oaks, pines, and California walnuts.

The trail crosses Davis Flat and Sampson Flat, passing a few scattered pieces of private property before finishing at the intersection with Central Mountains #2: Delilah Fire Lookout Trail. From there, it is a short distance to California 180.

The trail is suitable for high-clearance 2WDs in dry weather. In places it is eroded and rocky with some fairly deep ruts, but the grade is moderate throughout.

Current Road Information

Sequoia National Forest
Hume Lake Ranger District
35860 East Kings Canyon Road
Dunlap, CA 93621
(559) 338-2251

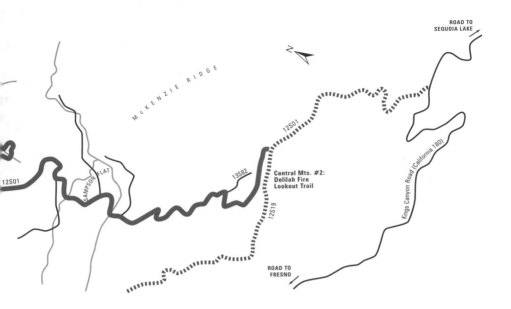

ROAD TO
SEQUOIA LAKE

McKENZIE RIDGE

12S01

Kings Canyon Road (California 180)

SAMPSON FLAT

12S01

13S82

Central Mts. #2:
Delilah Fire
Lookout Trail

12S19

ROAD TO
FRESNO

Davis Flat Trail commences on the south side of the steel bridge that spans Kings River

Davis Flat Trail accesses many fishing points along Kings River

Map References

BLM Fresno
USFS Sequoia National Forest
USGS 1:24,000 Luckett Mtn., Verplank
        Ridge
        1:100,000 Fresno
Maptech CD-ROM: Central Coast/Fresno
Southern & Central California Atlas &
        Gazetteer, p. 25
California Road & Recreation Atlas, p. 78

Route Directions

▼ 0.0   From Pine Flat Reservoir, continue east
         along paved Trimmer Springs Road.
         Zero trip meter 1.6 miles east of Kirch
         Flat USFS Campground and turn south-
         east on unmarked graded dirt road that
         heads along south bank of the Kings
         River. Turn is at the steel bridge that
         crosses river.
2.6 ▲   Trail finishes on paved Trimmer Springs
         Road. Turn left for Pine Flat Reservoir; turn
         right over steel bridge for Balch Camp.

GPS: N36°52.25' W119°07.81'

▼ 0.8   SO Cattle guard. Passing through Camp 4
             1/2 Work-station corral and cabin; then
             Camp 4½ USFS Campground on left
             and right alongside river.
1.8 ▲   SO Camp 4½ USFS Campground on left
             and right alongside river; then Camp
             4½ Workstation corral and cabin.
             GPS: N36°51.73' W119°07.26'

▼ 1.9   SO Camp 4 USFS Campground on left and
             right alongside river.
0.7 ▲   SO Camp 4 USFS Campground on left and
             right alongside river.
             GPS: N36°51.43' W119°06.37'

▼ 2.1   SO Green Cabin Flat Group Area on left.
0.5 ▲   SO Green Cabin Flat Group Area on right.
             GPS: N36°51.55' W119°06.16'
▼ 2.6   SO Cattle guard; then Mill Flat USFS
             Campground on left at confluence of
             Kings River and Davis Creek. Trail
             leaves Kings River and follows Mill Flat
             Creek. Zero trip meter.

0.0 ▲   Continue to the northwest.
GPS: N36°51.39' W119°05.78'

▼ 0.0   Continue to the south.
12.2 ▲   SO   Mill Flat USFS Campground on right at the confluence of Kings River and Davis Creek. Cross cattle guard and zero trip meter. Trail now leaves Mill Flat Creek and follows alongside Kings River.

▼ 0.6   SO   Cross over creek.
11.6 ▲   SO   Cross over creek.

▼ 1.8   SO   Small track on right and cabin on left.
10.4 ▲   SO   Small track on left and cabin on right.
GPS: N36°50.52' W119°05.30'

▼ 1.9   SO   Cross over Davis Creek on concrete ford at Crabtree; then private property on right.
10.3 ▲   SO   Private property on left; then cross over Davis Creek on concrete ford at Crabtree.

▼ 2.2   SO   Track on left turns into hiking trail almost immediately.
10.0 ▲   SO   Track on right turns into hiking trail almost immediately.

▼ 4.1   SO   Private property on right.
8.1 ▲   SO   Private property on left.
GPS: N36°49.30' W119°05.23'

▼ 4.5   SO   Cross over Davis Creek.
7.7 ▲   SO   Cross over Davis Creek.

▼ 4.7   SO   Corral on left; then gate.
7.5 ▲   SO   Gate; then corral on right.

▼ 5.7   SO   Track on left.
6.5 ▲   SO   Track on right.
GPS: N36°48.68' W119°05.27'

▼ 6.0   SO   Cross over creek.
6.2 ▲   SO   Cross over creek.

▼ 6.4   SO   Cross over creek.
5.8 ▲   SO   Cross over creek.

▼ 7.5   SO   Track on right.
4.7 ▲   SO   Track on left.
GPS: N36°48.58' W119°05.87'

▼ 7.8   SO   Cross over creek.
4.4 ▲   SO   Cross over creek.

▼ 8.6   SO   Track on left.
3.6 ▲   SO   Track on right.

GPS: N36°48.05' W119°05.29'

▼ 9.0   SO   Track on right.
3.2 ▲   SO   Track on left.
GPS: N36°47.93' W119°05.52'

▼ 9.4   SO   Cross over creek.
2.8 ▲   SO   Cross over creek.

▼ 9.6   SO   Cross over creek.
2.6 ▲   SO   Cross over creek.

▼ 9.9   SO   Track on left.
2.3 ▲   SO   Track on right.

▼ 10.2   SO   Cross over creek.
2.0 ▲   SO   Cross over creek.

▼ 10.3   SO   Track on right.
1.9 ▲   SO   Track on left.

▼ 10.4   SO   Track on left.
1.8 ▲   SO   Track on right.

▼ 11.7   SO   Track on right.
0.5 ▲   SO   Track on left.
GPS: N36°46.58' W119°05.33'

▼ 12.2   SO   Closure gate; then track on left is 13S82. Zero trip meter.
0.0 ▲   Continue to the northwest.
GPS: N36°46.36' W119°05.03'

▼ 0.0   Continue to the southwest.
1.3 ▲   SO   Track on right is 13S82; then closure gate. Zero trip meter.

▼ 0.2   SO   Private property on right.
1.1 ▲   SO   Private property on left.

▼ 0.4   SO   Track on right.
0.9 ▲   SO   Track on left.

▼ 1.3   Track on left; then trail ends at intersection with Central Mountains #2: Delilah Fire Lookout Trail. Turn right to continue along the trail; turn left to exit to Kings Canyon Road (California 180).
0.0 ▲   From Central Mountains #2: Delilah Fire Lookout Trail, 2.7 miles north of California 180, zero trip meter and turn northwest onto smaller graded road, marked 12S01—suitable for 4WDs, ATVs, and motorbikes. Zero trip meter. Track on right at intersection.
GPS: N36°46.09' W119°04.39'

Whitaker Research Forest Trail

STARTING POINT Generals Highway, 3.6 miles east of California 180

FINISHING POINT Central Mountains #5: Cherry Flat Trail, 0.1 miles from Eshom USFS Campground

TOTAL MILEAGE 5.4 miles

UNPAVED MILEAGE: 3.6 miles

DRIVING TIME 30 minutes

ELEVATION RANGE 4,900–6,900 feet

USUALLY OPEN Mid-April to November 15

BEST TIME TO TRAVEL Dry weather

DIFFICULTY RATING 1

SCENIC RATING 9

REMOTENESS RATING +0

Special Attractions

- Quiet trail within Kings Canyon National Park.
- Whitaker Research Forest.

Description

This short trail follows a lesser-traveled vehicle route in Kings Canyon National Park and the University of California-owned Whitaker Research Forest.

The trail leaves Generals Highway opposite Quail Flat Camp, 3.6 miles from the intersection with California 180. There is no sign for the turn and it is hard to see; initially, it looks like a pull-in, but once over the rise you will immediately see the trail descending into Kings Canyon National Park. The mainly single-track road is generally suitable for passenger vehicles in dry weather. In wet weather it should be avoided. The trail travels under the shady canopy of the forest, passing many large trees and granite outcroppings. The start of the Redwood Canyon Hiking Trail is passed on the edge of the national park before the main trail enters Whitaker Research Forest. The area is owned by the University of California and is dedicated to the study of forestry. The land was donated by

Horace Whitaker, who is buried opposite the center's gates beside the trail.

Several felled trees and a number of enormous old-growth stumps can be seen in the forest. Some of these stumps bear slots that were cut by loggers to use for the planks they balanced on as they worked. It was not uncommon for loggers of that time to spend days felling a single tree.

The grave of Horace Whitaker, donor of this forest, is shadowed by the giant trees that he loved

Hand-hewn sequoia felled from old-growth forest—lumberjacks balanced on planks inserted in the slots

Southern & Central California Atlas & Gazetteer, p. 25
California Road & Recreation Atlas, p. 85

Route Directions

▼ 0.0   From Generals Highway, 3.6 miles east of California 180, zero trip meter and turn southeast on unmarked dirt road. Turn is immediately before a closure gate and opposite the turn to Hume Lake and Horseshoe Bend Trail at Quail Flat Camp. Turn looks like it is just a pull-in, but the trail continues over the rise and immediately enters Kings Canyon National Park.

1.7 ▲   Trail ends at the intersection with Generals Highway. Turn left for Kings Canyon Visitor Center and Fresno; turn right for Sequoia National Park.
       GPS: N36°43.28′ W118°54.51′

▼ 1.7   SO   Track on left goes to Redwood Canyon Hiking Trailhead. Zero trip meter.

0.0 ▲   Continue to the north.
       GPS: N36°42.54′ W118°55.27′

▼ 0.0   Continue to the south.

3.7 ▲   SO   Track on right goes to Redwood Canyon Hiking Trailhead. Zero trip meter.

▼ 0.4   SO   Leaving Kings Canyon National Park. Entering Whitaker Research Forest.

3.3 ▲   SO   Leaving Whitaker Research Forest. Entering Kings Canyon National Park.
       GPS: N36°42.44′ W118°55.32′

▼ 1.5   BR   Track on left through closure gate.

2.2 ▲   BL   Track on right through closure gate.
       GPS: N36°41.91′ W118°55.96′

▼ 1.7   SO   Examples of cut trees showing slots made for planks below trail on right. Cross over creek.

2.0 ▲   SO   Cross over creek. Examples of cut trees showing slots made for planks below trail on left.

▼ 2.1   SO   Whitaker Forest Research Center on right. Horace Whitaker's grave is on the left, adjacent to large sequoias and surrounded by a wooden fence.

From the research facility, the road becomes roughly paved for the final couple of miles before it ends at the intersection with Central Mountains #5: Cherry Flat Trail, 0.1 miles from Eshom USFS Campground. Continue along the paved road for 7.5 miles to exit to Sierra Glen.

Current Road Information

Sequoia National Forest
Hume Lake Ranger District
35860 East Kings Canyon Road
Dunlap, CA 93621
(559) 338-2251

Map References

BLM   Mt. Whitney
USFS   Sequoia National Forest
USGS   1:24,000   General Grant Grove
         1:100,000 Mt. Whitney
Maptech CD-ROM: Kings Canyon/Death
         Valley

Northern end of Whitaker Research Forest Trail passes massive granite boulders

1.6 ▲	SO	Whitaker Forest Research Center on left. Horace Whitaker's grave is on the right, adjacent to large sequoias and surrounded by a wooden fence. **GPS: N36°42.16′ W118°56.02′**

▼ 2.7	SO	Gate. Exiting Whitaker Research Forest.
1.0 ▲	SO	Gate. Entering Whitaker Research Forest.
▼ 3.2	SO	Cabin on right behind fence.
0.5 ▲	SO	Cabin on left behind fence.
▼ 3.7		Trail ends at intersection with Central Mountains #5: Cherry Flat Trail, 7.5 miles northeast of Sierra Glen. Turn left to travel the Cherry Flat Trail; continue straight to exit to California 245 to Woodlake.
0.0 ▲		Trail commences on paved CR 465 at intersection with Central Mountains #5: Cherry Flat Trail, 7.5 miles northeast of Sierra Glen. The intersection is marked with a sign. Zero trip meter and continue north, following sign for Whitaker Forest. **GPS: N36°41.49′ W118°56.80′**

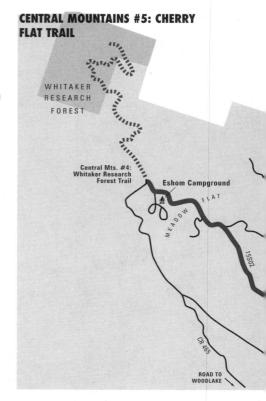

CENTRAL MOUNTAINS #5: CHERRY FLAT TRAIL

WHITAKER RESEARCH FOREST

Central Mts. #4: Whitaker Research Forest Trail

Eshom Campground

FLAT

MEADOW

15S02

CR 465

ROAD TO WOODLAKE

Cherry Flat Trail

STARTING POINT CR 465, 2 miles southwest of Whitaker Research Forest
FINISHING POINT Cherry Flat
TOTAL MILEAGE 9.9 miles
UNPAVED MILEAGE: 9.9 miles
DRIVING TIME 1.25 hours
ELEVATION RANGE 4,200–5,100 feet
USUALLY OPEN May to December
BEST TIME TO TRAVEL Dry weather
DIFFICULTY RATING 3
SCENIC RATING 8
REMOTENESS RATING +1

Special Attractions

- Views into Kings Canyon National Park and Kaweah River Valley.
- Small reed-fringed lake in Pierce Valley.

Description

This trail runs south from CR 465 near the Whitaker Research Forest and follows a lightly traveled trail to end near the national park boundary at Cherry Flat.

The first section of the trail is a well-used, graded dirt road, but after passing the last of the private property the trail is less maintained and becomes a formed, rutted trail. The ruts are deep, making wet-weather travel inadvisable. A few short sections through the manzanita and mountain mahogany vegetation can be a little brushy, but they are not long and with a bit of care the worst may be avoided.

The scenery is fairly typical of trails in this part of the Sierra Nevada—the views toward the granite domes of Kings Canyon National Park are worthwhile, as is the final view into the Kaweah River Valley.

The trail finishes on a spur overlooking the Kaweah River Valley. There is a small campsite here; otherwise camping along the

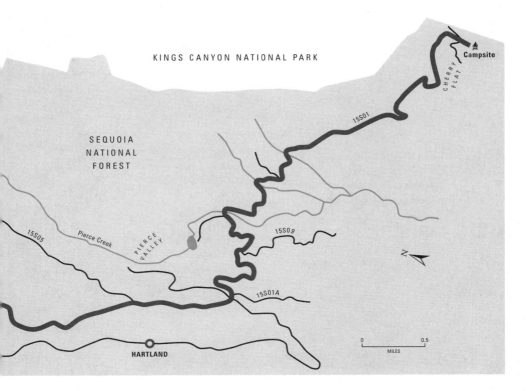

trail is very limited because of the abundant vegetation. Other trails lead slightly farther toward Cherry Flat and the large granite domes, but these are narrow and brushy.

One short, interesting spur from the main trail leads 0.4 miles to a small, unnamed lake in Pierce Valley. The reed-fringed lake has a couple of pleasant campsites nearby, but the tracks that continue past the lake quickly lead to dead ends. The coordinates of the lake are N36°39.03' W118°56.36'.

Current Road Information
Sequoia National Forest
Hume Lake Ranger District
35860 East Kings Canyon Road
Dunlap, CA 93621
(559) 338-2251

Map References
BLM   Mt. Whitney
USFS   Sequoia National Forest
USGS   1:24,000   General Grant Grove

1:100,000 Mt. Whitney
Maptech CD-ROM: Kings Canyon/Death Valley
Southern & Central California Atlas & Gazetteer, p. 25
California Road & Recreation Atlas, p. 85

Route Directions

▼ 0.0   Trail starts on California 465, 7.5 miles northeast of Sierra Glen. Zero trip meter and turn south on small paved road sign-posted to Eshom Campground. Road immediately turns to graded dirt.
4.2 ▲   Trail ends at intersection with CR 465. Turn right for Whitaker Research Forest and Kings Canyon National Park; turn left for Sierra Glen.
          GPS: N36°41.49' W118°56.78'

▼ 0.1   BL   Track on right into Eshom USFS Campground. Bear left through closure gate.

Cherry Flat Trail opens out of the forest toward the endpoint overlooking Kaweah River

4.1 ▲   SO   Closure gate; then track on left into
             Eshom USFS Campground.
             GPS: N36°41.41' W118°56.82'

▼ 0.6   SO   Track on right.
3.6 ▲   SO   Track on left.
▼ 0.8   BR   Bear right onto smaller graded road.
3.4 ▲   SO   Join larger graded dirt road.
             GPS: N36°40.89' W118°56.92'

▼ 0.9   BR   Track on left.
3.3 ▲   BL   Track on right.
             GPS: N36°40.85' W118°56.99'

▼ 1.2   SO   Cross over creek.
3.0 ▲   SO   Cross over creek.
▼ 3.4   SO   Track on left is 15S05.
0.8 ▲   BL   Track on right is 15S05.
▼ 3.5   BR   Bear right past track on left; then
             closure gate.
0.7 ▲   BL   Closure gate; then bear left past track
             on right.
             GPS: N36°39.23' W118°57.07'

▼ 4.2   TL   T-intersection. Turn left and join 15S01.

             Track on right returns to CR 465.
             Zero trip meter.
0.0 ▲   Continue to the northwest.
             GPS: N36°38.68' W118°56.79'

▼ 0.0   BL   Continue to the east. Immediately
             track on left; then bear left onto
             15S01. Ahead is private road 15S01A.
             GPS: N36°38.65' W118°56.75'

▼ 1.1   SO   Track on right is 15S09.
             GPS: N36°38.70' W118°56.33'

▼ 1.5   BR   Track on left goes 0.4 miles to a small
             lake in Pierce Valley. Bear right through
             closure gate.
             GPS: N36°38.86' W118°56.10'

▼ 1.6   SO   Cross over Pierce Creek.
▼ 2.3   SO   Cross over creek.
▼ 2.4   BR   Private road on left.
             GPS: N36°38.65' W118°55.63'

▼ 2.6   SO   Cross over creek.
▼ 2.9   SO   Cross over wash.

Spur trail off Cherry Flat Trail leads to a tranquil lake in Pierce Valley

▼ 5.5   SO   Track on left is a dead end.
         GPS: N36°37.85' W118°53.91'

▼ 5.6   BL   Track on right.
         GPS: N36°37.78' W118°53.93'

▼ 5.7   Trail ends at a campsite with views to the south over the Kaweah River Valley. Pierce Creek is to the west.
         GPS: N36°37.72' W118°53.93'

CENTRAL MOUNTAINS #6

Buck Rock Fire Lookout Trail

STARTING POINT Paved road14S11, 2.5 miles north of Generals Highway
FINISHING POINT Monarch Wilderness boundary
TOTAL MILEAGE 11.8 miles
UNPAVED MILEAGE: 11.7 miles
DRIVING TIME 1 hour
ELEVATION RANGE 6,700–8,200 feet
USUALLY OPEN Mid-April to November 15
BEST TIME TO TRAVEL Dry weather
DIFFICULTY RATING 2
SCENIC RATING 9
REMOTENESS RATING +0

Special Attractions

- Unusual fire lookout location on the large granite Buck Rock.
- Fantastic views on either side of the ridge trail.
- Wilderness access at several points along the trail.

History

The wonderfully located fire lookout on Buck Rock was constructed in 1923. It is referred to as a 4A construction-style tower, being approximately 14 feet by 14 feet in its layout. It is one of only three remaining 4A towers in California.

Burton Pass and Burton Meadow are named after an early rancher who worked in the region. Another local name appears farther down the trail at Evans Creek and Evans Grove. John Evans is remembered for having lived near this grove of sequoias and protecting the trees from the ravages of fire.

Groves of sequoias often take their names from nearby features. Horseshoe Bend Grove is named after a nearby bend in the Kings River. Windy Gulch Grove takes its name from the Windy Cliffs on the Kings River. The names of both Horseshoe Bend and Windy Gulch were first recorded on USGS topographic maps after a survey team worked its way through the rugged terrain in 1903.

Close to the point where Windy Gulch drains into the Kings River is a cave that lay hidden to pioneer settlers until after the turn of the twentieth century. Around 1907, Peter H. Boyden discovered a strikingly beautiful cave and started development. He intended to turn the cave into a tourist attraction. In 1912, the *Inyo Register* reported that Boyden was installing ladders to access the various chambers and electricity to illuminate the features within. Boyden Cavern is a series of interconnecting rooms with many natural features including an underground stream, stalactites and stalagmites, shield formations, crystalline helictites, and a bat cave.

Boyden Cavern is located within the 8,000-foot-deep Kings River Canyon, one of the deepest canyon in the United States. It is now open to the public between May and October and offers walking tours.

Description

The highlight of this trail is undoubtedly the Buck Rock Fire Lookout, perched as it is atop a large granite outcrop. It is accessible by a precarious ladder leading up the face of the rock.

The trail leaves from the small paved road that accesses the Big Meadows Hiking Trailhead. This extremely popular trail accesses the Jennie Lakes Wilderness. Initially the trail to the Buck Rock lookout is roughly graded as it passes Buck Rock USFS Campground. This is a relatively undeveloped camping area, with no numbered sites and only a few tables and fire rings. There are plenty of pleasant places to pitch a tent on either side of the road.

The trail past the campground is slightly rougher and better suited for high-clearance 2WD vehicles as it approaches the lookout.

As you drive north along the narrow ridge, there are fantastic views to the east and west. The lookout can be seen ahead, perched precariously on the large Buck Rock. Reaching the lookout requires a short, somewhat strenuous hike from the parking area at the bottom. The views from the lookout are well worth the effort.

Past the lookout, the trail is slightly rougher. The more difficult Central Mountains #7: Buck Road leads off into the boulder-strewn landscape to the east. The main trail continues as a formed trail down from the lookout to briefly cross the small paved road that travels over Burton Pass. It then follows the dirt road past the Kennedy Meadow Hiking Trailhead, which gives access to the Monarch Wilderness. The road continues as a small dirt trail past Tornado Meadows and

meanders around the hillside before becoming brushy. The trail ends at the boundary of the Monarch Wilderness.

Current Road Information

Sequoia National Forest
Hume Lake Ranger District
35860 East Kings Canyon Road
Dunlap, CA 93621
(559) 338-2251

Map References

BLM Mt. Whitney
USFS Sequoia National Forest
USGS 1:24,000 Muir Grove, Wren Peak
      1:100,000 Mt. Whitney
Maptech CD-ROM: Kings Canyon/Death Valley
Southern & Central California Atlas & Gazetteer, p. 25
California Road & Recreation Atlas, p. 86
Trails Illustrated, Sequoia and Kings Canyon (205)

Bear necessities! Good advice at Buck Rock USFS Campground

Route Directions

▼ 0.0   Trail starts on small paved road 14S11, 2.5 miles north of Generals Highway. 14S11 is the road that leads to Big Meadows Hiking Trailhead. Zero trip meter and turn northeast onto graded dirt road, following sign to Buck Rock Lookout. There is a corral and picnic area at intersection.

2.2 ▲   Trail ends at T-intersection with small paved road 14S11. Turn left for Big Meadows Hiking Trailhead; turn right to exit to Generals Highway.
       GPS: N36°43.02′ W118°50.89′

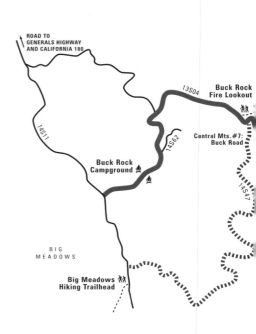

▼ 0.1   SO   Turnout area on left.
2.1 ▲   SO   Turnout area on right.
▼ 0.3   SO   Entering Buck Rock USFS Campground. Pull-in areas for camping on right and left.
1.9 ▲   SO   Leaving Buck Rock USFS Campground.
       GPS: N36°43.34′ W118°50.99′

▼ 0.5   SO   Cross over creek; then track on left. Leaving Buck Rock USFS Campground.
1.7 ▲   SO   Track on right; then cross over creek. Entering Buck Rock USFS Campground. Pull-in areas for camping on right and left.
▼ 0.7   SO   Track on right is 14S62.
1.5 ▲   SO   Track on left is 14S62.
       GPS: N36°43.47′ W118°51.21′

▼ 1.1   SO   Track on left.
1.1 ▲   SO   Track on right.
▼ 1.2   BR   Well-used track on left. Follow sign to lookout.
1.0 ▲   SO   Well-used track on right.
       GPS: N36°43.50′ W118°51.56′

▼ 2.1   BR   Track on left is 13S04B, which goes to Buck Rock Lookout—hiking access only. Parking for the tower on right. Remain on 13S04.
0.1 ▲   SO   Track on right is 13S04B, which goes to Buck Rock Lookout—hiking access only. Parking for the tower on left. Remain on 13S04.
       GPS: N36°44.11′ W118°51.45′

▼ 2.2   BL   Track on right is Central Mountains #7: Buck Road (14S47). Zero trip meter.
0.0 ▲   Continue to the southwest.
       GPS: N36°44.14′ W118°51.41′

▼ 0.0   Continue to the northwest.
2.3 ▲   SO   Track on left is Central Mountains #7: Buck Road (14S47). Zero trip meter.
▼ 1.0   SO   Track on right is 13S10.
1.3 ▲   SO   Track on left is 13S10.
       GPS: N36°44.53′ W118°51.23′

▼ 1.1   SO   Turnout on right with campsites and a great view.
1.2 ▲   SO   Turnout on left with campsites and a great view.
▼ 2.3   TL   T-intersection at Burton Pass. Turn left onto small paved road 14S02. Zero trip meter.
0.0 ▲   Turn southwest onto small formed trail 13S04, following sign to Buck Rock Lookout. Zero trip meter.
       GPS: N36°45.08′ W118°50.84′

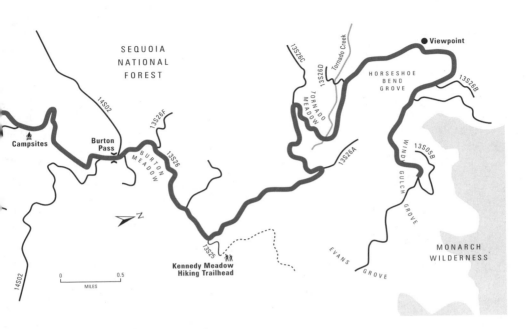

Buck Rock Fire Lookout perched like an eagle's nest

Everything up here is big—the granite boulders, weathered trees and vistas of the treeless Great Western Divide

▼ 0.0   Continue to the north.
▼ 0.1   TR   Turn right onto dirt road 13S26, following sign to Kennedy Meadow.
       GPS: N36°45.19′ W118°50.82′

▼ 0.2   SO   Closure gate.
▼ 0.3   BL   Bear left, following sign to Tornado Meadow.
       GPS: N36°45.26′ W118°50.83′

▼ 0.6   SO   Track on left is 13S26F.
▼ 1.2   SO   Track on left.
▼ 1.6   SO   Track on right is 13S25, which goes 0.25 miles to Kennedy Meadow Hiking Trailhead.
       GPS: N36°45.76′ W118°49.96′

▼ 2.8   BL   Track on right is 13S26A.
       GPS: N36°46.65′ W118°50.45′

▼ 3.7   BR   Track on left is 13S26C.
       GPS: N36°46.54′ W118°51.09′

▼ 4.2   SO   Cross over Tornado Creek. Tornado Meadow on left.
▼ 4.7   BR   Track on left is 13S26D. Zero trip meter.
       GPS: N36°46.92′ W118°51.20′

▼ 0.0   Continue to the north.
▼ 0.8   SO   Exceptional viewpoint with views over Kings River Canyon and the mountains and forest to the north.
       GPS: N36°47.56′ W118°51.46′

▼ 1.4   SO   Track on left is 13S26B.
       GPS: N36°47.59′ W118°51.07′

▼ 1.7   SO   Track on left.
       GPS: N36°47.37′ W118°50.95′

▼ 2.0   SO   Trail crosses old landslide area.
▼ 2.6   SO   Track on left is 13S05B. Trail continues past this point as far as the Monarch Wilderness boundary, but it can be brushy.
       GPS: N36°47.33′ W118°50.22′

Buck Road

STARTING POINT Central Mountains #6: Buck Rock Fire Lookout Trail, below lookout tower
FINISHING POINT Paved road 14S11, 0.2 miles west of Big Meadows Hiking Trailhead
TOTAL MILEAGE 3.6 miles
UNPAVED MILEAGE: 3.6 miles
DRIVING TIME 45 minutes
ELEVATION RANGE 7,600–8,200 feet
USUALLY OPEN Mid-April to November 15
BEST TIME TO TRAVEL Dry weather
DIFFICULTY RATING 5
SCENIC RATING 9
REMOTENESS RATING +0

Special Attractions

- Challenging, loose, and twisty trail.
- Trail travels through beautiful semi-open forest and granite boulders.

CENTRAL MOUNTAINS #7: BUCK ROAD

The loose gravel on the steep rock inclines will cause traction difficulty for some vehicles

Description

This trail is one of only a few designated 4WD trails through the recently dedicated Giant Sequoia National Monument. It is suitable for high-clearance 4WDs because of the loose surface, steep ascents and descents, and large rocks that need to be negotiated. In addition, there are off-camber sections that run around the hill where care must be taken; it is easy to slip sideways on the loose surface. The small formed trail is predominantly sandy.

The very twisty trail is exceptionally scenic and travels through semi-open forest past large granite boulders. There are also panoramic views and a couple of pleasant camping places.

The 5-rated part of the trail is the western end, where it leaves Central Mountains #6: Buck Rock Fire Lookout Trail. Here the dips, descents, and loose surface will challenge some vehicles. Decent tires are recommended. The second half of the trail is easier. It follows along smoother trails that were once used for logging to emerge on the small paved road

near the Big Meadows Hiking Trailhead, a popular access point for the Jennie Lakes Wilderness. Big Meadows got its name from hunters who found abundant game in the area over the years.

Current Road Information

Sequoia National Forest
Hume Lake Ranger District
35860 East Kings Canyon Road
Dunlap, CA 93621
(559) 338-2251

Map References

BLM   Mt. Whitney
USFS   Sequoia National Forest
USGS   1:24,000   Muir Grove
         1:100,000 Mt. Whitney
Maptech CD-ROM: Kings Canyon/Death
         Valley
Southern & Central California Atlas & Gazetteer, p. 25
California Road & Recreation Atlas, p. 86
Trails Illustrated, Sequoia and Kings
         Canyon (205)—route not shown

Route Directions

▼ 0.0   From Central Mountains #6: Buck Rock Fire Lookout Trail, directly below the lookout tower, zero trip meter and turn east on 14S47, marked as a designated vehicle route for 4WDs, ATVs, and motorbikes.

1.7 ▲   Trail ends on Central Mountains #6: Buck Rock Fire Lookout Trail, directly below the lookout tower. Turn left to visit Buck Rock Lookout and exit via Generals Highway.

     GPS: N36°44.14' W118°51.41'

▼ 0.5 BR Trail forks and rejoins. At times, the right-hand fork can be easier but this may change.

1.2 ▲ BL Trail forks and rejoins. At times, the left-hand fork can be easier but this may change.

▼ 1.1 TL Trail continues ahead. Turn left to avoid off-camber side slope.

0.6 ▲ TR Tracks rejoin.

     GPS: N36°44.06' W118°50.59'

▼ 1.2 SO Tracks rejoins.

0.5 ▲ SO Track on left. Continue straight ahead to avoid off-camber side slope.

     GPS: N36°44.03' W118°50.57'

▼ 1.6 SO Pull-off area on right. Remain on main trail marked by orange markers.

0.1 ▲ SO Pull-off area on left.

     GPS: N36°44.06' W118°50.24'

▼ 1.7 TR Track continues ahead. Zero trip meter.

0.0 ▲   Continue to the southwest.

     GPS: N36°44.07' W118°50.19'

▼ 0.0   Continue to the south.

1.9 ▲ TL Well-used track on right. Zero trip meter.

▼ 1.0 TR Well-used track on left.

0.9 ▲ TL Well-used track ahead.

     GPS: N36°43.61' W118°49.72'

Outcrops of granite and views deep into the Sierra Nevada are a feature of this trail

▼ 1.6	SO	Closure gate.
0.3 ▲	SO	Closure gate.
▼ 1.7	TL	T-intersection. Track on right is 14S01B. There are a couple of campsites with picnic tables opposite the intersection.
0.2 ▲	TR	Turn right onto unmarked trail. Track straight ahead is marked as 14S01B. There are a couple of campsites with picnic tables on left.
		GPS: N36°43.24′ W118°50.20′

▼ 1.9		Trail ends at T-intersection with paved road 14S11. Turn right to exit to Generals Highway.
0.0 ▲		Trail starts on small paved 14S11, 3.6 miles north of intersection with Generals Highway. Zero trip meter and turn northwest on small unmarked dirt trail at an informal camp area, 0.1 miles west of Big Meadows Workstation and 0.2 miles west of the Big Meadows Hiking Trailhead, which leads into Jennie Lakes Wilderness.
		GPS: N36°43.14′ W118°50.19′

Solo Peak Road

STARTING POINT California 190 at Camp Nelson
FINISHING POINT Solo Peak
TOTAL MILEAGE 14.3 miles
UNPAVED MILEAGE: 12.7 miles
DRIVING TIME 2 hours
ELEVATION RANGE 4,500–6,700 feet
USUALLY OPEN May to December
BEST TIME TO TRAVEL May to December
DIFFICULTY RATING 2
SCENIC RATING 8
REMOTENESS RATING +1

Special Attractions
■ Many large sequoias along the trail.
■ Lightly traveled trail.

History
Camp Nelson was named after pioneer John Milton Nelson, who first settled in the area in the early 1880s. He built a small sawmill and established an apple orchard. In the summer, ranchers moving their stock to higher meadows, hunters, and other travelers would visit Nelson on their way up the mountain. With so many visitors, Nelson built a two-story guesthouse and vacation cabins. The first post office was established in 1910 and operated until 1967. Rough mule train roads brought in the much-needed workforce for the sawmills in the summertime. A trafficable road was built by 1922, which opened up the area for further development. Many people built mountain retreats to escape the summer heat down in the valley. The area has many summer homes to this day.

Coy Creek and Coy Flat are named after Milton Coy, who settled this land in 1891. Rogers Camp is named after Henry Rogers, the original settler on land that is still privately owned.

Description
This trail through the Sequoia National Forest leaves the small settlement of Camp Nelson and travels along the north side of Solo Peak. It passes the forest service campground at Coy Flat, where there are very shady sites available under large pine trees. The trail turns to graded dirt at this point and follows a shelf road through dense forest. The road is mainly single vehicle width, but there are ample passing places.

Past the private property at Rogers Camp are some huge red-barked sequoias. The massive trees continue to be scattered throughout the forest until the end of the trail.

Past the turnoff for Central Mountains #9: Windy Gap Trail, the road continues to a dead end at Solo Peak. It follows along a shelf road for 7 miles before turning into small trails that become brushy, although they do continue farther than what is shown on maps.

Current Road Information
Sequoia National Forest
Tule River/Hot Springs Ranger District
32588 Highway 190
Springville, CA 93265
(559) 539-2607

Slate Mountain towers above Solo Peak Road near Camp Nelson

Sequoias stand out along Solo Peak Road

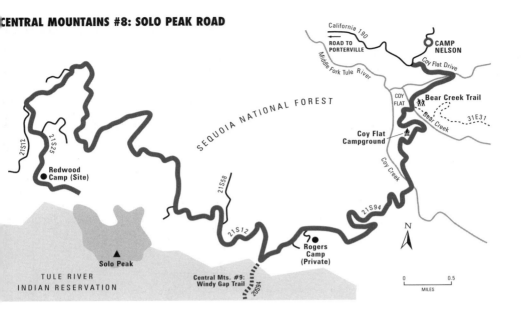

Map References

BLM   Three Rivers
USFS Sequoia National Forest
USGS 1:24,000 Camp Nelson, Sentinel
       Peak, Solo Peak, Camp Wishon
       1:100,000 Three Rivers
Maptech CD-ROM: Kings Canyon/Death
       Valley
Southern & Central California Atlas &
      Gazetteer, p. 38
California Road & Recreation Atlas, p. 86

Route Directions

▼ 0.0   From Camp Nelson on California 190,
           zero trip meter and turn east on paved
           Nelson Drive, following sign for Camp
           Nelson and Coy Flat. Immediately,
           paved road on left and paved road on
           right. Continue straight, following sign
           to Coy Flat. Remain on paved Coy Flat
           Drive, ignoring turns on right and left.
1.6 ▲   Trail ends at T-intersection with California
           190 in Camp Nelson. Turn left for Porterville.
           GPS: N36°08.19′ W118°37.10′

▼ 0.5   SO Cross over Middle Fork Tule River
           on bridge.
1.1 ▲ SO Cross over Middle Fork Tule River
           on bridge.

GPS: N36°08.14′ W118°36.66′

▼ 1.2   SO Bear Creek Trail (31E31) on left for hik-
           ing only; then cross over Bear Creek.
0.4 ▲ SO Cross over Bear Creek; then Bear
           Creek Trail (31E31) on right for hiking
           only.
           GPS: N36°07.81′ W118°37.07′

▼ 1.6   SO Coy Flat USFS Campground on right.
           Zero trip meter. Road turns to graded
           dirt.
0.0 ▲   Continue to the southwest.
           GPS: N36°07.67′ W118°37.09′

▼ 0.0   Continue to the east, following sign for
           Solo Peak Road through closure gate.
           Road is now marked 21S94.
4.4 ▲ SO Pass through closure gate. Coy Flat
           USFS Campground on left. Zero trip
           meter. Road is now paved.
▼ 1.2   SO Cross over Coy Creek.
3.2 ▲ SO Cross over Coy Creek.
▼ 2.4   SO Track on right; then cattle guard.
2.0 ▲ SO Cattle guard; then track on left.
           GPS: N36°06.76′ W118°37.67′

▼ 2.6   SO Cross over creek.
1.8 ▲ SO Cross over creek.

▼ 3.8	SO	Track on left is private property; then start of large sequoias.
0.6 ▲	SO	Track on right is private property.
		GPS: N36°06.54′ W118°38.26′

▼ 4.0	SO	Track on left.
0.4 ▲	SO	Track on right.
▼ 4.4	TR	Turn right onto 21S12. Ahead is Central Mountains #9: Windy Gap Trail (20S94), which enters the Tule River Indian Reservation. Zero trip meter.
0.0 ▲		Continue to the northeast.
		GPS: N36°06.24′ W118°38.65′

▼ 0.0		Continue to the north.
▼ 0.3	SO	Closure gate.
▼ 1.2	SO	Small trail on right is 21S58.
		GPS: N36°06.53′ W118°39.18′

▼ 1.4	SO	Track on right.
▼ 1.9	SO	Track on left.
		GPS: N36°06.73′ W118°39.63′

▼ 2.7	SO	Closure gate.
		GPS: N36°07.17′ W118°39.75′

▼ 6.0	BL	Well-used track on right. Remain on 21S12. Marker post at intersection.
		GPS: N36°07.97′ W118°40.96′

▼ 6.6	BL	Major track on right is 21S12. Bear left onto 21S25 and zero trip meter.
		GPS: N36°07.61′ W118°41.46′

▼ 0.0		Continue to the south.
▼ 0.5	SO	Track on left dead-ends in 1 mile at a previously cleared area where there are some large redwoods. Trail is used past this point, but it is narrow and brushy.
		GPS: N36°07.32′ W118°41.26′

▼ 1.1	BL	Track on right through fence line. This is the site of Redwood Camp.
		GPS: N36°06.86′ W118°41.28′

▼ 1.7		Trail ends in small clearing. Track does continue past this point, but is narrow, brushy, and little used.
		GPS: N36.06.77′ W118°40.76′

Windy Gap Trail

STARTING POINT Central Mountains #8: Solo Peak Road, 6 miles south of Camp Nelson

FINISHING POINT Western Divide Highway

TOTAL MILEAGE 13.5 miles

UNPAVED MILEAGE: Approximately 7 miles

DRIVING TIME 1 hour

ELEVATION RANGE 6,000–7,500 feet

USUALLY OPEN May to December

BEST TIME TO TRAVEL May to December

DIFFICULTY RATING 1

SCENIC RATING 8

REMOTENESS RATING +1

Special Attractions

- Access to Summit Hiking Trail at Windy Gap.
- Views of Slate Mountain.
- Quiet, lightly traveled trail connecting two areas of Sequoia National Forest.

History

The Tule River Indian Reservation was established in 1857 at a location close to Porterville. Initially known as the Monache Reservation, it accommodated Native Americans relocated after the Tule River War of 1856. The war was the climax of growing tension and discontent between local Indian tribes and white settlers. The Indians killed many cattle and hogs that they believed were grazing on their land and the settlers retaliated. The bloody war lasted six weeks and resulted in many fatalities on both sides. William Campbell, the sub-agent at Kings River, negotiated the peace settlement. Battle Mountain, a few miles northeast of Milo, is named after this war.

In 1873, the Tule River Indian Reservation was designated at its present location, because the original spot was thought to be unsuitable. Unscrupulous local merchants sold whisky on the reservation and some intoxicated Indians were subsequently responsible for the death of Mrs. J. Bonnsall and both of her young children. Those responsi-

The tea-color stain from water trickling down the granite rock of Mount Nelson along Windy Gap Trail

ble were hanged and the local people demanded the relocation of the reservation.

The move to the new location involved hundreds of Indians from the Tejon, Kaweah, Kings Tule, and Monache tribes. A school opened at the new location and farming knowledge was passed on to members of the tribes.

Description

Many of the trails within the Sierra Nevada are fairly short and link major areas with hiking and motorbike trails. This trail, an alternative to the paved Western Divide Highway, links the trails around Camp Nelson to the southern trails around California Hot Springs. It travels mainly through Sequoia National Forest and briefly into the Tule River Indian Reservation.

The trail leaves Central Mountains #8: Solo Peak Road, 6 miles south of Camp Nelson, and immediately enters the reservation. Travel is permitted on designated roads only.

The trail approaches the open western slope of Slate Mountain

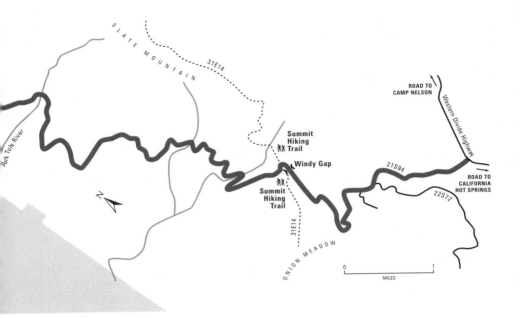

Please observe the regulations posted on entry. As the trail leaves the reservation and heads back into the national forest, the road surface is alternately graded dirt and single-lane paved. A passenger vehicle can generally travel this trail in dry weather. However, the trail is remote for the Sierra Nevada, and vehicles should be well prepared.

The shelf road winds its way along the west side of Slate Mountain, at times giving good views of the bare-topped mountain towering above. It then climbs up to Windy Gap to intersect with the Summit Hiking Trail, a popular trail that runs along the ridge tops of this part of the Sierra Nevada. From Windy Gap, it is an easy descent to join the Western Divide Highway.

Current Road Information

Sequoia National Forest
Tule River/Hot Springs Ranger District
32588 Highway 190
Springville, CA 93265
(559) 539-2607

Map References

BLM   Three Rivers
USFS   Sequoia National Forest
USGS   1:24,000   Solo Peak, Sentinel Peak
1:100,000 Three Rivers
Maptech CD-ROM: Kings Canyon/Death
Valley
Southern & Central California Atlas & Gazetteer, p. 38
California Road & Recreation Atlas, p. 86

Route Directions

▼ 0.0   From Central Mountains #8: Solo Peak
Road, 6 miles south of Camp Nelson,
zero trip meter and turn southwest on
20S94. Trail immediately enters the Tule
River Indian Reservation. Regulations
are posted at the gate.

9.8 ▲   Trail finishes at intersection with Central
Mountains #8: Solo Peak Road. Turn left
to continue to the end of this trail; continue straight to exit to Camp Nelson.
GPS: N36°06.24′ W118°38.65′

▼ 0.4   SO   Well-used track on right is Solo Road.
Remain on 20S94.

9.4 ▲   SO   Well-used track on left is Solo Road.
Remain on 20S94.

▼ 0.7 TL Turn left, remaining on 20S94 through closure gate. Track ahead goes to Cholollo Camp.

9.1 ▲ TR Closure gate; then immediately turn right. Track on left goes to Cholollo Camp.

GPS: N36°05.68' W118°38.73'

▼ 2.7 SO Cross over creek.

7.1 ▲ SO Cross over creek.

GPS: N36°05.62' W118°36.99'

▼ 4.4 SO Cross over South Fork Tule River.

5.4 ▲ SO Cross over South Fork Tule River.

▼ 7.7 SO Cross over creek.

2.1 ▲ SO Cross over creek.

GPS: N36°03.54' W118°35.62'

▼ 8.5 SO Cross over creek.

1.3 ▲ SO Cross over creek.

▼ 8.7 SO Well-used track on right. Windy Creek on right of trail.

1.1 ▲ BR Well-used track on left. Windy Creek on left of trail.

GPS: N36°03.01' W118°35.69'

▼ 8.8 SO Cross over Windy Creek.

1.0 ▲ SO Cross over Windy Creek.

▼ 9.8 SO Summit Hiking Trail (31E14) on left goes to Quaking Aspen. Trail now follows along road for a short distance. Zero trip meter at sign.

0.0 ▲ Continue to the southwest.

GPS: N36°02.71' W118°35.18'

▼ 0.0 Continue to the southeast.

2.4 ▲ SO Summit Hiking Trail (31E14) on right goes to Quaking Aspen. Zero trip meter at sign.

▼ 0.1 SO Cattle guard; then Summit Hiking Trail (31E14) on right goes to Onion Meadow. This is Windy Gap.

2.3 ▲ SO Summit Hiking Trail (31E14) on left goes to Onion Meadow; then cattle guard. This is Windy Gap. Trail now follows along road for a short distance.

GPS: N36°02.63' W118°35.19'

▼ 1.3 BL Well-used track on right. Remain on major road.

1.1 ▲ BR Well-used track on left. Remain on major road.

GPS: N36°01.76' W118°35.28'

▼ 1.6 SO Track on left is 21S94A.

0.8 ▲ SO Track on right is 21S94A.

GPS: N36°01.90' W118°35.23'

▼ 2.2 SO Track on right.

0.2 ▲ SO Track on left.

▼ 2.4 SO Small track on left and track on right is 22S72. Remain on 21S94 and zero trip meter.

0.0 ▲ Continue to the southwest.

GPS: N36°01.85' W118°34.69'

▼ 0.0 Continue to the northeast.

1.3 ▲ BR Track on left is 22S72 and small track on right. Bear right, remaining on 21S94 and zero trip meter.

▼ 1.2 SO Closure gate.

0.1 ▲ SO Closure gate.

▼ 1.3 Trail ends at T-intersection with Western Divide Highway. Turn right for California Hot Springs; turn left for Camp Nelson.

0.0 ▲ Trail starts on Western Divide Highway, 5.5 miles south of the turnoff to Peppermint USFS Campground. Zero trip meter and turn northwest on graded dirt road, marked as Crawford Road (21S94) to Windy Gap.

GPS: N36°01.27' W118°33.80'

CENTRAL MOUNTAINS #10

Packsaddle Meadow Trail

STARTING POINT M50, 9 miles north of Hot Springs Ranger Station

FINISHING POINT Paved road 23S16, 4.6 miles south of Johnsondale

TOTAL MILEAGE 7.5 miles

UNPAVED MILEAGE: 7.5 miles

DRIVING TIME 1 hour

ELEVATION RANGE 5,800–7,200 feet

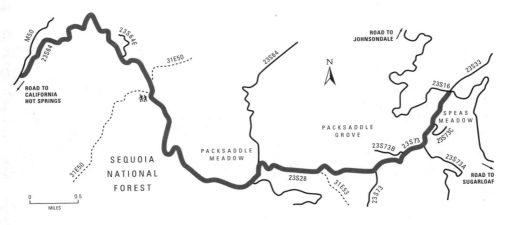

USUALLY OPEN May to December
BEST TIME TO TRAVEL May to December
DIFFICULTY RATING 2
SCENIC RATING 9
REMOTENESS RATING +0

Special Attractions
- Trail skirts the edge of a giant sequoia grove.
- Small, seldom-used trail within Giant Sequoia National Monument.
- Access to many trails suitable for hiking, horse, mountain bike, and motorbike use.

Description
Packsaddle Meadow Trail is contained within the newly established Giant Sequoia National Monument, designated by President Clinton in 2000. It travels along small tracks, following a single-track trail for much of the way. It leaves the paved M50 road, north of Hot Springs Ranger Station, and travels around the side of a mountain on a small graded road. There are extensive views over the ranges as the trail winds around large granite boulders, passing through a sequoia and pine forest that is interspersed with oaks. Packsaddle Meadow, a small tree-fringed meadow, is located roughly halfway along the trail. From there the trail climbs, passing the boundary of Packsaddle Grove on the left. The trail finishes a few miles south of Johnsondale, where there

is a small general store and restaurant (limited hours), but no fuel.

Current Road Information
Sequoia National Forest
Tule River/Hot Springs Ranger District
32588 Highway 190
Springville, CA 93265
(559) 539-2607

Map References
BLM   Isabella Lake
USFS   Sequoia National Forest
USGS 1:24,000   California Hot Springs,
             Johnsondale
             1:100,000 Isabella Lake
Maptech CD-ROM: Barstow/San
             Bernardino County
*Southern & Central California Atlas &
             Gazetteer*, p. 50
California Road & Recreation Atlas, p. 86

Route Directions

▼ 0.0 From M50, 9 miles north of Hot Springs Ranger Station, zero trip meter and turn east on graded dirt road marked 308018 and 23S64. Immediately track on right.

4.7 ▲ Track on left; then trail finishes on paved road M50. Turn left to exit to California Hot Springs.
       GPS: N35°56.35' W118°38.42'

Packsaddle Meadow is a quiet and pretty spot along the trail

▼ 0.1   SO   Closure gate.
4.6 ▲   SO   Closure gate.
▼ 2.1   SO   Track on left is 23S64E.
2.6 ▲   SO   Track on right is 23S64E.
        GPS: N35°56.43' W118°37.25'

▼ 2.5   SO   Trail on left is 31E50 for hikers, horses, mountain bikes, and motorbikes.
2.2 ▲   SO   Trail on right is 31E50 for hikers, horses, mountain bikes, and motorbikes.
        GPS: N35°56.23' W118°37.01'

▼ 2.6   SO   Trail on right is 31E50.
2.1 ▲   SO   Trail on left is 31E50.
▼ 4.2   SO   Closure gate.
0.5 ▲   SO   Closure gate.
        GPS: N35°55.29' W118°36.32'

▼ 4.5   SO   Track on right and small track on left.
0.2 ▲   SO   Small track on right and track on left.
        GPS: N35°55.25' W118°35.96'

▼ 4.7   BR   Fork in trail at Packsaddle Meadow.

        Track on left is 23S64. Zero trip meter.
0.0 ▲   Continue to the south.
        GPS: N35°55.40' W118°35.87'

▼ 0.0   Continue to the northeast.
1.5 ▲   SO   Track on right at Packsaddle Meadow is 23S64. Zero trip meter.
▼ 0.1   SO   Closure gate.
1.4 ▲   SO   Closure gate.
▼ 0.6   SO   Trail on right is Pup Meadow Trail (31E53) to Frog Meadow.
0.9 ▲   SO   Trail on left is Pup Meadow Trail (31E53) to Frog Meadow.
        GPS: N35°55.34' W118°35.33'

▼ 0.8   SO   Track on left.
0.7 ▲   SO   Track on right.
▼ 1.5   TL   Turn left and join 23S73. Track on right is also 23S73. Zero trip meter.
0.0 ▲   Continue to the west.
        GPS: N35°55.29' W118°34.58'

▼ 0.0   Continue to the north.
1.3 ▲   TR   Turn right, joining 23S28. Ahead is the

GIANT SEQUOIA

The giant sequoia trees of California are among the largest, and oldest, living things on earth. Almost all of these magnificent giants, remnants from the age of dinosaurs, are protected in Sequoia, Kings Canyon, and Yosemite National Parks. The trees have a tall, bare, reddish brown trunk; the diameter at the base sometimes exceeds 20 feet. The leaves are evergreen and scalelike, and the cones are pinelike. Sequoias grow to astonishing heights: usually between 150 and 250 feet tall. The largest of the species is a tree in Kings Canyon National Park named General Sherman, which is 275 feet tall, with a base diameter of 36 feet, a weight of about 2.7 million pounds, and an estimated age of 2,300 years. Rings on other trees imply ages of over 3,200 years old. Sequoia wood is no longer used as lumber, but many of these ancient trees were irresponsibly felled in earlier times.

The trees were named after a Cherokee Indian, Sequoya, the only inventor of a tribal alphabet in North America. Sequoya was the grandson of George Washington's personal guide, Christopher Gist.

Giant Sequoia

Lichen cover the trunk of this sequoia

Meadow.
GPS: N35°55.68' W118°33.89'

▼ 1.3　　Closure gate; then trail ends on small paved road 23S16. Turn left for Johnsondale; turn right for Sugarloaf. Small paved road 23S33 is opposite.

0.0 ▲　　Trail commences on small paved road 23S16, 4.6 miles south of Johnsondale, at the intersection with SM 99. Zero trip meter and turn southwest on graded dirt road, following sign for Speas Ridge Trail. Route is marked 23S73. Small paved road 23S33 is opposite.
GPS: N35°56.00' W118°33.70'

Capinero Saddle Trail

STARTING POINT CR 50, 0.8 miles north of Sugarloaf Sawmill, 6.7 miles north of Portuguese Pass
FINISHING POINT Intersection of M50 and M56, at the Hot Springs Ranger Station
TOTAL MILEAGE 8.2 miles
UNPAVED MILEAGE: 6.1 miles
DRIVING TIME 45 minutes
ELEVATION RANGE 3,600–5,300 feet
USUALLY OPEN April 15 to November 15
BEST TIME TO TRAVEL April 15 to November 15
DIFFICULTY RATING 1
SCENIC RATING 7
REMOTENESS RATING +0

Special Attractions

- Pleasant trail running between Sugarloaf and Pine Flat.
- Backcountry camping opportunities and developed campground at White River.

History

Sugarloaf Mill, formerly known as the Guernsey Mill and still marked as such on some maps, began operations in 1923 under the ownership of Roy Guernsey and his son Ralph. The mill was built close to the site of Parson's Mill, which had ceased operations in

continuation of 23S73. Zero trip meter.

▼ 0.4　SO　Track on left is 23S73B.

0.9 ▲　SO　Track on right is 23S73B.
GPS: N35°55.44' W118°34.25'

▼ 0.6　BL　Track on right is 23S73A. Remain on 23S73.

0.7 ▲　BR　Track on left is 23S73A. Remain on 23S73.
GPS: N35°55.50' W118°34.03'

▼ 0.9　SO　Track on right is 23S73C to Speas Meadow.

0.4 ▲　SO　Track on left is 23S73C to Speas

White River flows among pines, aspen and oaks

1905. The Guernseys improved many of the primitive roadways in the region in order to get their heavy milling machinery into place. However, truckers of the era still had their work cut out for them, sometimes taking a full day to travel a quarter of a mile through the worst areas. Getting stuck was a common occurrence. Pines, cedars, and firs were cut from the surrounding forests as well as from additional lands on Sugarloaf Mountain, which was the property of George Dooley, who had taken over some of Parson's former properties. The Guernseys sold their wood to traders in the region, who in turn brought the timber out of the forests to markets in Porterville and Bakersfield. The mill ran on gasoline until electricity was connected in 1947.

The Guernseys sold out to the Alexander family, who improved the mill to allow for proper finishing of the lumber on-site. The Alexanders had visited the area as early as 1908, and they constructed their first cabin in Spears Meadow around 1920. By the late 1930s, the Alexanders purchased some land and a cabin from the Guernseys and started constructing what would become the Sugarloaf Ski Lodge. Although low snowfalls hampered business during some winters, the Sugarloaf Ski Lodge soon became a popular resort. The lodge also attracted hunters who went after the region's abundant game. In later years, snowplows kept the roads open to enable guests to reach the lodge, which still used lanterns for lighting and wood-fired ranges for cooking until 1947. The Alexanders retired in the mid-1960s and sold the resort, which has changed hands several times since then and, when last visited, was closed.

Description

This short trail is one of a number of easy graded roads that crisscross Sequoia National Forest. Initially it travels through lush forest before entering more open, rolling hills, vegetated with small oaks and manzanitas. It continues to travel through a mixture of sug-

Open mountain ridges appear as Capinero Saddle Trail emerges from mature forests

CENTRAL MOUNTAINS #11: CAPINERO SADDLE TRAIL

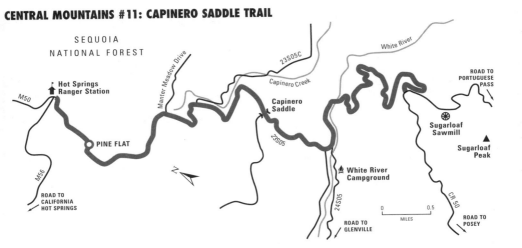

ar pines, black pines, oaks, and giant sequoias, offering good views and quiet backcountry driving. A number of smaller trails, unmarked on most maps, lead off from the main route. There are also a number of good backcountry campsites, as well as a forest service campground alongside the White River. The forest service closes this trail in the winter and when there is any danger or trail damage, such as after heavy rains.

Current Road Information
Sequoia National Forest
Tule River/Hot Springs Ranger District
32588 Highway 190
Springville, CA 93265
(559) 539-2607

Map References
BLM   Isabella Lake
USFS   Sequoia National Forest
USGS   1:24,000 Tobias Peak, Posey,
       California Hot Springs
       1:100,000 Isabella Lake
Maptech CD-ROM: Barstow/San
       Bernardino County
*Southern & Central California Atlas &
       Gazetteer,* p. 50
California Road & Recreation Atlas, p. 93

Route Directions

▼ 0.0   From CR 50, 0.8 miles north of
          Sugarloaf Sawmill, zero trip meter and
          turn northwest on graded dirt road
          23S05, sign-posted to California Hot
          Springs.
3.5 ▲   Trail ends on CR 50, 0.8 miles north of
          Sugarloaf Sawmill. Turn right for Posey.
          GPS: N35°50.46' W118°36.95'

▼ 0.2 SO Closure gate.
3.3 ▲ SO Closure gate.
▼ 0.3 SO Track on right.
3.2 ▲ SO Track on left.
▼ 1.8 SO Turnout on left.
1.7 ▲ SO Turnout on right.
▼ 2.9 BL Cross over White River on bridge; then
           track on right leads to a dead end.
0.6 ▲ BR Track on left leads to a dead end; bear
           right and cross over White River on
           bridge.
          GPS: N35°50.95' W118°37.39'

▼ 3.5 SO Graded road 24S05 on left crosses
           White River on bridge and goes to
           White River Campground and Glenville.
           Follow sign to Pine Flat. Zero trip
           meter.
0.0 ▲   Continue to the east on 23S05.
          GPS: N35°50.80' W118°37.87'

▼ 0.0   Continue to the west on 23S05.

4.7 ▲   SO   Graded road 24S05 on right crosses White River on bridge and goes to White River Campground and Glenville. Follow sign to Sugarloaf. Zero trip meter.

▼ 0.1   SO   Track on left.

4.6 ▲   SO   Track on right.

▼ 1.0   SO   Track on left.

3.7 ▲   SO   Track on right.

▼ 2.1   SO   Track on right alongside Capinero Creek is 23S05C into camping area; then cattle guard.

2.6 ▲   SO   Cattle guard; then track on left alongside Capinero Creek is 23S05C into camping area.

         GPS: N35°52.00′ W118°38.14′

▼ 2.6   SO   Track on right. Follow sign to Pine Flat. Road is now paved.

2.1 ▲   SO   Track on left. Road is now graded dirt.

         GPS: N35°52.09′ W118°38.36′

▼ 2.7   SO   Cattle guard.

2.0 ▲   SO   Cattle guard.

▼ 2.8   SO   Road passes through private housing. Paved road on right is Manter Meadow Drive. Remain on major paved road. Many small roads to houses on left and right.

1.9 ▲   SO   Paved road on left is Manter Meadow Drive. Remain on Pine Flat Drive.

▼ 4.0   SO   Grocery store and motel at Pine Flat.

0.7 ▲   SO   Grocery store and motel at Pine Flat.

         GPS: N35°52.65′ W118°39.05′

▼ 4.7   Trail ends at intersection of M56 and M50, 2 miles east of California Hot Springs. Hot Springs Ranger Station is at the intersection. Continue on M56 for California Hot Springs.

0.0 ▲   Trail starts on M56, 2 miles east of California Hot Springs. Zero trip meter at intersection with M50 and proceed southeast on paved M56 toward Pine Flat. Hot Springs Ranger Station is at the intersection.

         GPS: N35°53.17′ W118°38.83′

Rancheria Road

STARTING POINT California 178, 3 miles northeast of intersection with California 184

FINISHING POINT California 155 at Alta Sierra, 7.2 miles west of Wofford Heights

TOTAL MILEAGE 35.3 miles

UNPAVED MILEAGE: 29 miles

DRIVING TIME 3 hours

ELEVATION RANGE 600–6,800 feet

USUALLY OPEN April to November

BEST TIME TO TRAVEL Dry weather

DIFFICULTY RATING 1

SCENIC RATING 9

REMOTENESS RATING +0

Special Attractions

■ Historic Oak Flat Fire Lookout.

■ Alternative entry/exit for Sequoia National Forest.

■ Long trail through a variety of vegetation and scenery.

■ Access to a wide variety of backcountry campsites as well as 4WD, hiking, and equestrian trails.

History

At the start of the trail, a historical marker indicates that Francisco Garcés crossed the Kern River near this point on May 1, 1776. He was on an expedition to find a shorter route from Sonora, Mexico, to Monterey. Garcés named the river the San Felipe.

In 1986, private property just off of Rancheria Road was the site of a mysterious plane crash. The area was closed off and all remains of the plane were removed. The crash sparked a 120-acre blaze that firefighters fought to contain before they were removed from the scene. The plane, thought to be a top-secret stealth plane designed to be invisible to enemy radar, was on a test flight from Edwards Air Force Base. At the time, such technology was experimental and the government was keen to keep details secret.

Oak Flat Fire Lookout was constructed in 1934 as part of a chain of lookouts built to

Cold Spring catches fallen oak leaves

assist the forest service with communications and the detection of forest fires. This lookout tower ceased operations in 1984 because aircraft and truck patrols rendered it obsolete.

The idea for a ski area in the mountains of Kern County was first put forward in 1939. Possible locations were scouted by Kern County officials (initially by air) with the help of Wilfred Wiebe, president of the Bakersfield Ski Club. The team decided on Shirley Peak, and the location was developed for downhill skiing. In due course, the area opened, initially using an old towrope to pull skiers up the mountain. The first skier down the runs was Wilfred Wiebe.

Description

Rancheria Road is a highly scenic alternative route connecting Bakersfield to Alta Sierra. The graded dirt road is suitable for passenger vehicles in dry weather. There is no snow removal along the route, so it closes naturally with snowfall anytime from late November on. In addition, the forest service may gate it shut because of snow or rain.

Initially, the road passes through citrus groves and private land as it climbs up the valley alongside Rattlesnake Creek. These tight valleys and grassy hills are very pretty and an easy drive.

After 14 miles, the road enters Sequoia National Forest (the boundary is unmarked). A short spur trail leads to the historic Oak Flat Fire Lookout. The spur is gated shut after 0.4 miles, but the tower can be reached on foot, via a short walk from the gate. The 14-by-14-foot cabin is available for overnight rental for a small fee, which includes vehicle access to the tower. Contact the Greenhorn Ranger District in Lake Isabella (760-379-5646) for details.

The graded trail climbs gradually as it passes a number of oak trees and open boulder-strewn landscape. At the higher elevations near the end of the trail, the vegetation changes to pines and firs. There are many good campsites to be found along the trail in the open fire-safe areas as well as the developed campground at Evans Flat.

The northern end of the trail levels off as it travels near the top of the ridge in the

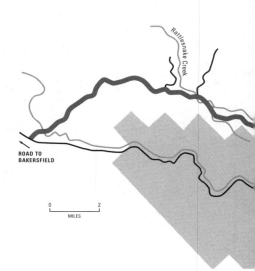

Greenhorn Mountains. Isabella Lake can be glimpsed through the trees from this end of the trail.

Shirley Meadows Ski Area operates during the winter months, with 70 percent of its runs catering to beginning and intermediate skiers. The quality of the season depends on snowfall—this quiet ski area has no snowmaking equipment.

A popular trail for hikers, mountain bikers, and equestrians is the Unal Trail, which heads off from the north end of Rancheria Road and climbs gently to travel over Unal Peak before dropping down past the site of a typical Native American home site. The entire trail is a loop of 3 miles and is dedicated to the Tubatulabal, early Native American occupants of the area.

Current Road Information

Sequoia National Forest
Kern River Ranger District-Lake Isabella
4875 Ponderosa Drive
PO Box 3810
Lake Isabella, CA 93240
(760) 379-5646

Map References

BLM   Isabella Lake, Tehachapi
USFS   Sequoia National Forest

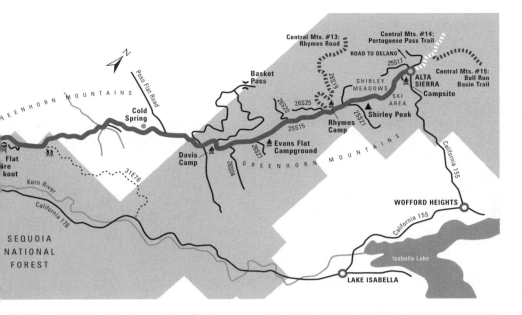

USGS 1:24,000 Rio Bravo Ranch, Pine
 Mtn., Democrat Hot Springs,
 Miracle Hot Springs, Alta Sierra
 1:100,000 Isabella Lake, Tehachapi
Maptech CD-ROM: Barstow/San
 Bernardino County
Southern & Central California Atlas &
 Gazetteer, pp. 63, 49, 50
California Road & Recreation Atlas, p. 93

Route Directions

▼ 0.0   From California 178, 3 miles northeast
           of intersection with California 184, zero
           trip meter and turn north on paved
           two-lane road marked Rancheria Road.
14.3 ▲   Trail ends at T-intersection with
           California 178. Turn right for
           Bakersfield; turn left for Lake Isabella.
           GPS: N35°25.01′ W118°49.83′

▼ 4.0   SO Road turns to graded dirt.
10.3 ▲   SO Road is now paved.
           GPS: N35°28.33′ W118°49.66′

▼ 6.2   SO Cattle guard.
8.1 ▲   SO Cattle guard.
▼ 6.5   SO Graded road on left.
7.8 ▲   SO Graded road on right.
           GPS: N35°29.50′ W118°47.72′

▼ 6.9   SO Road on right.
7.4 ▲   SO Road on left.
▼ 7.1   SO Road on right.
7.2 ▲   SO Road on left.
▼ 7.9   SO Graded road on left.
6.4 ▲   SO Graded road on right.
▼ 8.1   SO Cross over Rattlesnake Creek.
6.2 ▲   SO Cross over Rattlesnake Creek.
           GPS: N35°30.31′ W118°46.44′

▼ 8.6   SO Track on left.
5.7 ▲   SO Track on right.
▼ 8.7   SO Cross over creek; then cattle guard.
5.6 ▲   SO Cattle guard; then cross over creek.
▼ 10.3   SO Cattle guard.
4.0 ▲   SO Cattle guard.
▼ 13.6   SO Cattle guard. Entering Sequoia
           National Forest.
0.7 ▲   SO Cattle guard. Leaving Sequoia National
           Forest.
           GPS: N35°32.21′ W118°42.59′

▼ 14.1   SO Track on left.
0.2 ▲   SO Track on right.
▼ 14.3   SO Track on right is 27S20 to Oak Flat Fire
           Lookout. Closure gate at start of trail.
           Zero trip meter.
0.0 ▲   Continue to the west.
           GPS: N35°32.38′ W118°42.02′

Approaching Oak Flat Fire Lookout as morning haze fills the valley below

▼ 0.0   Continue to the north.
6.5 ▲   SO Track on left is 27S20 to Oak Flat Fire
            Lookout. Closure gate at start of trail.
            Zero trip meter.
▼ 0.3   SO Track on right.
6.2 ▲   SO Track on left.
▼ 0.4   SO Cattle guard.
6.1 ▲   SO Cattle guard.
▼ 1.1   SO Badger Gap Trail (31E76) on right for
            hikers, mountain bikes, horses, and
            motorbikes only.
5.4 ▲   SO Badger Gap Trail (31E76) on left for
            hikers, mountain bikes, horses, and
            motorbikes only.

▼ 2.3   SO Fence line.
4.2 ▲   SO Fence line.
▼ 2.4   SO Cattle guard.
4.1 ▲   SO Cattle guard.
▼ 3.7   SO Cattle guard.
2.8 ▲   SO Cattle guard.
▼ 4.6   SO Cross over creek.
1.9 ▲   SO Cross over creek.
▼ 4.8   SO Cross over creek.
1.7 ▲   SO Cross over creek.
▼ 5.0   SO Track on right is private.
1.5 ▲   SO Track on left is private.
▼ 5.6   SO Cattle guard.

0.9 ▲	SO	Cattle guard.
▼ 6.5	SO	Delonegha 4WD Trail (31E22) on right for 4WDs, ATVs, motorbikes, mountain bikes, horses, and hikers—rated black by the USFS. Zero trip meter.
0.0 ▲		Continue to the southeast.

GPS: N35°35.70' W118°39.35'

▼ 0.0		Continue to the northeast. Road is now marked 25S15.
1.9 ▲	SO	Delonegha 4WD Trail (31E22) on left for 4WDs, ATVs, motorbikes, mountain bikes, horses, and hikers—rated black. Zero trip meter.
▼ 0.2	SO	Track on left.
1.7 ▲	SO	Track on right.
▼ 0.6	SO	Cold Spring on left; then track on right.
1.3 ▲	SO	Track on left; then Cold Spring on right.

GPS: N35°35.86' W118°38.89'

▼ 1.6	SO	Cattle guard.
0.3 ▲	SO	Cattle guard.
▼ 1.9	SO	Graded road on left is Poso Flat Road. Remain on 25S15. Zero trip meter.
0.0 ▲		Continue to the southwest, following sign to State Highway 178.

GPS: N35°36.38' W118°38.23'

▼ 0.0		Continue to the northeast, following sign to State Highway 155.
5.3 ▲	BL	Graded road on right is Poso Flat Road. Remain on 25S15. Zero trip meter.
▼ 0.6	SO	Re-entering Sequoia National Forest at sign.
4.7 ▲	SO	Leaving Sequoia National Forest at sign.

GPS: N35°36.70' W118°37.83'

▼ 0.9	SO	Track on left.
4.4 ▲	SO	Track on right.
▼ 1.1	SO	Track on right; then small track on left.
4.2 ▲	SO	Small track on right; then track on left.
▼ 1.4	SO	Track on left is Basket Pass Road. Continue on Rancheria Road, following sign to Highway 155.
3.9 ▲	SO	Track on right is Basket Pass Road. Continue on Rancheria Road, following sign to Bakersfield.

GPS: N35°36.91' W118°37.26'

▼ 1.6	SO	Cattle guard.
3.7 ▲	SO	Cattle guard.
▼ 1.7	BL	Track on right and Davis Camp on right.
3.6 ▲	BR	Track on left and Davis Camp on left.

GPS: N35°36.93' W118°37.00'

| ▼ 1.8 | SO | Track on left is 26S13. Davis Camp Fire Safe Area on left; then track on right is 26S30 to Greenhorn Creek. |
| 3.5 ▲ | SO | Track on left is 26S30 to Greenhorn Creek; then Davis Camp Fire Safe Area on right. Track on right is 26S13. |

GPS: N35°37.00' W118°36.93'

| ▼ 2.5 | SO | Track on left is 26S13; then second track on left. |
| 2.8 ▲ | SO | Track on right; then second track on right is 26S13. |

GPS: N35°37.48' W118°36.61'

| ▼ 3.1 | SO | Track on right is Bradshaw Creek Road (26S04); then small track on left. |
| 2.2 ▲ | SO | Small track on right; then track on left is Bradshaw Creek Road (26S04). |

GPS: N35°37.41' W118°36.23'

▼ 3.5	SO	Closure gate.
1.8 ▲	SO	Closure gate.
▼ 3.7	SO	Track on right; then track on left is 26S05 marked to Basket Pass. Continue on 25S15.
1.6 ▲	SO	Track on right is 26S05 marked to Basket Pass; then track on left. Continue on 25S15.

GPS: N35°37.92' W118°36.02'

▼ 4.3	SO	Track on left is 26S18.
1.0 ▲	SO	Track on right is 26S18.
▼ 4.9	SO	Track on right is 26S27. Evans Flat USFS Campground on right; then track on left.
0.4 ▲	SO	Track on right; then Evans Flat USFS Campground on left. Track on left is 26S27.

GPS: N35°38.64' W118°35.48'

| ▼ 5.3 | SO | Track on right is Sawmill Road to California 178. Zero trip meter. |
| 0.0 ▲ | | Continue to the south, remaining on |

Oak Flat Fire Lookout

Rancheria Road.

GPS: N35°39.07' W118°35.29'

▼ 0.0   Continue to the north, remaining on Rancheria Road.

2.9 ▲   SO Track on left is Sawmill Road to California 178. Zero trip meter.

▼ 1.0 SO Track on left is 26S20 and track on right.

1.9 ▲ SO Track on right is 26S20 and track on left.

GPS: N35°39.87' W118°35°21'

▼ 2.9 SO Small track on left is 26S25. Second track on left is Central Mountains #13: Rhymes Road (26S19). Zero trip meter.

0.0 ▲   Continue to the south, following sign to Bakersfield.

GPS: N35°41.10' W118°34.40'

▼ 0.0   Continue to the northeast, following sign for State Highway 155. Rhymes Camp on left and track on right is Just Outstanding Trail.

4.4 ▲ SO Rhymes Camp on right and track on left is Just Outstanding Trail. Track on right is Central Mountains #13: Rhymes Road (26S19). Second smaller track on right is 26S25. Zero trip meter.

▼ 0.2 SO Track on left is 25S15D.

4.2 ▲ SO Track on right is 25S15D.

▼ 0.8 SO Track on left is 26S07 and track on right is 25S21.

3.6 ▲ SO Track on right is 26S07 and track on left is 25S21.

GPS: N35°41.65' W118°34.13'

▼ 1.1 SO Just Outstanding Trail crosses road. Track on left is 25S15B.

3.3 ▲ SO Just Outstanding Trail crosses road. Track on right is 25S15B.

▼ 1.7 SO Just Outstanding Trail (32E46) crosses road—no 4WDs or ATVs permitted.

2.7 ▲ SO Just Outstanding Trail (32E46) crosses road—no 4WDs or ATVs permitted.

▼ 2.0 SO Seasonal closure gate; then track on right.

2.4 ▲ SO Track on left; then seasonal closure gate.

▼ 2.1 SO Road becomes paved. Pass through Shirley Meadows Ski Area. Remain on paved road for next 2.3 miles.

2.3 ▲ SO Exit ski area. Road turns to graded dirt.

▼ 2.2 SO Seasonal closure gate. Exit ski area.

2.2 ▲ SO Seasonal closure gate. Pass through Shirley Meadows Ski Area.

GPS: N35°42.73' W118°33.52'

▼ 2.3 SO Track on left; then track on right.

2.1 ▲ SO Track on left; then track on right.

▼ 2.4 SO Track on left is used by snowmobiles and cross-country skiers in winter.

2.0 ▲ SO Track on right is used by snowmobiles and cross-country skiers in winter.

▼ 2.6 SO Track on right is 25S31.

1.8 ▲ SO Track on left is 25S31.

▼ 2.9 SO Track on right is 25S21.

1.5 ▲ SO Track on left is 25S21.

▼ 3.1 SO Turnout on right with views over Isabella Lake.

1.3 ▲ SO Turnout on left with views over Isabella Lake.

▼ 4.3 SO Track on left is 25S17 and track on right into campground. Unal Trail (31E58) for hikers, horses, and mountain bikes on left. Information boards mark the start.

0.1 ▲ SO Track on left into campground and track on right is 25S17. Unal Trail (31E58) for hikers, horses, and mountain bikes on right. Information boards mark the start. Follow sign for Shirley Meadows Ski Area.

▼ 4.4   Trail ends at T-intersection with California 155 at Greenhorn Summit, Alta Sierra. Turn right for Wofford Heights; turn left for Delano. Trail opposite is the start of Central Mountains #14: Portuguese Pass Trail.

0.0 ▲   Trail commences on California 155 at Greenhorn Summit, Alta Sierra, 7.2 miles west of Wofford Heights. Trail is opposite the start of Central Mountains #14: Portuguese Pass Trail at Kern County mile marker 53. Zero trip meter and turn south on paved road, following sign for Shirley Meadows Ski Area. Remain on paved road for next 2.3 miles.

GPS: N35°44.32' W118°33.31'

Rhymes Road

STARTING POINT Central Mountains #12: Rancheria Road, 2 miles south of Shirley Meadows

FINISHING POINT Intersection of Poso Park Drive and Old Stage Drive, 0.5 miles south of Poso Park

TOTAL MILEAGE 22.1 miles

UNPAVED MILEAGE: 22.1 miles

DRIVING TIME 2.5 hours

ELEVATION RANGE 4,000–6,100 feet

USUALLY OPEN May to December

BEST TIME TO TRAVEL May to December

DIFFICULTY RATING 2

SCENIC RATING 9

REMOTENESS RATING +0

Special Attractions

- Diverse trail running through Sequoia National Forest.
- Backcountry camping opportunities.

History

Rhymes Road commemorates James J. Rhymes, one of three people elected to office in the first Kern County election, which took place in 1866. That year, Democrats soundly defeated Republicans. Rhymes had been ranching in the area since the early 1860s. Another local name is encountered along the trail as it climbs to the north, away from California 155. The trail traverses the western face of Bohna Peak, passing just above the catchment area of Bohna Creek. Henry Bohna was an early settler who ranched between Rag and Gordon Gulches, just west of Glenville.

Peel Creek was the location of a sawmill by the same name. Previously, it was known as Greene Mill and prior to that, Redfield Mill. The mill operated from the late 1880s, and the lumber produced there was used for the construction of early properties in this mountain region. Ox teams used to haul timber and machinery were a common sight on the steep-sided hills. The difficult terrain, combined with the distance from markets in Bakersfield, Visalia, and Porterville, was a major factor contributing to the closure of the mill.

After sitting idle for some years, the Peel Mill was brought back to life in the early 1910s by the popular Jack Ranch Resort. Jack Ranch attracted campers who came on horseback to camp along Poso Creek. When automobiles started making the trek, the number of visitors increased. To accommodate these extra visitors, the owner came up with an ingenious way of increasing its water supply. The ranch utilized the steaming tubes and smokestack from the old abandoned mill to run water from Poso Creek to the kitchen. Mrs. Berry, who ran the kitchen in its early days, now had running water. The addition of heating coils to the furnace of the wood-fired range also provided hot water. Her excellent cooking gained a reputation among travelers. Soon, a number of fishermen, hunters, and campers were stopping for one of her home-cooked meals.

The ranch utilized the remaining lumber from the Peel Mill to construct platforms upon which campers could erect their canvas tents. During the summer, these campsites would attract 200 to 300 people at a fee of $1 to $1.50 per week, depending on the size of the platform base used. Many visitors became enamored of the region and returned in later years to purchase small plots for summer cabins. Many subdivisions, such as Panorama Heights and Poso Park, developed over the following decades.

Description

Rhymes Road is a small, single-track trail that runs down from Shirley Peak to follow alongside Alder Creek. At the start of the lightly traveled trail are sections of shelf road with good views back to Shirley Peak.

The very pleasant Alder Creek Campground is at the confluence of Alder Creek and Cedar Creek, with some shady sites down by the water. From here, the trail is well used as it climbs steadily to intersect with California 155.

North of the highway, the trail continues around the western side of the Greenhorn Mountains. There is a well-used, primitive

Shirley Peak is just visible among the pines on the southern end of the trail

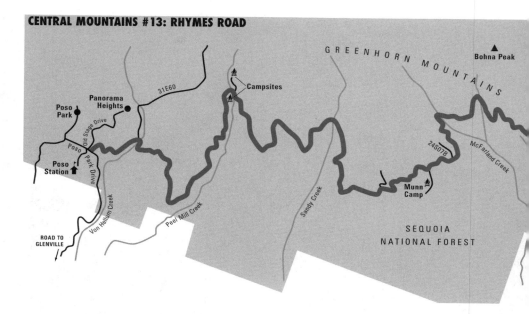

camping area at Munn Camp. The trail finishes at Poso Park, opposite Poso Station, a forest service property that is available for recreation rental. The cabin, constructed in 1933 as a base for national forest fire personnel, has one bedroom and sleeps five, with additional room outside for tents or a recreational vehicle. There is an overnight fee and reservations are required.

Current Road Information

Sequoia National Forest
Kern River Ranger District-Lake Isabella
4875 Ponderosa Drive
PO Box 3810
Lake Isabella, CA 93240
(760) 379-5646

Map References

BLM   Isabella Lake
USFS   Sequoia National Forest
USGS   1:24,000   Alta Sierra, Tobias Peak,
          Posey
          1:100,000 Isabella Lake
Maptech CD-ROM: Barstow/San
          Bernardino County
*Southern & Central California Atlas &
          Gazetteer,* p. 50
California Road & Recreation Atlas, p. 93

Route Directions

▼ 0.0   From Central Mountains #12: Rancheria Road, 2 miles south of Shirley Meadows, zero trip meter and turn west on graded dirt Rhymes Road, following sign to California 155. Rhymes Camp area is at the intersection. Immediately, track on left is 26S25. Rhymes Road is marked 26S19.

7.6 ▲   Trail ends at intersection with Central Mountains #12: Rancheria Road. Turn right to travel the trail to Bakersfield; turn left for Alta Sierra.
            GPS: N35°41.10′ W118°34.40′

▼ 0.1   SO Closure gate.
7.5 ▲   SO Closure gate.

▼ 0.8   SO Track on left. Continue straight ahead on 25S04.
6.8 ▲   SO Track on right.
            GPS: N35°41.14′ W118°35.06′

▼ 1.1   SO Track on left on right-hand switchback.
6.5 ▲   SO Track on right on left-hand switchback.
▼ 1.9   SO Cross over Bear Creek.
5.7 ▲   SO Cross over Bear Creek.
▼ 2.0   SO Boy Scouts of America Camp entrance on right.

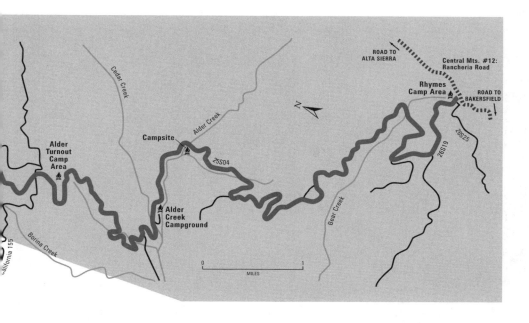

5.6 ▲	SO	Boy Scouts of America Camp entrance on left.	0.8 ▲	SO	Campsite on right.
▼ 2.4	SO	Track on right.	▼ 6.9	SO	Cross over creek.
5.2 ▲	SO	Track on left.	0.7 ▲	SO	Cross over creek.

▼ 2.4 SO Track on right.

5.2 ▲ SO Track on left.
   GPS: N35°41.63′ W118°35.09′

▼ 3.0 SO Faint track on right.

4.6 ▲ SO Faint track on left.

▼ 3.5 SO Track on right.

4.1 ▲ SO Track on left.
   GPS: N35°41.96′ W118°35.86′

▼ 3.8 SO Track on right and track on left.

3.8 ▲ SO Track on right and track on left.
   GPS: N35°42.03′ W118°36.04′

▼ 4.3 BR Track on left. Remain on main trail.

3.3 ▲ BL Track on right. Remain on main trail.

▼ 5.2 SO Track on left to viewpoint.

2.4 ▲ SO Track on right to viewpoint.

▼ 5.6 SO Cross over creek.

2.0 ▲ SO Cross over creek.

▼ 6.6 SO Track on right; then cross over Alder Creek.

1.0 ▲ SO Cross over Alder Creek; then track on left.
   GPS: N35°43.16′ W118°35.88′

▼ 6.8 SO Campsite on left.

0.8 ▲ SO Campsite on right.

▼ 6.9 SO Cross over creek.

0.7 ▲ SO Cross over creek.

▼ 7.1 SO Entering Alder Creek Fire Safe Area.

0.5 ▲ SO Leaving fire safe area at sign.
   GPS: N35°43.27′ W118°36.27′

▼ 7.4 SO Cattle guard.

0.2 ▲ SO Cattle guard.
   GPS: N35°43.19′ W118°36.51′

▼ 7.6 SO Track on left into Alder Creek Campground; then main trail exits campground across bridge over Cedar Creek. Zero trip meter.

0.0 ▲ Continue to the northeast.
   GPS: N35°43.17′ W118°36.81′

▼ 0.0 Continue to the southwest.

3.0 ▲ SO Entering Alder Creek Campground across bridge over Cedar Creek; then track on right into campground. Zero trip meter at bridge.

▼ 0.1 SO Exiting fire safe area; then cattle guard.

2.9 ▲ SO Cattle guard; then entering Alder Creek Fire Safe Area around campground.

▼ 0.3 SO Track on right and track on left.

2.7 ▲ SO Track on right and track on left.

▼ 1.1 SO Cross over creek.

Rhymes Road winds in and out of the forest, descending to Alder Creek

1.9 ▲ SO Cross over creek.
▼ 2.7 SO Two tracks on right.
0.3 ▲ SO Two tracks on left.
▼ 2.9 SO Alder Turnout Camp on right.
0.1 ▲ SO Alder Turnout Camp on left.
       GPS: N35°44.20' W118°36.72'

▼ 3.0 SO Closure gate; then intersection with paved California 155. Zero trip meter and continue across paved road onto graded dirt Safety Creek Fire Road, following sign to Panorama Heights. Immediately pass through closure gate.
0.0 ▲ Continue to the south.
       GPS: N35°44.25' W118°36.71'

▼ 0.0 Continue to the northwest. Road is marked 24S07.
3.8 ▲ SO Closure gate; then intersection with paved California 155. Zero trip meter and continue across paved road onto graded dirt road sign-posted to Alder Creek Campground. Immediately pass through closure gate.
▼ 0.9 SO Track on right.
2.9 ▲ SO Track on left.

▼ 1.9 SO Cross over creek.
1.9 ▲ SO Cross over creek.
▼ 2.0 SO Track on right.
1.8 ▲ SO Track on left.
       GPS: N35°45.30' W118°36.49'

▼ 2.3 SO Cross over creek.
1.5 ▲ SO Cross over creek.
▼ 2.9 SO Cross over McFarland Creek.
0.9 ▲ SO Cross over McFarland Creek.
       GPS: N35°45.76' W118°36.67'

▼ 3.4 SO Track on right is 24S07B.
0.4 ▲ SO Track on left is 24S07B.
       GPS: N35°45.49' W118°37.05'

▼ 3.8 BR Track on left goes 0.1 miles to Munn Camp—primitive camp and corral. Zero trip meter.
0.0 ▲ Continue to the southeast.
       GPS: N35°45.66' W118°37.23'

▼ 0.0 Continue to the northeast.
7.7 ▲ BL Track on right goes 0.1 miles to Munn Camp—primitive camp and corral. Zero trip meter.

▼ 0.1	SO	Cross over creek.
7.6 ▲	SO	Cross over creek.
▼ 0.5	SO	Cross over creek twice.
7.2 ▲	SO	Cross over creek twice.
▼ 0.7	SO	Track on right.
7.0 ▲	SO	Track on left.
▼ 1.1	SO	Cross over creek.
6.6 ▲	SO	Cross over creek.
▼ 2.3	SO	Cross over Sandy Creek.
5.4 ▲	SO	Cross over Sandy Creek.
▼ 3.6	SO	Track on left through clearing.
4.1 ▲	SO	Track on right through clearing.

GPS: N35°47.09′ W118°37.68′

▼ 4.3	SO	Leaving Greenhorn Ranger District at sign.
3.4 ▲	SO	Entering Greenhorn Ranger District at sign.

GPS: N35°47.47′ W118°37.23′

▼ 4.4	SO	Track on right to campsite; then cross over Peel Mill Creek; then campsite on left.
3.3 ▲	SO	Campsite on right; then cross over Peel Mill Creek; then track on left to campsite.

GPS: N35°47.50′ W118°37.22′

▼ 6.2	SO	Track on left to viewpoint.
1.5 ▲	SO	Track on right to viewpoint.
▼ 6.9	SO	Cross over Von Hellum Creek; then trail on right is 31E60 to Portuguese Pass.
0.8 ▲	SO	Trail on left is 31E60 to Portuguese Pass; then cross over Von Hellum Creek.

GPS: N35°48.09′ W118°38.02′

▼ 7.1	SO	Cross over creek.
0.6 ▲	SO	Cross over creek.
▼ 7.2	SO	Cattle guard; entering private property.
0.5 ▲	SO	Cattle guard; leaving private property.
▼ 7.6	SO	Cattle guard.
0.1 ▲	SO	Cattle guard.
▼ 7.7		Trail ends at intersection of Poso Park Drive and Old Stage Drive, 0.5 miles south of Poso Park. Continue straight ahead to exit to Poso Park.
0.0 ▲		Trail starts at the intersection of Poso Park Drive and Old Stage Drive, 0.5 miles south of Poso Park, 11.5 miles

northeast of Glenville. Zero trip meter and turn east on unmarked graded dirt road. Turn for Poso Station is opposite, and the CDF fire station and Panorama Heights are to the southeast. The turn is unmarked.

GPS: N35°48.47′ W118°38.35′

Portuguese Pass Trail

STARTING POINT California 155 at Alta Sierra
FINISHING POINT CR 50 at Portuguese Pass
TOTAL MILEAGE 6.9 miles
UNPAVED MILEAGE: 6.8 miles
DRIVING TIME 45 minutes
ELEVATION RANGE 5,900–7,400 feet
USUALLY OPEN April to November 15
BEST TIME TO TRAVEL April to November 15
DIFFICULTY RATING 1
SCENIC RATING 8
REMOTENESS RATING +0

Special Attractions
- Views of the Kern River Valley.
- Easy trail through the Greenhorn Mountains.
- Snowmobile, cross-country skiing, and snowshoe route in winter.

History
Cattle were driven on government trails past the old Parson Mill (located near the site of present-day Sugarloaf Mill) to summer pastures at Tobias Meadow to the north and Portuguese Meadow to the south. Early hunting and fishing pack trains carried visitors from the Jack Ranch on the western side of the Greenhorn Mountains through this region. Horses and mules were picked for their quiet demeanor and confidence on the narrow trails. Going rates were around $2 a day for a pack animal. Hiring a guide who would tend the animals cost about $5 a day. It was apparently quite an art to keep the animals moving in the correct direction and to keep them grouped at night. These pack trains continued until

Portuguese Pass Trail passes through mature forests along the ridge of the Greenhorn Mountains

approximately 1950, when the construction of better roads enabled visitors to visit the region in their own vehicles.

The Greenhorn Mountains were thought to hold gold and were named after two miners who prospected there—one called Green, the other called Horn.

Description

This short, easy trail travels through Sequoia National Forest between the community of Alta Sierra and the paved road on top of Portuguese Pass. The trail meanders through the forest, passing through stands of sequoias, sugar pines, and black pines. It travels alongside Penney Plantation, where a fire destroyed the vegetation about 10 years ago. There are views over the Kern River Valley to the mountains beyond. Black bears, coyotes, and deer are often seen in this region.

Like all of the trails in the national forest, this trail is closed by the forest service if there is any danger of trail damage from rain or snow. In winter, the trail is marked as a snowmobile route and is also used by snowshoers and cross-country skiers.

Current Road Information

Sequoia National Forest
Kern River Ranger District-Lake Isabella
4875 Ponderosa Drive
PO Box 3810
Lake Isabella, CA 93240
(760) 379-5646

Map References

BLM   Isabella Lake
USFS   Sequoia National Forest
USGS 1:24,000   Alta Sierra, Tobias Peak
          1:100,000 Isabella Lake

New growth of oak and manzanita is evident in fire-ravaged areas above Bull Run Creek

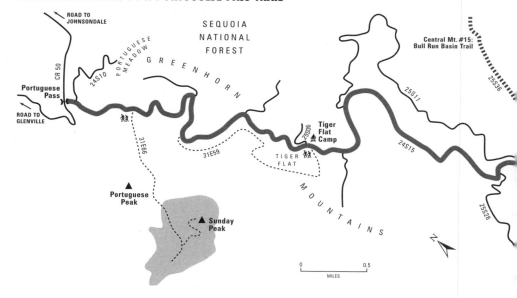

Maptech CD-ROM: Barstow/San
    Bernardino County
*Southern & Central California Atlas &
    Gazetteer,* p. 50
California Road & Recreation Atlas, p. 93

Route Directions

▼ 0.0   From California 155 at Greenhorn
Summit, Alta Sierra, 7.2 miles west of
Wofford Heights, zero trip meter and
turn north on small paved road. Trail is
opposite Central Mountains #12:
Rancheria Road. There is a sign after
the intersection for Portuguese Pass.
Route is marked as 24S15.

1.1 ▲   Trail ends at California 155 on
Greenhorn Summit, Alta Sierra, opposite Central Mountains #12: Rancheria
Road. Turn right for Glenville; turn left
for Wofford Heights and Lake Isabella.
     GPS: N35°44.32' W118°33.31'

▼ 0.1   SO   Closure gate. Road is now graded dirt.
1.0 ▲   SO   Closure gate. Road is now paved.
▼ 1.1   BL   Two tracks on right are 25S16 to Black
Mountain Saddle and Central
Mountains #15: Bull Run Basin Trail

(25S36). Follow sign to Tiger Flat. Zero
trip meter.
0.0 ▲   Continue to the west.
     GPS: N35°45.19' W118°33.24'

▼ 0.0   Continue to the northeast.
5.8 ▲   SO   Two tracks on left are 25S16 to Black
Mountain Saddle and Central
Mountains #15: Bull Run Basin Trail
(25S36). Remain on main graded road.
Zero trip meter.
▼ 0.2   SO   Track on right is 25S11 and track
on left.
5.6 ▲   SO   Track on left is 25S11 and track
on right.
     GPS: N35°45.36' W118°33.26'

▼ 0.5   SO   Track on left is 25S28.
5.3 ▲   SO   Track on right is 25S28.
▼ 2.1   SO   Track on right is 25S11.
3.7 ▲   SO   Track on left is 25S11.
     GPS: N35°46.55' W118°33.65'

▼ 2.6   SO   Track on left is marked Rockpile.
3.2 ▲   SO   Track on right is marked Rockpile.
▼ 2.8   SO   Portuguese Trail (31E59) on left for
hikers, horses, mountain bikes, and
motorbikes.
3.0 ▲   SO   Portuguese Trail (31E59) rejoins on right.

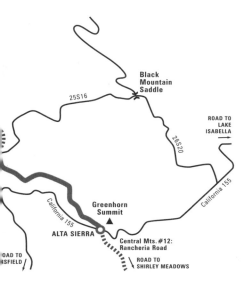

▼ 2.9   SO   Track on right is 25S06, which leaves through Tiger Flat Camp.

2.9 ▲   SO   Track on left is 25S06, which leaves through Tiger Flat Camp.

▼ 3.1   SO   Track on right.

2.7 ▲   SO   Track on left.

▼ 3.5   SO   Track on right.

2.3 ▲   SO   Track on left.

▼ 4.2   SO   Portuguese Trail (31E59) rejoins on left.

1.6 ▲   SO   Portuguese Trail (31E59) on right for hikers, horses, mountain bikes, and motorbikes.

GPS: N35°47.37' W118°34.57'

▼ 4.5   SO   Two tracks on right on left-hand bend.

1.3 ▲   SO   Two tracks on left on right-hand bend.

GPS: N35°47.45' W118°34.24'

▼ 5.2   SO   Track on left is Sunday Peak Trail (31E66) for hikers, horses, mountain

These trees are the lone survivors of fires that cleared many acres of forest in the Greenhorn Mountains

bikes, and motorbikes. Also track on left is 24S28 and track on right.

0.6 ▲ SO Track on right is 24S28 and track on left. Second track on right is Sunday Peak Trail (31E66) for hikers, horses, mountain bikes, and motorbikes.
GPS: N35°47.69' W118°34.56'

▼ 5.7 SO Closure gate; then track on right is 24S10 and track on left.

0.1 ▲ SO Track on left is 24S10 and track on right; then closure gate.
GPS: N35°48.04' W118°34.82'

▼ 5.8 Trail ends at T-intersection with small paved CR 50 at Portuguese Pass. Turn right for Johnsondale; turn left for Glenville.

0.0 ▲ Trail commences on CR 50 at Portuguese Pass, 8 miles east of Sugarloaf Village. Zero trip meter and proceed southeast on graded dirt road at sign for Portuguese Pass, following sign for Greenhorn Summit and California 155.
GPS: N35°48.12' W118°34.81'

CENTRAL MOUNTAINS #15

Bull Run Basin Trail

STARTING POINT Central Mountains #14: Portuguese Pass Trail, 1.1 miles from the southern end
FINISHING POINT Silver Strand Mine
TOTAL MILEAGE 2.3 miles (one-way)
UNPAVED MILEAGE: 2.3 miles
DRIVING TIME 20 minutes (one-way)
ELEVATION RANGE 5,000–6,000 feet
USUALLY OPEN May to December
BEST TIME TO TRAVEL May to December
DIFFICULTY RATING 3
SCENIC RATING 8
REMOTENESS RATING +0

Special Attractions

■ Remains of the Black Sambo Mine.
■ Access to the Bull Run Motorbike Trail.

History

The Black Sambo Mine was originally staked as an antimony prospect but in 1954 it was thought to contain tungsten. However, neither mineral was successfully mined from it. Two single-compartment shafts 20 to 30 feet deep were dug along the fault line; they have since caved in. Two open cuts were also made along a gully on the eastern side of Cow Creek. These open cuts, named Susie Q, were set about 300 feet apart and had faces 10 to 15 feet in height with the longest cut being about 75 feet. A pump station operated just below the lowest Susie Q cutting. It pumped water to a holding tank that was located above the upper cutting.

The Silver Strand Mine was also a tungsten mine seemingly with little recorded success.

Description

This short trail travels a much smaller track than many of the trails within this region of the Sierra Nevada. The surface is formed, undulating, and rough in spots as it descends along the narrow valley of Cow Creek. The trail passes beside large granite boulders as well as the creek as it travels through part of an area burned in a fire a few years ago. The creek contains trout but is not stocked for fishermen.

The large wooden headframe of the Black Sambo Mine can be found alongside the trail in the narrow valley. A short distance from the trail on the left are more mining remains, including an old crusher perched on the hillside.

As the valley opens out slightly for the final vehicle section, the trail becomes narrower and more brushy. It ends for vehicles alongside the creek at the Silver Strand Mine. The adits at the mine have steel gates on them. Motorbikes, hikers, and horses can follow the trail to connect through to Bull Run Basin and farther to finish at road 24S35.

Current Road Information

Sequoia National Forest
Kern River Ranger District-Lake Isabella
4875 Ponderosa Drive
PO Box 3810
Lake Isabella, CA 93240
(760) 379-5646

The headframe of the Black Sambo Mine near Cow Creek among slender sequoias

CENTRAL MOUNTAINS #15: BULL RUN BASIN TRAIL

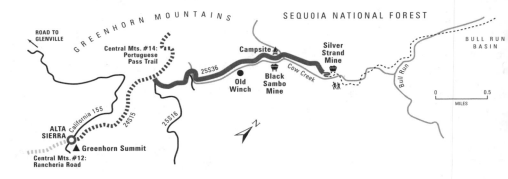

Map References

BLM   Isabella Lake
USFS   Sequoia National Forest
USGS   1:24,000   Tobias Peak
       1:100,000 Isabella Lake
Maptech CD-ROM: Barstow/San
       Bernardino County
*Southern & Central California Atlas &
       Gazetteer,* p. 50
California Road & Recreation Atlas, p. 93

Route Directions

▼ 0.0   From Central Mountains #14:
         Portuguese Pass Trail, 1.1 miles from
         the southern end, zero trip meter and
         turn north on small formed trail follow-
         ing sign for Bull Run Basin. Trail is
         marked 25S36.
         GPS: N35°45.21' W118°33.23'

▼ 0.2   SO Pass through fence line.
▼ 0.5   SO Track on right; then cross over creek;
         then track on left.
▼ 1.0   SO Old winch on right of trail.
         GPS: N35°45.77' W118°32.75'

▼ 1.4   SO Wooden headframe and small cabin of
         the Black Sambo Mine alongside the trail.
         GPS: N35°46.06' W118°32.51'

▼ 1.5   SO Track on left and campsite on left; then
         cross through creek. Track on left goes
         short distance to many mine remains
         on hillside.
▼ 1.6   SO Adit below trail on right.

▼ 1.8   BR Track on left stops just over the rise.
         GPS: N35°46.26' W118°32.28'

▼ 2.3   Trail ends for vehicles beside Cow
         Creek at the Silver Strand Mine. From
         here the trail continues for hikers, hors-
         es, and motorbikes only.
         GPS: N35°46.30' W118°32.07'

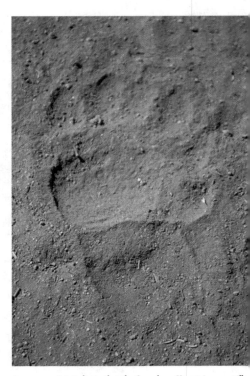

Bear paw prints indicate that the Greenhorn Mountains are still habitat for these shy creatures

Piute Mountain Road

STARTING POINT Kelso Valley Road at Sageland,
  17 miles south of California 178

FINISHING POINT California 483, 2.5 miles
  south of Bodfish

TOTAL MILEAGE 30.5 miles

UNPAVED MILEAGE: 30.5 miles

DRIVING TIME 3.5 hours

ELEVATION RANGE 4,000–8,200 feet

USUALLY OPEN March to December

BEST TIME TO TRAVEL Dry weather

DIFFICULTY RATING 2

SCENIC RATING 9

REMOTENESS RATING +0

Special Attractions

- Trail traverses a wide variety of vegetation
  and scenery.
- Long shelf road offers views of Isabella
  Lake and the Sierra Nevada.
- Access to wilderness areas and the Pacific
  Crest National Scenic Trail.

History

The first section of the route, from Kelso
Creek to the Piute Mountains, partly follows
a trail that early prospectors traveled while exploring the mountains. A prospector named
Bob Palmer made his way west from Missouri, hoping to cash in on the mineral boom
in California. In 1860, he staked his first
claim near Erskine Creek, on the northwest
side of the Piute Mountains. The claim did-
n't pay off so he moved on, feeling there were
too many miners in that general area. Palmer
made his way to Kelso Creek, which is
named after John W. Kelso, an early settler
who carted much-needed goods to and from
Los Angeles during the years of the Kern River gold rush.

Palmer found that the specks in his pan
grew in size as he worked his way up Kelso
Creek toward Piute Mountain. He joined
with a part-Cherokee friend of his, Hamp
Williams, and together they established what
became known as the Hamp Williams Mine.

This mine flourished and was joined by others such as the Bright Star Mine, which was
located in the canyon of the same name to the
north of the trail. By 1862, mining and logging activities in the region encouraged the
development of a settlement originally known
as Kelso. By 1864, it was known as Claraville,
renamed after Clara Munckton, a miner's
daughter. The town grew to a population of
nearly 500 by the mid-1860s.

By 1868, Claraville was quite the place to
be. Besides having the obligatory saloons,
stores, and hotels, it had its own courthouse
and even an opera company that gave per-
formances in town as well as in Sageland.
However, the Bright Star Mine was running
into financial problems around that time because its owners were ignoring their investment and were instead squandering their for-
tunes living the high life. It was declared
bankrupt a year later and Claraville suffered
from the lack of trade. By the early 1870s, the
town died out and its residents moved on to
more profitable ventures. Landers Creek and
Landers Meadow, to the east of Claraville, are
named after early settlers who grazed their cattle on the high pastures in the favorable summer months.

The starting point for the trail is marked
as Sageland on some maps. This was the site
of a small settlement that supplied miners
working in the mountain ranges. Sageland
supplied much of the labor force for nearby
mines, including the St. John, Burning
Moscow, and Hortense Mines. Like Claraville, Sageland suffered from the closure of
the Bright Star Mine and was deserted by the
early 1870s.

Liebel Peak, located close to the trail, was
named in the 1930s in remembrance of
prospector-turned-settler Michael Otto
Liebel, who entered the region in the 1870s.
Liebel married an Indian girl and settled on
land near the base of this mountain to raise a
large family of 11 children.

The name Walker is also prominent in the
region. The Joe Walker Mine and Walker
Basin are both named after renowned explorer Joseph Reddeford Walker (see page 127).
His earliest trip through the region took place

Climbing out of Kelso Valley near the Harris Grade

in 1833. During this expedition, he located what is now Walker Pass (northeast of the trail in the Scodie Mountains). In 1844, John C. Frémont suggested that the pass be named after Walker in recognition of the discovery of such an important route.

Description

This long trail traverses Piute Mountain, running from Kelso Valley to Rancheria Creek Valley. The trail leaves paved Kelso Valley Road and follows a roughly graded dirt road that climbs steadily into Sequoia National Forest. This section of trail is also known as the Harris Grade. Initially the trail climbs through a pinyon and juniper forest before entering a pine forest on top of the plateau. The trail gradually narrows to a single-lane dirt road as it enters the forest and passes the small settlement of Claraville—now private property and cabins. There are many side trails for 4WDs to explore, as well as an alternative exit back to Kelso Valley via Central Mountains #17: Jawbone Canyon Road.

The long Pacific Crest National Scenic Trail crosses the road a couple of times. There are also many pleasant backcountry campsites, although you do need to be aware of bears.

Eventually the trail descends a long shelf road, dropping nearly 4,000 feet in the last few miles down a steady grade to the highway near Isabella Lake. The views are excellent; the lake can be seen far below and the southern tip of the Sierra Nevada can be seen to the north.

The grade is moderate all the way, and although some sections are only wide enough for a single vehicle, there are ample passing places. Parts of the original trail (a harder, alternative 4WD route) are still open to travel up the ridge from Kelso Valley Road. This route runs close to the graded road and occasionally crosses it. The trail is best suited to high-clearance vehicles because of the eroded surface and some ruts that would make it difficult for passenger vehicles.

Current Road Information

Sequoia National Forest
Kern River Ranger District-Lake Isabella
4875 Ponderosa Drive

PO Box 3810
Lake Isabella, CA 93240
(760) 379-5646

Map References

BLM   Tehachapi
USFS Sequoia National Forest
USGS 1:24,000   Pinyon Mtn., Claraville,
      Piute Peak, Lake Isabella South,
      Miracle Hot Springs
      1:100,000 Tehachapi
Maptech CD-ROM: Barstow/San
      Bernardino County
Southern & Central California Atlas & Gazetteer, pp. 65, 64, 51
California Road & Recreation Atlas, pp. 93, 94

Route Directions

▼ 0.0   From California 178, 5 miles southwest of Onyx, zero trip meter and turn southeast on paved Kelso Valley Road. Remain on paved road for 17 miles; then zero trip meter and turn southwest on graded dirt road sign-posted for Piute Mountain. This is Sageland town site

4.9 ▲   Trail ends at T-intersection with paved Kelso Valley Road. Turn left for Weldon and California 178; turn right for Mojave.
     GPS: N35°28.80′ W118°12.71′

▼ 1.0   SO   Track on right.
3.9 ▲   SO   Track on left.
▼ 1.1   SO   Track on right.
3.8 ▲   SO   Track on left.
▼ 2.1   SO   Two tracks on right.
2.8 ▲   SO   Two tracks on left.
     GPS: N35°28.31′ W118°13.60′

▼ 2.8   SO   Track on left.
2.1 ▲   SO   Track on right.
▼ 2.9   SO   Track on right.
2.0 ▲   SO   Track on left.
▼ 3.4   SO   Track on left.
1.5 ▲   SO   Track on right.
▼ 3.6   SO   Track on right.
1.3 ▲   SO   Track on left.
▼ 4.1   SO   Track on left.
0.8 ▲   SO   Track on right.

▼ 4.9 SO Entering Sequoia National Forest at sign. Zero trip meter.

0.0 ▲ Continue to the south.

GPS: N35°27.89' W118°15.83'

▼ 0.0 Continue to the west. Road is now marked 27S02. Immediately track on right.

2.2 ▲ SO Track on left; then leaving Sequoia National Forest. Zero trip meter.

▼ 0.4 SO Track on right.

1.8 ▲ SO Track on left.

▼ 0.7 SO Cross over wash.

1.5 ▲ SO Cross over wash.

▼ 1.2 SO Track on right.

1.0 ▲ SO Track on left.

▼ 1.5 SO Pacific Crest National Scenic Trail crosses road. Left goes to Kelso Valley Road, Willow Spring, and Sequoia National Forest.

0.7 ▲ SO Pacific Crest National Scenic Trail crosses road. Right goes to Kelso Valley Road, Willow Spring, and Sequoia National Forest.

▼ 2.1 SO Track on left.

0.1 ▲ SO Track on right.

▼ 2.2 SO Graded road on left is Sorrell Peak Road (27S04). Zero trip meter.

0.0 ▲ Continue to the northeast, remaining on 27S02 and following the sign for Kelso Valley Road.

GPS: N35°26.95' W118°17.18'

▼ 0.0 Continue to the southwest, remaining on 27S02 and following the sign for Jawbone Canyon Road.

2.2 ▲ SO Graded road on right is Sorrell Peak Road (27S04). Zero trip meter.

▼ 0.9 BL Graded road on right is 29S05 to Landers Station Camp.

1.3 ▲ SO Graded road on left is 29S05 to Landers Station Camp.

GPS: N35°26.93' W118°18.16'

▼ 1.2 SO Entering private property.

1.0 ▲ SO Entering national forest.

▼ 1.4 SO Corral on left.

Blind corners are encountered as the shelf road cuts around massive granite outcroppings

0.8 ▲   SO Corral on right.

▼ 1.5   SO Re-entering national forest.

0.7 ▲   SO Entering private property.

▼ 1.6   SO Pacific Crest National Scenic Trail crosses road. Left goes 0.75 miles to Waterhole Trail Camp.

0.6 ▲   SO Pacific Crest National Scenic Trail crosses road. Right goes 0.75 miles to Waterhole Trail Camp.

GPS: N35°26.69′ W118°18.83′

▼ 1.7   SO Track on right; then cross over Landers Creek.

0.5 ▲   SO Cross over Landers Creek; then track on left.

▼ 1.8   SO Track on left is 29S07, which goes 0.6 miles to Waterhole Mine Campsite.

0.4 ▲   SO Track on right is 29S07, which goes 0.6 miles to Waterhole Mine Campsite.

GPS: N35°26.69′ W118°19.03′

▼ 1.9   SO Entering private property.

0.3 ▲   SO Entering national forest.

▼ 2.1   SO Cross over wash.

0.1 ▲   SO Cross over wash.

▼ 2.2   SO Graded road on left is Central Mountains #17: Jawbone Canyon Road to Kelso Valley. Zero trip meter. This is the site of Claraville.

0.0 ▲   Continue to the east.

GPS: N35°26.65′ W118°19.50′

▼ 0.0   Continue to the west. Remain on main road through private property.

1.8 ▲   SO Graded road on right is Central Mountains #17: Jawbone Canyon Road to Kelso Valley. Zero trip meter. This is the site of Claraville.

▼ 0.5   SO Cross over wash.

1.3 ▲   SO Cross over wash.

▼ 0.7   SO Re-entering national forest.

1.1 ▲   SO Entering private property. Remain on main road.

▼ 1.1   SO Track on right and track on left.

0.7 ▲   SO Track on right and track on left.

▼ 1.3   SO Track on left is 28S40.

0.5 ▲   SO Track on right is 28S40.

GPS: N35°27.22′ W118°20.51′

▼ 1.6   SO Track on right.

0.2 ▲   SO Track on left.

▼ 1.8   BL 5-way intersection. Take the second left, remaining on 27S02 and following the sign to Walker Basin. Major track on right is 28S27 to Steve Spring. Zero trip meter.

0.0 ▲   Continue to the southeast.

GPS: N35°27.59′ W118°20.69′

▼ 0.0   Continue to the west.

3.6 ▲   BR 5-way intersection. Take the second right, remaining on 27S02. Zero trip meter.

▼ 0.3   SO Cross over wash.

3.3 ▲   SO Cross over wash.

▼ 0.7   SO Cross over creek.

2.9 ▲   SO Cross over creek.

▼ 1.2   SO Track on left is 28S40.

2.4 ▲   SO Track on right is 28S40.

GPS: N35°27.45′ W118°21.45′

▼ 3.3   SO Graded road on right is 28S17, which goes 2 miles to Piute Vista and then stops. Also track on left.

0.3 ▲   SO Graded road on left is 28S17, which goes 2 miles to Piute Vista and then stops. Also track on right.

GPS: 35°26.98′ W118°22.43′

▼ 3.6   BR Bear right, remaining on 27S02 and following sign to Lake Isabella. Graded road on left is 28S01. Zero trip meter.

0.0 ▲   Continue to the southeast.

GPS: N35°26.88′ W118°22.64′

▼ 0.0   Continue to the north.

5.8 ▲   SO Remain on 27S02, following sign to Kelso Valley Road. Graded road on right is 28S01. Zero trip meter.

▼ 0.2   SO Track on right.

5.6 ▲   SO Track on left.

▼ 0.3   SO Camping areas on right and left as trail travels around Piute Peak.

5.5 ▲   SO Camping areas on right and left as trail travels around Piute Peak.

GPS: N35°27.14′ W118°22.79′

▼ 0.6   SO Closure gate; then turnout on left.

5.2 ▲   SO Turnout on right; then closure gate.

▼ 1.2   SO Track on left is 28S23; also track on right.

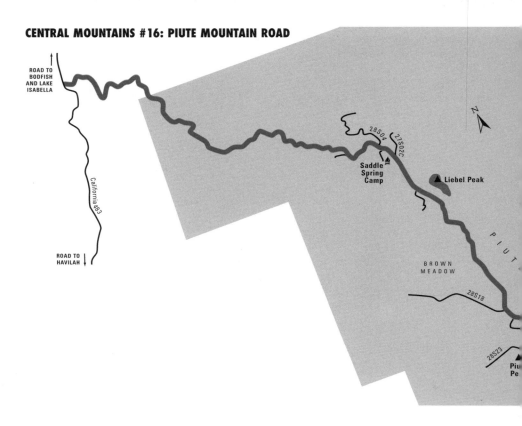

4.6 ▲	SO	Track on right is 28S23; also track on left. **GPS: N35°27.73' W118°23.23'**
▼ 1.4	BR	Track on right; then track forks. Track on left is 28S18 to Brown Meadow.
4.4 ▲	SO	Track on right is 28S18 to Brown Meadow; then track on left. **GPS: N35°27.88' W118°23.34'**
▼ 1.7	SO	Track on right.
4.1 ▲	SO	Track on left.
▼ 3.4	SO	Track on right is 27S02F and track on left is 27S02D.
2.4 ▲	SO	Track on left is 27S02F and track on right is 27S02D. **GPS: N35°29.56' W118°23.66'**
▼ 4.7	SO	Track on right is 28S19; then track on left.
1.1 ▲	SO	Track on right; then track on left is 28S19. **GPS: N35°30.39' W118°24.26'**

▼ 4.8	SO	Track on right is 27S02G.
1.0 ▲	SO	Track on left is 27S02G. **GPS: N35°30.49' W118°24.33'**
▼ 5.2	SO	Track on left is 27S02B.
0.6 ▲	SO	Track on right is 27S02B. **GPS: N35°30.82' W118°24.43'**
▼ 5.5	SO	Track on right is 27S02C; then track on left.
0.3 ▲	SO	Track on right; then track on left is 27S02C. **GPS: N35°31.06' W118°24.51'**
▼ 5.8	SO	Saddle Spring Camp on left at the start of 27S02A. Zero trip meter.
0.0 ▲		Continue to the east. **GPS: N35°31.25' W118°24.67'**
▼ 0.0		Continue to the west.
6.9 ▲	SO	Saddle Spring Camp on right at the start of 27S02A. Zero trip meter.

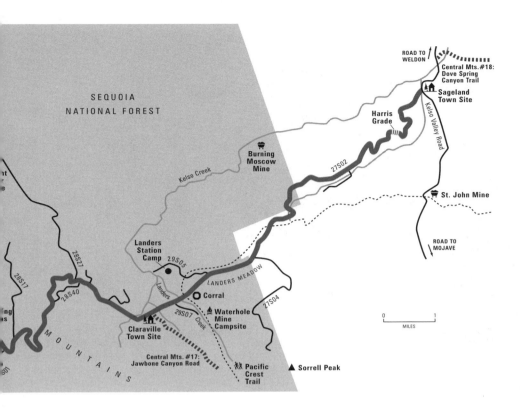

▼ 0.1	SO	Track on right is 28S04.
6.8 ▲	SO	Track on left is 28S04.
▼ 0.8	SO	Track on left.
6.1 ▲	SO	Track on right.
▼ 0.9	SO	Track on left.
6.0 ▲	SO	Track on right.
▼ 1.2	SO	Entering private property through closure gate. Remain on main road.
5.7 ▲	SO	Re-entering national forest through closure gate.
▼ 1.5	SO	Re-entering national forest.
5.4 ▲	SO	Entering private property. Remain on main road.
▼ 4.1	SO	Start to descend shelf road.
2.8 ▲	SO	End of climb.
▼ 6.9	SO	Leaving Sequoia National Forest at sign. Zero trip meter.
0.0 ▲		Continue to the south.

GPS: N35°33.45' W118°28.82'

▼ 0.0		Continue to the north.
3.1 ▲	SO	Entering Sequoia National Forest at sign. Zero trip meter.

▼ 1.2	SO	Track on right.
1.9 ▲	SO	Track on left.
▼ 2.1	SO	Track on right; then second track on right.
1.0 ▲	SO	Track on left; then second track on left.
▼ 2.5	SO	Three tracks on right.
0.6 s	SO	Three tracks on left.

GPS: N35°34.20' W118°30.04'

▼ 3.0	SO	Closure gate.
0.1 ▲	SO	Closure gate.
▼ 3.1		Trail ends at T-intersection with California 483, 2.5 miles south of Bodfish. Turn left for Havilah; turn right for Lake Isabella.
0.0 ▲		Trail starts on California 483, 2.5 miles south of Bodfish. Zero trip meter and turn south on graded dirt road. There is a sign after the intersection for Kelso Canyon.

GPS: N35°34.16' W118°30.36'

The trail riding the ridge within the Sequoia National Forest

Jawbone Canyon Road

STARTING POINT California 14 at Jawbone Station, 19.1 miles northeast of the intersection with California 58

FINISHING POINT Central Mountains #16: Piute Mountain Road, 10 miles west of Kelso Valley Road

TOTAL MILEAGE 30.3 miles

UNPAVED MILEAGE: 29.4 miles

DRIVING TIME 2 hours

ELEVATION RANGE 2,100–6,900 feet

USUALLY OPEN April to November

BEST TIME TO TRAVEL April to November

DIFFICULTY RATING 2

SCENIC RATING 9

REMOTENESS RATING +0

Special Attractions

- Jawbone Canyon OHV Area—an open area with a number of trails for 4WDs, ATVs, and motorbikes.

- Trail travels through a variety of scenery from desert to pine forest.
- The historic Geringer Grade.

History

In the 1860s, a German emigrant named Frederick Butterbredt settled in the region, took a Native American wife, and worked as a ranchero. Butterbredt Spring, Well, Peak, and Canyon are all named after his large family. In the late 1990s, the Jawbone-Butterbredt Area of Critical Environmental Concern was established on some of the weathered landscape once frequented by the family.

Jawbone Canyon Trail drops down through Kelso Valley at the foot of the Piute Mountains. John W. Kelso was a merchant who operated a store in the small mining town of Keyesville. Jawbone Canyon Trail follows a section of the trail used by Kelso to transport his merchandise into these mountains. His route took him through Jawbone Canyon, on to Kelso Valley, and then up and over St. John Ridge, which is visible from the trail at the northern end of Kelso Valley. From there he traveled down Kelso Creek to the South Fork Valley, and farther west to Keyesville. His ox team was a familiar sight to the miners and settlers of the Kern River region. Even in the worst weather conditions, he and others managed to bring supplies from Los Angeles to the gold rush camps in the area.

St. John Ridge is named after a gold mine of the same name, which was established in 1860 by a Mr. St. John and Jonnie Bonner. The partners sold out for an estimated $30,000. However, the mine flourished, supporting two mills and producing nearly $700,000 worth of gold by 1875.

The Geringer Grade on the southeast side of the Piute Mountains was a route established to connect the mining settlement of Claraville with Kelso Valley. The steep grade was named after Ott and Jack Gehringer, mining engineers who ran the Gwynne Mine, located 3 miles south of Claraville just west of the trail. They mined gold- and tungsten-bearing quartz that could be found in veins throughout the granitic bedrock. They staked six claims with a total recorded output of $770,000 in gold. Operations ceased in 1942.

In the late 1940s, the White Rock Mine was one of the active mines in the Jawbone Canyon region. Rhyolite, or pottery clay, was extracted with the use of earthmoving machinery and trucks. Antimony was also mined at Antimony Flat, just south of the prominent Cross Mountain, at the head of Jawbone Canyon.

The eastern end of the trail passes over a huge black pipeline known as the Jawbone Siphon, which is part of the Los Angeles Aqueduct. Also visible at the eastern end of the trail are the thousands of windmills that form the Tehachapi Pass Wind Farm. Scattered along the ridge tops around Tehachapi Pass, in one of the world's windiest areas, more than 5,000 wind turbines supply electricity for more than 500,000 people in Southern California. Winds over Tehachapi Pass average 14 to 20 miles per hour, and the various kinds of wind turbines operate individually, depending on conditions and the needs of each turbine.

Trail crosses into Kelso Valley with the Piute Mountains in the distance

Description

Jawbone Canyon Road is a roughly graded dirt road that connects the desert areas of Jawbone Canyon with the pine-covered Piute Mountain region in the Sequoia National Forest. Initially the road is paved as it travels through the Jawbone Canyon OHV Area, where there are formed trails and open areas for 4WDs, ATVs, and motorbikes. At the start of the trail, the staffed Jawbone Station offers an excellent selection of maps, books, and free information.

One noteworthy feature along the early stages of the trail is Blue Point—a prominent ridge of rock that gains its distinctive blue color from copper in the rock. Blue Point was considered sacred to the Native Americans who lived in Jawbone Canyon. The scenery within the canyon is spectacular in its own right, with rugged hills surrounding the open canyon. The windmills of the Tehachapi Pass Wind Farm are visible on the ridge to the southwest.

Once outside the open Jawbone Canyon OHV Area, the route climbs alongside Hoffman Canyon, offering spectacular views back over Jawbone Canyon, Blue Point, and the Fremont Valley beyond. It continues to wind through boulder-strewn hills before descending to cross the wide, flat Kelso Valley. To the west of the valley, the Piute Mountains rise up behind it. The route passes through some private property within Kelso Valley, which is not clearly marked; be sure you are on public land before following any side trails or setting up camp.

Upon entering Sequoia National Forest, the road starts to climb up the Geringer Grade, a series of narrow steep switchbacks that swiftly takes the road up 2,500 feet to the upper reaches of the Piute Mountains. Once on top, the trail travels through pine forests before finishing at the T-intersection with Central Mountains #16: Piute Mountain Road.

Typically, the trail surface is fairly even and graded with areas in Jawbone Canyon that can be sandy in spots. At the higher elevations, the trail is narrower and receives less maintenance. However it is still easily passable in dry weather by high-clearance vehicles. There are no closure gates along the trail; it closes naturally during the winter months depending on snowfall. It is often open for longer than the stated times. Check with the Sequoia National Forest for details.

Current Road Information

Sequoia National Forest
Kern River Ranger District-Lake Isabella
4875 Ponderosa Drive
PO Box 3810
Lake Isabella, CA 93240
(760) 379-5646

BLM Ridgecrest Field Office
300 South Richmond Road
Ridgecrest, CA 93555
(760) 384-5400

Map References

BLM   Tehachapi
USFS   Sequoia National Forest
USGS   1:24,000   Cinco, Cross Mtn.,
       Pinyon Mtn., Emerald Mtn.,
       Claraville
       1:100,000 Tehachapi
Maptech CD-ROM: Barstow/San
       Bernardino County
Southern & Central California Atlas &
       Gazetteer, pp. 65, 64
California Road & Recreation Atlas, p. 94
Other: East Kern County OHV Riding
       Areas and Trails—Jawbone Canyon

Route Directions

▼ 0.0   From California 14, 19.1 miles northeast of intersection with California 58, zero trip meter and turn northwest at the sign for Jawbone Station. The paved road immediately passes beside Jawbone Station on right—BLM and OHV information and maps are available. Trail initially passes through Jawbone Canyon OHV Area. Remain on paved road. Many small tracks on left and right through open area.

4.5 ▲   Trail passes Jawbone Station on left before finishing at T-intersection with California 14. Turn left for Randsburg;

LOS ANGELES–OWENS RIVER VALLEY AQUEDUCT

From its inception, Los Angeles was plagued by a shortage of water. Periods of drought were common; one report from 1841 claims that no rain fell on the town for 18 months. Still, for many years, Angelenos could meet their water needs by using water from the Los Angeles River. The population explosion at the end of the nineteenth century meant that the city was starting to outgrow its water supply. William Mulholland, superintendent of the city's water department, decided to look for an alternative source. Mulholland soon noticed the Owens River Valley, a picturesque agricultural region to the north of Los Angeles on the east side of the Sierra Nevada. Farmers in the area had a large surplus of water, and the Bureau of Reclamation was already considering damming the Owens River for future irrigation use.

Mulholland began to secretly purchase land in the quiet valley. He persuaded business associates such as Fred Eaton to do the same. The purchases prevented a dam from being built without angering local farmers. Many willingly sold their land to the Los Angeles prospectors, unaware of their intentions. Eventually the Los Angeles Department of Water and Power controlled 302,000 acres of land in Inyo and Mono Counties. Before long it became apparent what the city intended to do with the land and water rights.

Construction of the Los Angeles Aqueduct began in 1907 and was completed in 1913. At the time it was considered quite an engineering feat; 233 miles long, including 52 miles of tunnels, it carried 320,000 acre-feet of water annually to Los Angeles. A second aqueduct, finished in 1970, increased the supply.

In 1928, disaster struck the San Francisquito Canyon. The Saint Francis Dam, part of the system that provided Los Angeles with its water, began to reveal a fault in its wall. Mulholland and his inspectors rushed to inspect the dam but decided the structure was secure and returned to Los Angeles. That night, the dam gave way and water flooded 7,900 acres of land. Many downstream communities were destroyed and at least 385 people lost their lives in the torrent of water. Although Los Angeles gave $1 million for relief, local residents were infuriated, blaming poor engineering for the dam's failure. Some Angelenos countered, implying the disaster was the result of terrorism by Owens Valley activists. Only years later was a natural landslide revealed to have been the cause of the dam's collapse.

Before the aqueduct to Los Angeles, the Owens River Valley was a fertile and prosperous farming region, but this changed when the land was robbed of its water. Owens Lake dried, and local residents suffered economically. Beautiful Mono Lake has also lost much of its water because streams feeding it have been diverted to feed the coastal metropolis. The aqueduct was bombed several times during the 1920s. In addition to an increased water supply, Los Angeles had gained the ill will of some of California's rural inhabitants.

	turn right for Mojave.		3.3 ▲	SO Graded road on left.
	GPS: N35°18.01′ W118°00.00′		▼ 1.9	SO Graded road on right is SC175 for 4WDs, ATVs, and motorbikes.
▼ 0.6	SO Graded road on right goes to Dove Spring.		2.6 ▲	SO Graded road on left is SC175 for 4WDs, ATVs, and motorbikes.
3.9 ▲	SO Graded road on left goes to Dove Spring.			**GPS: N35°18.76′ W118°01.71′**
	GPS: N35°18.34′ W118°00.51′			
▼ 1.1	SO Graded road on right follows pipeline.		▼ 2.7	SO Cross over pipeline.
3.4 ▲	SO Graded road on left follows pipeline.		1.8 ▲	SO Cross over pipeline.
▼ 1.2	SO Graded road on right.		▼ 3.1	SO Track on left.

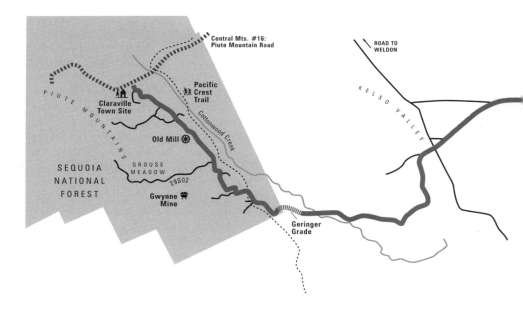

1.4 ▲	SO	Track on right.	
▼ 3.8	SO	Cattle guard.	
0.7 ▲	SO	Cattle guard.	
▼ 3.9	SO	Road turns to graded dirt.	
0.6 ▲	SO	Road is now paved.	
▼ 4.5	SO	Track on right is SC176 for 4WDs, ATVs, and motorbikes. Zero trip meter. Blue Point is directly ahead.	
0.0 ▲		Continue to the southeast.	
		GPS: N35°19.02' W118°04.49'	

▼ 0.0		Continue to the northwest.
6.8 ▲	SO	Track on left is SC176 for 4WDs, ATVs, and motorbikes. Zero trip meter.
▼ 0.4	SO	Blue Point on right; then track on right.
6.4 ▲	SO	Track on left; then Blue Point on left.
		GPS: N35°19.06' W118°04.97'

▼ 1.4	BR	Graded road on left leads through a closed area.
5.4 ▲	BL	Graded road on right leads through a closed area.
		GPS: N35°18.53' W118°05.89'

▼ 1.6	SO	Cross through Jawbone Canyon Wash.
5.2 ▲	SO	Cross through Jawbone Canyon Wash.
▼ 2.0	SO	Cross through Hoffman Canyon Wash.
4.8 ▲	SO	Cross through Hoffman Canyon Wash.
▼ 2.1	SO	Exiting Jawbone Canyon OHV Area at sign.

4.7 ▲	SO	Entering Jawbone Canyon OHV Area at sign. Many tracks on left and right through open area.
		GPS: N35°18.91' W118°06.47'

▼ 2.3	SO	Cross through wash.
4.5 ▲	SO	Cross through wash.
▼ 3.1	SO	Track on right.
3.7 ▲	SO	Track on left.
▼ 3.3	SO	Track on right.
3.5 ▲	SO	Track on left.
▼ 3.5	SO	Track on right.
3.3 ▲	SO	Track on left.
▼ 6.0	SO	Cross through wash; then track on right.
0.8 ▲	SO	Track on left; then cross through wash.
		GPS: N35°21.77' W118°06.72'

▼ 6.2	SO	Two tracks on right are both SC251 for 4WDs, ATVs, and motorbikes.
0.6 ▲	SO	Two tracks on left are both SC251 for 4WDs, ATVs, and motorbikes.
		GPS: N35°21.92' W118°06.69'

▼ 6.8	BL	Track on right is SC123, which enters Butterbredt Spring Wildlife Sanctuary, and is suitable for 4WDs, ATVs, and motorbikes. Zero trip meter.
0.0 ▲		Continue to the southeast.
		GPS: N35°22.35' W118°06.95'

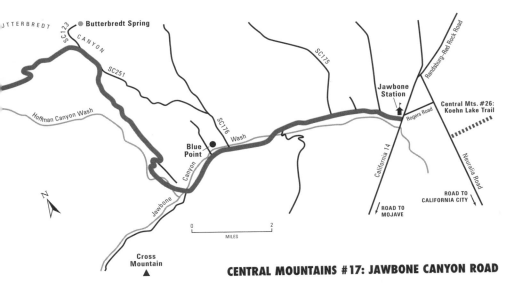

CENTRAL MOUNTAINS #17: JAWBONE CANYON ROAD

▼ 0.0   Continue to the northwest.
6.0 ▲   SO   Track on left is SC123, which enters Butterbredt Spring Wildlife Sanctuary, and is suitable for 4WDs, ATVs, and motorbikes. Zero trip meter.

▼ 0.1   SO   Cattle guard.
5.9 ▲   SO   Cattle guard.
▼ 4.6   SO   Track on right.

1.4 ▲   SO   Track on left.
▼ 6.0   BL   Graded road on right travels along Kelso Valley to Weldon. Zero trip meter.
0.0 ▲   Continue to the northeast.
       GPS: N35°22.76′ W118°12.64′

▼ 0.0   Continue to the southwest, following sign to Piute Mountain.

The dry, rugged landscape of Jawbone Canyon is popular with 4WD vehicles, dirt bikes and ATVs

6.5 ▲   SO Graded road on left travels along Kelso Valley to Weldon. Zero trip meter.

▼ 0.3   SO 4-way intersection of graded dirt roads. Road on right leads to Weldon.

6.2 ▲   SO 4-way intersection of graded dirt roads. Road on left leads to Weldon. Follow sign to Highway 14.

▼ 0.7   SO Cattle guard; then track on left and track on right along fence line.

5.8 ▲   SO Track on left and track on right along fence line; then cattle guard.

▼ 1.7   SO Track on left and track on right along fence line; then cattle guard.

4.8 ▲   SO Cattle guard; then track on left and track on right along fence line.

▼ 2.1   SO Track on left.

4.4 ▲   SO Track on right.

▼ 2.2   SO Track on right.

4.3 ▲   SO Track on left.

▼ 3.0   SO Track on left; then track on right.

3.5 ▲   SO Track on left; then track on right.

▼ 3.7   SO Track on right.

2.8 ▲   SO Track on left.

▼ 3.8   SO Track on right.

2.7 ▲   SO Track on left.

▼ 4.9   SO Cross through Cottonwood Creek. Trail now starts to switchback up the Geringer Grade.

1.6 ▲   SO End of descent. Cross through Cottonwood Creek.
GPS: N35°22.41' W118°16.48'

▼ 6.5   SO Entering Sequoia National Forest at sign. Zero trip meter.

0.0 ▲   Continue to the east.
GPS: N35°22.80' W118°17.24'

▼ 0.0   Continue to the west.

3.5 ▲   SO Leaving Sequoia National Forest at sign. Zero trip meter.

▼ 0.9   SO Track on right to campsite.

2.6 ▲   SO Track on left to campsite.

▼ 1.3   TR Track on left and track straight ahead. Remain on main graded road.

2.2 ▲   TL Track on right and track straight ahead. Remain on main graded road.
GPS: N35°23.18' W118°17.87'

▼ 1.7   SO Track on right; then Pacific Crest National Scenic Trail crosses road, for hikers and horses only.

1.8 ▲   SO Pacific Crest National Scenic Trail crosses road, for hikers and horses only; then track on left.
GPS: N35°23.43' W118°17.89'

▼ 2.1   SO Track on left.

1.4 ▲   SO Track on right.
GPS: N35°23.54' W118°18.16'

▼ 2.6   SO End of climb onto Piute Mountain.

0.9 ▲   SO Begin descent to Kelso Valley along the Geringer Grade.

▼ 3.1   SO Track on right.

0.4 ▲   SO Track on left.

▼ 3.2   SO Track on left.

0.3 ▲   SO Track on right.

▼ 3.3   SO Track on right.

0.2 ▲   SO Track on left.

▼ 3.5   SO Graded road (29S02) on left goes to Grouse Meadow. Zero trip meter.

0.0 ▲   Continue to the south, following sign to Kelso Valley.
GPS: N35°24.33' W118°18.43'

▼ 0.0   Continue to the north, following sign to Piute Mountain Road.

3.0 ▲   SO Graded road (29S02) on right goes to Grouse Meadow. Zero trip meter.

▼ 1.0   SO Old mill on left.

2.0 ▲   SO Old mill on right.

▼ 1.6   SO Track on left; then track on right.

1.4 ▲   SO Track on left; then track on right.

▼ 1.9   SO Track on right.

1.1 ▲   SO Track on left.

▼ 2.1   SO Track on left.

0.9 ▲   SO Track on right.

▼ 2.9   SO Track on left.

0.1 ▲   SO Track on right.

▼ 3.0   Trail ends at T-intersection with Central Mountains #16: Piute Mountain Road. Turn right to return to Kelso Valley Road and Weldon; turn left for Bodfish.

0.0 ▲   Trail commences on Central Mountains #16: Piute Mountain Road, 10 miles west of Kelso Valley Road. Zero trip meter and turn east onto Jawbone Canyon Road, following sign for Kelso Valley.
GPS: N35°26.64' W118°19.52'

Dove Spring Canyon Trail

STARTING POINT Kelso Valley Road, 17 miles south of Weldon

FINISHING POINT California 14, 7.6 miles north of Jawbone Station

TOTAL MILEAGE 18.1 miles

UNPAVED MILEAGE: 17.4 miles

DRIVING TIME 1.5 hours

ELEVATION RANGE 2,700–5,300 feet

USUALLY OPEN Year-round

BEST TIME TO TRAVEL Year-round

DIFFICULTY RATING 3

SCENIC RATING 8

REMOTENESS RATING +0

Special Attractions

- Dove Springs OHV Area.
- Picturesque sandy trail situated within a high desert area.
- Red Rock Canyon State Park.

History

The red-striped, tilted layers of Red Rock Canyon are the result of an uplift that occurred approximately 10 million years ago. The sediments packed within these layers are the remnants of earlier geological activities that had occurred in the surrounding regions. Time has compacted the layers and the elements have weathered them into the striking fluted shapes we see today.

Located along an old Indian trade route, the red canyon has been used as a meeting point by the native Kawaiisu people for thousands of years. In 1850, the spot was used as a resting and watering point for Illinois Jayhawkers who were escaping the harsh conditions of Death Valley.

Heading south from Death Valley in 1867, a German prospector named Goler stumbled upon gold nuggets while drinking at a spring. Unfamiliar with the land and fearful of an attack by Indians, he quickly mapped his find and headed for Los Angeles. He arranged Grant Price Cuddeback as his financial backer and made two unsuccessful expeditions back to the area in search

Some of the spectacular formations in Red Rock Canyon State Park

of his original find. However, on their third attempt, Cuddeback and Goler struck gold in Red Rock Canyon. They mined in the canyon for several years, but Goler eventually moved on, still disappointed at not finding his original strike of 1867. In time, a collection of rich mines in the nearby El Paso Mountains became known as the Goler Mining District, seemingly at the location of the prospector's original find. However, Goler himself was long gone by then and never profited from the mines.

Red Rock Canyon was also a watering point for cattle and sheep drovers on their way to greener pastures and markets. El Tejon Ranch was one of a number of ranches whose teamsters took advantage of this rest stop. As the Kern River goldfields grew, Red Rock Canyon became a stage stop for travelers coming from Los Angeles. A trade route developed from Owens Valley and Cerro Gordo through to Bakersfield and Ventura. The station was run by a gold miner named Rudolf Hagen, who named it after his son. The station, of which no trace remains, offered relief from the sweltering summer heat and icy winter winds. Hay and water were available for pack trains and a teamster could take a welcome rest after he tended to his stock. Stories were shared of events along the harsh trail, what conditions lay ahead, and where the latest washout or gunfight had occurred. A post office opened at Ricardo in 1898. A railroad was put through the canyon and at one time, a truck stop as well.

The railroad was constructed to bring cement, piping, and equipment to Dove Spring, where a small city was built as the center of construction for the Los Angeles Aqueduct. The project, which began in 1907, was completed in 1913.

Hollywood took advantage of the badlands scenery for movie backdrops. Red Rock Canyon has been the setting for many Westerns. Episodes of *Bonanza* and a number of TV commercials have also been filmed there.

Description

Dove Spring Canyon Trail connects Kelso Valley Road with California 14 and the old settlements in Kern County. For those with a high-clearance 4WD, the trail makes an easy and picturesque shortcut between the two areas.

The trail leaves Kelso Valley Road up one of the clearly marked OHV trails that traverses BLM land. It follows a formed sandy trail through stands of Joshua trees, and runs mainly in a wash until it reaches a saddle at the high point of the trail at a little over 5,300 feet. A side trail to the north at that point leads to the remains of the Sunset Mine.

The main trail gradually descends along Dove Spring Canyon, passing by Dove Spring, before entering the open OHV area at Gold Peak Well. Within the open area there are many unmarked trails to the right and left. Only numbered routes are mentioned as side trails in the route directions unless there is the potential for confusion. Remain on the major through-route, which is periodically marked with posts that read SC103.

The trail finishes in the extremely picturesque Red Rock Canyon State Park (which was established in 1968 as the first state park in Kern County), at the entrance to Ricardo Campground and the old site of the Ricardo Stage Station. The campground is situated at the base of the eroded White House Cliffs and makes a wonderful place to camp for the night. Alternatively, undeveloped backcountry campsites can be found at other points along the trail.

Current Road Information

BLM Ridgecrest Field Office
300 South Richmond Road
Ridgecrest, CA 93555
(760) 384-5400

Map References

BLM   Tehachapi, Cuddeback Lake
USGS   1:24,000   Pinyon Mtn., Dove
            Spring, Saltdale NW
            1:100,000 Tehachapi, Cuddeback
            Lake
Maptech CD-ROM: Barstow/San
            Bernardino County
*Southern & Central California Atlas &
            Gazetteer*, p. 65

Spectacular scenery within Red Rock Canyon State Park

California Road & Recreation Atlas, p. 94
Other: East Kern County OHV Riding
Areas and Trails—Jawbone Canyon

Route Directions

▼ 0.0   From Kelso Valley Road, 17 miles
south of Weldon on California 178, zero
trip meter and turn southeast on
formed dirt trail marked SC103 for
4WDs, ATVs, and motorbikes.

3.8 ▲   Trail ends on Kelso Valley Road. Turn
right for Weldon; turn left to continue
to Central Mountains #17: Jawbone
Canyon Road or Central Mountains
#16: Piute Mountain Road.
GPS: N35°29.30′ W118°12.21′

▼ 0.4 SO Track on left.
3.4 ▲ SO Track on right.
▼ 0.5 SO Track on left is SC36 for 4WDs, ATVs,
and motorbikes.
3.3 ▲ SO Track on right is SC36 for 4WDs,
ATVs, and motorbikes.
GPS: N35°29.22′ W118°11.88′

▼ 0.6 SO Track on left is SC102 for ATVs and
motorbikes only.
3.2 ▲ SO Track on right is SC102 for ATVs and
motorbikes only.

▼ 1.6 SO Cross through wash.
2.2 ▲ SO Cross through wash.

▼ 1.9 BR Bear right and enter wash, remaining
on SC103; then track on left is SC111
for motorbikes only.
1.9 ▲ BL Track on right is SC111 for motorbikes
only; then bear left and exit wash,
remaining on SC103.
GPS: N35°28.62′ W118°10.59′

▼ 2.2 SO Willow Spring on left.
1.6 ▲ SO Willow Spring on right.
GPS: N35°28.39′ W118°10.40′

▼ 2.8 SO Exit wash.
1.0 ▲ SO Enter wash.

▼ 3.8 SO Saddle. Track on left goes to the
Sunset Mine. Pinyon Mountain is on
the right. Pacific Crest National Scenic
Trail crosses the road at this point.
Zero trip meter.
0.0 ▲   Continue to the northwest.
GPS: N35°27.85′ W118°08.95′

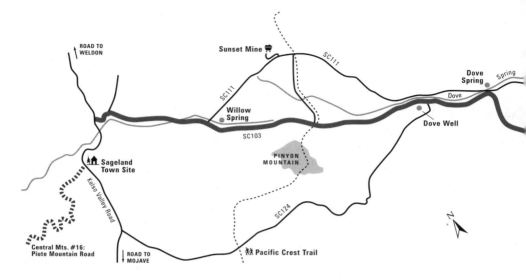

▼ 0.0   Continue to the southeast.

1.7 ▲   SO   Saddle. Track on right goes to the Sunset Mine. Pinyon Mountain is on the left. Pacific Crest National Scenic Trail crosses the road at this point. Zero trip meter.

▼ 1.2   SO   Track on left.

0.5 ▲   SO   Track on right.

▼ 1.7   SO   Track on left, which runs parallel with main route, is SC111 for 4WDs, ATVs, and motorbikes. Track on right is SC102 for ATVs and motorbikes only. Trail now enters Dove Spring Canyon Wash. Dove Well on right. Zero trip meter.

0.0 ▲   Continue to the west, remaining on SC103.

      GPS: N35°27.52' W118°07.23'

▼ 0.0   Continue to the east, remaining on SC103.

3.3 ▲   SO   Track on right, which runs parallel with main route, is SC111 for 4WDs, ATVs, and motorbikes. Track on left is SC102 for ATVs and motorbikes only. Trail leaves Dove Spring Canyon Wash. Dove Well on left. Zero trip meter.

▼ 0.2   SO   Track on right is SC124 for 4WDs, ATVs, and motorbikes.

3.1 ▲   SO   Track on left is second entrance to SC124.

▼ 0.3   SO   Track on right is second entrance to SC124.

3.0 ▲   SO   Track on left is SC124 for 4WDs, ATVs, and motorbikes.

▼ 1.2   SO   Track on left is SC111 for 4WDs, ATVs, and motorbikes.

2.1 ▲   BL   Track on right is SC111 for 4WDs, ATVs, and motorbikes.

      GPS: N35°27.17' W118°06.05'

▼ 1.3   BR   Track ahead is SC328 for 4WDs, ATVs, and motorbikes. Remain on SC103. Dove Spring on left.

2.0 ▲   BL   Track ahead is SC328 for 4WDs, ATVs, and motorbikes. Remain on SC103. Dove Spring on right.

      GPS: N35°27.17' W118°05.97'

▼ 1.4   SO   Cattle guard.

1.9 ▲   SO   Cattle guard.

▼ 1.5   SO   Track on left.

1.8 ▲   SO   Track on right.

      GPS: N35°27.04' W118°05.94'

▼ 3.3   BL   Track ahead is SC99 for 4WDs, ATVs, and motorbikes. Remain on SC103 and zero trip meter.

0.0 ▲   Continue to the northwest.

      GPS: N35°25.87' W118°04.92'

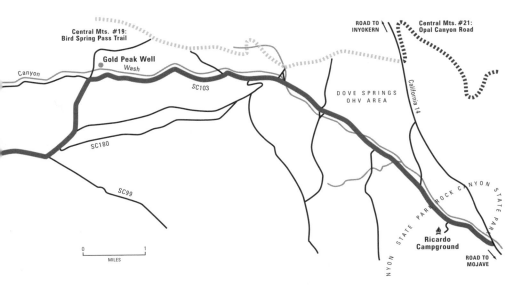

▼ 0.0   Continue to the northeast.

1.7 ▲   BR   Track on left is SC99 for 4WDs, ATVs, and motorbikes. Remain on SC103 and zero trip meter.

▼ 0.2   SO   Track on right opposite rocky outcrop is SC180.

1.5 ▲   SO   Track on left opposite rocky outcrop is SC180.

▼ 0.8   TL   4-way intersection. Remain on SC103. Track on right and track straight ahead.

0.9 ▲   TR   4-way intersection. Remain on SC103. Track on left and track straight ahead.

A sandy section of trail descending to Dove Spring Canyon

▼ 1.7 BR Marked track on left; then enter Dove Springs OHV Area at sign. Track on left goes to Gold Peak Well. Zero trip meter at sign.

0.0 ▲   Continue to the southwest on SC103.
GPS: N35°26.61' W118°03.58'

▼ 0.0   Continue to the southeast. Many tracks on right and left in open area. Remain on main trail, which travels along the valley floor.

3.1 ▲ BL Leave Dove Springs OHV Area at sign. Track on right goes to Gold Peak Well; then second marked track on right. Zero trip meter at sign.

▼ 2.3 SO Well-used track on left.

0.8 ▲ BL Well-used track on right.
GPS: N35°25.83' W118°01.49'

▼ 2.7 SO Well-used track on right.

0.4 ▲ SO Well-used track on left.
GPS: N35°25.65' W118°01.21'

▼ 3.1 BR Track on left is SC94 for 4WDs, ATVs, and motorbikes. Zero trip meter.

0.0 ▲   Continue to the northwest on SC103.
GPS: N35°25.45' W118°00.82'

▼ 0.0   Continue to the southeast on SC103.

3.8 ▲ SO Track on right is SC94 for 4WDs, ATVs, and motorbikes. Zero trip meter.

▼ 0.2 SO Track on left; then cross through wash—vehicles travel up and down wash.

3.6 ▲ SO Cross through wash—vehicles travel up and down wash; then track on right.

▼ 0.9 SO Track on right before pipeline; then well-used track on left and track on right. Remain on marked SC103.

2.9 ▲ SO Track on left and well-used track on right before pipeline; then track on left. Remain on marked SC103.
GPS: N35°24.69' W118°00.38'

▼ 1.7 SO Cross through wash—vehicles travel up and down wash.

2.1 ▲ SO Cross through wash—vehicles travel up and down wash.

▼ 1.8 SO Track on left and track on right under power lines.

2.0 ▲ SO Track on left and track on right under power lines.

▼ 2.0 SO Track on right.

1.8 ▲ SO Track on left.

▼ 2.2 SO Cattle guard; entering Red Rock Canyon State Park. End of OHV area.

1.6 ▲ SO Leaving state park and entering Dove Springs OHV Area over cattle guard. Many tracks on right and left in open area. Remain on main trail, which travels along the valley floor.
GPS: N35°23.74' W117°59.75'

▼ 2.4 SO Cross through wash.

1.4 ▲ SO Cross through wash.

▼ 2.9 SO Old section of US 6 on left is being re-vegetated. Enter wash.

0.9 ▲ SO Old section of US 6 on right is being re-vegetated. Exit wash.

▼ 3.8 TR Turn right out of wash; then turn left onto paved road. Vehicles can continue in the wash, which exits at the end of the trail. Zero trip meter. Paved road on right goes immediately into Ricardo Campground.

0.0 ▲   Continue to the northeast.
GPS: N35°22.45' W117°59.28'

▼ 0.0   Continue to the west.

0.7 ▲ TR Turn right opposite parks work area and sign for Ricardo Campground; then turn left up wash. Vehicles travel to the right down wash. Zero trip meter. Paved road continues into Ricardo Campground.

▼ 0.7   Track on left is alternate exit from wash and track on right. Trail ends at T-intersection with California 14. Turn right for Mojave; turn left for Inyokern.

0.0 ▲   Trail commences on California 14, 7.6 miles north of Jawbone Station. Zero trip meter and turn northwest onto paved Abbott Drive at sign for Red Rock Canyon State Park, Ricardo Campground. Track on left. Track on right is alternate beginning that avoids paved road by traveling up the wash.
GPS: N35°21.89' W117°58.88'

Bird Spring Pass Trail

STARTING POINT California 14, 3.5 miles north of the turn to Ricardo Campground

FINISHING POINT Kelso Valley Road, 10.7 miles south of California 178

TOTAL MILEAGE 20.8 miles, plus 2.9-mile spur

UNPAVED MILEAGE: 20.8 miles, plus 2.9-mile spur

DRIVING TIME 2 hours

ELEVATION RANGE 2,600–5,500 feet

USUALLY OPEN Year-round

BEST TIME TO TRAVEL Year-round

DIFFICULTY RATING 3

SCENIC RATING 9

REMOTENESS RATING +0

Special Attractions

- Historic route through Bird Spring Pass.
- Dove Springs OHV Area.
- Joshua tree forest and spectacular high desert scenery.

History

Located at the eastern end of the trail, Indian Wells Valley was known to Native Americans for many years. However, a waterhole farther up the valley was a welcome surprise to the Manly-Rogers Death Valley escape party of 1850 (see page 120) because it was the first water they had found since crossing the Argus Range north of Trona.

By the 1860s a stage station was located at Indian Wells. Operated by James Bridger, it catered to the mule teams coming from the mines in the Cerro Gordo and Coso regions.

Stagecoach holdups, bandits, and outlaw activity seemingly came hand in hand with any region being settled in the West. Indian Wells was an important stopping point for many travelers in the region, and it managed to attract its share of shady characters. One of these marauding outlaws was Tiburcio Vasquez. After he attacked a number of travelers, a warrant was issued for his arrest. Vasquez and his mob took to a hiding place that would later come to be known as Robber's Roost (located close to Freeman Junction near Indian Wells). In the 1870s, they

A remote stretch of trail approaching Bird Spring Pass

would lie in wait behind the roost's rocky crags before ambushing stagecoaches, travelers, and pack trains. By the time a military party was sent to end their activities, the Vasquez gang had relocated to the thriving community of Los Angeles. In 1875, Vasquez was finally cornered at what would later become known as Hollywood. From there he was transported to San Jose to face trial for murder. He was convicted and hanged in March of the same year.

The Los Angeles Aqueduct and Second Los Angeles Aqueduct, which supply water from the Owens Valley to Los Angeles, pass just below the crags of Robber's Roost.

Joseph Reddeford Walker, a renowned pathfinder of the American West, is credited with finding a passage through the Scodie Mountains in 1833. The pass chosen by Walker is situated north of Bird Spring Pass along the ridge tops of the Scodie Mountains. The Pacific Crest National Scenic Trail crosses this trail at Bird Spring Pass, and takes hikers to Walker Pass—now on the busy route of California 178.

On his fifth trip to California in March 1854, John Charles Frémont was blocked by snow at Walker Pass. He found an alternate, southern route through the Scodie Mountains that crossed over Bird Spring Pass.

In 1874, a former forty-niner from Boston, Freeman S. Raymond, established a stage station at the important junction that gained his name. Located at the eastern end of the route over Walker Pass, the station adopted Raymond's first name in 1889 when it received a post office. Raymond passed away in 1909 and the post office was moved south to Ricardo, located in Red Rock Canyon. California 14 now runs along the original north-south stage route.

Description

Bird Spring Pass Trail travels between the Dove Springs OHV Area and the Kelso Valley. Along the way, it traverses some spectacular high desert country.

The well-formed sandy trail leaves California 14 at the main entry point into Dove Springs OHV Area. This popular area has a wide variety of trails and is designed to handle 4WDs, ATVs, and motorbikes. Throughout the OHV area there are many unmarked trails; these are not mentioned in the route directions unless there is a chance for confusion with the main route.

The trail leads north of Central Mountains #18: Dove Spring Canyon Trail and follows the smaller, sandy SC94 toward Bird Spring Pass. The trail is well formed and gets its difficulty rating from the frequent sections of loose sand that must be negotiated. Although it is in a popular area, the trail has a remote feel and once away from the OHV area is seldom traveled. A good portion of the trail passes through thick Joshua tree forests before swinging west to travel along the southern boundary of the Kiavah Wilderness toward Bird Spring Pass.

The Pacific Crest National Scenic Trail crosses on the pass, and a spur trail to the south climbs higher up to the communications towers on Wyleys Knob. From the towers there are excellent views in all directions: east over the Indian Wells Valley, west over the Kelso Valley to the Piute Mountains, and south over the high desert hills.

Motorbikes have the option of traveling one of the smaller marked trails from this spur that allows them to cross over to the Dove Springs OHV Area.

West of the pass, the trail is less sandy as it switchbacks down a narrow shelf road to Kelso Valley Road. Passing places are limited on the shelf road, so you may need to back up if you encounter oncoming traffic. The trail passes around the boundary of the Jawbone-Butterbredt Area of Critical Environmental Concern, which was established to protect the region's desert wildlife and Indian artifacts. The area is also used for livestock, with sheep and cattle allowed to graze under a permit system.

Current Road Information

BLM Ridgecrest Field Office
300 South Richmond Road
Ridgecrest, CA 93555
(760) 384-5400

Crossing the creosote-covered flats en route to Bird Spring Pass

Map References

BLM   Cuddeback Lake, Tehachapi,
      Isabella Lake
USGS   1:24,000   Saltdale NW, Dove Spring,
      Horse Canyon, Cane Canyon
      1:100,000 Cuddeback Lake,
      Tehachapi, Isabella Lake
Maptech CD-ROM: Barstow/San
      Bernardino County
Southern & Central California Atlas &
      Gazetteer, pp. 65, 51
California Road & Recreation Atlas, p. 94
Other: East Kern County OHV Riding
      Areas and Trails—Jawbone Canyon

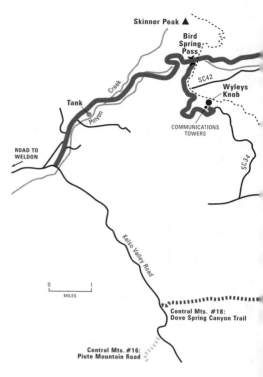

Route Directions

▼ 0.0   From California 14, 3.5 miles north of
       the turn to Ricardo Campground in Red
       Rock Canyon State Park, zero trip
       meter and turn northwest on SC94 at
       sign for Dove Springs OHV Area.
       Central Mountains #21: Opal Canyon
       Road is opposite.Road turns to graded
       dirt over cattle guard. Many tracks on
       left and right through OHV area.

1.9 ▲   Trail ends on California 14. Central
       Mountains #21; Opal Canyon Road is
       opposite. Turn left for Inyokern; turn
       right for Mojave.
       GPS: N35°24.85' W117°58.81'

▼ 0.7   SO   Track on left and track on right under
           power lines. Remain on SC94.
1.2 ▲   SO   Track on left and track on right under
           power lines. Remain on SC94.

▼ 1.1   SO   Well-used track on left and track on
           right. Continue on Bird Spring Road.
0.8 ▲   SO   Track on left and well-used track on
           right. Continue on Bird Spring Road.
           GPS: N35°25.33' W117°59.86'

▼ 1.9   TR   Cross through wash; then turn sharp
           right, following marker for SC94. Track
           straight ahead and small tracks at
           intersection. Zero trip meter.
0.0 ▲   Continue to the northeast.
           GPS: N35°25.43' W118°00.64'

▼ 0.0   Continue to the north.

7.0 ▲   TL   Turn sharp left; then cross through
           wash, remaining on SC94. Track on
           right and small tracks at intersection.
           Zero trip meter.

▼ 0.3   BL   Roughly graded road on right. Follow
           sign for SC94.
6.7 ▲   SO   Roughly graded road on left.
           GPS: N35°25.70' W118°00.72'

▼ 0.8   SO   Track on right; then tank on left. Cross
           cattle guard, remaining on SC94. Track
           on right after cattle guard is SC5.
6.2 ▲   BR   Track on left is SC5; then cattle guard.
           Tank on right; then track on left.
           Remain on SC94.
           GPS: N35°26.05' W118°00.86'

▼ 2.7   SO   Track on left and track on right are
           both SC161 for ATVs and motorbikes
           only.
4.3 ▲   SO   Track on left and track on right are both
           SC161 for ATVs and motorbikes only.
           GPS: N35°27.08' W118°02.60'

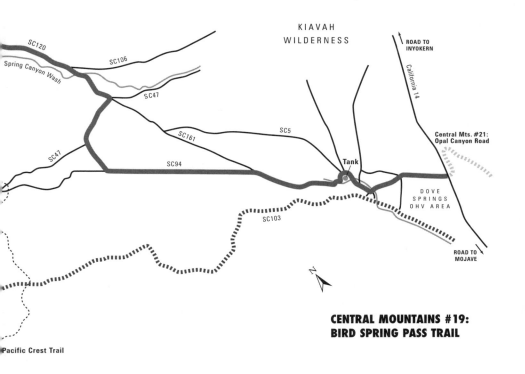

KIAVAH WILDERNESS

ROAD TO INYOKERN

California 14

SC120

Spring Canyon Wash

SC106

SC47

SC161

SC5

SC47

SC94

Central Mts. #21:
Opal Canyon Road

Tank

DOVE
SPRINGS
OHV AREA

SC103

ROAD TO
MOJAVE

N

CENTRAL MOUNTAINS #19:
BIRD SPRING PASS TRAIL

Pacific Crest Trail

▼ 2.9   SO   Track on left and track on right.
4.1 ▲   SO   Track on left and track on right.
▼ 3.1   SO   Track on left and track on right.
3.9 ▲   SO   Track on left and track on right.
▼ 5.1   SO   Track on left and track on right.
1.9 ▲   SO   Track on left and track on right.
▼ 6.1   BR   Track on left.
0.9 ▲   BL   Track on right.
           GPS: N35°28.94′ W118°05.69′

▼ 7.0   SO   4-way intersection. Tracks on left and straight ahead are SC47 for 4WDs, ATVs, and motorbikes. Track on right is SC44 for motorbikes only. Zero trip meter.
0.0 ▲   Continue to the south on SC94.
           GPS: N35°29.63′ W118°05.72′

▼ 0.0   Continue to the north on SC47.
1.4 ▲   SO   4-way intersection. Track on right is SC47 for 4WDs, ATVs, and motorbikes. Track on left is SC44 for motor-bikes only. Track ahead is SC94 for 4WDs, ATVs, and motorbikes. Zero trip meter.

▼ 1.0   SO   Track on left. Stone and concrete foundations at intersection. Then track on right.
0.4 ▲   SO   Track on left; then track on right. Stone and concrete foundations at intersection.
           GPS: N35°30.10′ W118°04.90′

▼ 1.1   SO   Track on left.
0.3 ▲   SO   Track on right.
▼ 1.4   TL   4-way intersection. SC47 continues ahead. Track on right is SC161 for 4WDs, ATVs, and motorbikes. Track on left is SC120 for 4WDs, ATVs, and motorbikes. Zero trip meter.
0.0 ▲   Continue to the west on SC47 and leave the boundary of the Kiavah Wilderness.
           GPS: N35°30.15′ W118°04.50′

▼ 0.0   Continue to the northwest on SC120

FIRST DEATH VALLEY WAGON TRAIN

The story of the first wagon train to enter Death Valley is mixed with heroism and tragedy. Most of the train belonged to a group of forty-niners who had left a large party led by Captain Jefferson Hunt. Hunt was an experienced trailsman paid to guide groups to the California goldfields. He strongly cautioned his party not to attempt a supposed shortcut recommended by O. K. Smith, the leader of a passing pack train. Nevertheless, a third of Hunt's party decided to deviate from the known route west of Salt Lake City.

Included in the fated wagon train were a group of about 40 men known as the Jayhawkers. The Jayhawkers discovered that the uncharted route added several months to their journey and led them through forbidding desert expanses. They reached Death Valley late in December 1849, and spent a hot Christmas Day trudging down Furnace Creek Wash. Forced to burn their wagons and eat their oxen, the Jayhawkers escaped Death Valley by a northerly route via Towne's Pass. Jayhawker Canyon is named after the unfortunate group. Several members perished during the journey, but several survivors later returned to Death Valley as some of the region's first prospectors.

Accompanying the Jayhawkers were Reverend Brier, his wife, and their three sons—the youngest just four years old. The trip was especially hard for the family, who were particularly ill suited to desert travel. Juliet Brier later described her travels: "I was sick and weary and the hope of a good camping place was the only thing that kept me up." Despite having to abandon their possessions, eat all their beasts of burden, and carry their exhausted children, the Brier family made it through Death Valley intact. On February 5, 1850, the Briers and Jayhawkers found civilization at the San Francisquito Ranch.

Several groups had split from Hunt's original party. One group included two families—the Bennetts and Arcanes—and 11 bachelors. Hopelessly lost in the arid wilderness, this party was also forced to slaughter their oxen to survive. On Christmas Day 1849, the group reached Travertine Springs at the base of the Panamint Range. They decided to camp there while two bachelors, William Lewis Manly and John Rogers, set out to look for a settlement. They succeeded in obtaining supplies and pack animals from Mission San Fernando. When they made it back the group's campsite, they found the Bennetts and Arcanes alone; the bachelors had left to attempt their own escape from Death Valley. One man perished in the journey.

Manly and Rogers guided the families through Galena Canyon, Warm Spring Canyon, and Butte Valley before exiting Death Valley via Redlands Canyon. Fresh water was extremely limited along the route and the terrain was deadly. Leather boots on the oxen's feet soon wore out. The adults' shoes were destroyed, too, and all group members trudged on with blistered feet. It took three weeks and 250 miles of travel before the families reached civilization. Despite their ordeal, the group was happy to escape with their lives. As she departed the area she thought would be her grave, one woman cried "goodbye, Death Valley." This was the first recorded usage of the region's present-day name.

Manly and Rogers had saved the group from the well-known fate of the Donner Party. Their heroism in this tragic journey is remembered by several regional place names, including Rogers Peak, Manly Peak, Manly Fall, and Manly Pass. Manly later published his recollections of the ordeal in Death Valley in '49. Several trails in this book follow sections of the Bennett-Arcane escape route.

Trail SC44, for dirt bikes only, crosses Bird Spring Pass Trail and follows the sandy wash between Joshua trees and granite outcroppings

along the southern boundary of the Kiavah Wilderness.

▼			
5.2 ▲	TR	4-way intersection. Tracks on left and right are SC47 for 4WDs, ATVs, and motorbikes. Track ahead is SC161 for 4WDs, ATVs, and motorbikes. Zero trip meter.
▼ 0.1	SO	Track on left.
5.1 ▲	SO	Track on right.
▼ 0.6	SO	Track on left and track on right.
4.6 ▲	SO	Track on left and track on right.
▼ 0.8	SO	Track on left.
4.4 ▲	SO	Track on right.
▼ 0.9	SO	Track on left; then cross through Bird Spring Canyon wash.
4.3 ▲	SO	Cross through Bird Spring Canyon wash; then track on right.

GPS: N35°30.90′ W118°04.77′

▼ 1.4	SO	Track on right is SC106 for 4WDs, ATVs, and motorbikes.
3.8 ▲	BR	Track on left is SC106 for 4WDs, ATVs, and motorbikes.

GPS: N35°31.21′ W118°05.00′

▼ 1.6	SO	Track on left.
3.6 ▲	SO	Track on right.
▼ 3.4	SO	Track on left.
1.8 ▲	SO	Track on right.
▼ 5.2	BR	Bird Spring Pass. Pacific Crest National Scenic Trail crosses road. To the left it goes to Sequoia National Forest; to the right it goes to Walker Pass. Skinner Peak on right. Track on left is spur to Wyleys Knob (SC0228) for 4WDs and motorbikes only. Remain on SC120. Zero trip meter.
0.0 ▲		Continue to the east on SC 120.

GPS: N35°33.18′ W118°07.98′

Spur to Wyleys Knob (SC0228)

▼ 0.0		Proceed to the southwest.
▼ 0.8	SO	Track on left is SC42 for motorbikes only.
▼ 1.8	BL	Track on right is SC124 for motorbikes only.

GPS: N35°32.35′ W118°09.03′

▼ 2.0	SO	Track on right is SC48 for motorbikes only.
▼ 2.7	BL	Track on right is SC34 for motorbikes only.
▼ 2.9	UT	Spur ends at communications towers

on Wyleys Knob. Retrace your route
back to Bird Spring Pass.
GPS: N35°32.15' W118°08.38'

Continuation of Main Trail

▼ 0.0   Continue to the west on SC120.
5.3 ▲   SO   Bird Spring Pass. Pacific Crest National
              Scenic Trail crosses road. To the right
              it goes to Sequoia National Forest; to
              the left it goes to Walker Pass. Skinner
              Peak on left. Track on right is spur to
              Wyleys Knob (SC0228) for 4WDs and
              motorbikes only. Remain on SC120.
              Zero trip meter.
              GPS: N35°33.18' W118°07.98'

▼ 1.0   BR   Track on left.
4.3 ▲   BL   Track on right.
              GPS: N35°33.30' W118°08.36'

▼ 1.4   BR   Track on left.
3.9 ▲   BL   Track on right.
▼ 2.1   SO   Cross through Pinyon Creek.
3.2 ▲   SO   Cross through Pinyon Creek.
▼ 2.9   SO   Track on left.
2.4 ▲   SO   Track on right.
▼ 3.1   SO   Cross through Pinyon Creek.
2.2 ▲   SO   Cross through Pinyon Creek.
▼ 3.8   SO   Tank on left.
1.5 ▲   SO   Tank on right.
              GPS: N35°33.58' W118°10.90'

▼ 4.1   SO   Track on left.
1.2 ▲   SO   Track on right.
▼ 4.3   SO   Track on left.
1.0 ▲   BL   Track on right.
              GPS: N35°33.46' W118°11.50'

▼ 4.5   SO   Two tracks on right.
0.8 ▲   SO   Two tracks on left.
▼ 4.7   SO   Track on right.
0.6 ▲   SO   Track on left.
▼ 4.8   SO   Track on left.
0.5 ▲   SO   Track on right.
▼ 5.0   SO   Track on left is SC36 for 4WDs, ATVs,
              and motorbikes.
0.3 ▲   SO   Track on right is SC36 for 4WDs,
              ATVs, and motorbikes.
              GPS: N35°33.12' W118°12.04'

▼ 5.3   Trail ends at T-intersection with paved
              Kelso Valley Road. Turn right for Weldon
              and California 178; turn left for Central
              Mountains #16: Piute Mountain Road.
0.0 ▲   Trail commences on Kelso Valley Road,
              10.7 miles south of California 178. Zero
              trip meter and turn east on well-used
              formed trail at sign for Bird Spring
              Pass. The Jawbone-Butterbredt Area
              of Critical Environmental Concern is on
              south side of road.
              GPS: N35°32.97' W118°12.39'

CENTRAL MOUNTAINS #20

Chimney Peak Byway

STARTING POINT Kennedy Meadows Road,
    11 miles west of US 395
FINISHING POINT California 178, 2 miles east of
    the South Fork Fire Station, 7.8 miles
    east of Onyx
TOTAL MILEAGE 14 miles
UNPAVED MILEAGE: 14 miles
DRIVING TIME 1 hour
ELEVATION RANGE 3,300–6,600 feet
USUALLY OPEN Year-round
BEST TIME TO TRAVEL Year-round
DIFFICULTY RATING 1
SCENIC RATING 8
REMOTENESS RATING +0

Special Attractions

■ Trail follows one section of the Chimney
Peak Back Country Byway.
■ Excellent views into the Owens Peak
Wilderness and Chimney Peak Wilderness.

History

The southern end of this trail finishes near
Canebrake, just across California 178 from
Canebrake Flat, where Chimney Creek flows
into Canebrake Creek. This was a popular gathering place for the local Tubatulabal Indians.
The spot had remained unknown to settlers until Captain Joseph Reddeford Walker traveled
through the region in 1834. He was responsible

for finding a reliable route across the Sierra Nevada through what is now called Walker Pass. Today, California 178 traces Walker's route through the mountains.

The name Canebrake Creek is attributed to Lieutenant Robert S. Williamson, who passed by here in 1853 while surveying a potential railroad route through the Sierra Nevada. Williamson witnessed the Indians gathering the cane-like bulrush in the creek bed and learned that they referred to the creek in their native tongue as Chay-o-poo-ya-pah, which he understood to mean a creek of bulrushes. The route through Canebrake Creek Valley and Walker Pass was to become an important commercial route for early ox teams heading east to supply the developing mines on the eastern side of the Sierra Nevada. By the 1860s miners and ranchers were finding the South Fork Valley (located west of Walker Pass along present-day California 178) to be a suitable place to settle. In the 1870s, stage-coaches were kicking up dust as they crossed the dry Canebrake Flat at the start of the climb to Walker Pass.

In 1910, Billy and Ava James developed a stage station nearby and grew vegetables, which they sold to miners in Randsburg and other communities east of the Sierra Nevada.

A Tubatulabal Indian named Quigam, who as a child had witnessed Captain Walker passing through the region in 1834, remained in the area as an adult. He lived in the tribe's Canebrake tribal rancheria with his wife and family. One of their children was swept away in a flashflood in Canebrake Creek shortly after the turn of the twentieth century. Quigam died when their shanty home accidentally burned down a number of years later. Reminders of the Tubatulabal people and their long residence here linger on in the form of grinding circles worn into the rocks near the creek. The area was also a traditional gathering place for harvesting pinyon nuts and was later used for mining, cattle grazing, and barite mining.

The green around Canebrake Creek makes it hard to imagine the fires that recently ravaged the upper reaches of this trail

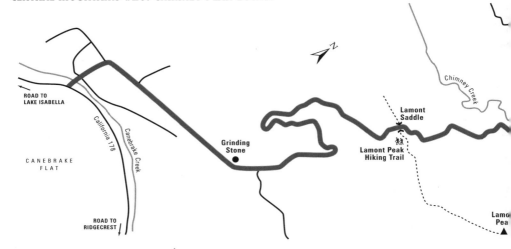

Description

This trail forms part of the designated Chimney Peak Back Country Byway. The graded dirt road travels through a wide variety of scenery between Chimney Peak Wilderness and Owens Peak Wilderness. Although the road is often washboardy, it is generally suitable for a passenger vehicle in dry weather.

The trail passes by the popular Chimney Creek BLM Campground. It enters Lamont Meadow and travels briefly alongside Chimney Creek, before climbing to Lamont Saddle where the Pacific Crest National Scenic Trail crosses again. The trail then descends a series of switchbacks to finish on California 178.

The route described is not the complete byway. A major loop, which travels past Chimney Peak itself, is not included but is well worth visiting. The trail is normally open year-round, but sections may become impassable in the winter and early spring.

Current Road Information

BLM Ridgecrest Field Office
300 South Richmond Road
Ridgecrest, CA 93555
(760) 384-5400

Map References

BLM   Isabella Lake
USFS   Sequoia National Forest

USGS   1:24,000   Lamont Peak
          1:100,000 Isabella Lake
Maptech CD-ROM: Barstow/San
          Bernardino County
Southern & Central California Atlas & Gazetteer, p. 51
California Road & Recreation Atlas, p. 94

Route Directions

▼ 0.0   From Kennedy Meadows Road, 11 miles west of intersection with US 395, zero trip meter and turn south onto graded gravel Chimney Peak Back Country Byway. Intersection is sign-posted and is immediately north of the Chimney Peak Work Center and Fire Station.
3.6 ▲   Trail ends on Kennedy Meadows Road. Turn right to exit to US 395; turn left to travel to Kennedy Meadows.
              GPS: N35°52.16' W118°00.74'

▼ 0.2   SO   Track on left.
3.4 ▲   SO   Track on right.
▼ 1.6   SO   Two tracks on right into weather site.
2.0 ▲   SO   Two tracks on left into weather site.
              GPS: N35°51.04' W118°01.55'

▼ 3.6   SO   Chimney Creek Campground on left of trail. Zero trip meter.
0.0 ▲   Continue to the west.
              GPS: N35°50.34' W118°02.53'

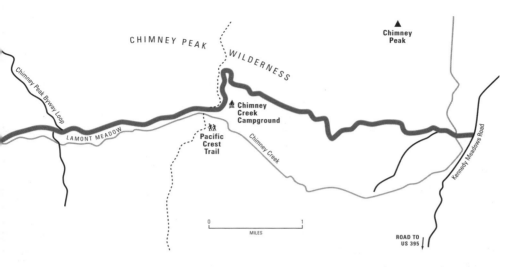

CHIMNEY PEAK
WILDERNESS

▲ Chimney
Peak

Chimney Peak Byway Loop

LAMONT MEADOW

🏕 Chimney
Creek
Campground

Chimney Creek

Pacific
Crest
Trail

Kennedy Meadows Road

ROAD TO
US 395

0 ———— 1
MILES

▼ 0.0   Continue to the east.
1.8 ▲ SO Chimney Creek Campground on right
        of trail. Zero trip meter.

▼ 0.3 SO Pacific Crest National Scenic Trail
        crosses road.

1.5 ▲ SO Pacific Crest National Scenic Trail
        crosses road.
        GPS: N35°50.15′ W118°02.59′

▼ 1.8 SO Graded road on right is the end of
        Chimney Peak Byway loop to Rock

Chimney Peak Byway landscape

Chimney Peak Byway winds through a green valley below Lamont Peak

JOSEPH REDDEFORD WALKER

Joseph Reddeford Walker was born December 13, 1798, in eastern Tennessee's Roan County. Soft-spoken, disciplined, and never a braggart, Walker stood 6 feet tall. For four years he served as a sheriff in Jackson County, Missouri, before leaving the area to head west. Here, on the frontiers of North America, he established his reputation as one of the greatest figures of American expansion.

Joseph Reddeford Walker

In 1832, Walker met Captain Benjamin Bonneville, who was planning a trapping expedition in the Rocky Mountains. Walker joined Bonneville's party as they moved west toward Green River. After wintering on the Salmon River, Walker and a group of 40 men left the main party and headed to California. The motives for the trip are unknown, but the exploration was a resounding success. The group found the Humboldt River, in what is now Nevada, crossed the Sierra Nevada, and made its way to the Pacific Coast. On the way, they passed through the Yosemite Valley and its huge sequoia trees. It was along Walker's route that many of the forty-niners reached California during the gold rush.

Once rested in the Mexican mission of San Juan Bautista (near present-day Monterey), the group moved down the San Joaquin Valley and through the mountains at Walker Pass, before heading north to reconnect with Bonneville's party. California 178 roughly retraces his steps today.

Walker returned to California many times, often as a guide to migrants from the East, and notably as a member of John Frémont's explorative expeditions. He mined gold in the state for several years. A prospecting trip to southern Arizona in the 1860s yielded much wealth and sparked a gold rush to the area around present-day Prescott. In 1867, Walker retired to his nephew's ranch in Contra Costa County, California. The old pathfinder died in 1876 at the age of 78. By then, his trailblazing had helped open California to many Americans.

	House Basin Trail. This is Lamont Meadow. Lamont Peak on left. Zero trip meter.	
0.0 ▲	Continue to the north, following sign to Kennedy Meadows. **GPS: N35°48.89′ W118°03.18′**	
▼ 0.0	Continue to the south, following sign to Highway 178.	
2.4 ▲	SO Graded road on left is the start of Chimney Peak Byway loop to Rock House Basin Trail. Lamont Peak on right. Zero trip meter.	
▼ 0.1	SO Track on left.	
2.3 ▲	SO Track on right.	

▼ 0.8	SO Cross over Chimney Creek.
1.6 ▲	SO Cross over Chimney Creek. This is Lamont Meadow.
▼ 2.4	SO Lamont Saddle. Lamont Peak Hiking Trail leads off on left and right. Zero trip meter at sign.
0.0 ▲	Continue to the north. **GPS: N35°47.27′ W118°04.27′**
▼ 0.0	Continue to the south.
6.2 ▲	SO Lamont Saddle. Lamont Peak Hiking Trail leads off on left and right. Zero trip meter at sign.
▼ 2.9	SO Track on left.
3.3 ▲	SO Track on right.

▼ 3.2	SO	Turnout on right.
3.0 ▲	SO	Turnout on left.
▼ 3.7	SO	Cattle guard; then track on left.
2.5 ▲	SO	Track on right; then cattle guard.
▼ 4.0	SO	Turnout on right is the site of an Indian grinding stone.
2.2 ▲	SO	Turnout on left is the site of an Indian grinding stone.

GPS: N35°45.79' W118°04.86'

▼ 5.7	SO	Track on right.
0.5 ▲	SO	Track on left.
▼ 6.0	SO	BLM information board on left and track on left. Road is now paved.
0.2 ▲	SO	Road turns to graded dirt. BLM information board on right and track on right.
▼ 6.1	SO	Track on left and track on right; then cross through wash.
0.1 ▲	SO	Cross through wash; then track on left and track on right.
▼ 6.2		Trail ends at T-intersection with California 178. Turn left for Ridgecrest; turn right for Lake Isabella.
0.0 ▲		Trail commences on California 178, 2 miles east of the South Fork Fire Station and 7.8 miles east of Onyx. Zero trip meter and turn north on paved road. Intersection is well marked for Chimney Peak Recreation Area.

GPS: N35°44.93' W118°06.70'

CENTRAL MOUNTAINS #21

Opal Canyon Road

STARTING POINT California 14, 7.4 miles north of intersection with Randsburg–Red Rock Road

FINISHING POINT Central Mountains #23: Last Chance Canyon Trail at Cudahy Camp, 4.4 miles north of Randsburg–Red Rock Road

TOTAL MILEAGE 6.3 miles

UNPAVED MILEAGE: 6.3 miles

DRIVING TIME 1 hour

ELEVATION RANGE 2,700–3,300 feet

USUALLY OPEN Year-round

BEST TIME TO TRAVEL Year-round

DIFFICULTY RATING 5

SCENIC RATING 9

REMOTENESS RATING +0

Special Attractions

- Rough, scenic trail within Red Rock Canyon State Park.
- Can be combined with Central Mountains #23: Last Chance Canyon Trail and other trails in the area for a full day's outing.
- Rockhounding for opals at two sites (fees required).

History

John Goler, one of the forty-niners who struggled out of Death Valley (see page 120), also lived to tell of the gold he had seen in the El Paso Mountains during his epic trip. After regaining his strength, Goler took a job as a blacksmith in the San Fernando Valley, but he could never forget the memory of gold in the El Paso Mountains. Goler traveled back toward Death Valley time and time again for nearly 20 years, sticking as close as he could remember to his original route. However, he never found the gold he talked of so much. Fellow prospectors finally believed his story when a find in 1893 seemed to match Goler's description. The miners decided to call the location Goler Gulch.

This strike at the eastern end of the El Paso Mountains triggered the second mild rush into the El Paso region. Mining camps sprang up in Last Chance Canyon, Jawbone Canyon, Summit Diggings, and Red Rock Canyon. With little water to work their ores, miners turned to the mushrooming town of Garlock on the south side of the range. The town had an ample water supply and as many as a half dozen mills were operating at its peak in the late 1800s. Up to a thousand men were combing the hills in search of a big strike. As usual, most of the prospectors had little luck and moved on to the next promising sign of fortune.

As the trail's name suggests, opals are plentiful in this region. Though much of the area is off-limits to rock collecting, because of its location within the boundaries of Red Rock

The dry and rugged El Paso Mountains

Canyon State Park, it is still possible to chase down some opals at two locations just north of the trail. The two old private mine sites are well sign-posted and allow you to chip and sledgehammer away to uncover those fire opals that have not yet been found (fees required). Volcanic activity in this once lush region resulted in flows that repeatedly covered the area with layers of volcanic ash. Petrified wood found close to the trail is associated with these ash layers.

Description

Opal Canyon Road is a small, formed trail that runs through Red Rock Canyon State Park, connecting California 14 with Central Mountains #23: Last Chance Canyon Trail. The trail leaves California 14 opposite Dove Springs OHV Area. Initially, it is a wide graded road, but it soon drops in standard to become a rough, formed trail that travels down the sandy wash of Opal Canyon.

A short distance from the trail, there are two privately owned rockhounding areas. Barnett Mine and Nowak Opal Area are open to the public on weekends, and it is possible to search for opals for a small fee. Small signs point the way to the claims.

The road travels in the wash, through the western El Paso Mountains, before swinging sharply and steeply out of the wash to climb a ridge. This section of the trail is where it earns its difficulty rating of 5. Low-traction, steep climbs, and off-camber side slopes will test the tire tread and wheel articulation of your vehicle. Although the trail is narrow, most vehicles will be able to negotiate this section with care.

There are panoramic views from the ridge top over the Nightmare Gulch Area, the El Paso Mountains, and east to the pink- and rose-colored rocks of Last Chance Canyon.

The trail passes the northern end of Central Mountains #22: Nightmare Gulch Over-

The El Paso Mountains are extremely rugged and popular with recreationalists

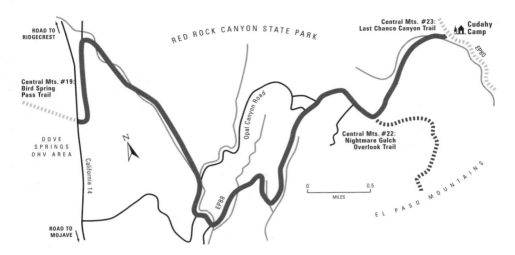

look Trail, and drops down to travel along a small wash to Cudahy Camp, located along Last Chance Canyon Trail. The final steep pinch to join this trail can have deep holes and the sandy soil offers little traction. However most high-clearance 4WD vehicles with good tires will manage the ascent.

Current Road Information

BLM Ridgecrest Field Office
300 South Richmond Road
Ridgecrest, CA 93555
(760) 384-5400

Map References

BLM   Cuddeback Lake
USGS 1:24,000   Saltdale NW
        1:100,000 Cuddeback Lake
Maptech CD-ROM: Barstow/San
        Bernardino County
*Southern & Central California Atlas &
        Gazetteer*, p. 65
California Road & Recreation Atlas, p. 94
Other: East Kern County OHV Riding
        Area and Trails—Jawbone Canyon

Route Directions

▼ 0.0   At mile marker 44 on California 14, 7.4 miles north of intersection with Randsburg–Red Rock Road, zero trip

meter and turn east onto graded dirt road over cattle guard. The entrance to Dove Springs OHV Area and Central Mountains #19: Bird Spring Pass Trail is opposite. Road immediately swings north, following alongside the highway.

2.7 ▲   Trail ends on California 14, opposite the entrance to Dove Springs OHV Area and Central Mountains #19: Bird Spring Pass Trail. Turn left for Randsburg and Mojave; turn right for Ridgecrest.
           GPS: N35°24.83' W117°58.77'

▼ 0.5   SO   Enter Red Rock Canyon State Park at sign.
2.2 ▲   SO   Exit Red Rock Canyon State Park at sign.
▼ 0.7   BR   Track on left.
2.0 ▲   BL   Track on right.
           GPS: N35°25.37' W117°58.55'

▼ 0.9   SO   Cross through wash.
1.8 ▲   SO   Cross through wash.
▼ 1.0   SO   Cross through wash.
1.7 ▲   SO   Cross through wash.
▼ 1.3   SO   Enter wash.
1.4 ▲   SO   Exit wash.
▼ 2.1   SO   Well-used track on left up side wash is Opal Canyon Road, which goes to Barnett Opal Mine (privately owned, fee required).
0.6 ▲   BL   Well-used track on right up side wash

Opal Canyon Road descends to join Last Chance Canyon Trail

is Opal Canyon Road, which goes to Barnett Opal Mine (privately owned, fee required).

GPS: N35°24.20' W117°57.93'

▼ 2.5   BL   Track on right. Bear left and join unmarked EP88, remaining in wash.
0.2 ▲   BR   Track on left. Bear right, remaining in wash.

GPS: N35°23.92' W117°58.08'

▼ 2.7   TL   Turn left and climb steeply out of wash. Track continues ahead in wash. Zero trip meter.
0.0 ▲   Continue to the north.

GPS: N35°23.84' W117°57.97'

▼ 0.0   Continue to the southeast.
2.5 ▲   TR   Descend and turn right up wash. Track on left down wash. Zero trip meter.
▼ 0.2   SO   Enter wash.
2.3 ▲   SO   Exit wash.
▼ 0.4   SO   Exit wash up ridge to the right.
2.1 ▲   SO   Enter wash.

GPS: N35°24.01' W117°57.68'

▼ 0.7   BR   Small track on left.
1.8 ▲   BL   Small track on right.
▼ 0.8   SO   Cross through wash.
1.7 ▲   SO   Cross through wash.
▼ 1.1   SO   Enter wash.
1.4 ▲   SO   Exit wash.
▼ 1.2   SO   Exit wash to the left.
1.3 ▲   SO   Enter wash.
▼ 1.3   SO   Enter wash.
1.2 ▲   SO   Exit wash to the right.
▼ 1.6   SO   Exit wash.
0.9 ▲   SO   Enter wash.
▼ 1.8   SO   Two tracks on left join main Opal Canyon Road.
0.7 ▲   SO   Two tracks on right join main Opal Canyon Road.
▼ 1.9   SO   Opal Canyon Road on left. Track on right on saddle goes 0.1 miles to viewpoint.
0.6 ▲   SO   Track on left on saddle goes 0.1 miles to viewpoint. Opal Canyon Road on right.

GPS: N35°24.46' W117°56.83'

▼ 2.3   SO   Track on left goes to mine; then track on right.

0.2 ▲   SO   Track on left; then track on right goes to mine.

GPS: N35°24.36' W117°56.51'

▼ 2.5   TL   Small track on right; then turn left on well-used trail descending to the north-east. Track ahead is Central Mountains #22: Nightmare Gulch Overlook Trail. Zero trip meter.
0.0 ▲   Continue to the northwest.

GPS: N35°24.23' W117°56.39'

▼ 0.0   Continue to the northeast.
1.1 ▲   TR   T-intersection. Central Mountains #22: Nightmare Gulch Overlook Trail on left; then small track on left. Zero trip meter.
▼ 0.2   SO   Enter line of wash.
0.9 ▲   SO   Exit wash.
▼ 0.6   SO   Track on right.
0.5 ▲   SO   Track on left.
▼ 1.0   SO   Exit line of wash; then track on left by old water tank joins Central Mountains #23: Last Chance Canyon Trail. Track on right.
0.1 ▲   SO   Track on left. Track on right by old water tank joins Central Mountains #23: Last Chance Canyon Trail; then enter line of wash.
▼ 1.1   Cross through Last Chance Canyon Wash; then trail ends at T-intersection with Central Mountains #23: Last Chance Canyon Trail at Cudahy Camp. Turn right to exit via Last Chance Canyon Trail to Randsburg–Red Rock Road; turn left to continue along Last Chance Canyon Trail to either Central Mountains #24: Burro Schmidt Tunnel Trail or Central Mountains #25: Sheep Spring Trail.
0.0 ▲   Trail commences on Central Mountains #23: Last Chance Canyon Trail at Cudahy Camp, 4.4 miles north of Randsburg–Red Rock Road. Zero trip meter and turn southwest on unmarked trail that immediately dips down to cross through Last Chance Canyon Wash.

GPS: N35°24.66' W117°55.55'

Nightmare Gulch Overlook Trail

STARTING POINT Central Mountains #21: Opal Canyon Road, 1.1 miles from Cudahy Camp

FINISHING POINT Randsburg–Red Rock Road, 4.5 miles northeast of California 14

TOTAL MILEAGE 5 miles, plus 1.1-mile spur

UNPAVED MILEAGE: 7.2 miles

DRIVING TIME 1 hour

ELEVATION RANGE 1,900–3,400 feet

USUALLY OPEN Year-round

BEST TIME TO TRAVEL Year-round

DIFFICULTY RATING 4

SCENIC RATING 8

REMOTENESS RATING +0

Special Attractions

- Access to the difficult canyon trail along Nightmare Gulch.
- Panoramic ridge top views.
- Scenic, small trail within Red Rock Canyon State Park.

History

Nightmare Gulch Overlook Trail offers a unique insight into the region's ancient landscape. The area, once full of lush vegetation, displays signs of high erosion. Early Native Americans may have camped by lakeshores in the vicinity prior to evolving climatic changes. Local volcanic activity resulted in heavy layers of ash that settled throughout the surrounding region. Nearby pumice mines such as the Holly Ash Cleanser Mine and Dutch Cleanser Mine, active from early last century, were dug deep into these fine white, chalk-like layers to produce the finest abrasive cleansing agents. Petrified wood, a result of such volcanic activity, can still be seen in the region. Early miners in the El Paso Mountains discovered petrified forests, and carted pieces off for collectors. Today, there are only sparse reminders of these once lush forests, and the remnants are just for

The slightly off-camber trail runs high above Nightmare Gulch

Tumbleweed gathers at the old talc mine above Nightmare Gulch

Nightmare Gulch lies far below the trail

CENTRAL MOUNTAINS #22: NIGHTMARE GULCH OVERLOOK TRAIL

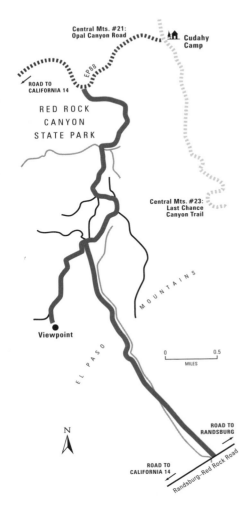

Please respect this closure to ensure that the trail remains open to vehicles on its current basis.

The trail travels around the ridge tops between Nightmare Gulch and Last Chance Canyon, offering panoramic views of both. Some of the climbs are steep and eroded, and there are several sections that are off-camber, tilting a vehicle toward the drop. The trail descends from the first ridge to pass alongside the extensive workings of an old mine. Many trails leave in all directions here, and the route makes a sharp turn to climb a rough, uneven trail to the top of the ridge. Once on the ridge there are 360-degree views: To the east is Last Chance Canyon and the Rand Mountains, to the west is Nightmare Gulch and the Piute Mountains, to the north are the Scodie Mountains, and to the south is the Fremont Valley.

The trail descends the ridge again to rejoin the track it left a short distance south of the mine. Those not wanting to take the ridge top route can remain on the main trail through the mining area.

A spur leads off from this point and climbs to another panoramic viewpoint that looks south over the canyons to Koehn Lake. The difficult trail into Nightmare Gulch leaves through the mining area a short distance to the north.

From here, the trail follows a roughly graded road down to the canyon to exit to Randsburg–Red Rock Road.

Current Road Information
BLM Ridgecrest Field Office
300 South Richmond Road
Ridgecrest, CA 93555
(760) 384-5400

looking and admiring. No rock collection of any sort is permitted within Red Rock Canyon State Park.

Map References
BLM   Cuddeback Lake
USGS 1:24,000   Saltdale NW, Cantil
         1:100,000 Cuddeback Lake
Maptech CD-ROM: Barstow/San
         Bernardino County
Southern & Central California Atlas & Gazetteer, p. 65
California Road & Recreation Atlas, p. 94
Other: East Kern County OHV Riding
         Area and Trails—Jawbone Canyon

Description
Nightmare Gulch is a small, highly scenic canyon in Red Rock Canyon State Park. The area attracts many raptors, which can often be seen riding the thermals above the canyons and mountains. A difficult 4WD trail leads down into Nightmare Gulch. However, to protect raptor nesting sites, the gulch is closed to vehicle travel for the first 15 days of each month.

Route Directions

▼ 0.0   From Central Mountains #21: Opal Canyon Road, 1.1 miles from the eastern end at Cudahy Camp (the intersection with Central Mountains #23: Last Chance Canyon Trail), zero trip meter and turn southeast onto unmarked, well-used formed trail; then track on right.

1.6 ▲   Track on left; then trail ends at intersection with Central Mountains #21: Opal Canyon Road. Turn right to exit to Central Mountains #23: Last Chance Canyon Trail; continue straight to exit to California 14.

     GPS: N35°24.23' W117°56.39'

▼ 0.1   SO   Track on left.
1.5 ▲   SO   Track on right.
▼ 0.5   BR   Track on left.
1.1 ▲   BL   Track on right.
▼ 0.7   BR   Track on left.
0.9 ▲   BL   Track on right.

     GPS: N35°23.89' W117°55.94'

▼ 0.8   BL   Track on right.
0.8 ▲   SO   Track on left.
▼ 0.9   SO   Enter wash; track on left.
0.7 ▲   SO   Track on right; exit wash.
▼ 1.1   SO   Exit wash up ridge to the left.
0.5 ▲   SO   Drop down to enter wash.
▼ 1.6   TL   Track on right toward mine. Large adit is visible directly ahead; then turn sharp left up unmarked, rough uneven trail and zero trip meter. Track straight ahead rejoins main trail in a short distance. Track ahead also passes the start of limited-access Nightmare Gulch Trail.

0.0 ▲   Continue to the northwest past track on left toward mine.

     GPS: N35°23.30' W117°56.23'

▼ 0.0   Continue to the north.
0.9 ▲   TR   Turn sharp right onto well-used trail and zero trip meter. Large adit is visible ahead. Track straight ahead rejoins main trail (in opposite direction) in a short distance.

▼ 0.2   SO   Two tracks on left and two tracks on right.
0.7 ▲   SO   Two tracks on left and two tracks on right.
▼ 0.4   TR   T-intersection. Turn right along ridge.
0.5 ▲   TL   Turn left and descend from ridge. Track continues straight ahead.

     GPS: N35°23.25' W117°56.02'

▼ 0.5   SO   Track on left.
0.4 ▲   SO   Track on right.
▼ 0.9   TL   5-way intersection. Track straight ahead is spur to viewpoint. Turn first left and zero trip meter. First track on right rejoins main trail (in opposite direction) in a short distance. Second track on right is private.

0.0 ▲   Continue to the northeast.

     GPS: N35°22.92' W117°56.36'

Spur to Viewpoint

▼ 0.0   Proceed to the southwest.
▼ 0.3   BL   Two tracks on right go to private property.
▼ 0.4   BL   Track on right.
▼ 1.0   BL   Track on right.
▼ 1.1   UT   Spur ends at viewpoint. Retrace your steps back to the 5-way intersection.

     GPS: N35°22.23' W117°56.71'

Continuation of Main Trail

▼ 0.0   Continue to the southeast.
2.5 ▲   TR   5-way intersection. First track on left is spur to viewpoint. Second track on left is private. Turn first right and start to climb up ridge. Zero trip meter. Track ahead rejoins main trail in a short distance. Track ahead also passes the start of limited-access Nightmare Gulch Trail.

     GPS: N35°22.92' W117°56.36'

▼ 0.1   SO   Enter line of wash.
2.4 ▲   SO   Exit line of wash.
▼ 1.6   SO   Exit canyon and Red Rock Canyon State Park at small sign.
0.9 ▲   SO   Enter canyon and Red Rock Canyon State Park at small sign.

     GPS: N35°21.65' W117°55.74'

▼ 1.7	SO	Exit wash.
0.8 ▲	SO	Enter wash.
▼ 2.5		Trail ends on Randsburg—Red Rock Road. Turn left for Randsburg; turn right for California 14.
0.0 ▲		Trail commences on Randsburg-Red Rock Road, 4.5 miles northeast of California 14. Zero trip meter and turn northwest onto unmarked formed trail.

GPS: N35°21.04' W117°55.13'

Last Chance Canyon Trail

STARTING POINT Randsburg–Red Rock Road, 6 miles northeast of California 14

FINISHING POINT Central Mountains #24: Burro Schmidt Tunnel Trail, 4.8 miles from the eastern end

TOTAL MILEAGE 10.6 miles

UNPAVED MILEAGE: 10.6 miles

DRIVING TIME 2 hours

ELEVATION RANGE 2,000–3,600 feet

USUALLY OPEN Year-round

BEST TIME TO TRAVEL September to May

DIFFICULTY RATING 5

SCENIC RATING 10

REMOTENESS RATING +0

Special Attractions

■ Open-air museum at Bickel Camp.
■ Beautiful scenery within Red Rock Canyon State Park.
■ Rockhounding for agate, jasper, and opalized wood.

History

North of Cudahy Camp is the Old Dutch Cleanser Mine. The pumice found here is a result of ongoing volcanic activity in the region. Many layers of fine volcanic ash settled on an area that was once lushly vegetated. Early miners removed petrified wood, and only small segments are still visible today. These pieces are not for collecting anymore, just admiring. A series of tunnels were cut into the white, chalky rock layer through openings in the cliff face. The large tunnels sloped nearly 45 degrees down to a transverse tunnel deep within the volcanic layer. A tramway carried the diggings through the main tunnel and down the cliff face into Last Chance Canyon. Mining trucks then transported the diggings all the way down Last Chance Canyon. Some sections of the old road that have endured decades of erosion are still visible in the canyon.

In the early 1900s, storekeepers across the country proudly hung metal "Old Dutch Cleanser" signs above their doors. The same signs are now prized antiques. Dutch Cleanser as a brand name is still popular as a fine polishing and cleansing agent. It has a multitude of uses, including the meticulous preparation of fish for *gyotaku,* the oriental art of fish printing.

The name Last Chance is generally associated with explorers and prospectors who found water at the brink of death by dehydration. In some prospectors' cases, it also referred to finding worthwhile ore deposits during their last search of a region. In this instance, Last Chance Canyon also may have reflected how hard it was for prospectors to find anything worth mining. Near the northern end of the canyon lies what was called Grubstake Hill. Prospectors who had spent all their time and money searching the El Paso Mountains and had run dry in all respects would turn to Grubstake Hill. The locality was known to contain gold, but the ore was so hard to extract that prospectors turned to it only as a last resort. It was their last chance to buy the new supplies it would take to move on to more promising areas.

Description

Last Chance Canyon is a beautiful, remote canyon within Red Rock Canyon State Park that combines breathtaking scenery, historical interest, and an exciting drive.

The trail leaves Randsburg–Red Rock Road opposite the dry Koehn Lake and the site of Saltdale. The trail is a clearly defined, formed road as it climbs up the bajada, providing views back over Koehn Lake and the

Walt Bickel's Camp, now an open-air museum

Fremont Valley, before it drops down to enter the wash in Last Chance Canyon. It follows in or alongside the wash for the next few miles. For the most part, the trail is well formed and remains out of the wash itself. Some sections offer the choice of traveling in the sandy wash or along the formed trail. The sand in the wash is deep and loose; some will slow down a vehicle. The sand is interspersed with rocky sections that will require careful wheel placement to avoid underbody damage. However, the most challenging rocky section can be avoided by remaining on the formed trail.

All that remains of Cudahy Camp are concrete and stone foundations scattered around an open area. Central Mountains #21: Opal Canyon Road leaves the old mining camp to the west, heading toward California 14. A short distance farther, the adits of the Dutch Cleanser Mine can be seen high on the cliffs to the northwest. This mine can be reached via a network of small trails on the west side of the cliffs.

North of Cudahy Camp, the trail leaves the wash, where work is under way to re-vegetate the area. Be sure to remain on the correct trail to avoid damage to the wash area. This is one of the most scenic parts of the canyon, with pink- and rose-colored canyon walls and sculpted rock formations. Rockhounds can search the side washes in the area, where it is possible to find samples of agate, jasper, and petrified wood. However, collecting is prohibited in Red Rock Canyon State Park, and any specimens should be admired and left in place.

The trail leaves the wash area and heads up a short, steep low-traction climb. This stretch is the part that earns the trail its 5-rating for difficulty. The remainder of the trail is rated up to a 4 for difficulty. Farther north, the standard becomes easier and smoother as you approach Bickel Camp.

Walt Bickel donated the open-air museum at Bickel Camp to the BLM upon his death in 1995. Walt used to prospect in the region, and he lived in the cabin, which was built in

Weathered sign guides the way to Schmidt Tunnel

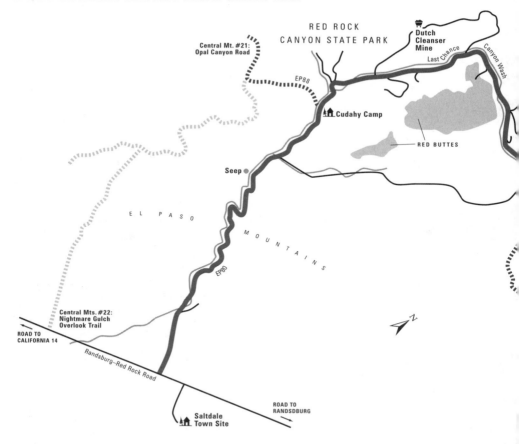

1937. The cabin and mining memorabilia are open for people to enjoy. There is a caretaker on site.

North of Bickel Camp, the trail becomes smooth and well-used as it loops around to finish near the eastern end of Central Mountains #24: Burro Schmidt Tunnel Trail. You have the choice there of exiting a short distance to the south to the paved Randsburg–Red Rock Road, or meeting up with Central Mountains #25: Sheep Spring Trail and heading north to exit near Ridgecrest.

Current Road Information

BLM Ridgecrest Field Office
300 South Richmond Road
Ridgecrest, CA 93555
(760) 384-5400

Map References

BLM   Cuddeback Lake
USGS   1:24,000   Cantil, Saltdale NW, Garlock
          1:100,000 Cuddeback Lake
Maptech CD-ROM: Barstow/San Bernardino County
Southern & Central California Atlas & Gazetteer, pp. 65, 66
California Road & Recreation Atlas, p. 94
Other: East Kern County OHV Riding Areas and Trails—Jawbone Canyon

Route Directions

▼ 0.0   From paved Randsburg–Red Rock Road, 6 miles northeast of California 14 and 0.3 miles southwest of small signed Saltdale Road, zero trip meter

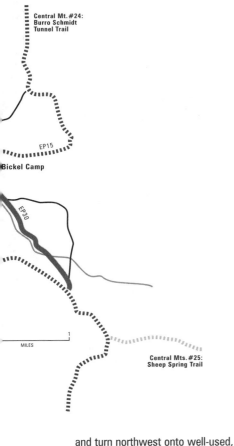

Central Mt. #24:
Burro Schmidt
Tunnel Trail

EP15

Bickel Camp

EP30

MILES

Central Mts. #25:
Sheep Spring Trail

▼ 2.4   SO Track on right.
2.0 ▲ SO Track on left.
          GPS: N35°23.28' W117°55.08'

▼ 2.5   SO Short, rocky 4-rated section.
1.9 ▲ SO Short, rocky 4-rated section.
▼ 3.2   SO Seep on right.
1.2 ▲ SO Seep on left.
          GPS: N35°23.70' W117°55.29'

▼ 3.6   SO Well-used track on right travels up side
          wash, south of Red Buttes.
0.8 ▲ SO Well-used track on left travels up side
          wash, south of Red Buttes.
          GPS: N35°23.98' W117°55.35'

▼ 4.3   SO Open area is Cudahy Camp. Track is
          generally less rocky.
0.1 ▲ SO Open area is Cudahy Camp. Track
          ahead is somewhat more rocky.
          GPS: N35°24.60' W117°55.51'

▼ 4.4   SO Track on right and concrete slab founda-
          tions from Cudahy Camp. Then track
          on left is Central Mountains #21: Opal
          Canyon Road (EP88). Intersection is
          unmarked but well used. Zero trip meter.
0.0 ▲   Continue to the southeast.
          GPS: N35°24.66' W117°55.55'

▼ 0.0   Continue to the northwest.
3.2 ▲ SO Track on right is Central Mountains
          #21: Opal Canyon Road (EP88).
          Intersection is unmarked but well
          used. Track on left and concrete slab
          foundations from Cudahy Camp. Zero
          trip meter.
▼ 0.2   BL Bear left out of wash up steep, loose
          pinch. Track on left to mine at top
          of rise.
3.0 ▲ BR Track on right to mine on top of rise.
          Descend steep pinch and bear right
          along Last Chance Canyon wash.
▼ 0.4   SO Cross through side wash; then well-
          used track on left past tanks. There are
          three tracks ahead at this point. Take
          the right-hand track, bearing north,
          and re-enter wash.
2.8 ▲ SO Exit wash, bearing south, past tracks
          on right. Well-used track on right past

and turn northwest onto well-used,
formed Last Chance Canyon Road
(EP80). Road is marked by a Red Rock
Canyon State Park OHV sign.
4.4 ▲   Trail ends at T-intersection with paved
          Randsburg–Red Rock Road, opposite
          the dry Koehn Lake. Turn left for
          Randsburg; turn right for California
          14 and Mojave.
          GPS: N35°21.70' W117°53.86'

▼ 0.8   SO Track on right up ridge.
3.6 ▲ SO Track on left up ridge.
▼ 0.9   SO Cross through wash.
3.5 ▲ SO Cross through wash.
▼ 1.0   SO Enter Last Chance Canyon wash.
3.4 ▲ SO Exit Last Chance Canyon wash.
▼ 2.0   SO Start of rocky sections in canyon wash.
2.4 ▲ SO End of rocky sections.

Red rocks and an undulating trail make for an interesting ride

tanks. Continue straight ahead and cross through side wash to climb a small rise on the far side.

GPS: N35°24.88' W117°55.66'

▼ 0.9	SO	Track on right goes to mining camp and track on left.
2.3 ▲	SO	Track on left goes to mining camp and track on right.
▼ 1.0	SO	Track on left.
2.2 ▲	SO	Track on right.
▼ 1.1	SO	Track on right to private mining camp.
2.1 ▲	BR	Track on left to private mining camp.

GPS: N35°25.38' W117°55.42'

▼ 1.4	SO	Track on right to mine adits.
1.8 ▲	SO	Track on left to mine adits.
▼ 1.5	SO	Track on right and track on left.
1.7 ▲	SO	Track on right and track on left.
▼ 1.7	SO	Track on right.
1.5 ▲	BR	Track on left.

▼ 1.9	SO	Track on left; then trail forks and rejoins in a short distance.
1.3 ▲	SO	Trail rejoins; track on right.

GPS: N35°26.03' W117°55.09'

▼ 2.0	SO	Trail rejoins; then track on left.
1.2 ▲	SO	Track on right; then trail forks and rejoins in a short distance.
▼ 2.1	SO	Track on left.
1.1 ▲	SO	Track on right.

GPS: N35°26.22' W117°55.07'

▼ 2.6	SO	Track on right.
0.6 ▲	SO	Track on left.
▼ 2.7	SO	Small track on left.
0.5 ▲	SO	Small track on right.
▼ 3.2	SO	Two well-used tracks on left. Zero trip meter and continue straight ahead, following wooden sign for Schmidt Tunnel.
0.0 ▲		Continue to the west.

The open-air museum at Bickel Camp

▼ 0.0   Continue to the east.

0.8 ▲   SO   Two well-used tracks on right. Zero trip meter and continue straight ahead. There is a small wooden sign for Schmidt Tunnel at the intersection.

▼ 0.4   SO   Small track on right; then well-used track on left. Follow sign for Schmidt Tunnel, leaving the wash.

0.4 ▲   SO   Well-used track on right; then small track on left. There is a sign for Schmidt Tunnel at the intersection. Enter line of wash.

GPS: N35°25.99' W117°53.86'

▼ 0.6   SO   Leaving Red Rock Canyon State Park at sign.

0.2 ▲   SO   Entering Red Rock Canyon State Park at sign.

GPS: N35°25.95' W117°53.68'

▼ 0.7   SO   Enter line of wash.

0.1 ▲   SO   Exit line of wash.

▼ 0.8   SO   Track on left; then 4-way intersection. Continue straight ahead on well-used trail in wash, following BLM sign for EP30. Track on right and left is Central Mountains #24: Burro Schmidt Tunnel Trail (EP15). Zero trip meter.

0.0 ▲   Continue to the southwest past track on right.

GPS: N35°25.99' W117°53.39'

▼ 0.0   Continue to the northeast on EP30.

2.2 ▲   SO   4-way intersection. Continue straight ahead on well-used trail marked by a BLM sign designating the trail suitable for 4WDs, ATVs, and motorbikes. Track on left and right is Central Mountains #24: Burro Schmidt Tunnel Trail (EP15). Zero trip meter.

▼ 0.1   SO   Track on left beside mine adits in hillside.

2.1 ▲   SO   Track on right beside mine adits in hillside.

▼ 0.3   SO   Bickel Camp on left—many old, interesting mining remains. Please do not take anything. Track on right.

1.9 ▲   SO   Bickel Camp on right—many old, interesting mining remains. Please do not take anything. Track on left.

▼ 0.6   SO   Track on left.

1.6 ▲   SO   Track on right.

▼ 0.9   SO   Track on left.

1.3 ▲   SO   Track on right.

GPS: N35°26.13' W117°52.57'

▼ 1.4   SO   Track on left.

0.8 ▲   SO   Track on right.

▼ 1.7   SO   Exit line of wash.

0.5 ▲   SO   Enter line of Last Chance Canyon wash.

▼ 2.1   SO   Track on left and track on right.

0.1 ▲   SO   Track on left and track on right.

GPS: N35°26.14' W117°51.28'

▼ 2.2   Trail ends at intersection with Central Mountains #24: Burro Schmidt Tunnel Trail (EP15). Turn right to continue to Burro Schmidt Tunnel; turn left to exit to Randsburg–Red Rock Road.

0.0 ▲   Trail commences on Central Mountains #24: Burro Schmidt Tunnel Trail, 4.8 miles from intersection with Randsburg–Red Rock Road. Zero trip meter at 4-way intersection and proceed east on small formed trail marked EP30. Burro Schmidt Tunnel Trail continues to the southwest, following EP15. Also small track on left and pull-in on right.

GPS: N35°26.13' W117°51.20'

Burro Schmidt Tunnel Trail

STARTING POINT California 14, 13.5 miles north of intersection with Randsburg–Red Rock Road

FINISHING POINT Randsburg–Red Rock Road at mile marker 11, 1.1 miles west of intersection with Garlock Road

TOTAL MILEAGE 14.9 miles, plus 0.9-mile spur

UNPAVED MILEAGE: 14.9 miles, plus 0.9-mile spur

DRIVING TIME 1.5 hours

ELEVATION RANGE 2,100–4,000 feet

USUALLY OPEN Year-round

Burro Schmidt's cabin, built in 1902

BEST TIME TO TRAVEL Year-round
DIFFICULTY RATING 2
SCENIC RATING 9
REMOTENESS RATING +0

Special Attractions
- Remains of the Holly Ash Cleanser Mine and Bonanza Gulch post office.
- Trail intersects with other 4WD, ATV, and motorbike trails in the El Paso Mountains.
- Burro Schmidt Tunnel and cabin.

History
Garlock, located near the eastern end of the trail, was formerly known as Cow Wells and it was just that. Early settlers and teamsters used it as a watering hole and staging station for haulage teams headed north to the Panamint Mines on the edge of Death Valley. After the 1893 gold strike at Goler Gulch, Cow Wells flourished because of the availability of water. Eugene Garlock established a 5-stamp mill in 1895 to cater to the burgeoning mines in the El Paso Mountains. In the same year, the big gold strike that was to put Randsburg on the map also fueled Garlock's progress. By 1899 several hundred people had taken up residency in the town now known as Garlock. Hotels offered quality accommodations to travelers and the saloons were bustling. Yet Randsburg's mining boom would turn out to be the death of Garlock. Large quantities of ore from the Yellow Aster Mine were hauled by 20-mule teams across the Fremont Valley to the mill at Garlock. Such a productive mine needed its own mill. By 1897, Randsburg and the newly developed Johannesburg had their own small mills in operation. Garlock's days were numbered.

Garlock Fault, which runs through this region, may not have shifted for more than a thousand years, yet it is capable of causing a tremor of magnitude 8 on the Richter scale. The fault marks a striking geologic division in the region. To the north of the line, high mountains follow a north-south trend, interspersed with deep valleys such as Death Valley. To the south of the fault, less striking mountains combine with wide basins and plains to make up the Mojave Desert. Most faults throughout the state run in a north-north-

Burro Schmidt's hand-dug tunnel took 32 years to complete

westerly direction, yet the Garlock Fault generally runs east to west. Where it meets the southern reaches of the Sierra Nevada (close to Cantil), it bears southwest until it intercepts the San Andreas Fault near Gorman.

Mesquite Canyon, so-named by miners because of the mesquite growth at its entrance, was an old Indian entrance to the El Paso Mountains. Prospectors used it to enter and exit the mountains as well. As such it became a reliable ambush point for gunslingers who sought the prospectors' gold. Mines such as the Golden Badger and Decker in the side canyons on the south face of Mesquite Canyon were just a couple of the low-profit claims in the region. Located at the top of Mesquite Canyon, Gerbracht Camp was a place generally avoided because in her later years, Della Gerbracht guarded the area with her rifle and was reputedly none too shy about using it! The nearby Colorado Camp, just to the west, produced low-grade coal that took a lot of effort to keep burning. It gained no great commercial sales and quickly petered out. Copper and gold claims were also worked nearby.

William Henry Schmidt, born in Rhode Island in 1871, moved to California in his early twenties, just before the gold strike in the Rand Mining District. Like several other rookie prospectors enticed by the 1893 Goler gold find, Schmidt established mining claims in the Last Chance Canyon area. As the years passed, Schmidt toiled in the remote location as small finds made him ever hopeful of an eventual "big one." He worked in the Kern River region during the warmer months, saving every penny he could earn as a hired hand. Every winter he took his meager wages and returned to work his own claims.

It occurred to Schmidt that he might need a better transportation route out of the El Paso Mountains if he ever did find a mother lode. He thought to himself, "Why not dig a tunnel through the mountain to the southwest and look for precious metals along the way?" Though seemingly a good idea at the time, no worthwhile seams were revealed in the entire 1,872 feet of the monumental tunnel he finally built. It seems tunnel fever over-

took his gold fever. Schmidt, who was of slight build, had moved from back East partially for health reasons. (Several members of his family had died of tuberculosis, and he was advised to move to a better climate.) Yet he managed to dig the tunnel almost entirely by hand. His main tools were a pick, a four-pound hammer, and a hand drill. These were later complemented by occasional use of dynamite, a wheelbarrow, and later still a set of rails and an ore cart.

Over the years, Schmidt was forced to sell off his other claims in order to survive. He led the life of a hermit in his lone cabin and was known as Burro Schmidt to others because his main companions were his burros. Schmidt started his tunnel in 1906 and saw daylight on the south side of Copper Mountain in 1938. Although many people asked him his reasons, he would never say exactly why he kept digging. Schmidt sold his tunnel claim and moved to his other claims in the region. He died in 1954 and was laid to rest in the Joburg Cemetery.

Toward the northeastern end of the trail lies the Holly Ash Cleanser Mine. Discovered in the early 1930s, this large ledge of volcanic ash and white pumice became a direct competitor of the Dutch Cleanser Mine, located just to the south. Their products were used in a variety of items; the finest quality ore went into polishing substances and the coarser forms were used in plaster and agricultural products.

Description

The trail leaves California 14 and bears southwest across the wide Indian Wells Valley. It gradually rises along a steady grade toward the El Paso Mountains. At the base of the mountains are the remains of the old Holly Ash Cleanser Mine. A tank and several mining relics surround huge white caverns hollowed into the cliff.

The trail enters the El Paso Mountains, passing the sturdy wooden building of the Bonanza Gulch post office before descending into Bonanza Canyon. The trail crosses Central Mountains #23: Last Chance Canyon Trail, immediately southwest of Bickel Camp. If you do not intend to travel the full

GARLOCK

Garlock came into being when an enterprising settler made the unlikely decision to dig a well on the edge of the barren El Paso Mountains. Surprisingly, water was found only 30 feet below the surface. For decades, the settlement then known as Cow Wells was a reliable watering stop for travelers through Death Valley. The town's ample water resources prompted Eugene Garlock to install a 5-stamp gold mill, the Garlock Pioneer Mill, in 1895, the same year prospectors struck gold at Randsburg. Garlock's mill processed the first ore from Randsburg's Yellow Aster Mine and other burgeoning mines in the area.

By 1899, six stamp mills and several hundred people resided in town. The legendary 20-mule teams hauled ore from the Yellow Aster Mine across the Fremont Valley. Garlock thrived. Two hotels offered accommodations to travelers. The town supported assayers, two saloons, a couple general stores, a Wells Fargo office, a school, and mine promoters. The two-story Doty Hotel gave the best view of the region, but that apparently was not terribly impressive. As one guest commented, "one could look farther and see less than at any point in the surrounding country."

Garlock's prosperity was short lived. In 1898, a railroad spur was completed to connect Johannesburg in the Rand Mining District to the Atchison, Topeka & Santa Fe line at Kramer. In the same year a water pipe was extended from Goler Wash to Randsburg. These two projects eliminated the region's need for Garlock's mills and water. By 1903, its little school had only three pupils; the post office closed in 1904. Garlock, once a town full of activity, was now deteriorating. Many of Garlock's residents and structures relocated to Randsburg.

Garlock did have two small revivals. In 1911, workers laying track for the Southern Pacific's line from Mojave to Keeler camped in the abandoned buildings. The crews moved on when the section of track was completed. Then in the early 1920s a salt company started to work deposits in nearby Kane Lake. The post office reopened in 1923, but by 1926 the salt project had failed and the office was forced to close again. Today, a rock and adobe structure known as Jennie's Bar remains, as does an automated Mexican arrastra.

Approximately 5 miles northwest of Garlock is evidence of a prehistoric Indian village, discovered in the 1880s. Some experts believe the same tribe who built sites in Arizona and New Mexico inhabited the village. (Stone carvings resemble those found on the famous Posten Butte near Florence, Arizona.) Other experts believe the site was a religious center used intermittently.

length of Last Chance Canyon Trail, it is worth the short detour to see the cabin and open-air museum at Bickel Camp.

The main trail continues in the wash to the start of the spur to Burro Schmidt's cabin and tunnel. Pass by the private property and follow signs to the tunnel itself. There are two cabins side by side, the second of which is Burro Schmidt's old one-room house. The cabin still has a stove and the walls and ceiling are lined with old magazine and newspaper pages dating back to the 1920s. Outside there is a spread of old artifacts to admire. Stop here and register; donations are appreciated. An on-site caretaker lives in the first cabin.

The tunnel itself is a short distance past the cabin. Past the tunnel, a network of steep narrow trails crisscrosses the ridge to many fine vantage points.

The main trail passes the eastern end of Last Chance Canyon Trail and the southern end of Central Mountains #25: Sheep Spring Trail, before swinging south into Mesquite Canyon. It passes by the remains of a few old mines before crossing the bajada to end on the Randsburg–Red Rock Road near the settlement of Garlock.

Current Road Information
BLM Ridgecrest Field Office
300 South Richmond Road
Ridgecrest, CA 93555
(760) 384-5400

Map References
BLM   Cuddeback Lake
USGS   1:24,000   Saltdale NW, Garlock
          1:100,000 Cuddeback Lake
Maptech CD-ROM: Barstow/San
          Bernardino County
*Southern & Central California Atlas &
          Gazetteer*, pp. 65, 66
California Road & Recreation Atlas, p. 94
Other: East Kern County OHV Riding
          Areas and Trails—Jawbone Canyon

Route Directions

▼ 0.0   From California 14, 13.5 miles north of
                  intersection with Randsburg–Red Rock
                  Road, zero trip meter and turn south-
                  east onto graded dirt road. There is a
                  small wooden sign for Schmidt Tunnel
                  at the intersection and the trail is
                  marked EP15 by a BLM marker. Trail is
                  suitable for 4WDs, ATVs, and motor-
                  bikes. Cross cattle guard.
3.3 ▲   Cross cattle guard; then trail ends on
                  California 14. Turn right for Ridgecrest;
                  turn left for Mojave.
                  GPS: N35°30.04' W117°56.87'

▼ 1.0   SO   Cross through Little Dixie Wash.
2.3 ▲   SO   Cross through Little Dixie Wash.
▼ 1.3   SO   Track on right.
2.0 ▲   SO   Track on left.
▼ 1.6   SO   Cross over graded dirt Red
                  Rock–Inyokern Road. There is a sign at
                  the intersection for Bonanza Trail and
                  Burro Schmidt Tunnel.
1.7 ▲   SO   Cross over graded dirt Red
                  Rock–Inyokern Road. There is a sign at
                  the intersection for Bonanza Trail and
                  Burro Schmidt Tunnel.
                  GPS: N35°28.84' W117°55.84'

▼ 1.9   SO   Track on right.
1.4 ▲   BR   Track on left.

▼ 2.5   SO   Track on left.
0.8 ▲   SO   Track on right rejoins.
▼ 2.7   SO   Track on left rejoins.
0.6 ▲   SO   Track on right.
▼ 2.8   SO   Track on right.
0.5 ▲   SO   Track on left.
▼ 3.3   BL   Well-used track on right. Zero trip meter.
0.0 ▲   Continue to the northwest.
                  GPS: N35°27.49' W117°54.63'

▼ 0.0   Continue to the east and cross through
                  wash. Track on right up wash.
1.2 ▲   BR   Cross through wash. Track on left up
                  wash. Then well-used track on left.
                  Zero trip meter.
▼ 0.2   SO   Track on right.
1.0 ▲   SO   Track on left.
▼ 0.6   SO   Track on right.
0.6 ▲   SO   Track on left.
▼ 0.8   SO   Two tracks on right at tank.
0.4 ▲   SO   Two tracks on left at tank.
▼ 1.0   SO   Track on right to large stone tank and
                  many mining remains of the Holly Ash
                  Cleanser Mine; then second track
                  on right.
0.2 ▲   SO   Track on left; then second track on left
                  to large stone tank and many mining
                  remains of the Holly Ash Cleanser
                  Mine.
                  GPS: N35°27.06' W117°53.76'

▼ 1.2   TL   5-way intersection. Turn first left on
                  saddle, remaining on marked EP15.
                  Also second track on left, track on
                  right, and track straight ahead. Zero
                  trip meter.
0.0 ▲   Continue to the north.
                  GPS: N35°26.93' W117°53.67'

▼ 0.0   Continue to the northeast.
2.5 ▲   TR   5-way intersection. Turn first right on
                  saddle, remaining on marked EP15.
                  Two tracks on left and track straight
                  ahead. Zero trip meter.
▼ 0.7   SO   Track on right.
1.8 ▲   SO   Track on left.
▼ 1.0   TL   4-way intersection. Turn left; then
                  rusty corrugated iron cabin on right is
                  Bonanza Gulch post office; then enter
                  Bonanza Canyon.

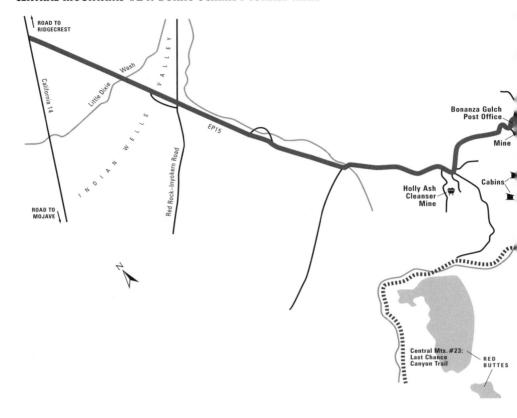

1.5 ▲   TR   Trail has exited Bonanza Canyon.
Rusty corrugated iron cabin on left is
Bonanza Gulch post office; then 4-way
intersection.
GPS: N35°27.02' W117°52.86'

▼ 1.1   TR   Track on left. Remain on EP15.
1.4 ▲   TL   Track on right. Remain on EP15.
▼ 1.2   SO   Track on left. Enter line of wash.
1.3 ▲   SO   Track on right. Exit line of wash.
▼ 1.3   SO   Mine on right; then track on right; then
track on left to cabin.
1.2 ▲   SO   Track on right to cabin; then track on
left; then mine on left.
GPS: N35°26.84' W117°52.81'

▼ 1.7   SO   Stone and timber cabin on right.
0.8 ▲   SO   Stone and timber cabin on left.
GPS: N35°26.57' W117°53.05'

▼ 1.8   SO   Track on right up side wash.

0.7 ▲   SO   Track on left up side wash.
▼ 2.0   SO   Corrugated iron cabin on right.
0.5 ▲   SO   Corrugated iron cabin on left.
GPS: N35°26.40' W117°53.21'

▼ 2.4   SO   Track on left and track on right. Remain
on EP15.
0.1 ▲   SO   Track on right and track on left. Remain
on EP15.
▼ 2.5   SO   Exit Bonanza Canyon and cross
through wide Last Chance Canyon
wash. Central Mountains #23: Last
Chance Canyon Trail crosses here. To
the left it is marked EP30. Zero trip
meter and continue straight ahead,
remaining on marked EP15.
0.0 ▲   Continue to the northwest up Bonanza
Canyon wash.
GPS: N35°25.99' W117°53.37'

▼ 0.0   Continue to the southeast up side wash.

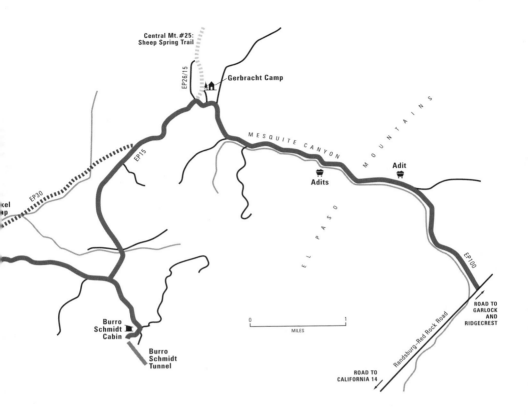

1.4 ▲   SO Central Mountains #23: Last Chance
                Canyon Trail crosses here. To the right
                it is marked EP30. Zero trip meter and
                continue straight ahead, remaining on
                marked EP15. Cross through wide Last
                Chance Canyon wash.
▼ 0.1   BL Track on right.
1.3 ▲   SO Track on left.
▼ 0.4   SO Adit on left.
1.0 ▲   SO Adit on right.
▼ 0.8   SO Mine on left.
0.6 ▲   SO Mine on right.
▼ 1.2   SO Track on right.
0.2 ▲   SO Track on left.
▼ 1.3   SO Track on left to mine.
0.1 ▲   SO Track on right to mine.
▼ 1.4   TL Track continuing straight ahead up
                wash is spur to Burro Schmidt's
                Tunnel and cabin. Turn left and exit
                wash, remaining on EP15, to continue
                along main trail. Zero trip meter. There

is a sign for Burro Schmidt Tunnel at
the intersection.
0.0 ▲   Continue to the northwest.
             GPS: N35°25.20' W117°52.28'

Spur to Burro Schmidt's Tunnel and Cabin

▼ 0.0   Proceed southeast up wash, following
             sign to Burro Schmidt Tunnel.
▼ 0.1   SO Track on left.
▼ 0.5   SO Track on right.
▼ 0.6   SO Track on right to Burro Schmidt Camp
                is private. BLM sign at intersection.
                GPS: N35°24.70' W117°52.35'

▼ 0.7   TR Track on left and track straight ahead.
▼ 0.8   SO Burro Schmidt's cabin on right. Stop
                and register in Burro's old cabin
                (second cabin on right of trail).
                GPS: N35°24.63' W117°52.43'

▼ 0.9   UT   Burro Schmidt's Tunnel on left. Retrace your steps back to the start of the spur.
GPS: N35°24.64' W117°52.51'

Continuation of Main Trail

▼ 0.0   Continue to the northeast.
1.7 ▲   TR   T-intersection with track in wash. Track on left up wash is spur to Burro Schmidt's Tunnel and cabin. Turn right down wash, remaining on EP30, to continue along main trail. Zero trip meter. There is a sign for Burro Schmidt Tunnel at the intersection.
GPS: N35°25.20' W117°52.28'

▼ 0.1   SO   Track on right.
1.6 ▲   SO   Track on left.
▼ 0.3   SO   Cross through wash. Track on left and track on right in wash.
1.4 ▲   SO   Cross through wash. Track on left and track on right in wash.
GPS: N35°25.34' W117°52.02'

▼ 1.0   SO   Track on right.
0.7 ▲   SO   Track on left.
▼ 1.5   SO   Track on right.
0.2 ▲   SO   Track on left.
▼ 1.7   SO   Track on left is Central Mountains #23: Last Chance Canyon Trail. Zero trip meter.
0.0 ▲   Continue to the southwest on EP15.
GPS: N35°26.13' W117°51.20'

▼ 0.0   Continue to the east on EP15.
0.8 ▲   BL   Track on right is Central Mountains #23: Last Chance Canyon Trail. Zero trip meter.
▼ 0.1   SO   Track on left to mine.
0.7 ▲   SO   Track on right to mine.
▼ 0.2   SO   Track on left; then track on right.
0.6 ▲   SO   Track on left; then track on right.
▼ 0.5   SO   Track on left.
0.3 ▲   SO   Track on right.
▼ 0.7   BL   Bear left onto EP26/15. Track straight ahead.
0.1 ▲   BR   Track on left.
GPS: N35°26.19' W117°50.51'

▼ 0.8   TR   4-way intersection. Track straight ahead is Central Mountains #25: Sheep Spring Trail; track on left is marked EP26/15. Zero trip meter and turn right onto EP26.
0.0 ▲   Continue southwest on EP26/15.
GPS: N35°26.20' W117°50.42'

▼ 0.0   Continue south on EP26. Immediately track on left.
4.0 ▲   TL   Track on right; then 4-way intersection. Track straight ahead is EP26/15. Track on right is Central Mountains #25: Sheep Spring Trail. Zero trip meter and turn left onto formed trail, also marked EP26/15.
▼ 0.1   TL   T-intersection with graded road. To the right is EP15; to the left is EP100. Sign for Schmidt Tunnel at intersection; then track on left goes into Gerbracht Camp.
3.9 ▲   TR   Track on right goes into Gerbracht Camp; then turn right onto EP26/15. Track ahead is EP15. Sign for Schmidt Tunnel at intersection.
GPS: N35°26.15' W117°50.42'

▼ 0.2   SO   Well-used track on left for 4WDs, ATVs, and motorbikes. Also track on right.
3.8 ▲   SO   Well-used track on right for 4WDs, ATVs, and motorbikes. Also track on left.
GPS: N35°26.05' W117°50.26'

▼ 0.6   SO   Track on right. Enter line of wash.
3.4 ▲   SO   Track on left. Exit line of wash.
▼ 0.8   SO   Track on right; then track on left.
3.2 ▲   SO   Track on right; then track on left.
▼ 1.1   SO   Track on left.
2.9 ▲   SO   Track on right.
▼ 1.3   SO   Track on right; then track on left.
2.7 ▲   SO   Track on right; then track on left.
▼ 1.7   SO   Adits on right.
2.3 ▲   SO   Adits on left.
▼ 1.8   SO   Track on right is old road.
2.2 ▲   SO   Old road rejoins on left.
▼ 1.9   SO   Old road rejoins on right.
2.1 ▲   BR   Track on left is old road.
▼ 2.1   SO   Track on right.
1.9 ▲   SO   Track on left.

▼ 2.5	SO	Adit on left.
1.5 ▲	SO	Adit on right.
		GPS: N35°24.54' W117°49.08'

▼ 2.6	SO	Track on left.
1.4 ▲	SO	Track on right.
		GPS: N35°24.44' W117°48.96'

▼ 3.2	SO	Track on right.
0.8 ▲	SO	Track on left.
▼ 3.5	SO	Track on right. Exiting Mesquite Canyon.
0.5 ▲	SO	Track on left. Entering Mesquite Canyon.
▼ 3.8	SO	Two tracks on left.
0.2 ▲	SO	Two tracks on right.
▼ 4.0		Trail ends at T-intersection with RandsburgRed Rock Road. Turn right for California 14 and Mojave; turn left for Ridgecrest.
0.0 ▲		Trail commences on Randsburg–Red Rock Road at mile marker 11, 1.1 miles west of intersection with Garlock Road. Zero trip meter and turn north on well-used formed trail, marked EP100.
		GPS: N35°23.32' W117°48.96'

CENTRAL MOUNTAINS #25

Sheep Spring Trail

STARTING POINT Browns Road, 4 miles northeast of intersection with US 395

FINISHING POINT Central Mountains #24: Burro Schmidt Tunnel Trail, 4 miles north of the Randsburg–Red Rock Road

TOTAL MILEAGE 12 miles

UNPAVED MILEAGE: 10.9 miles

DRIVING TIME 2 hours

ELEVATION RANGE 2,700–4,000 feet

USUALLY OPEN Year-round

BEST TIME TO TRAVEL Year-round

DIFFICULTY RATING 3

SCENIC RATING 9

REMOTENESS RATING +0

Special Attractions

- Petroglyphs near Sheep Spring.
- Remote trail through the El Paso Mountains.

- Sites of Gerbracht Camp and Colorado Camp.
- Collecting petrified wood.
- Hiking through the rugged Black Hills.

History

The old railroad grade at the northern end of the trail was once the route of the Nevada & California Railroad. Construction began in 1908 on the line that was needed to deliver construction materials for the ambitious Los Angeles Aqueduct project. The railroad was built from Mojave, passing through Inyokern, on its way to Lone Pine. The line also connected with the Carson & Colorado Railroad, which came in from Nevada and passed through Owenyo Station near Lone Pine. Union Pacific took over the railroad at a later stage.

Construction of the aqueduct continued until 1913. In 1914, increasing production at the Searles Lake chemical plant required an improved system of transportation. The mule teams that were in use at the time could no longer meet the needs of the expanding industry. The American Trona Corporation financed and built its own railroad from Searles Lake to Searles Station. From the station it joined the Union Pacific Railroad (located east of this trail).

Gold was discovered close to the trail in 1893, in what became known as Goler Canyon. It gained its name from forty-niner John Goler, one of many prospectors on their way to the California goldfields in the winter of 1849 who just managed to escape death while on a shortcut through Death Valley. Goler survived to tell the tale of sighting gold nuggets in the general area, but fearful of an attack by the Indians, he had moved on in a lost and confused state of mind. Goler spent the following two decades looking for the elusive gold, but to no avail. News of the 1893 discovery prompted a rush of prospectors into the El Paso Mountains. Three of those prospectors would go on to find what would become the Yellow Aster Mine, giving birth to the nearby settlement of Randsburg.

Evidence of Native Americans in the region dates back thousands of years. Pottery shards and grinding stones appear to the west of this

Many petroglyphs adorn the boulders near Sheep Spring

trail in the Black Mountain region. Petroglyphs can be found along the trail, often etched into the black rock near watering points. Many of the rock art designs are difficult to interpret. However, other images are more readily deciphered, often depicting wild animals that were encountered and hunted. As you travel through these colorful canyons and mountains, it becomes obvious that you are not the first to sample the breathtaking land.

Description

Sheep Spring Trail winds alongside the eastern edge of the El Paso Wilderness, passing through some exceptionally beautiful and rugged scenery. The trail leaves Browns Road southwest of Ridgecrest. To reach the trailhead from Ridgecrest, proceed south on South China Lake Boulevard to the intersection with US 395. Continue southwest, across US 395, onto the unmarked paved Browns Road, CR 655 (on some maps this is called Randsburg—Inyokern Road) and drive 4 miles to the start of the trail.

The first mile of the road is paved because it serves as access for a sandpit. Afterwards, it turns into a well-used, winding formed trail. Navigation is generally easy because the El Paso Mountains Wilderness limits vehicle trails leaving to the west. However, there are many opportunities for hikers to head west into the wilderness.

One very interesting feature of the trail is the large group of petroglyphs that can be found up and down the shallow wash near Sheep Spring. The images are etched into darker volcanic boulders along the sides of the wash. You will find quite a few interesting figures and shapes, including many images of bighorn sheep, after which the spring is named.

Rockhounds will enjoy hunting for agate, petrified wood, and jasper in dry washes and around the base of sandstone domes along the trail.

The trail is best traveled in dry weather. Rain or snow can turn stretches of road into sticky mud. The surface is rough and undulating, but it has no major obstacles along the way. In dry weather, stock SUVs should encounter no difficulties.

South of Sheep Spring the trail follows along ridge tops and wash lines, at times providing panoramic views into the El Paso Mountains. The rock formations are both colorful and interesting, with many weathered holes in the sandstone domes that border the trail. At the site of Colorado Camp, a stone chimney and some scattered stone foundations are all that remain of this once active mining camp. Even less remains at the site of Gerbracht Camp, located at the trail's southern end.

The trail ends at the intersection with Central Mountains #24: Burro Schmidt Tunnel Trail. From here you can exit via the easy Mesquite Canyon or to the west by following the more difficult Central Mountains #23: Last Chance Canyon Trail.

This trail is considered to be part of Mesquite Canyon Road on some maps.

Current Road Information

BLM Ridgecrest Field Office
300 South Richmond Road
Ridgecrest, CA 93555
(760) 384-5400

Map References

BLM Ridgecrest, Cuddeback Lake
USGS 1:24,000 Inyokern SE, Garlock
1:100,000 Ridgecrest, Cuddeback Lake
Maptech CD-ROM: Barstow/San Bernardino County
Southern & Central California Atlas & Gazetteer, pp. 52, 66
California Road & Recreation Atlas, p. 94
Other: East Kern County OHV Riding Areas and Trails—Jawbone Canyon

Route Directions

▼ 0.0	Trail commences on Browns Road, 4 miles northeast of intersection with US 395. Zero trip meter and turn southwest on unmarked paved road and immediately cross over old railroad grade. Trail is marked as EP26 a short distance from the start.
6.6 ▲	Trail finishes on paved Browns Road.

Turn right for Ridgecrest; turn left for Inyokern.

GPS: N35°34.03' W117°46.68'

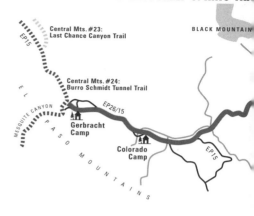

▼ 0.5   SO   Track on left.
6.1 ▲   SO   Track on right.
▼ 1.1   SO   Road turns to graded dirt.
5.5 ▲   SO   Road is now paved.
▼ 1.6   SO   Track on right.
5.0 ▲   SO   Track on left.
▼ 1.8   SO   Track on right is EP18 for 4WDs, ATVs, and motorbikes.
4.8 ▲   SO   Track on left is EP18 for 4WDs, ATVs, and motorbikes.

GPS: N35°32.68' W117°48.01'

▼ 2.0   SO   Track on left into sandpit and small track on right. Trail is now small, formed trail.
4.6 ▲   SO   Track on right into sandpit and small track on left. Trail is now graded dirt.

GPS: N35°32.62' W117°48.05'

▼ 2.2   BR   Trail forks; track on left.
4.4 ▲   SO   Track rejoins on right.
▼ 2.3   SO   Track rejoins on left.

4.3 ▲   BL   Trail forks; track on right.
▼ 2.4   SO   El Paso Mountains Wilderness on right.
4.2 ▲   SO   End of El Paso Mountains Wilderness on left.
▼ 2.7   SO   Track on left. Remain on marked EP26.
3.9 ▲   BL   Track on right. Remain on marked EP26.
▼ 3.0   SO   Enter line of wash.
3.6 ▲   SO   Exit line of wash.

GPS: N35°31.83' W117°48.19'

Sandstone rock formations along the trail

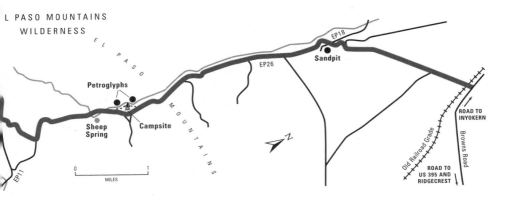

▼ 3.2   SO   Track on left.
3.4 ▲   SO   Track on right.
▼ 4.1   SO   Exit line of wash; then track on left.
2.5 ▲   SO   Track on right; then enter line of wash.
▼ 4.9   SO   Track on left. Remain on marked EP26. On the right at this point is a sign for a closed vehicle trail. Park here and hike 0.2 miles in a southwest direction along old vehicle trail down into the wash. Petroglyphs are on the dark volcanic rocks along west bank of the wash. The easiest ones to find are facing down into the wash. Coordinates of petroglyphs are GPS: N35°30.11' W117°48.22'
1.7 ▲   SO   Track on right. Remain on marked EP26. On the left at this point is a sign for a closed vehicle trail. Park here and follow the above directions to find the petroglyphs.
    GPS: N35°30.23' W117°48.10'

▼ 5.0   SO   Track on left. Remain on marked EP26.
1.6 ▲   SO   Track on right. Remain on marked EP26.
▼ 5.1   SO   Track on left. Bear right into wash toward Sheep Spring, remaining on EP26.
1.5 ▲   TL   Track continues straight ahead. Remain on EP26.
▼ 5.2   SO   Campsite on right. More petroglyphs can be found on boulders above the wash, both to the north and south of the campsite. Enter line of wash.
1.4 ▲   SO   Campsite on left. More petroglyphs

can be found on boulders above the wash, both to the north and south of the campsite. Exit line of wash.
    GPS: N35°29.99' W117°48.18'

▼ 5.3   SO   Cross through wash. More petroglyphs can be found on boulders on hill to the right.
1.3 ▲   SO   Cross through wash. Petroglyphs can be found on boulders on hill to the left.
▼ 5.4   SO   Cross through wash; then Sheep Spring on left and track on left opposite El Paso Mountains Wilderness sign.
1.2 ▲   SO   Sheep Spring on right and track on right opposite El Paso Mountains Wilderness sign; then cross through wash.
    GPS: N35°29.84' W117°48.23'

▼ 5.8   SO   Exit line of wash.
0.8 ▲   SO   Enter line of wash.
▼ 5.9   SO   Track on left. Remain on marked EP26.
0.7 ▲   SO   Track on right. Remain on marked EP26.
    GPS: N35°29.45' W117°48.35'

▼ 6.6   BR   Well-used track on left is EP11 (signed by BLM marker post) for 4WDs, ATVs, and motorbikes. Remain on marked EP26 and zero trip meter.
0.0 ▲   Continue to the northwest.
    GPS: N35°28.94' W117°48.25'

▼ 0.0   Continue to the south.
3.5 ▲   BL   Well-used track on right is EP11 (signed by BLM marker post) for

This stone chimney and diggings are all that remain of the Colorado Camp

4WDs, ATVs, and motorbikes. Remain on marked EP26 and zero trip meter.

▼ 0.1   SO Cross through wash.
3.4 ▲   SO Cross through wash.

▼ 0.6   SO Cross through wash.
2.9 ▲   SO Cross through wash.

▼ 0.7   SO Track on left. Remain on marked EP26.
2.8 ▲   BL Track on right. Remain on marked EP26.
         GPS: N35°28.66' W117°48.75'

▼ 1.1   SO Cross through wash.
2.4 ▲   SO Cross through wash.

▼ 1.7   SO Cross through wash.
1.8 ▲   SO Cross through wash.

▼ 3.0   SO Cross through wash.
0.5 ▲   SO Cross through wash.
         GPS: N35°27.70' W117°49.32'

▼ 3.1   SO Track on left.
0.4 ▲   SO Track on right.

▼ 3.5   TR T-intersection with EP15. Zero trip meter and turn right onto EP15. Intersection is marked with trail numbers.
0.0 ▲   Continue to the west.
         GPS: N35°27.47' W117°49.27'

▼ 0.0   Continue to the south.
1.9 ▲   TL Turn left onto EP26 and zero trip meter.

EP15 continues ahead. Intersection is marked with trail numbers.

▼ 0.4　SO　Track on left; then cross through wash; then second track on left.

1.5 ▲　SO　Track on right; then cross through wash; then second track on right.

▼ 0.7　BL　Bear left, leaving main EP26/15 to pass beside remains of Colorado Camp.

1.2 ▲　SO　Rejoin main EP26/15.

▼ 0.75　SO　Remains of Colorado Camp on left at sign—stone chimney and various diggings. Track on left.

1.15 ▲　SO　Remains of Colorado Camp on right at sign—stone chimney and various diggings. Track on right.

GPS: N35°26.88′ W117°49.63′

▼ 0.8　SO　Rejoin main EP15.

1.1 ▲　BR　Bear right, leaving main EP15 to pass beside remains of Colorado Camp.

▼ 0.9　SO　Track on right and track on left.

1.0 ▲　SO　Track on right and track on left.

▼ 1.2　SO　Track on right.

0.7 ▲　SO　Track on left.

▼ 1.4　BL　Small track on left; then bear left, leaving EP15/26 to the right.

0.5 ▲　SO　Track on left is EP15/26. Continue straight ahead, joining EP15/26; then small track on right.

GPS: N35°26.53′ W117°50.15′

▼ 1.7　SO　Track on left and track on right.

0.2 ▲　SO　Track on right and track on left.

▼ 1.8　BR　Flat open area is site of Gerbracht Camp. Track on left.

0.1 ▲　BL　Flat open area is site of Gerbracht Camp. Track on right.

GPS: N35°26.22′ W117°50.32′

▼ 1.9　Trail ends at 4-way intersection with Central Mountains #24: Burro Schmidt Tunnel Trail, which is straight ahead and to the left. To the right is EP26/15. Turn left to exit via Mesquite Canyon to Randsburg–Red Rock Road; continue straight to travel Central Mountains #24: Burro Schmidt Tunnel Trail.

0.0 ▲　Trail commences at a 4-way intersection on Central Mountains #24: Burro Schmidt Tunnel Trail, 4 miles north of paved Randsburg–Red Rock Road. Zero trip meter and turn northeast on well-used, unmarked trail at intersection. Central Mountains #24: Burro Schmidt Tunnel Trail continues to the southwest along marked EP15. To the north is EP26/15.

GPS: N35°26.20′ W117°50.42′

CENTRAL MOUNTAINS #26

Koehn Lake Trail

STARTING POINT Neuralia Road at Rancho Seco
FINISHING POINT Randsburg–Red Rock Road, 1.5 miles east of intersection with Garlock Road
TOTAL MILEAGE 24.9 miles
UNPAVED MILEAGE: 21.1 miles
DRIVING TIME 2 hours
ELEVATION RANGE 1,900–3,900 feet
USUALLY OPEN Year-round
BEST TIME TO TRAVEL Year-round
DIFFICULTY RATING 3
SCENIC RATING 8
REMOTENESS RATING +0

Special Attractions

- Wildlife viewing for desert tortoise.
- Access to a network of 4WD, ATV, and motorbike trails.

History

A German emigrant named Charley Koehn was en route to the goldfields of the Panamint region in search of work when opportunity came knocking. Koehn set up a way station near Red Rocks to supply passing freight teams traveling south from the Panamint Range. He was also fortunate enough to be in operation before the Goler gold rush of 1893 hit the nearby El Paso Mountains. Realizing another market was close at hand, Koehn would load up his newly purchased wagon and head for the hills to sell his wares. As the local mines flourished, so did Koehn's market. His way station also delivered news of the latest mineral strikes throughout the surrounding region. The Rand Mine was getting underway by the late 1890s, and he could relate its progress to miners while out selling wagonloads of food and merchandise around the El Paso and Randsburg mining regions.

The desert region surrounding Koehn Lake Trail is home to the desert tortoise. Not always visible, this animal retreats to its cool underground burrow during hotter parts of the summer and hibernates there during long, cold winters. The desert tortoise is currently protected to help increase the number of maturing animals. They are most vulnerable when young. As they age, their shells thicken, and by age 10, they have a good chance of survival. Desert tortoises can live as long as humans. To the early Native Americans the desert tortoise was a delicacy when roasted over a bed of hot ashes. Tortoise population numbers are thought to have been even lower then than now.

Description

Koehn Lake Trail takes a winding path through the Rand Mountains, traveling mainly through the Rand Mountain Fremont Valley Management Area. This area is prime habitat for the desert tortoise, and patient travelers will have a good chance of seeing one of these elusive animals, particularly when traveling between March and September.

To reach the trailhead, turn east on the paved Rogers Road from California 14, opposite Jawbone Station and the entrance to the OHV area, 1 mile south of the intersection with Randsburg–Red Rock Road. After 0.7 miles, turn south on Neuralia Road. Proceed 0.9 miles to Rancho Seco and then turn east on Munsey Road. The trail leaves along the paved Munsey Road before swinging north along the shores of the dry Koehn Lake. The Desert Tortoise Natural Area is on the east side of the trail at this point; no vehicles are allowed within the area, but hikers may walk inside and attempt to spot one of the creatures. Many tracks to the west lead down to the edge of Koehn Lake. Only hikers are allowed on the surface of the lake.

The trail enters the Rand Mountain Fremont Valley Management Area—another prime desert tortoise habitat. Vehicle travel within the area is restricted to roads and trails that are designated with numbered brown posts. Camping is restricted to areas marked with white signs and camping symbols. There are five such spots within the management area, although none of them are located along this trail. Camping is not permitted outside of these areas. Firearm use is limited to shotguns for seasonal hunting of upland game birds.

The route follows a mixture of sandy and rocky trails, traveling in wash bottoms and along ridge tops. The area has a very remote feel and is normally very quiet. There are panoramic views along the trail: into the Rand Mountains, north to the El Paso Mountains, and west to Koehn Lake. The trail ends by dropping down to finish on Randsburg–Red Rock Road.

Current Road Information

BLM Ridgecrest Field Office
300 South Richmond Road
Ridgecrest, CA 93555
(760) 384-5400

Map References

BLM   Cuddeback Lake
USGS   1:24,000 Cantil, Saltdale SE,
          Garlock, Johannesburg
          1:100,000 Cuddeback Lake
Maptech CD-ROM: Barstow/San
          Bernardino County
*Southern & Central California Atlas &
          Gazetteer,* pp. 65, 66
California Road & Recreation Atlas, p. 94
Other: East Kern County OHV Riding
          Areas and Trails—Jawbone Canyon

Route Directions

▼ 0.0   Trail commences on Neuralia Road in
           Rancho Seco. Turn east onto paved
           Munsey Road and zero trip meter.
5.6 ▲   Trail ends at the intersection with
           Neuralia Road in Rancho Seco. Turn
           right to exit to California 14.

On the western side of the Rand Mountains the trail weaves through the creosote bushes

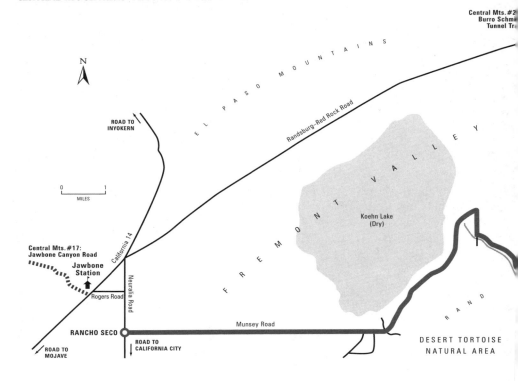

GPS: N35°17.20' W117°59.09'

▼ 3.8   SO   Road turns to graded dirt.
1.8 ▲   SO   Road is now paved. Remain on paved road until end of trail.
▼ 5.2   SO   Track on left.
0.4 ▲   SO   Track on right.
▼ 5.3   SO   Track on right.
0.3 ▲   SO   Track on left.
▼ 5.5   SO   Track on right.
0.1 ▲   SO   Track on left.
▼ 5.6   BL   Track on right goes to the edge of Desert Tortoise Natural Area. Zero trip meter.
0.0 ▲   Continue to the west.

GPS: N35°17.23' W117°52.93'

▼ 0.0   Continue northeast around the shores of Koehn Lake. Desert Tortoise Natural Area is now on the right and Rand Mountain Fremont Valley Management Area is on the left. Track on left.
3.9 ▲   SO   Track on right; then track on left goes to the edge of Desert Tortoise Natural Area. Bear right and zero trip meter.

▼ 0.3   SO   Track on right and track on left.
3.6 ▲   SO   Track on left and track on right.
▼ 1.9   SO   Track on left.
2.0 ▲   SO   Track on right.
▼ 2.2   SO   Track on left. Many tracks on left to edge of lakeshore for next 1.7 miles. Vehicle travel on lakebed is prohibited.
1.7 ▲   SO   Track on right.
▼ 3.9   TR   Turn sharp right around fence line that marks the boundary of Desert Tortoise Natural Area onto small formed trail marked R5, suitable for 4WDs, ATVs, and motorbikes. Entering Rand Mountain Fremont Valley Management Area. There is an information board at the intersection. Vehicle travel in this area is limited to trails marked with brown numbered posts. Zero trip meter.
0.0 ▲   Continue southwest, following shoreline of Koehn Lake. Many tracks on right to edge of lakeshore for next 1.7

miles. Vehicle travel on lakebed is prohibited.

GPS: N35°19.88' W117°50.57'

▼ 0.0   Continue to the south.

3.5 ▲   TL   Turn sharp left around fence line that marks the boundary of Desert Tortoise Natural Area onto large graded road. There is an information board at the intersection. Desert Tortoise Natural Area is now on the left. Zero trip meter.

▼ 0.6   BL   Bear away from the edge of Desert Tortoise Natural Area. Enter line of wash

2.9 ▲   BR   Fence on left marks the boundary of Desert Tortoise Natural Area. Exit line of wash.

▼ 1.6   SO   Track on left is R50 for 4WDs, ATVs, and motorbikes.

1.9 ▲   SO   Track on right is R50 for 4WDs, ATVs, and motorbikes.

GPS: N35°18.80' W117°49.74'

▼ 2.0   SO   Track on left is R50 for 4WDs, ATVs, and motorbikes.

Koehn Lake as seen from the El Paso Mountains

1.5 ▲   BL   Track on right is R50 for 4WDs, ATVs, and motorbikes.
         GPS: N35°18.46' W117°49.51'

▼ 3.3   BR   Track on left is R6 for 4WDs, ATVs, and motorbikes.

0.2 ▲   SO   Track on right is R6 for 4WDs, ATVs, and motorbikes.
         GPS: N35°17.35' W117°49.26'

▼ 3.5   TL   Turn left up side wash onto R40 for 4WDs, ATVs, and motorbikes. Zero trip meter.

0.0 ▲   Continue to the northwest.
         GPS: N35°17.21' W117°49.20'

▼ 0.0   Continue to the east.

4.2 ▲   TR   T-intersection with R5. Turn right down main wash and zero trip meter.

▼ 1.7   SO   Track on left and track on right are both R15 for 4WDs, ATVs, and motorbikes.

2.5 ▲   SO   Track on left and track on right are both R15 for 4WDs, ATVs, and motorbikes.
         GPS: N35°17.18' W117°47.36'

▼ 2.0   SO   Exit line of wash.

2.2 ▲   SO   Enter line of wash.

▼ 2.5   SO   Pass through fence line, leaving Rand Mountain Fremont Valley Management Area. Track on right is R10 for 4WDs, ATVs, and motorbikes. Continue straight ahead on R 40/10.

1.7 ▲   SO   Track on left is R10 for 4WDs, ATVs, and motorbikes. Continue straight ahead through fence line on R40, re-entering Rand Mountain Fremont Valley Management Area.
         GPS: N35°17.20' W117°46.54'

▼ 2.7   TL   Turn left along fence line, remaining on R40/10. Track straight ahead.

1.5 ▲   TR   T-intersection. Turn right along fence line, remaining on R40/10.
         GPS: N35°17.20' W117°46.32'

▼ 2.8   TL   Turn left onto R40 and pass through fence line, re-entering Rand Mountain Fremont Valley Management Area. R10 continues straight ahead. Track on right.

1.4 ▲   TR   Pass through fence line, leaving Rand

Mountain Fremont Valley Management Area. T-intersection. Track on left is R10. Turn right onto R40/10. Small track straight ahead.
         GPS: N35°17.27' W117°46.24'

▼ 3.2   SO   Track on right and track on left are both R25 for 4WDs, ATVs, and motorbikes.

1.0 ▲   SO   Track on right and track on left are both R25 for 4WDs, ATVs, and motorbikes.
         GPS: N35°17.55' W117°46.00'

▼ 4.2   TR   T-intersection with R37. Track on left goes 0.4 miles to viewpoint. Zero trip meter.

0.0 ▲   Continue to the southwest.
         GPS: N35°18.08' W117°45.23'

▼ 0.0   Continue to the south.

3.9 ▲   TL   R37 continues 0.4 miles to viewpoint. Zero trip meter and turn left onto R40.

▼ 0.3   TL   Turn left onto R48. R37 continues straight ahead.

3.6 ▲   TR   T-intersection with R37.

▼ 0.5   SO   Track on left and track on right are both R12. It is marked as suitable for 4WDs, ATVs, and motorbikes but to the left it becomes too narrow for vehicles after 1 mile.

3.4 ▲   SO   Track on left and track on right are both R12. It is marked as suitable for 4WDs, ATVs, and motorbikes but to the right it becomes too narrow for vehicles after 1 mile.
         GPS: N35°17.86' W117°45.07'

▼ 0.7   BL   Trail forks; both are marked R48.

3.2 ▲   SO   Track on left is R48.

▼ 0.8   BL   Bear left onto wider formed trail R43 for 4WDs, ATVs, and motorbikes, and proceed down line of wash in canyon.

3.1 ▲   BR   Exit line of wash and bear right onto smaller formed trail R48 for 4WDs, ATVs, and motorbikes.
         GPS: N35°17.95' W117°44.80'

▼ 1.9   BL   Track on right is R49.

2.0 ▲   BR   Track on left is R49.

DESERT TORTOISE

Desert tortoises have high-domed shells and stocky legs that are covered with large coni-cal scales. Adult males grow to about 15 inches and weigh about 20 pounds; females are slightly smaller. These completely terrestrial creatures are masters at conserving water and energy in the harshest of conditions. They derive most of their water from food and can store up to a cup in their bladders for use during dry seasons. After heavy rains, tortoises will drink so much water that one tortoise was documented as having weighed 43 percent more after drinking! To minimize water loss they incur from breathing, desert tortoises hi-bernate in humid burrows, occupied by one or many individuals, as far as 30 feet under-ground—ideally beneath a wash. Their hard, domed shells serve as insulation against moisture loss and temperature fluctuation in addition to providing armorlike protection from predators. Tortoises breed after 15 years of age. Their eggs—which are the size and

Desert Tortoise

shape of Ping-Pong balls—hatch into fully formed, self-sufficient young turtles. However, youngsters remain vulnerable to predators because their protective shells do not develop until after the first five years. It takes 15 to 20 years for one to reach maturity. Desert tor-toises prefer rocky foothills; they live in burrows they have dug in firm soil or between and under large rocks. Native Americans considered their meat a delicacy but never seriously endangered their population. Desert tortoises have become threatened in recent years be-cause native plants have been replaced by less nutritionally satisfying exotic species.

Two of the tortoises' relatives, the western pond turtle and the spiny softshell turtle, can be found in California lakes and ponds.

The flat expanse of dry Koehn Lake sits on the western side of the Rand Mountains

GPS: N35°18.73' W117°44.49'

▼ 2.2 SO Game water tank on right.
1.7 ▲ SO Game water tank on left.

▼ 2.4 SO Track on left is R12. Although marked for 4WDs, ATVs, and motorbikes, it becomes too narrow for vehicles.
1.5 ▲ SO Track on right is R12. Although marked for 4WDs, ATVs, and motorbikes, it becomes too narrow for vehicles.
GPS: N35°18.81' W117°45.05'

▼ 3.0 SO Track on right is R45 for 4WDs, ATVs, and motorbikes.
0.9 ▲ SO Track on left is R45 for 4WDs, ATVs, and motorbikes.
GPS: N35°19.29' W117°45.12'

▼ 3.1 SO Track on right is R46 for 4WDs, ATVs, and motorbikes.
0.8 ▲ SO Track on left is R46 for 4WDs, ATVs, and motorbikes.
GPS: N35°19.41' W117°45.21'

▼ 3.7 SO Track on left is R37 for 4WDs, ATVs, and motorbikes. Exit canyon, but continue in line of wash.

0.2 ▲ SO Track on right is R37 for 4WDs, ATVs, and motorbikes. Enter canyon.
GPS: N35°19.90' W117°45.27'

▼ 3.9 SO Track on left and track on right are both R50 for 4WDs, ATVs, and motorbikes. Zero trip meter.
0.0 ▲ Continue east, entering line of wash.
GPS: N35°20.04' W117°45.38'

▼ 0.0 Continue west, exiting line of wash.
3.8 ▲ SO Track on left and track on right are both R50 for 4WDs, ATVs, and motorbikes. Zero trip meter.

▼ 0.7 SO Cross through wash.
3.1 ▲ SO Cross through wash.

▼ 2.8 SO Cross through wash.
1.0 ▲ SO Cross through wash.

▼ 3.6 SO Cross through wash. Track on right up wash is R60 for 4WDs, ATVs, and motorbikes.
0.2 ▲ SO Cross through wash. Track on left up wash is R60 for 4WDs, ATVs, and motorbikes.
GPS: N35°23.19' W117°46.30'

▼ 3.8 Trail ends at intersection with paved

Descending through creosote and mojave yuccas toward Koehn Lake

Randsburg–Red Rock Road, 1.5 miles east of intersection with Garlock Road. Turn right for Randsburg; turn left for California 14.

0.0 ▲ Trail commences on paved Randsburg–Red Rock Road, 1.5 miles east of intersection with Garlock Road. Zero trip meter and turn south onto graded dirt road marked R43. R43 also goes north of Randsburg–Red Rock Road. Enter Rand Mountain Fremont Valley Management Area. There is an information board at the intersection.
GPS: N35°23.39′ W117°46.30′

CENTRAL MOUNTAINS #27

Government Peak Trail

STARTING POINT Randsburg–Red Rock Road, 1.5 miles west of Randsburg
FINISHING POINT Randsburg–Mojave Road, 4.7 miles west of US 395
TOTAL MILEAGE 7.9 miles
UNPAVED MILEAGE: 7.9 miles
DRIVING TIME 1.5 hours
ELEVATION RANGE 3,100-4,700 feet
USUALLY OPEN Year-round
BEST TIME TO TRAVEL Year-round
DIFFICULTY RATING 5
SCENIC RATING 10
REMOTENESS RATING +0

Special Attractions

■ Far-reaching views from Government Peak.
■ A network of trails around the mining region.
■ Famous Yellow Aster Mine.

History

The gold strike of 1893 at Goler Gulch, just across the Fremont Valley in the El Paso Mountains, brought a surge of eager prospectors to the region. Two of them found placer gold on the side of Rand Mountain in 1894 and returned the next year to make good on their findings. Fredrick Mooers and John Singleton had struck a big one indeed. They teamed up with Charles Burcham, who owned a wagon, and the three men started to work the mine. Financially, they were at rock bottom. They first had to dig enough gold to afford the registration fee for a claim on what they called the Rand Mine. The name was a reminder of the big find in South Africa about ten years earlier. They nearly sold their mine because they did not have the start-up money to properly work the claim. But Mooers's wife put her foot down and joined the men in the camp, working with them in the mine.

The Rand Mine's need for a mill proved to be good fortune for the nearby settlement of Garlock. The region was now teeming with prospectors. From as close as the Panamint Mines to as far away as Los Angeles, miners were coming into the region in droves. The Johannesburg Mines were also carting ore to Garlock, whose saloon and hotel were busy quenching thirsts and filling rooms.

By 1897, Randsburg had its own 30-stamp mill, which later extended to 100-stamp. The town's population leapt to nearly 2,500, including settlers who came from all over the world. Wooden stores with ornate facades were tightly packed together and sold a wide variety of goods. Johannesburg was also a growing settlement in the booming region, which was being compared by many to the famed Comstock in Nevada. Investors were eager to purchase wherever they could.

In 1898, the Randsburg Railroad Company wasted no time in extending a track north to Johannesburg from the Santa Fe line at Kramer, another reason for wild celebration. By 1906, the Rinaldi & Clark freight partnership was established locally and teams were hauling goods from the rail depot at Johannesburg all the way to the Panamint Mines. Their stagecoaches carried passengers, feed, supplies, and much-welcomed mail deliveries. The World War I years brought competition to the freight teams in the form of the Ford and Moreland trucks. Transportation modes in remote regions were about to change.

In 1905, tungsten was discovered at Red Mountain, and the town of Atolia was born.

Randsburg Post Office

Another boom followed for the Randsburg Mining District. The Rand Mine, later known as the Yellow Aster Mine, which is the name shown on maps today, had produced more than $6 million in gold by 1911. By 1919, it was silver that was making history at the Kelly Silver Mine near Red Mountain. This mine went on to produce more than $15 million worth of silver, making it one of the largest producers in California. The 1930s marked the decline of the mining district. In 1933, the rail line was torn up between Kramer and Johannesburg in order to be used elsewhere. The old embankment is still visible.

The 1940s rekindled life in the Randsburg region with the War Department's demand for tungsten, molybdenum, and potash. Once again, the mines reportedly ran 24 hours a day and Randsburg teemed with life.

Fire has plagued Randsburg since its earliest days, and the wooden houses and stores were reduced to ash on several occasions. Though the population continued to grow to 3,500 by the start of the twentieth century, most of the buildings are now gone.

Today, as you climb the shelf trail to the top of Government Peak (4,755 feet), you can overlook the modern mining activity of the Yellow Aster Mine, in full swing once again. The Rand Mining Company (now called Glamis Gold Limited) brought in heavy machinery in 1984. Using a cyanide leaching process, the company extracted more than 94,000 ounces of gold by 1997. Like many mining districts, the claim names in this region keep you wondering—Red Bird Mine, Tam O' Shanter Mine, Ben Hur Mine, Orphan Girl Mine, Sophie Moren Mine, and Winnie Mine are only a few of the colorful names.

Description

This short, high-interest trail takes the intrepid traveler high into the Rand Mountains along the face of Government Peak. The trail passes several mines before dropping down on the south side of the mountain to finish on graded dirt Randsburg-Mojave Road.

The trail leaves Randsburg–Red Rock Road 1.5 miles west of the ghost town of Randsburg. It travels through the Rand Mountain Fremont Valley Management Area; vehicle travel is restricted to roads and trails that are designated by brown, numbered posts. Camping is restricted to areas marked with white signs and camping emblems. There are five such sites within the management area, two of which are near the start of this trail. Firearm use is limited to shotguns for seasonal hunting of upland game birds.

The brown marker posts aid in navigation, but there are still a number of intersecting side trails that make it easy to miss a turn. The trail heads toward the base of Government Peak and ascends a wash for a short way before wrapping around the large, recently reworked Yellow Aster Mine. The narrow road is well formed with a limited number of passing places. As it starts the steep climb around the face of Government Peak, the trail passes several old mining remains—mainly wooden ore hoppers and tailings piles. Sections of the trail are rough and uneven, which, combined with the loose traction and narrow shelf road, gives the trail its difficulty rating of 5.

From Government Peak, there are panoramic views over the open-pit Yellow Aster Mine, Fremont Valley, and El Paso Mountains. The trail continues along the ridge tops before descending a rough track down to Randsburg-Mojave Road. The final off-camber descent will tilt vehicles toward a drop-off, with side slopes up to 20 degrees.

Note that because of recent mining activity, the route does not completely follow trails marked on topographic maps of the region.

Current Road Information

BLM Ridgecrest Field Office
300 Sooth Richmond Road
Ridgecrest, CA 93555
(760) 384-5400

Map References

BLM   Cuddeback Lake
USGS 1:24,000 El Paso Peaks,
        Johannesburg
        1:100,000 Cuddeback Lake

Expansive views over Fremont Valley as you descend from Government Peak

Maptech CD-ROM: Barstow/San
     Bernardino County
Southern & Central California Atlas &
     Gazetteer, p. 66
California Road & Recreation Atlas, p. 94
Other: East Kern County OHV Riding
     Areas and Trails—Jawbone Canyon

Route Directions

▼ 0.0   From Randsburg—Red Rock Road, 1.5
          miles west of Randsburg and 6.9 miles
          east of intersection with Garlock Road,
          zero trip meter and turn southwest on
          formed dirt trail marked R44. Trail is suit-
          able for 4WDs, ATVs, and motorbikes.
          There is an information board at the inter-
          section and R110 also crosses paved
          road at this point. Enter Rand Mountain
          Fremont Valley Management Area.

3.4 ▲   Trail ends at paved Randsburg—Red
          Rock Road. Turn right for Randsburg;
          turn left to exit to California 14.
          GPS: N35°22.82' W117°40.61'

▼ 0.1 SO Cross through wash.
3.3 ▲ SO Cross through wash.
▼ 0.2 SO Cross through wash.
3.2 ▲ SO Cross through wash.
▼ 0.5 TL Cross through wash; then turn left up
           wash onto R30 for 4WDs, ATVs, and
           motorbikes. R44 continues straight
           ahead. Track on right is also R30.
2.9 ▲ TR Turn right out of wash onto R44 for
           4WDs, ATVs, and motorbikes. R30
           continues straight ahead. Track on left
           is also R44.
           GPS: N35°22.60' W117°41.02'

▼ 1.1 TR T-intersection. Turn right and exit
           wash, remaining on R30. Mining
           works on left.
2.3 ▲ TL Turn left down wash, remaining on
           R30. Mining works at intersection.
           GPS: N35°22.13' W117°40.56'

▼ 1.2 BL Track on right is R97. Remain on R30.
2.2 ▲ BR Track on left is R97. Remain on R30
           and drop down to the wash.
▼ 1.7 BL Track on right is R34 for 4WDs, ATVs,

and motorbikes. Remain on R30.
1.7 ▲ BR Track on left is R34 for 4WDs, ATVs,
           and motorbikes. Remain on R30.
           GPS: N35°21.66' W117°40.65'

▼ 2.1 BR Graded track on left. Trail leaves
           mining area.
1.3 ▲ BL Graded track on right. Trail follows
           edge of mining area.
           GPS: N35°21.53' W117°40.47'

▼ 2.2 BR Bear right in front of wooden ore hop-
           per, remaining on R30.
1.2 ▲ BL Bear left in front of wooden ore hopper.
           GPS: N35°21.43' W117°40.51'

▼ 2.3 TL Track on right is R34.
1.1 ▲ TR Track straight ahead is R34.
           GPS: N35°21.42' W117°40.62'

▼ 2.5 BR Track on left goes to ore hopper.
0.9 ▲ BL Track straight ahead goes to ore hopper.
           GPS: N35°21.28' W117°40.55'

▼ 2.8 SO Viewpoint on right on tight left-hand
           switchback.
0.6 ▲ SO Viewpoint on left on tight right-hand
           switchback.
▼ 2.9 SO Track on right is R85/34 for 4WDs,
           ATVs, and motorbikes.
0.5 ▲ BR Track on left is R85/34 for 4WDs,
           ATVs, and motorbikes.
           GPS: N35°21.10' W117°40.81'

▼ 3.1 SO Track on left to mine.
0.3 ▲ SO Track on right to mine.
▼ 3.3 SO Saddle. Track on left to communica-
           tions tower and overlook above Yellow
           Aster Mine. Turnout on right. Remain
           on R85/30.
0.1 ▲ BL Saddle. Track on right to communica-
           tions tower and overlook above Yellow
           Aster Mine. Turnout on left. Remain on
           R85/30.
           GPS: N35°20.87' W117°40.50'

▼ 3.4 TR 4-way intersection. Track on left. Track
           straight ahead is R85. Remain on R30
           and zero trip meter.
0.0 ▲   Continue to the northwest.

Old wooden ore hopper

GPS: N35°20.80′ W117°40.47′

▼ 0.0   Continue to the southwest.

0.8 ▲   TL   4-way intersection. Track straight ahead. Track on right is R85. Remain on R30 and zero trip meter.

▼ 0.1   SO   Track on right and track on left are both R83 for 4WDs, ATVs, and motorbikes.

0.7 ▲   SO   Track on right and track on left are both R83 for 4WDs, ATVs, and motorbikes.

▼ 0.5   SO   Track on left is R24 for 4WDs, ATVs, and motorbikes.

0.3 ▲   SO   Track on right is R24 for 4WDs, ATVs, and motorbikes.
GPS: N35°20.50′ W117°40.75′

▼ 0.7   BR   Track on left to communications tower.

0.1 ▲   BL   Track on right to communications tower.

▼ 0.8   BL   Communications tower on left; then bear left onto R77 for 4WDs, ATVs, and motorbikes. Track on right is R30/77. Zero trip meter.

0.0 ▲   Continue to the northeast. End of climb.
GPS: N35°20.31′ W117°40.99′

▼ 0.0   Continue to the southeast. Trail starts to descend.

3.7 ▲   BR   Track on left is R30/77 for 4WDs, ATVs, and motorbikes; then communications tower on right. Bear right onto R30 and zero trip meter.

▼ 0.3   SO   Track on right is R75 for 4WDs, ATVs, and motorbikes.

3.4 ▲   SO   Track on left is R75 for 4WDs, ATVs, and motorbikes.
GPS: N35°20.12′ W117°41.04′

▼ 0.9   BL   Track on right is R20 for 4WDs, ATVs, and motorbikes. Bear left onto R77/20.

2.8 ▲   SO   Track on left is R20 for 4WDs, ATVs, and motorbikes. Bear right onto R77/20.
GPS: N35°19.72′ W117°41.40′

▼ 1.2   SO   Track on right is R75 for 4WDs, ATVs, and motorbikes.

2.5 ▲   BR   Track on left is R75 for 4WDs, ATVs, and motorbikes.

▼ 1.3   BL   Track on right goes to private property.

2.4 ▲   BR   Track on left goes to private property.

▼ 1.8   SO   Track on left to mine.

1.9 ▲   SO   Track on right to mine.

▼ 2.0   TR   Turn right, remaining on R77. R20 continues straight ahead.

1.7 ▲   TL   Turn left at T-intersection onto R77. R20 is on the right.
GPS: N35°19.55′ W117°40.77′

▼ 2.1   SO   Track on left.

1.6 ▲   BL   Track on right.

▼ 2.2   SO   Track on left goes 0.1 miles to mine.

1.5 ▲   SO   Track on right goes 0.1 miles to mine.

▼ 2.7   SO   Trail starts to descend to Randsburg-Mojave Road.

1.0 ▲   SO   End of climb.

▼ 2.8	SO	Cross through wash.
0.9 ▲	SO	Cross through wash.
▼ 3.2	SO	Tailings heap on right. End of descent.
0.5 ▲	SO	Tailings heap on left. Start to climb.
▼ 3.3	TL	Turn left onto graded dirt road, which is also R77. R69 is on the right.
0.4 ▲	TR	Turn right onto small formed trail R77. Straight ahead is R69.

GPS: N35°18.46' W117°40.97'

▼ 3.7		Trail ends at intersection with graded dirt Randsburg—Mojave Road. Turn right for California City and California 14; turn left for Johannesburg and US 395.
0.0 ▲		Trail commences on graded dirt Randsburg-Mojave Road, 4.7 miles west of US 395. Note that Randsburg-Mojave Road leaves US 395 as Osdick Road, which then becomes Randsburg—Mojave Road. Zero trip meter and turn northwest on graded dirt road. Road is marked R77 and immediately enters Rand Mountain Fremont Valley Management Area. There is a notice board at the intersection.

GPS: N35°18.21' W117°40.69'

CENTRAL MOUNTAINS #28

Frazier Mountain Trail

STARTING POINT Lockwood Valley Road, 5.5 miles southwest of Lake of the Woods

FINISHING POINT Lockwood Valley Road, 1 mile southwest of Lake of the Woods

TOTAL MILEAGE 15.3 miles, plus 4.1-mile spur

UNPAVED MILEAGE: 15.3 miles, plus 4.1-mile spur

DRIVING TIME 3 hours

ELEVATION RANGE 5,000–8,000 feet

USUALLY OPEN April to November

BEST TIME TO TRAVEL Dry weather

DIFFICULTY RATING 4

SCENIC RATING 8

REMOTENESS RATING +0

Special Attractions

■ Rocky 4WD route through Los Padres

National Forest.
■ Frazier Mountain Fire Lookout.
■ Access to other trails for 4WDs, ATVs, and motorbikes.

History

William T. Frazier is the man after whom this mountain and associated trails are named. Frazier was a miner in these hills in the 1850s; the remains of one of his mines are located a short distance away from the trail. Names such as Arrastra Flat, at the bottom of the canyon below Frazier Mountain, and Gold Dust Mine farther to the south are reminders of the predominant pioneer activity in this region.

In anticipation of a mining boom, a town by the name of Lexington was laid out in 1887. The settlement was located on Piru Creek, south of Frazier Mountain. However, the town never developed, and little remains of it.

Borax deposits were found at the southern end of the trail in Lockwood Valley and have been mined by the Frazier Borate Company. A settlement in the valley was named Stauffer after John Stauffer, co-founder of the borax business. Stauffer and his partner, Thomas Thorkildsen, established a company camp and store, which lasted until they were surpassed by the larger borax mines of Death Valley in the 1880s. A post office was established at Stauffer in 1905. It temporarily closed between 1933 and 1937, and shut its doors for good in 1942.

Frazier Mountain overlooks Tejon Pass and Peace Valley to the east. One of the major early routes to and from Los Angeles crossed the San Emigdio Mountains through these valleys. Tejon Pass was formerly called Fort Tejon Pass, in association with the historic Fort Tejon to the north in Kern County. The fort was established in the summer of 1854. By 1855, Phineas Banning's wagon trains were carting supplies from Los Angeles via Fort Tejon to Fort Miller in Fresno. With the Kern River gold rush also luring many away from the city, traffic out of Los Angeles was becoming heavy.

For a few years, a herd of camels was maintained at Fort Tejon. Under the suggestion of Edward F. Beale, the camels were shipped from Africa and stationed at Fort Tejon. Beale had convinced Secretary of War Jefferson Davis that a camel corps would be well suited for duty in the California desert. The camels remained at Fort Tejon until 1861.

Fort Tejon was located along the Butterfield stagecoach route. The first stagecoach stopped there in the middle of the night on October 8, 1858. The stage was en route from St. Louis, heading for San Francisco via Los Angeles. From the fort, the journey became quite dangerous. It followed the shelf road through Grapevine Canyon past Comanche Point, and then went on to cross the San Joaquin Valley. The fort finally closed in September 1864. The property was later to become an important part of Edward Beale's ranch.

After his discharge in 1864, a soldier by the name of Henry Gorman settled in the area. Having served at Fort Tejon, Gorman knew the region well. In 1877, he operated the first post office south of the pass, Gorman's Station. This post office opened and closed five times by the 1910s.

A settlement to the north of Tejon Pass, Lebec, gained its first post office in 1895. In its early days, many bears roamed the region around Lebec. A carved inscription on an old oak tree related the tale of Peter Lebeck, a traveler who was killed by a bear in October 1837. It is thought that Lebeck, possibly spelled Lebec, may have been part of a Hudson's Bay party led by Michael La Framboise.

Description

The route past Frazier Peak combines a number of different trails to form a loop. The standard varies slightly, ranging from 2 to 4 over the course of the trail.

The trail commences on Lockwood Valley Road and initially follows a graded dirt road that runs alongside Seymour Creek. It then turns off onto one of the designated 4WD routes that crisscross the region, the blue-rated West Frazier Mine Route. This trail gradually climbs around some of the lower slopes of Frazier Mountain, becoming more uneven and eroded as it climbs through scrub oak, pine, and juniper. The grade is moderate and

should not cause any trouble. The surface alternates between loose gravel and embedded rocks.

The route then turns onto West Frazier Tie Route, again blue-rated, which climbs a steeper grade onto Frazier Mountain. In places the grade reaches 25 percent, but it is usually more level. Although a bit loose and rocky in places, the trail will be within the crawling capabilities of most 4WDs.

On top of the mountain, the trail standard is easier as it travels around the eastern edge of Frazier Mountain through open pine forest. There are views south to Hungry Valley State Vehicular Recreation Area and Angeles National Forest. An old wooden fire lookout still stands on Frazier Mountain, now dwarfed by communications towers surrounding it. Like other lookouts in the region, it is no longer in use; the fire watch is carried out more efficiently from airplanes.

The trail follows a less direct route down from the mountain along a smaller road than others in the area. A spur trail heads off from this point, running out for 4 miles to end at a small loop. A popular blue-rated motorbike route connects through to Hungry Valley State Vehicular Recreation Area. All other vehicles must travel the roughly graded road back down to rejoin Lockwood Valley Road. The route exits past the Chuchupate National Forest Ranger Station near Lake of the Woods.

The trails in this region are closed during winter depending on snowfall, and they may close during or after heavy rains the rest of the year.

Current Road Information

Los Padres National Forest
Mt. Pinos Ranger District
34580 Lockwood Valley Road
Frazier Park, CA 93225
(661) 245-3731

Map References

BLM   Cuyama, Lancaster
USFS Los Padres National Forest: Mt.
      Pinos, Ojai and Santa Barbara
      Ranger Districts

Mine shaft and boiler remains on mountainside off Frazier Mountain Trail

USGS 1:24,000 Cuddy Valley,
          Lockwood Valley, Frazier Mtn.
          1:100,000 Cuyama, Lancaster
Maptech CD-ROM: Barstow/San
          Bernardino County; San Luis
          Obispo/Los Padres National Forest
*Southern & Central California Atlas &
          Gazetteer*, p. 77
California Road & Recreation Atlas, p. 102

Route Directions

▼ 0.0   From Lockwood Valley Road, 5.5 miles
           southwest of Lake of the Woods, zero
           trip meter and turn south on graded
           dirt road 8N12 at sign for Lockwood
           Creek Campground.
1.4 ▲   Trail ends at T-intersection with
           Lockwood Valley Road. Turn left for
           California 33; turn right for Lake of the
           Woods.
           GPS: N34°45.58' W119°02.94'

▼ 0.3   SO Cross through Seymour Creek wash.
1.1 ▲   SO Cross through Seymour Creek wash.
▼ 0.4   SO Cattle guard.
1.0 ▲   SO Cattle guard.
▼ 0.8   SO Track on right.
0.6 ▲   SO Track on left.
▼ 0.9   SO Cross through creek.
0.5 ▲   SO Cross through creek.
▼ 1.0   SO Closure gate.
0.4 ▲   SO Closure gate.
           GPS: N34°44.89' W119°02.68'

▼ 1.3   SO Cross through wash.
0.1 ▲   SO Cross through wash.
▼ 1.4   TL Track on right is Lockwood Mine Road.
               Turn left onto West Frazier Mine Road
               #118—rated green for motorbikes and
               ATVs, rated blue for 4WDs. Zero trip
               meter.
0.0 ▲   Continue to the west.
           GPS: N34°44.74' W119°02.32'

▼ 0.0   Continue to the north through closure
           gate.
3.4 ▲   TR Closure gate; then track straight ahead
               is Lockwood Mine Route. Turn right,
               joining graded road, and zero trip meter.

▼ 0.1   SO Cross through wash.
3.3 ▲   SO Cross through wash.
▼ 0.2   SO Cross through wash.
3.2 ▲   SO Cross through wash.
▼ 0.4   SO Track on left.
3.0 ▲   SO Track on right.
           GPS: N34°45.04' W119°02.13'

▼ 0.6   SO Cross through two washes.
2.8 ▲   SO Cross through two washes.
▼ 0.8   SO Cross through wash.
2.6 ▲   SO Cross through wash.
▼ 1.0   BR Turnout on left.
2.4 ▲   BL Turnout on right.
▼ 1.6   BL Track on right. Follow trail route marker.
1.8 ▲   SO Track on left.
           GPS: N34°45.61' W119°01.17'

▼ 1.8   SO Cross through wash and start to climb.
1.6 ▲   SO End of descent. Cross through wash.
▼ 2.1   SO Cross over creek.
1.3 ▲   SO Cross over creek.
▼ 2.2   SO Trail does a sharp switchback to the
               left. Remains of mine ahead—little
               remains except adit in hillside.
1.2 ▲   SO Trail does a sharp switchback to the
               right. Remains of mine ahead—little
               remains except adit in hillside.
           GPS: N34°45.71' W119°00.80'

▼ 2.4   BL Two tracks on right go 0.1 miles to
               mine adits.
1.0 ▲   SO Two tracks on left go 0.1 miles to mine
               adits.
           GPS: N34°45.79' W119°00.81'

▼ 3.2   SO Track on right.
0.2 ▲   SO Track on left.
           GPS: N34°46.02' W119°00.23'

▼ 3.3   SO Gate.
0.1 ▲   SO Gate.
▼ 3.4   BR Track on left is continuation of West
               Frazier Mine Trail for 4WDs, ATVs, and
               motorbikes—rated green. Bear right
               onto West Frazier Tie Trail for 4WDs,
               ATVs, and motorbikes—rated blue.
               Zero trip meter.
0.0 ▲   Continue to the southwest. End of
               descent.

The decommissioned Frazier Mountain Lookout Tower sits high above historic Tejon Pass

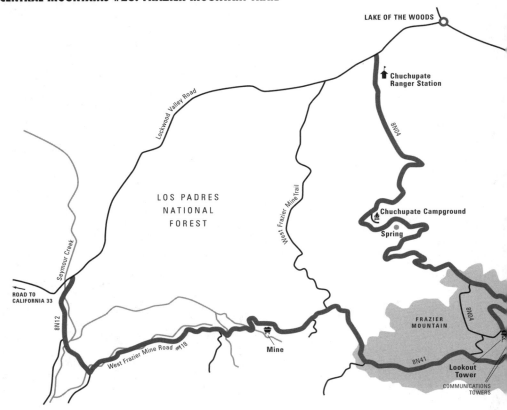

GPS: N34°46.17' W119°00.13'

▼ 0.0   Continue to the northeast and start to climb steeply.

3.1 ▲   BL   Track on right and left is West Frazier Mine Trail for 4WDs, ATVs, and motorbikes—rated green. Zero trip meter.

▼ 0.7   SO   End of climb.

2.4 ▲   SO   Trail starts to descend.

▼ 1.1   TL   T-intersection. Track on right. Turn left onto 8N41.

2.0 ▲   TR   Turn right onto West Frazier Tie Trail for 4WDs, ATVs, and motorbikes—rated blue. Trail continues ahead.

         GPS: N34°45.78' W118°59.48'

▼ 2.3   BR   Track on left is continuation of 8N41. Bear right, following trail sign.

0.8 ▲   SO   Track on right is 8N41. Continue straight, joining 8N41.

GPS: N34°46.21' W118°58.40'

▼ 3.0   SO   Track on left and communications tower on left.

0.1 ▲   BL   Track on right and communications tower on right.

▼ 3.1   BR   Frazier Mountain Fire Lookout and two communications towers on left. Bear right onto trail sign-posted to East Frazier Road. Zero trip meter. Track on left is 8N04.

0.0 ▲   Continue to the east.

         GPS: N34°46.53' W118°58.13'

▼ 0.0   Continue to the northwest.

1.0 ▲   BL   Track on right is 8N04. Zero trip meter and bear left toward communications towers. Two towers and Frazier Mountain Fire Lookout on right.

▼ 0.4   BR   Track on left.

trail accesses Hungry Valley State Vehicular Recreation Area.
GPS: N34°46.92' W118°55.76'

▼ 4.1 UT Trail ends at a small loop. Retrace your steps back to the main trail.
GPS: N34°46.85' W118°55.81'

Continuation of Main Trail

▼ 0.0   Continue to the west.
4.0 ▲ TR Turn right onto smaller, formed trail marked with a trail sign to continue on main trail. Zero trip meter. Continue straight ahead to travel Frazier Mine Spur.
GPS: N34°46.78' W118°57.92'

▼ 0.9 SO Track on left is 8N04 to Frazier Mountain Fire Lookout. Continue straight, joining 8N04.
3.1 ▲ SO Track on right is 8N04 to Frazier Mountain Fire Lookout. Continue straight on 8N24, following sign to East Frazier Trail.
GPS: N34°46.88' W118°58.70'

▼ 3.4 SO Tank and spring on left.
0.6 ▲ SO Tank and spring on right.
GPS: N34°47.16' W118°59.78'

▼ 3.6 SO Closure gate.
0.4 ▲ SO Closure gate.
▼ 4.0 SO Track on right goes into Chuchupate USFS Campground. Zero trip meter.
0.0 ▲   Continue west on 8N04. Road is now graded dirt.
GPS: N34°47.17' W119°00.06'

▼ 0.0   Continue to the northeast on 8N04. Road is now paved. Remain on paved road, ignoring turns on left and right.
2.4 ▲ BR Track on left goes into Chuchupate USFS Campground. Zero trip meter.
▼ 2.2 SO Closure gate; then Chuchupate Ranger Station on left.
0.2 ▲ SO Chuchupate Ranger Station on right; then closure gate.
▼ 2.4   Trail ends at intersection with Lockwood Valley Road. Turn left for

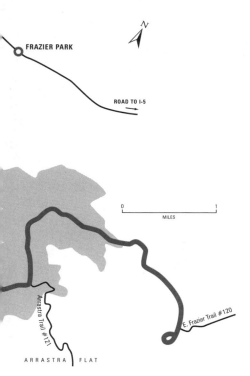

0.6 ▲ BL Track on right.
▼ 1.0 TL T-intersection with roughly graded dirt East Frazier Road. Turn left to continue along main trail; turn right to travel the Frazier Mine Spur. Zero trip meter.
0.0 ▲   Continue to the southwest.
GPS: N34°46.78' W118°57.92'

Frazier Mine Spur

▼ 0.0   Continue to the east.
▼ 0.5 SO Track on right is Arrastra Trail #121. It is a vehicle route for 0.4 miles before becoming a black-rated trail for motorbikes only. Frazier Mine is below the motorbike trail.
GPS: N34°46.85' W118°57.51'

▼ 4.0 SO Track on left is East Frazier Trail #120 for motorbikes only—rated blue. This

Views through Lockwood Valley, an old borax mining area

California 33 and Ojai; turn right for Lake of the Woods.

0.0 ▲   Trail commences along Lockwood Valley Road, 1 mile west of Lake of the Woods. Zero trip meter and turn southeast on paved road at sign for Chuchupate Ranger Station and Frazier Mountain Lookout.
GPS: N34°48.57' W119°00.69'

CENTRAL MOUNTAINS #29

San Emigdio Mountain Trail

STARTING POINT Cerro Noroeste Road, 4 miles west of Pine Mountain Club
FINISHING POINT Cerro Noroeste Road, 2.2 miles west of Pine Mountain Club
TOTAL MILEAGE 14.9 miles (round-trip) including both spurs
UNPAVED MILEAGE: 14.9 miles
DRIVING TIME 2 hours (round-trip) including both spurs

ELEVATION RANGE 5,700–7,400 feet
USUALLY OPEN Year-round
BEST TIME TO TRAVEL Dry weather
DIFFICULTY RATING 4, 5 for spur to San Emigdio Peak
SCENIC RATING 8
REMOTENESS RATING +0

Special Attractions

■ Loop trail offering two more-challenging spurs.
■ National forest campgrounds and backcountry campsites.
■ Wide-ranging views from the narrow ridge trail.

History

Considering that this trail runs mainly within the San Andreas Fift zone, it is no surprise that there are frequent earth movements in the region. The name San Emigdio Mountain was chosen with this in mind. St. Emidius was a German martyr believed to offer protection from earthquakes. The name San Emigdio, also known as San Emidio, first appeared on a land grant in 1842. In July of that year, California governor Juan B. Alvarado granted a total of 17,709 acres of land to José Antonio Dominguez. In 1866, half of this parcel was patented to John C. Frémont, and the other half went to the heirs at law of José Antonio Dominguez, who had died of smallpox about one year after gaining the original land grant. It is commonly thought that this particular San Emigdio land grant was, in effect, the start of rancho days in what was to become Kern County. This property is visible way below the trail as it passes over San Emigdio Mountain. Look down through Doc Williams Canyon on the northern side of the range.

Beginning with San Diego in 1769, Spanish missionaries and soldiers established a string of missions and presidios in what was then known as Alta (Upper) California. Jesuit missionaries had been expelled from Baja (Lower) California by the king of Spain and were instructed to explore and settle the coast to the north. As missions developed up and down coastal California, they began to have a noticeable effect on native lifestyles. Some Indians chose to move away toward the San Joaquin Valley. Many traveled along El Camino Viejo. Spanish deserters moving between the San Francisco Bay area and Los Angeles also traveled this road in the late 1700s because it enabled them to travel from north to south and avoid the coastal missions. El Camino Viejo (literally "the old road" in Spanish) climbs up the spectacular eastern side of San Emigdio Mountain and enters the San Andreas Fault. It roughly follows the course of San Emigdio Creek through what is known as Devils Kitchen, which is below the eastern spur off this trail. From there, El Camino Viejo followed close to today's Mil Potrero Highway, passing by Frazier Park en route to Los Angeles.

Traffic along the inland route varied over the years. Beaver trappers and missionaries were among the more frequent travelers along the road. However, their presence in the area began to push the native Yokuts farther inland. The Yokuts quickly adapted to the European intrusion. They found that the

Descending San Emigdio Mountain toward El Camino Veijo 3,000 feet below

settlers' horses, as well as being good eating, were an excellent form of transportation that made it easier to avoid conflict with troops or rancheros. The Yokuts, with the assistance of other native people who had moved inland to avoid the missionaries, stole the settlers' horses. The settlers retaliated, often taking the Yokuts for slave labor.

Pine Mountain Club, a residential development begun in the mid-1970s, was once a marble quarry that produced a very pure white marble with a fine gray vein running through it. Marble from this quarry was used for many of the tombstones in Taft's Cemetery. The quarry closed in 1962, when a source was found near Mammoth Lakes that was easier and cheaper to access.

Description

The San Emigdio Mountain Trail is a short loop with two more difficult spur trails running off from it along the ridge, one at either end. Initially the trail is uneven as it leaves Cerro Noroeste Road (also numbered FR 95 at this point) and travels up toward the ridge of San Emigdio Mountain. There are two very pleasant campgrounds that a high-clearance 2WD can access—Caballo and Marian. Both are open areas with some shade.

From Marian Campground, the first spur heads up along the ridge to Brush Mountain. This spur immediately starts to climb steeply with grades as high as 25 percent. Once on the ridge, it winds along, offering views over Doc William Canyon and northeast along Blue Ridge, which parallels the San Andreas Fault.

The main trail continues east along the ridge from Marian Campground along a narrow formed section of the San Emigdio Jeep Trail, before joining the graded road, 9N34, which winds back down to join Cerro Noroeste Road.

The second, longer spur initially continues along the graded 9N34 to San Emigdio Mountain, where it picks up the San Emigdio Jeep Trail again. Viewpoints from San Emigdio Mountain offer excellent views to the north, down a drop of nearly 3,000 feet into Cloudburst Canyon. The narrow,

A steep climb west from Marian Campground provides views of San Emigdio Mountain

CENTRAL MOUNTAINS #29: SAN EMIGDIO MOUNTAIN TRAIL

sheer ridge continues along the first part of the trail and includes some steep, loose grades. The first descent, 0.3 miles from the mountain peak, is one of the steepest with a grade of 25 percent and a very deep, loose, low-traction surface, made more difficult by moguls at the top. Be sure that you feel confident about returning up this slope before you commit yourself to descending it; the trail is a dead end.

The trail winds along the ridge, passing other steep pinches. Care is needed on the sandy surface. It is easy to bog down and quickly dig yourself into a hole. The trail ends on the ridge and turns into an area for non-motorized recreation only.

Current Road Information
Los Padres National Forest
Mt. Pinos Ranger District
34580 Lockwood Valley Road
Frazier Park, CA 93225
(661) 245-3731

Map References
BLM   Cuyama
USFS Los Padres National Forest: Mt.
      Pinos, Ojai and Santa Barbara
      Ranger Districts
USGS 1:24,000   Sawmill Mtn.,
      Eagle Rest Peak
      1:100,000 Cuyama
Maptech CD-ROM: San Luis Obispo/Los

Padres National Forest
Southern & Central California Atlas & Gazetteer, p. 76, 77
California Road & Recreation Atlas, p. 101

Route Directions

▼ 0.0   From Cerro Noroeste Road (FR 95), 20 miles southeast of the intersection with California 33/166 and 4 miles west of Pine Mountain Club, zero trip meter and turn west onto graded dirt road 9N27, following sign for Marian Campground. Immediately pass through closure gate. Cerro Noroeste Road is 9 miles south of Maricopa along California 33/166.

1.8 ▲   Pass through closure gate; then trail finishes on Cerro Noroeste Road (FR 95). Turn left for Pine Mountain Club; turn right for California 33/166 and Maricopa.
        GPS: N34°51.80′ W119°13.63′

▼ 0.5   SO Caballo Campground on right and left.
1.3 ▲   SO Caballo Campground on right and left.
        GPS: N34°52.12′ W119°13.53′

▼ 1.8   TR Turn right at sign into Marian Campground. Track ahead is the start of Brush Mountain Spur along San Emigdio Jeep Trail #107. Zero trip meter.
0.0 ▲   Continue to the southwest.

Fallen trees slowly succumb to the harsh weather on San Emigdio Mountain

GPS: N34°52.83' W119°12.99'

Brush Mountain Spur

▼ 0.0   Continue north at sign for Marian Campground.

▼ 0.1   TL   T-intersection. Turn left onto San Emigdio Jeep Trail #107—rated green for ATVs and motorbikes, rated blue for 4WDs. Track on right goes into Marian Campground.
GPS: N34°52.88' W119°12.96'

▼ 1.0   SO   Track on left.
▼ 1.4   UT   Track on left is the end of small loop. Trail runs around a small loop and returns to this point. Retrace your route back toward the campground.
GPS: N34°53.51' W119°13.68'

Continuation of Main Trail

▼ 0.0   Continue to the east.
▼ 1.2   TL   Turn left at sign for Marian Campground. Track on right is the start of Brush Mountain Spur along San

Emigdio Jeep Trail #107. Zero trip meter.
GPS: N34°52.83' W119°12.99'

▼ 0.1   BR   Keeping the campground on your left, bear right past sign for the San Emigdio Jeep Road, suitable for 4WDs, ATVs, and motorbikes—rated green.
1.1 ▲   BL   Keeping the campground on your right, leave track on right through campground.
GPS: N34°52.81' W119°12.93'

▼ 1.2   TR   Turn right onto better graded trail 9N34 (unmarked), and zero trip meter. Road ahead is San Emigdio Mountain Spur.
0.0 ▲   Continue to the northwest.
GPS: N34°52.33' W119°12.12'

San Emigdio Mountain Spur

▼ 0.0   Proceed southeast on graded road from intersection with San Emigdio Jeep Trail #107.
▼ 1.6   SO   Track on right goes to quarry.

SAN ANDREAS FAULT

Faults, fractures in the earth's crust, occur in California because the state is situated on the boundary of the oceanic Pacific plate and the continental North American plate. Earthquakes occur when the plates shift and grind against each other along the faults. The San Andreas Fault is the most significant one in California. It extends nearly 700 miles from Cape Mendocino in the north, through San Francisco, west of San Jose, south through Parkfield and Tejon Pass, east of the San Jacinto Mountains, and into Mexico.

The San Andreas Fault revealed itself dramatically during the legendary San Francisco earthquake on April 18, 1906. The powerful quake and the ensuing fire claimed the lives of at least 3,000 people and moved land on either side of the fault as much as 21 feet. Another powerful earthquake, perhaps just as strong, occurred in 1857 near Fort Tejon.

Approximately 20 million people now live in the vicinity of the San Andreas Fault. Hundreds of small earthquakes occur along the fault each year, though most are very low in magnitude. The fault is clearly visible from the air, marked by a linear arrangement of lakes and valleys. One of the best places to see it from the ground is on the Carrizo Plain, west of Bakersfield.

▼ 1.8   SO   Turnout on left is San Emigdio Peak. Continue onto San Emigdio Trail—rated green for motorbikes, rated blue for ATVs and 4WDs. Zero trip meter.
GPS: N34°52.32′ W119°10.48′

▼ 0.0   Continue to the east.
▼ 0.3   BL   Trail forks.
GPS: N34°52.18′ W119°10.27′

▼ 1.6   SO   Suggested turnaround point. The last 0.4 miles of the trail are tight, twisty, and brushy, and do not go to a particular viewpoint.
GPS: N34°51.93′ W119°09.31′

▼ 2.0   UT   Trail ends at closure sign.
GPS: N34°51.90′ W119°09.06′

Continuation of Main Trail

▼ 0.0   Continue to the west.
1.5 ▲   TL   Turn left onto San Emigdio Jeep Trail #107 at sign. Trail is suitable for 4WDs, ATVs, and motorbikes—rated green. Track on right is San Emigdio Mountain Spur. Zero trip meter.
GPS: N34°52.33′ W119°12.12′

▼ 1.4   SO   Closure gate.
0.1 ▲   SO   Closure gate.

▼ 1.5   SO   Trail ends at T-intersection with Cerro Noroeste Road. Turn left for Pine Mountain Club; turn right for Maricopa and California 33/166.
0.0 ▲   Trail commences on Cerro Noroeste Road (FR 95), 0.2 miles west of Apache Saddle Forest Station and 2.2 miles west of Pine Mountain Club. Zero trip meter and turn north on unsigned, graded dirt road 9N34.
GPS: N34°51.69′ W119°12.71′

CENTRAL MOUNTAINS #30

Cuyama Peak Trail

STARTING POINT California 33, 0.5 miles south of the intersection with Ballinger Canyon Road
FINISHING POINT Cuyama Peak Fire Lookout
TOTAL MILEAGE 16.3 miles (one-way)
UNPAVED MILEAGE: 12.1 miles
DRIVING TIME 1.5 hours (one-way)
ELEVATION RANGE 2,700–5,800 feet
USUALLY OPEN Year-round, may be closed briefly after snowfall
BEST TIME TO TRAVEL Dry weather
DIFFICULTY RATING 3
SCENIC RATING 8
REMOTENESS RATING +0

Cuyama Peak Fire Lookout—its fire-spotting days are over, but it remains rewarding for bird-watchers

Special Attractions

- Cuyama Peak Fire Lookout and shingle cabin.
- Rough, unmaintained shelf road climbing to Cuyama Peak.
- Popular trail for hunters (in season) and bird-watchers.

History

The tower on Cuyama Peak was built in 1934. Its structure, known as a modified L-4 style, is set on top of a 20-foot steel tower that is H-braced for rigidity. During World War II, this facility was occupied by members of the Aircraft Warning Service. The small cabin they lived in still stands alongside the lookout tower. Unfortunately, the cabin has attracted its share of vandals, who remove more and more as the years go by. This shingle-covered building is apparently one of only four such buildings still standing.

Like most lookout towers in the region, the Cuyama Peak lookout ceased operations in the 1960s, when it proved more efficient to spot fires from airplanes instead.

From the lookout tower, Ventucopa is visable to the north. The settlement is located close to the starting point of this trail and the wide wash of the Cuyama River. In 1926, when residents were trying to register a name for the post office, a local named Dean Parady came up with the name that was laughed at by many, but still stuck. After all, the settlement lay between Ventura and Maricopa. So why not call it Ventucopa?

Description

Cuyama Peak Trail climbs a long spur to the old lookout tower on Cuyama Peak. The lookout is not maintained and the road up to it sees correspondingly little maintenance, making it rougher than many other such lookout trails.

The trail leaves California 33 at an unmarked intersection, 0.5 miles south of marked Ballinger Canyon Road. The sandy trail runs across a river flat before crossing the wide, sandy wash of the Cuyama River. It then joins the paved Santa Barbara Canyon Road. If the Cuyama River crossing is impassable for any reason, an alternative entry/exit to the trail can be found at the junction of Santa Barbara Canyon Road and California 166, a couple of miles east of New Cuyama. This route is longer but avoids the sandy river crossing.

Initially, the trail passes through ranchland before entering Los Padres National Forest. It follows Santa Barbara Canyon before turning off into the narrower, rougher Dry Canyon. The Santa Barbara Canyon Trail, for hikers and horses, can be accessed from a major intersection near the start of Dry Canyon. There are some reasonable campsites along this spur, which goes 1.8 miles before stopping at a closure gate. Hikers can continue past the closure gate to McPherson Peak.

The main trail crosses the creek a number of times as it winds along Dry Canyon. Campers are better off selecting a site in the lower portion of the canyon; as it climbs and becomes tighter, there is less space available. The creek crossings can be rough and sandy. Water can race down this canyon, rearranging the creek crossings as it does so.

The trail climbs away from the creek for the final 3 miles to the old Cuyama Peak Fire Lookout and shingle cabin. The grades are moderate, but the shelf road can be loose in places. There are panoramic views from the lookout over the Dick Smith Wilderness, Chumash Wilderness, Cuyama Valley, and Los Padres National Forest.

The trail is popular with deer hunters (in season) and bird-watchers, who keep a special eye out for the pinyon jay.

Current Road Information
Los Padres National Forest
Mt. Pinos Ranger District
34580 Lockwood Valley Road
Frazier Park, CA 93225
(661) 245-3731

Map References
BLM   Cuyama
USFS Los Padres National Forest: Mtn. Pinos, Ojai and Santa Barbara Ranger Districts

View from the Cuyama Peak Fire Lookout

USGS 1:24,000 Ballinger Canyon,
         Cuyama, Fox Mt., Cuyama Peak
         1:100,000 Cuyama
Maptech CD-ROM: San Luis Obispo/Los
         Padres National Forest
Southern & Central California Atlas &
         Gazetteer, p. 76
California Road & Recreation Atlas, p. 101

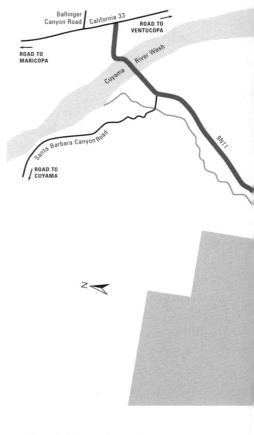

Route Directions

▼ 0.0   From California 33, 0.5 miles south of
         intersection with Ballinger Canyon
         Road and 4 miles south of California
         166, zero trip meter and turn west on
         unmarked, formed dirt trail.
1.4 ▲   Trail ends at T-intersection with
         California 33. Turn left for Maricopa;
         turn right for Ventucopa.
         GPS: N34°52.78′ W119°29.79′

▼ 0.3   SO Track on left.
1.1 ▲   SO Track on right.
▼ 0.6   BL Track on right.
0.8 ▲   BR Track on left.
         GPS: N34°52.76′ W119°30.37′

▼ 0.7   SO Start to cross wide sandy wash of
             Cuyama River.
0.7 ▲   SO Exit Cuyama River Wash.
         GPS: N34°52.68′ W119°30.34′

▼ 1.0   SO Exit Cuyama River Wash.
0.4 ▲   SO National forest route marker—road not
             maintained for low-clearance vehicles.
             Start to cross wide sandy wash of
             Cuyama River.

▼ 1.4   SO Track on right opposite private proper-
             ty; then bear left on small paved road,
             following sign to Santa Barbara
             Canyon Road, and cross cattle guard.
             Road is now marked 9N11. Road
             crosses private property. Remain on
             main road. Road on right is also Santa
             Barbara Canyon Road to Cuyama. Zero
             trip meter.
0.0 ▲   Continue to the north.
         GPS: N34°52.12′ W119°30.81′

▼ 0.0   Continue to the south.

▼ 0.8   SO Two cattle guards.
▼ 2.6   SO Cattle guard. Entering Los Padres
             National Forest. Track on left to well.
         GPS: N34°50.38′ W119°32.50′

▼ 2.7   SO Second track on left to well.
▼ 3.0   SO Cross through wash.
▼ 3.1   SO Cattle guard.
▼ 3.3   SO Cattle guard. Entering private property.
             Remain on paved road.
         GPS: N34°49.83′ W119°32.88′

▼ 3.7   SO Cross through wash.
▼ 4.2   BR Bear right on paved road and zero trip
             meter. Road ahead goes into private
             property.
         GPS: N34°49.13′ W119°33.37′

▼ 0.0   Continue to the southwest. Pass
         through gate; then cross through
         creek. Road turns to graded dirt.

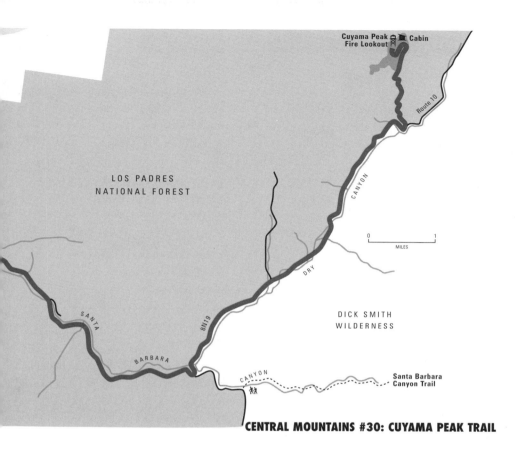

CENTRAL MOUNTAINS #30: CUYAMA PEAK TRAIL

▼ 0.3   SO   Cattle guard.
▼ 0.7   SO   Cattle guard.
▼ 0.8   SO   Cross through wash.
▼ 2.0   SO   Cattle guard.
▼ 2.4   SO   Track on right.
▼ 3.1   TL   Turn left onto 8N19, following sign to
              Cuyama Peak Lookout. Track ahead
              passes some campsites and accesses
              the Santa Barbara Canyon Trail for hik-
              ers and horses before reaching a
              locked gate in 1.8 miles. Zero trip
              meter.
              GPS: N34°47.13' W119°34.25'

▼ 0.0   Continue to the northeast.
▼ 0.2   SO   Cross through wide wash.
▼ 0.3   SO   Gate.
▼ 1.7   SO   Track on left.
▼ 2.1   SO   Cross through wash and track on left.
▼ 2.2   SO   Cross through wash.
              GPS: N34°46.27' W119°32.44'

▼ 2.3   SO   Cross over wash.
▼ 2.7   SO   Cross through wash.
▼ 3.1   SO   Cross through wash.
▼ 3.9   SO   Cross through wash.
▼ 4.9   SO   Trail leaves creek and starts to climb
              shelf road.
              GPS: N34°45.36' W119°30.02'

▼ 5.1   SO   Saddle.
▼ 5.2   SO   Cross through wash.
▼ 5.5   SO   Cross through wash. Lesser-used track
              on right at left-hand switchback is
              Route #10 for motorbikes.
              GPS: N34°44.96' W119°29.80'

▼ 7.6   Trail ends at old lookout tower and
              cabin on Cuyama Peak.
              GPS: N34°45.24' W119°28.52'

Potrero Seco Trail

STARTING POINT California 33, 31 miles north of Ojai, 3.6 miles north of Pine Mountain Inn

FINISHING POINT Monte Arido

TOTAL MILEAGE 13.7 miles (one-way)

UNPAVED MILEAGE: 13.7 miles

DRIVING TIME 1.5 hours (one-way)

ELEVATION RANGE 4,700–5,600 feet

USUALLY OPEN Year-round, closed after rain or snow

BEST TIME TO TRAVEL Dry weather

DIFFICULTY RATING 3

SCENIC RATING 8

REMOTENESS RATING +1

Special Attractions

- Lightly traveled, permit-only trail within Los Padres National Forest.
- Trail travels around the edge of Dick Smith Wilderness and Matilija Wilderness.
- Beautiful, winding ridge top trail.

Description

This trail sees a maximum of 10 vehicles a day, so your chances of meeting other travelers are slim. The trail is in good condition with a fairly smooth surface. The 3-rating is mainly for some moderately steep sections and the forest service's requirement for 4WD vehicles.

The trail leaves California 33 and immediately enters the permit area through a gate. The first couple of miles are roughly graded because they access private property. The trail then runs along the boundary of two separate wilderness areas, the Dick Smith Wilderness to the north and the Matilija Wilderness to the east. Hiking trails access both wilderness areas.

There is one forest service camping area near the start of the trail, immediately past private property at Potrero Seco. There are two sites, both with shade. Both have picnic tables and either a fire ring or BBQ.

Once past the camping area, the trail starts to climb onto the ridge top. When the trail passes the Don Victor Hiking Trail, the conditions of

the permit require that 4WD be engaged. Seco Peak is on the left as the trail proceeds toward the Three Sisters, prominent rock formations that stand on either side of the trail.

From here the trail winds along open ridge tops, offering views down Diablo Canyon to the west and toward Matilija Canyon to the east. The vegetation is low scrub—California scrub oak, manzanita, and sagebrush. Animals that might be seen include the elusive bobcat, deer, and many different raptors, including the endangered California condor.

The trail finishes at a closure gate below Monte Arido. From here you must retrace your steps back to the entry point on California 33.

Permit Information

It is essential to obtain the free permit necessary to drive this trail prior to travel. This will provide you with the code to the combination lock on a gate before the area. The code is changed frequently. The maximum number of permits issued is 10 vehicles per day and is strictly enforced. Please adhere to the regulations available at Ojai Ranger Station so that this trail remains open to public use. Too many other, similar trails in Los Padres National Forest are limited to Administration Use Only and are not open to the public. Let's retain the access we have to this one. Permits can be obtained from:

Los Padres National Forest
Ojai Ranger District
1190 East Ojai Avenue
Ojai, CA 93023
(805) 646-4348

Call the Ojai office for permit availability between 8 A.M. and 4:30 P.M. Monday through Friday during winter months, and seven days a week during summer months. Reservations are made by phone only, but permits are available on a walk-in basis if there are some still available for that day. Reservations may be made up to 14 days prior to the date of use. During hunting season there is a lot of competition for permits; other times use can be very light. One vehicle permit is issued per person with a maximum of 4 people per vehicle. A Forest Adventure Pass is also required.

Near vertical granite fins called the Three Sisters rise up along Potrero Seco Trail

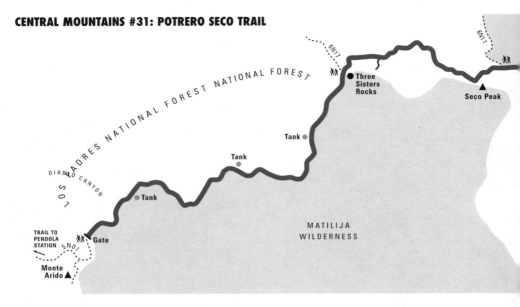

Permits are free and are valid for up to 3 days at any one time. Permits must be picked up by 10 A.M. the day of the trip or reservations will be canceled and released to others. One permit for up to 3 days will be issued per person in a 7-day period. After hours pickup can be arranged if desired.

Current Road Information

Los Padres National Forest
Ojai Ranger District
1190 East Ojai Avenue
Ojai, CA 93023
(805) 646-4348

Map References

BLM   Cuyama
USFS   Los Padres National Forest: Mtn.
       Pinos, Ojai and Santa Barbara
       Ranger Districts
USGS   1:24,000   Rancho Nuevo Creek,
       Old Man Mt.
       1:100,000 Cuyama
Maptech CD-ROM: San Luis Obispo/Los
       Padres National Forest
*Southern & Central California Atlas &
       Gazetteer,* p. 76
California Road & Recreation Atlas, p. 101

Route Directions

▼ 0.0   From California 33, 31 miles north of Ojai and 3.6 miles north of Pine Mountain Inn, zero trip meter and turn west onto graded dirt road. The turn is opposite sign-posted road to Pine Mountain. Pass through closure gate using combination given to you with your permit.
         GPS: N34°38.95' W119°23.08'

▼ 0.6   SO Track on left.
         GPS: N34°38.50' W119°23.18'

▼ 1.5   SO Cattle guard.
▼ 2.1   SO Cattle guard.
▼ 3.1   SO Cattle guard. Entering Los Padres National Forest.
         GPS: N34°38.25' W119°25.41'

▼ 3.3   SO Track on right to Potrero Seco Campground.
         GPS: N34°38.27' W119°25.56'

▼ 3.4   SO Gate.
         GPS: N34°38.19' W119°25.69'

▼ 4.7   SO Hiking trail on right is Don Victor Trail (6N11), which enters the Dick Smith

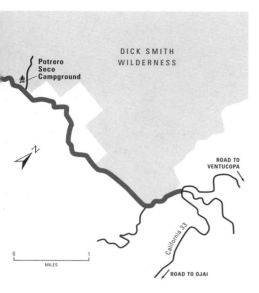

DICK SMITH
WILDERNESS

Potrero
Seco
Campground

ROAD TO
VENTUCOPA

California 33

0   1
MILES

ROAD TO OJAI

Wilderness. Zero trip meter at 4x4 only
sign. 4WD must be engaged past this
sign to comply with permit requirements.

GPS: N34°37.89' W119°26.44'

▼ 0.0   Continue to the south.
▼ 1.8   SO Track on right.
▼ 2.4   SO Faint track on left.
         GPS: N34°36.81' W119°27.69'

▼ 3.2   SO Track on right is 6N17 (closed to
            vehicles). Zero trip meter at Three
            Sisters Rocks.
            GPS: N34°36.33' W119°27.84'

▼ 0.0   Continue to the southeast.
▼ 0.5   SO Gate.
         GPS: N34°35.99' W119°27.62'

▼ 1.1   SO Game water tank on right.
         GPS: N34°35.59' W119°27.37'

▼ 2.8   SO Game water tank on right.
         GPS: N34°34.67' W119°27.72'

▼ 4.7   SO Game water tank below track on left.

Winding away from Potrero Seco along the ridge top

Potrero Seco Trail follows ridgeline above the upper reaches of Agua Caliente Canyon

GPS: N34°33.58' W119°28.35'

▼ 5.8   Trail ends at closure gate below Monte Arido. Track on right goes short distance to dam. Hiking trail 5N01, 0.2 miles south of the closure gate, goes to Pendola Station.
GPS: N34°32.81' W119°28.26'

Nordhoff Ridge Trail

STARTING POINT Rose Valley Road, 3 miles east of California 33 at Lower Rose Lake
FINISHING POINT Nordhoff Peak/Sespe Wilderness boundary
TOTAL MILEAGE 28.8 miles (round-trip) including both spurs
UNPAVED MILEAGE: 27.6 miles
DRIVING TIME 2 hours for both legs
ELEVATION RANGE 4,600–5,100 feet

USUALLY OPEN Year-round
BEST TIME TO TRAVEL Dry weather
DIFFICULTY RATING 3 for Chief Peak spur, 4 for Nordhoff Peak spur
SCENIC RATING 9
REMOTENESS RATING +1

Special Attractions

- Lightly traveled, permit-only trail within Los Padres National Forest.
- Excellent ocean views as well as views over Lion Canyon and the Sespe Wilderness.
- Lookout tower on Nordhoff Peak.
- Rose Valley Falls.
- Popular mountain bike route that can be combined with the Gridley Trail.

History

At one time, Nordhoff Peak and Nordhoff Ridge overlooked a town of the same name. R. G. Surdam established the town in 1874. The Germanic name came from Charles Nordhoff. A writer of renown in his day, Nordhoff had written favorably about the features within the

Narrow shelf road up to Nordhoff Ridge

Past Nordhoff Peak, the trail is less used and is overgrown with scrub vegetation

Ojai Valley. His grandson, Charles B. Nordhoff, was also a writer. Charles co-authored with James N. Hall, the 1932 best-seller, *Mutiny on the Bounty.* In 1916, the town of Nordhoff changed its name to Ojai, a Chumash-derived word referring to the moon.

Ojala, located at the foot of Nordhoff Ridge, was reported as having the smallest post office premises in the nation at the time. The tiny post office was reputed to be the size of a phone booth.

Nordhoff Ridge Trail becomes a hiking trail when it enters the Sespe Wilderness. At this point, it passes the end of the eye-catching Topatopa Bluff. This name, along with many others, is taken from a Chumash word of similar pronunciation. A rancheria (a native village or community) was noted as being located nearby in the upper reaches of the Ojai Valley. Indications are that the rancheria name may refer to a brushy place.

In 1947, the Sespe Condor Sanctuary was established to the east of the bluff. This refuge encompassed 53,000 acres, mainly within the southeastern corner of Los Padres National Forest. Except for two through corridors, public access was closed in an effort to protect the habitat of these magnificent birds.

In 1944, a P-51 aircraft crashed into the mountains below the Nordhoff Peak lookout tower. With the passing of time, natural re-vegetation, and official and unofficial salvaging, little evidence of the crash remains today.

Description

This lightly traveled trail sees a maximum of 20 vehicles a day, often fewer. Your chances of meeting anyone, especially if you travel outside the hunting season, are remote. The trail leaves Rose Valley Road opposite Lower Rose Lake. It travels a short distance to the Rose Valley Campground and then leaves through the locked gate. From the campground, a valid permit is essential. A short, marked foot trail also leads off through the campground to the fern-covered Rose Valley Falls. It is a 10-minute walk to the base of the falls.

Once you're through the gate, the trail starts to climb steeply. The road was once paved, but has fallen into disrepair and is now a mix of paved patches and loose, scrabbly dirt. The forest service requires 4WD to be engaged for the surfaced parts of this climb, and for this reason will issue permits only to 4WD vehicles. The trail climbs up the steep spur to Nordhoff Ridge, where it forks along the top. Both trails are well worth the trip.

The first spur travels along Nordhoff Ridge and is rated 4 for difficulty, because of the loose, rough climb up to Nordhoff Peak. There is an excellent picnic and camping spot perched right on top of the ridge with views in all directions. Although it is very exposed, it is an excellent place to stop when the weather is good.

On top of Nordhoff Peak is an old metal lookout tower. It is possible to climb the tower for an even more elevated view of the coastline and inland valleys. The trail contin-ues past the tower to hiking trail 23W09, which heads steeply down the valley to join Signal Road. Past the hiking trail, the vehicle trail is less used and brushy. It continues for approximately 2 miles along Nordhoff Ridge.

The second spur, which is rated a 3 for difficulty, winds around the side of Chief Peak to finish at the boundary of the Sespe Wilderness. Like the spur along Nordhoff Ridge, there are panoramic views over the Pacific Coastline and Channel Islands National Park—the islands of Santa Cruz and Anacapa. This spur also offers views down into Lion Canyon and over toward the Sespe Wilderness, as well as views of Topatopa Bluff—a prominent striated ridge of mainly bare rock.

Permit Information

It is essential to obtain the free permit necessary to drive this trail prior to travel. This will provide you with the code to the combination lock on a gate before the area. The code is changed frequently. The maximum number of permits

The trail runs out on a ridge—Lake Casitas is visible on clear days

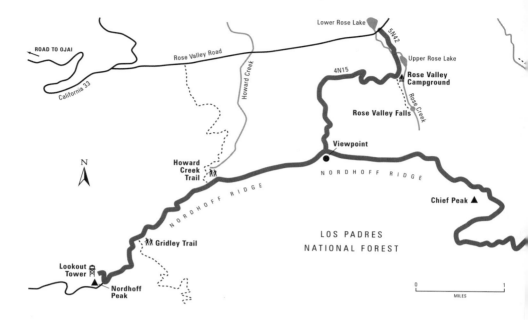

issued is limited to 20 vehicles per day and is strictly enforced. Please adhere to the regulations available at Ojai Ranger Station so that this trail remains open to public use. Too many other, similar trails in Los Padres National Forest are limited to Administration Use Only and are not open to the public. Let's retain the access we have to this one. Permits can be obtained from:

Los Padres National Forest
Ojai Ranger District
1190 East Ojai Avenue
Ojai, CA 93023
(805) 646-4348

Call the Ojai office for permit availability 8 A.M. to 4:30 P.M. Monday through Friday during winter months, and seven days a week during summer months. Reservations are made by phone only, but are available on a walk-in basis if there are some still available for that day. Reservations may be made up to 14 days prior to the date of use. During hunting season there is a lot of competition for permits; other times use can be very light. One vehicle permit is issued per person with a maximum of 4 people per vehicle. A Forest Adventure Pass is also required.

Permits are free and are valid for up to 3 days at any one time. Permits must be picked up by 10 A.M. on the day of the trip or reservations will be canceled and released to others. One permit for up to 3 days will be issued per person in a 7-day period. After hours pickup can be arranged if desired.

Current Road Information
Los Padres National Forest
Ojai Ranger District
1190 East Ojai Avenue
Ojai, CA 93023
(805) 646-4348

Map References
BLM   Cuyama, Santa Barbara
USFS   Los Padres National Forest: Mt. Pinos, Ojai and Santa Barbara Ranger Districts
USGS   1:24,000   Lion Canyon, Ojai, Santa Paula Peak
1:100,000   Cuyama, Santa Barbara
Maptech CD-ROM: San Luis Obispo/Los Padres National Forest; Ventura/Los Angeles/Orange County

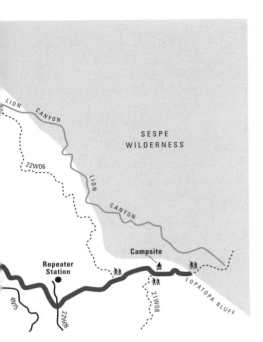

Southern & Central California Atlas & Gazetteer, pp. 76, 77
California Road & Recreation Atlas, p. 102

Route Directions

▼ 0.0   From Rose Valley Road at Lower Rose Lake, 3 miles east of California 33, zero trip meter and turn southeast on the paved road 5N42 at the 4-way intersection. Intersection is unmarked. Lower Rose Lake is on the left. Rose Valley Road is 14 miles north of Ojai on California 33.
         GPS: N34°32.38' W119°11.11'

▼ 0.3   SO   Cross through Rose Creek on concrete ford.

▼ 0.5   SO   Rose Valley Campground. Road passes through campground.
         GPS: N34°32.01' W119°10.87'

▼ 0.6   BR   Bear right through campground and cross through creek. Then pass through closure gate onto 4N15. Permit and valid combination number required

past this point. Zero trip meter.
         GPS: N34°31.93' W119°10.95'

▼ 0.0   Continue to the northwest on paved road.

▼ 2.1   TR   Cattle guard; then track on right is spur to Nordhoff Peak. Track on left is spur to Chief Peak. Viewpoint ahead. Turn right onto Nordhoff Peak Spur and zero trip meter.
         GPS: N34°31.14' W119°11.77'

Nordhoff Peak Spur

▼ 0.0   Continue to the southwest on Nordhoff Peak Spur from the T-intersection at the top of climb from Rose Valley Campground.
         GPS: N34°31.14' W119°11.77'

▼ 1.3   SO   Track on left goes around dam.

▼ 1.4   SO   Well-used track on right to campsite with picnic table and fire ring. Well-used track on left rejoins. Continue up the middle track.
         GPS: N34°30.86' W119°13.11'

▼ 1.6   SO   Howard Creek Trail on right for hikers, horses, and mountain bikes.
         GPS: N34°30.81' W119°13.24'

▼ 2.0   SO   Track on right is blocked.

▼ 2.7   SO   Gridley Trail on left for hikers, horses, and mountain bikes.
         GPS: N34°30.34' W119°13.97'

▼ 3.7   TR   Turn right to travel to the lookout tower.
         GPS: N34°29.85' W119°14.47'

▼ 3.9   Trail ends at lookout tower on Nordhoff Peak.
         GPS: N34°29.90' W119°14.47'

Chief Peak Spur

▼ 0.0   Continue to the east on Chief Peak Spur from the T-intersection at the top of climb from Rose Valley Campground.
         GPS: N34°31.14' W119°11.77'

▼ 1.1   SO   Dam on left.

▼ 2.0   SO   Chief Peak on right.
             GPS: N34°30.77′ W119°09.96′

▼ 4.7   TL   Unmarked track ahead is a continua-
             tion of 4N15. Turn left onto unmarked
             trail 5N08. Zero trip meter.
             GPS: N34°30.03′ W119°09.24′

▼ 0.0   Continue to the northeast.
▼ 1.2   SO   Track on right is 22W08 to Thacher
             School. Track on left goes to Repeater
             Station.
             GPS: N34°29.70′ W119°08.43′

▼ 2.0   SO   Lion Canyon Hiking Trail (22W06) on
             left to Middle Lion Campground.
             GPS: N34°29.97′ W119°07.70′

▼ 2.5   SO   Hiking trail 21W08 on right to Upper Ojai.
             GPS: N34°30.03′ W119°07.27′

▼ 2.6   SO   Campsite on left with picnic table
             and fire ring.
▼ 3.1   Trail ends at boundary of the Sespe
             Wilderness.
             GPS: N34°30.01′ W119°06.86′

CENTRAL MOUNTAINS #33

Big Caliente Spring Trail

STARTING POINT California 154, 5.6 miles
   north of Santa Barbara
FINISHING POINT Big Caliente Hot Springs
TOTAL MILEAGE 28.9 miles (one-way),
   plus 5.6-mile spur to Little Caliente
   Hot Springs
UNPAVED MILEAGE: 10.6 miles, plus 5.6-mile
   spur
DRIVING TIME 2.5 hours (one-way),
   including spur
ELEVATION RANGE 400–3,600 feet
USUALLY OPEN Year-round
BEST TIME TO TRAVEL Year-round
DIFFICULTY RATING 1, 2 for spur to Little
   Caliente Hot Springs
SCENIC RATING 9
REMOTENESS RATING +0

Special Attractions
■ Painted Cave State Historic Park.
■ Natural hot springs for soaking at Big and
  Little Caliente Hot Springs.
■ Long ridge top trail above Santa Barbara.
■ Access to Divide Peak OHV Trail.
■ Birding along the Santa Ynez River.

History
This trail commences at the historic San
Marcos Pass in the Santa Ynez Mountains.
In 1846, soldiers of the Presidio of Santa
Barbara went to great lengths to block the
path of Lieutenant Colonel John C. Frémont and his troops. Frémont was en route
to Los Angeles to support the push for California's independence from Mexico. Tales
vary. Some say Mexican soldiers lay in wait
to ambush Frémont at Gaviota Pass, located
20 miles west on the present route of US 101
where it passes over the Santa Ynez Mountains. Other reports say the soldiers were already in Los Angeles. Hearing of the sus-
pected ambush, Frémont instead made his
way up and over San Marcos Pass, guided by
Benjamin Foxen and his son. They descend-
ed from the pass to capture Santa Barbara on
Christmas Day.

By the late 1860s, a stagecoach route ran
through San Marcos Pass. The pass was a
steep, difficult climb for horses, and rough
grooves were carved into the sandstone to
give traction on the climb out of Santa Barbara. Horse teams were changed at the top
before the stagecoaches proceeded down the
north side of the Santa Ynez Mountains via
Cold Spring Tavern. By the early 1890s, an
improved toll road was constructed over the
pass with fees so high that travelers and
haulers thought it was daylight robbery. Gen-
uine robberies were not uncommon on San
Marcos Pass. There was also the danger of
frightened horses getting away from the
stagecoach driver on the steep terrain and
overturning the coach.

Though the large concrete bridge over
Cold Spring Canyon (north of the pass) was
constructed in the 1960s, it is still possible to
get an insight about the original San Marcos
Pass route. The old pass road, set below the

Arroyo Burro Road, which is closed to vehicles to assist red-legged toad survival, is a pleasant hike

Little Caliente Spring—the upper level is hottest

more modern high bridge, passes the door of the Cold Spring Tavern. The tavern is still operating in its original buildings in the shade of the narrow oak-lined canyon. A nearby small cabin once housed a bottling plant for the natural spring water that was greatly valued by passing travelers.

The feast day of St. Barbara, a fourth-century woman beheaded by her father for converting to Christianity, is celebrated on December 4. On this date in 1602, Vizcaíno passed through the area and named the waters between the Channel Islands and the mainland Canal de Santa Bárbara. In 1782, this name was applied to the newly established Presidio de Santa Bárbara, now referred to as the birthplace of the town of Santa Barbara. On December 4, 1786, the site of the mission at Santa Barbara was declared by placing a cross at the location referred to as Pedregoso, meaning stony.

Santa Cruz Island, the largest of the visible islands offshore, had a number of names given to it over the centuries. In 1543, Juan Cabrillo called it San Sebastian. Vizcaíno, on his voyage of 1602, named it Isla de Gente Barbuda after some bearded people seen on the island. By the latter half of the eighteenth century it had become informally known as Santa Cruz, because a friar who had visited the island lost his cross-bearing staff there. A native found the staff for the friar, and the incident was well remembered until finally the name of the holy cross stuck. Santa Rosa, formerly Isla de San Lucas, and the other islands of this group also had a number of names over the years. Prior to the arrival of Europeans, the Chumash inhabited several of these islands. Santa Rosa was known as Wimat to the Chumash, San Miguel was Tukan, and Santa Cruz was Limu.

European diseases took their toll on the mainland tribal populations. The Tongva people of the Los Angeles region, the Humaliwu division of the Chumash, and the Tejon Chumash of the hinterland succumbed in great numbers to plagues of the white man. The same also happened on the islands. It is thought that the Limu islanders were the most resilient against disease.

Many of the island people were taken to the mainland to be used as labor for the construction of missions. Santa Barbara, Santa Ynez, and Purisimo were relocation centers for such people. The Limu fought to retain independence, but they too were drafted against their will into the workforce.

Today the islands of San Miguel, Santa Rosa, Santa Cruz, Anacapa, and Santa Barbara comprise Channel Islands National Park. Originally established as a national monument in 1938, the islands were classified as a national biosphere reserve in 1976, before gaining national park status in 1980.

As you take in the ocean views from high up along the aptly named Camino Cielo (Spanish for "Sky Road"), cast your eyes and mind some 95 miles south of the eastern end of Santa Cruz Island. Here is the lonely San Nicholas Island. Now try to imagine being stranded there for 18 years by yourself. This was the case for one native woman in the nineteenth century.

In 1835, Chumash living on San Nicholas were moved to the mainland to become part of the workforce building Spanish missions. Realizing that her baby was not on the ship, one woman jumped overboard in a fierce storm. The ship was not very sturdy, and Captain George Nidever did not return for her because he was worried about his ship weathering the storm.

Over the years, Captain Nidever made efforts to find the woman. The island is about 25 square miles in area, and although searchers found evidence of a human inhabitant, the woman always managed to elude them. For 18 years she lived alone, surviving on a diet of fish and edible plants. However, the persistent captain eventually found her. She was dressed in skins and huddled in a small shelter made of sagebrush. The only dialect she could speak was not comprehended by anyone, including local Indians, whose dialect had changed and evolved through contact with mainland tribes and Europeans. No evidence of the baby was ever found, and she was unable to tell her rescuers about her life over the past 18 years.

View from Blue Canyon Pass

Named Juana Maria by her guardians, she was housed the Santa Barbara community. Sadly she died after only six or seven weeks; the abrupt change of diet was a likely cause. She was buried in the cemetery of the Santa Barbara Mission. The artifacts that she had brought with her from San Nicholas were made available for scientific study but were lost in the fires of San Francisco in the early twentieth century. Sometimes referred to as the lone woman, her time on the island was the inspiration behind the book *Island of the Blue Dolphins* (1990), by Scott O'Dell.

Though it is also a naval reservation, the San Nicholas Island Archaeological District covers the entire island. It was recorded in 1984 as having 355 prehistoric sites listed throughout the island.

Description

Big Caliente and Little Caliente Springs are natural hot springs, located a short distance apart in beautiful natural settings. The springs, which are suitable for bathing, are reached by a long and winding ridge top road that travels along the Santa Ynez Mountains.

There are plenty of interesting things along the way. Near the start of the trail is Chumash Painted Cave, a rock shelter lavishly decorated with rock art. A small sign on a tree points to the cave; the state historic park sign is farther along and hard to see in the forward direction of this trail. There is limited parking alongside the road, which is narrow and twisting at this point.

On a clear day you can see Santa Barbara below and the numerous oil-drilling platforms in the Pacific Ocean. The turnoff for Arroyo Burro Road enables you to travel to the campground and recreation area on the Santa Ynez River to the north. The road is currently closed at the lower end to protect the habitat of the red-legged toad.

On the main trail, the winding road travels along a narrow spine on top of the range and offers great views to the north and south. There are many turnouts for admiring the view. The trail passes the start of the Divide Peak OHV Route, for motorbikes and ATVs only, before starting the long descent to the Santa Ynez River. The ford through the river is concrete, and the water is normally very shallow. The national forest map shows Juncal Campground at this point, but the campground has been closed since May 2000 to protect the habitat of the red-legged toad. Those wishing to camp can proceed to the P-Bar Campground, where there are some pleasant open sites under large pine trees. No primitive camping is permitted along this route.

Birders have a chance to spot many species along the river. The endangered Bell's vireo, a small migratory bird, visits the Santa Ynez River. The southern spotted owl, black chinned hummingbird, hairy woodpecker, spotted sandpiper, and yellow-breasted chat are just some of the other species found here.

The trail divides at Pendola Guard Station. The main route continues for 2.5 miles to Big Caliente Spring. A parking area, pit toilet, and changing area are located at the end of the trail. Beside the parking area, there is a rectangular concrete tub about 3 feet deep for soaking—the water is warm to hot. The trail to Little Caliente Spring continues past the parking area to Caliente Debris Dam and Potrero Seco. This is for hikers only. A second spring is found only a short distance up the trail on the far side of the creek. The tub is built out of river rocks. No camping is permitted at the springs.

Debris dams were constructed by the forest service to trap debris from the Coyote Fire of September 1964 before it washed into Gibraltar Lake and reduced its capacity for water storage.

The trail to Little Caliente requires a high-clearance 2WD vehicle. The final section can be deeply rutted and is not suitable for passenger vehicles. They can, however, access the P-Bar Campground. Little Caliente Spring tends to be quieter than Big Caliente, and is set in a narrow creek valley. There are three soaking pools, set one above the other on the hillside; each holds two to four people. The water is hot and the view fabulous. The stone pools are well constructed and there are a couple of wooden platforms and benches for your clothes but no other facilities. The de facto dress code for both these springs is "clothing optional."

Big Caliente Spring Trail crosses the Santa Ynez River

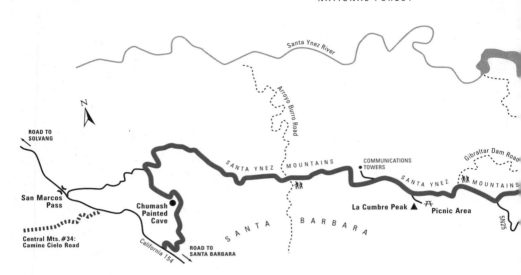

Current Road Information

Los Padres National Forest
Santa Barbara Ranger District
3505 Paradise Road
Santa Barbara, CA 93105
(805) 967-3481

Map References

BLM   Santa Barbara, Cuyama
USFS   Los Padres National Forest: Mt.
       Pinos, Ojai and Santa Barbara
       Ranger Districts
USGS   1:24,000   Goleta, San Marcos Pass,
       Little Pine Mt., Santa Barbara,
       Carpinteria, White Ledge Peak,
       Hildreth Peak
       1:1100,000 Santa Barbara, Cuyama
Maptech CD-ROM: San Luis Obispo/Los
       Padres National Forest; Ventura/Los
       Angeles/Orange County
*Southern & Central California Atlas &
       Gazetteer,* pp. 89, 90, 76
California Road & Recreation Atlas, p. 101

Route Directions

▼ 0.0   From California 154, 5.6 miles north of
          Pacific Coast Highway in Santa Barbara,
          zero trip meter and turn north on paved
          road at sign for Painted Cave Road.
3.2 ▲   Trail ends on California 154. Turn left
          for Santa Barbara.
          GPS: N34°29.48′ W119°47.67′

▼ 1.9 SO Chumash Painted Cave on left of
          paved road.
1.3 ▲ SO Chumash Painted Cave on right of
          paved road.
          GPS: N34°30.25′ W119°47.20′

▼ 3.2 TR Turn sharp right onto unmarked paved
          road. Zero trip meter.
0.0 ▲   Continue to the east.
          GPS: N34°30.81′ W119°47.76′

▼ 0.0   Continue to the northeast.
3.9 ▲ TL Turn sharp left onto unmarked, paved
          road. Zero trip meter.

▼ 3.9 SO Track on left is Arroyo Burro Road. Zero

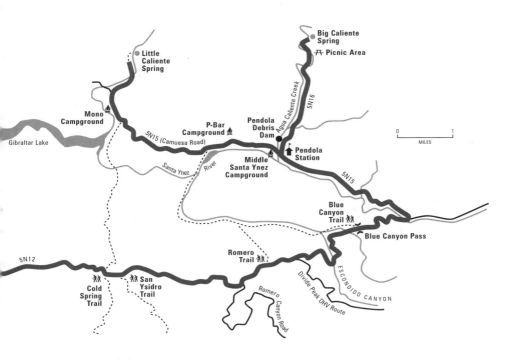

trip meter at sign. Hiking trail on right for hikers, horses, and mountain bikes.

0.0 ▲ Continue to the south.
GPS: N34°30.31' W119°45.12'

▼ 0.0 Continue to the north.

4.7 ▲ SO Track on right is Arroyo Burro Road. Zero trip meter at sign. Hiking trail on left for hikers, horses, and mountain bikes.

▼ 2.2 SO Track on left to communications towers.

2.5 ▲ SO Track on right to communications towers.
GPS: N34°30.06' W119°43.42'

▼ 2.6 SO Turnout on right for communications towers.

2.1 ▲ SO Turnout on left for communications towers.

▼ 2.9 SO La Cumbre Peak on right. Picnic area is 0.25 miles behind locked gate.

1.8 ▲ SO La Cumbre Peak on left. Picnic area is 0.25 miles behind locked gate.
GPS: N34°29.73' W119°42.80'

▼ 4.1 SO Track on left is Gibraltar Dam Road— closed to motor vehicles.

0.6 ▲ SO Track on right is Gibraltar Dam Road—

closed to motor vehicles.
GPS: N34°29.78' W119°41.89'

▼ 4.7 BL Paved road on right is Gibraltar Road (5N25) to Santa Barbara. Zero trip meter and bear left, following sign to Big Caliente Hot Spring.

0.0 ▲ Continue to the west.
GPS: N34°29.47' W119°41.36'

▼ 0.0 Continue to the east on 5N12.

▼ 3.5 SO Cold Spring Hiking Trail crosses road. Left goes to Mono Campground and right to Mountain Drive.
GPS: N34°29.06' W119°38.29'

▼ 3.7 SO San Ysidro Hiking Trail on right to Mountain Drive.
GPS: N34°29.01' W119°38.05'

▼ 6.5 SO Romero Canyon on right. Trail is now graded dirt.

▼ 7.1 SO Romero Hiking Trail on left to Blue Canyon Trail.
GPS: N34°28.82' W119°35.25'

THE CHUMASH AND THEIR ROCK ART AT PAINTED CAVE

The Chumash were the first of California's tribes encountered by Europeans. Portuguese conquistador Juan Rodriguez Cabrillo landed in Chumash territory in 1542. At that time, the tribal group, a network of 75 to 100 villages united by common language and culture, numbered between 20,000 and 30,000 members. They inhabited a 7,000-square-mile region of Southern California, along the shore between present-day San Luis Obispo and Ventura, on several of the Channel Islands, and inland along the streams and valleys of what is now Santa Barbara County. The Chumash are thought to have entered California quite early, perhaps 10,000 years ago. The last 1,000 years of pre-colonial Chumash civilization was a golden age for the culture,

A Chumash camp

and evidence of their expressive artwork can be seen scattered around their ancestral homeland, most famously at Painted Cave northwest of Santa Barbara.

The Chumash survived by exploiting the abundant resources of this region. They were the best seafarers of the California Indians and stood alone among those tribes in their use of boats made out of conjoined plants, instead of carved tree trunks or hide-covered frames. From these boats, the Chumash caught ocean fish using both nets and spears. They made harpoons by putting an antler tip or bone on a wooden spear and tying a string to it. With these weapons they hunted sea otters, seals, and sea lions.

The Chumash were technically advanced when compared to their neighbors. Spanish missionaries viewed them as the most "civilized" of the various mission tribes. The British Museum in London has preserved a Chumash bow, harpoon, and spear-thrower obtained by George Vancouver on an early expedition in the Pacific. All three weapons reveal a craftsmanship superior to that of other Southern California tribes. Chumash basketry and stone working were also quite advanced.

Five Spanish missions were established on Chumash territory—San Buenaventura, Santa Barbara, Santa Inés, La Purísma Conception, and San Luis Obispo. Though the tribe was apparently quite receptive to Spanish influence, mission life seems to have somewhat demoralized the Chumash. Missionaries complained that abortion became alarmingly common among the tribe. Clearly the Indians were reluctant to bring new members into a world so removed from their traditional life. Secularization of the missions only led to disorder for the Chumash, and by the time California became a U.S. state in 1850, their survivors were scattered and few. Nevertheless, there remain today a relatively large number of people who claim at least partial Chumash ancestry.

Painted Cave

Although Chumash populations dwindled and much of their cultural identity was lost during the period of Spanish missions, the tribe left an indelible mark on the California landscape in the form of several cave paintings. In order to protect these historical treasures, state authorities generally refrain from releasing their locations. One notable exception is Painted Cave, in the hills above Santa Barbara.

Painted Cave was likely a religious site, with drawings representing spiritual themes. The painting also appears to mark the winter solstice; a triangular beam of light shines onto the panel on the first day of winter each year. One theory, supported by dating of the paint substances, claims that the central black disc outlined in white commemorated a solar eclipse that took place on November 24, 1677. Other symbols include wheels, halos, crosses, horned animals, humans, and fantastical beasts.

Most Chumash paintings were drawn on sandstone cave walls using natural materials. Red paint was made from hematite, an iron oxide; black paint was made from charcoal or manganese oxide. The pigments were mixed with animal fat or plant juices and the resulting substance was applied to the rock using fingers or brushes made from feathers or animal tails. At other times, the pigment was dried and applied directly as a type of chalk.

The Painted Cave can be viewed, free of charge, every day in the Chumash Painted Cave State Historic Park. The cave is protected by a gate, but the paintings are clearly visible from outside. Some visitors claim that at sunrise and sunset, the echoes of bone flutes and soft chanting resound around the painted walls.

▼ 7.5 SO Pull-in on left.

▼ 7.8 SO Track on left to parking area for Divide
Peak OHV Route; then track on right is
Divide Peak OHV Route for ATVs and
motorbikes only. Zero trip meter.
GPS: N34°28.86' W119°34.61'

▼ 0.0 Continue east through seasonal closure gate.

▼ 1.1 SO Cross over Escondido Canyon Creek.
GPS: N34°28.62' W119°33.98'

▼ 2.3 SO Cross over creek on bridge.
GPS: N34°29.16' W119°33.56'

▼ 2.4 SO Trail 26W12 on left for hikers and horses.
GPS: N34°29.19' W119°33.52'

▼ 2.5 SO Blue Canyon Pass.
GPS: N34°29.18' W119°33.35'

▼ 3.8 SO Cross over wash.

▼ 3.9 BL Cross over Santa Ynez River on concrete
ford; then bear left, following sign to Big
Caliente Canyon. Zero trip meter.
GPS: N34°29.20' W119°32.41'

▼ 0.0 Continue to the north on 5N15.

▼ 1.1 SO Cross over wash on concrete ford.
GPS: N34°29.76' W119°33.18'

▼ 2.9 TR Graded road straight ahead is 5N15.
Turn right onto 5N16, following sign to
Caliente Hot Spring and zero trip meter.
GPS: N34°30.50' W119°34.56'

Spur to Little Caliente Spring (Camuesa Road)

▼ 0.0 Continue to the northwest through closure gate and cross Agua Caliente
Creek on concrete ford. Road is
marked 5N15 to Little Caliente.
GPS: N34°30.50' W119°34.56'

▼ 0.1 SO Middle Santa Ynez Campground on left.
GPS: N34°30.56' W119°34.66'

▼ 0.3 SO Closure gate.

▼ 1.1 SO P-Bar Campground on right.
GPS: N34°30.88' W119°35.41'

▼ 1.7 SO Trail 26W12 on left for hikers.
GPS: N34°30.80' W119°35.98'

▼ 3.4 SO Closure gate.
GPS: N34°31.19' W119°37.26'

▼ 4.0 SO Trail on left is Cold Spring Trail to
Gibraltar Lake for hikers and horses.
GPS: N34°31.48' W119°37.48'

▼ 4.4 SO Mono Campground on left. Trail on left
through campground is 5N15 for hikers
and horses.
GPS: N34°31.69' W119°37.61'

▼ 4.8 BR Bear right onto smaller trail, following
sign for Little Caliente. Track on left
goes 0.2 miles then stops at closure
gate.
GPS: N34°31.98' W119°37.60'

▼ 5.3 SO Cross through wash.
▼ 5.4 SO Cross through creek.
▼ 5.5 SO Cross through wash.
▼ 5.6 UT Trail ends at turnaround and parking
area for Little Caliente Hot Spring. To
reach the spring, follow the unmarked
hiking trail to the northeast for a short
distance. Retrace your steps back to
the Pendola Forest Station.
GPS: N34°32.43' W119°37.16'

Continuation of Trail to Big Caliente Spring

▼ 0.0 Continue to the north.
GPS: N34°30.50' W119°34.56'

▼ 0.1 SO Pendola Forest Station on right.
▼ 0.3 SO Closure gate. Pendola Debris Dam
on left.
▼ 0.7 SO Cross through wash.
▼ 1.5 SO Cross through wash.
▼ 2.1 SO Cross Agua Caliente Creek on
concrete ford.
GPS: N34°32.07' W119°33.75'

▼ 2.2 SO Picnic area on right is Lower Caliente.
GPS: N34°32.14' W119°33.74'

▼ 2.3   SO Cross over Agua Caliente Creek on concrete ford.

▼ 2.5   Cross over Agua Caliente Creek on concrete ford. Then trail ends at Big Caliente Spring.

GPS: N34°32.35′ W119°33.83′

Camino Cielo Road

STARTING POINT California 154, 7 miles north of US 101

FINISHING POINT US 101 at Refugio State Beach

TOTAL MILEAGE 25.2 miles

UNPAVED MILEAGE: 9.2 miles

DRIVING TIME 1.5 hours

ELEVATION RANGE 100–4,200 feet

USUALLY OPEN Year-round

BEST TIME TO TRAVEL Year-round

DIFFICULTY RATING 2

SCENIC RATING 9

REMOTENESS RATING +0

Special Attractions

- Gun club target shooting—open to the public.
- Extensive views of the Pacific Ocean and coastline.

History

Refugio Pass, at the western end of the trail, has many colorful stories attached to its surrounding area. In the 1850s, Don Nicholás Den was leased the College Ranch, Cañada de los Pinos, which was part of the Santa Inés Mission holdings north of the Santa Ynez Mountains. For the grazing rights, he paid the Roman Catholic Church $3,000 a year. Den's wealth caught the eye of a disreputable character by the name of Jack Powers. Powers made plans to steal the thousand head of cattle that had been rounded up for sale to a dealer in Los Angeles. While Den was negotiating the sale in Los Angeles, Powers rode to the College Ranch and informed the majordomo that he had purchased the cattle and had come to take possession of them. The majordomo did not believe this outrageous tale

Camino Cielo Road offers views north toward the San Rafael Wilderness

The trail runs just below a ridge top in the Santa Ynez Mountains

but, realizing he was outnumbered by Powers' armed men, he quietly ordered the cattle to be released from their pen, thereby delaying attempts to remove them from the ranch.

The majordomo made his way to Den's house in Santa Barbara to relay the news. He was greeted by Den's foreman, an Irishman named Tom Meehan. Meehan wanted to take the law into his own hands and go after Powers and his gang himself. Den forbade this course of action and persuaded the sheriff to visit the College Ranch and oust Powers from his land. When the posse arrived, Powers realized that he was outnumbered. He left, but not before issuing many threats to both Den and Meehan.

Den returned to Los Angeles, leaving Meehan in charge of the ranch. Over the next few weeks, Meehan had several encounters with Powers and his gang but always managed to escape. Eventually, Meehan was forced to leave the ranch to secure more food and supplies. His intention was to ride over to Nuestra Señora del Refugio on the southern side of Refugio Pass. As he approached the pass, his horse spooked, and he came face to face with one of Powers men. Others approached and surrounded Meehan. He and his horse were gunned down without ever firing a shot in return.

A passing shepherd discovered Meehan's body trapped under his horse. He managed to tie him onto a burro and bring him back to nearby Dos Pueblos Ranch. Meehan's killers had gone straight to the sheriff claiming they had been ambushed and that they had acted in self-defense. Although it was obviously a lie, there was no way of proving it without a witness. Again, Don Nicholás refused to take the law into his own hands. However, two of Meehan's killers were quietly gunned down later by two of Den's ranch hands.

In 1951, Refugio Pass was the scene of an aircraft crash. A Douglas DC-3C en route from Santa Maria to Santa Barbara did not maintain the sufficient minimum altitude of 4,000 feet and crashed into the mountain near the pass. All 19 passengers and 3 crew members onboard died in the accident.

Description

Camino Cielo (Spanish for "Sky Road") follows a ridge top path through the Santa Ynez Mountains, the closest range to the Pacific Ocean. The trail is initially a single-lane, paved road as it heads west from California 154 through a small group of houses to travel into Los Padres National Forest. Once past the popular Winchester Canyon Gun Club, which is open to the public when its gate is open, the road turns to uneven, roughly graded dirt. There are good views of Lake Cachuma to the north, with the San Rafael Wilderness behind. It winds down toward the head of Ellwood Canyon, gradually descending some switchbacks, before running around the head of the canyon. Ellwood Canyon opens directly to the ocean. From here, the trail travels mainly on the south side of the ridge, providing great views over the coastline, back to Santa Barbara, and west over the less populated state beach areas. Several drilling rigs can be seen out at sea.

The road services a series of communications towers along the ridge, so the area is well traveled. Although there are several trails, the forest service has been attempting to close many of the smaller trails. Please respect these closures and travel only on marked trails. Motorbike riders will find a couple of trails marked specifically for their use.

At Santa Ynez Peak, the trail reverts to a small, single-lane paved road as it descends toward Refugio Pass. It then becomes a wider road, finishing on US 101 at Refugio Beach State Park.

Current Road Information
Los Padres National Forest
Santa Barbara Ranger District
3505 Paradise Road
Santa Barbara, CA 93105
(805) 967-3481

Map References
BLM Santa Barbara, Santa Maria,
      Cuyama, Point Conception
USFS Los Padres National Forest: Mt.
      Pinos, Ojai and Santa Barbara
      Ranger Districts

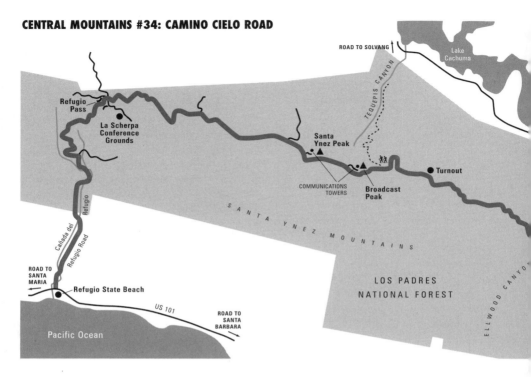

USGS 1:24,000 San Marcos Pass, Lake
     Cachuma, Santa Ynez, Tajiguas
     1:100,000 Santa Barbara, Santa
     Maria, Cuyama, Point Conception
Maptech CD-ROM: San Luis Obispo/Los
     Padres National Forest; Ventura/Los
     Angeles/Orange County
*Southern & Central California Atlas &
     Gazetteer,* pp. 75, 74, 88
California Road & Recreation Atlas,
     pp. 100, 101

Route Directions

▼ 0.0   From California 154, 7 miles north of
          US 101, 0.2 miles east of mile marker
          25, zero trip meter and turn west on
          West Camino Cielo at sign. Road is ini-
          tially paved.
3.8 ▲   Trail ends at T-intersection with
          California 154. Turn right for Santa
          Barbara.
          GPS: N34°30.26′ W119°48.69′

▼ 0.1   SO Cross over San Jose Creek on bridge.
3.7 ▲   SO Cross over San Jose Creek on bridge.

▼ 0.2   BL Bear left on Camino Cielo. Paved road
              on right is Kinevan Road.
3.6 ▲   BR Bear right on Camino Cielo. Paved road
              on left is Kinevan Road.
              GPS: N34°30.27′ W119°48.89′

▼ 0.6   SO Paved road on left.
3.2 ▲   SO Paved road on right.
▼ 1.4   SO Road on left.
2.4 ▲   SO Road on right.
▼ 3.8   SO Winchester Canyon Gun Club (trap and
              skeet range) entrance on right. Public
              is welcome when gate is open. Zero
              trip meter.
0.0 ▲   Continue to the southeast.
          GPS: N34°30.34′ W119°51.86′

▼ 0.0   Continue to the northwest.
7.8 ▲   SO Winchester Canyon Gun Club (trap and
              skeet range) entrance on left. Public is
              welcome when open. Zero trip meter.
▼ 0.2   SO Road turns to graded dirt.
7.6 ▲   SO Road is now paved.
▼ 0.3   SO View of Lake Cachuma on right.
7.5 ▲   SO View of Lake Cachuma on left.
▼ 1.3   SO Track on right through gate.

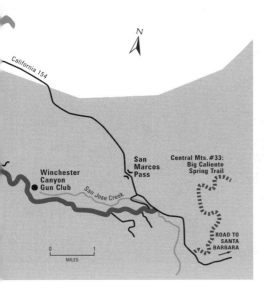

1.1 ▲ SO Track on left.
▼ 6.9 SO Trail on right for hikers, horses, and mountain bikes goes to Tequepis Canyon.
0.9 ▲ SO Trail on left for hikers, horses, and mountain bikes goes to Tequepis Canyon.
       GPS: N34º31.60' W119º56.98'

▼ 7.8 BL Well-used track on right goes to communications towers. Zero trip meter.
0.0 ▲   Continue to the southeast.
       GPS: N34º31.53' W119º57.82'

▼ 0.0   Continue to the west.
6.9 ▲ BR Well-used track on left goes to communications towers. Zero trip meter.
▼ 0.5 SO Track on right goes to communications towers.
6.4 ▲ BR Track on left goes to communications towers.
       GPS: N34º31.58' W119º58.37'

▼ 1.2 SO Road on right goes to communications tower.
5.7 ▲ BL Road on left goes to communications tower.
       GPS: N34º31.68' W119º58.87'

▼ 1.6 SO Paved road on right. Road is now paved.
5.3 ▲ BR Paved road on left. Road is now graded dirt.
       GPS: N34º31.83' W119º59.33'

▼ 3.8 SO Road on right goes into private property.
3.1 ▲ BL Road on left goes into private property.
       GPS: N34º32.00' W120º01.44'

▼ 6.9 TL Turn left on top of Refugio Pass, remaining on paved road. Two roads on right and entrance of La Scherpa Conference Grounds on left. Zero trip meter.
0.0 ▲   Continue to the east.
       GPS: N34º32.01' W120º03.67'

▼ 0.0   Continue to the south.
6.7 ▲ TR Entrance of La Scherpa Conference Grounds on right; then turn right on top of Refugio Pass. Road continues ahead and second track on right. Zero trip meter.

6.5 ▲ SO Track on left through gate.
       GPS: N34º30.57' W119º52.61'

▼ 1.5 SO Track on left under power lines.
6.3 ▲ SO Track on right under power lines.
▼ 3.8 SO Track on right.
4.0 ▲ SO Track on left.
       GPS: N34º31.25' W119º54.68'

▼ 4.1 SO Two tracks on right.
3.7 ▲ SO Two tracks on left.
       GPS: N34º31.32' W119º54.96'

▼ 4.6 SO Track on left.
3.2 ▲ SO Track on right.
▼ 5.2 SO Track on right.
2.6 ▲ SO Track on left.
▼ 5.3 SO Turnout on right.
2.5 ▲ SO Turnout on left.
       GPS: N34º31.64' W119º55.91'

▼ 5.8 SO Track on right.
2.0 ▲ SO Track on left.
▼ 5.9 SO Turnout on left and track on left.
1.9 ▲ SO Track on right and turnout on right.
▼ 6.7 SO Track on right.

Ocean clouds blanket Camino Cielo Road near Santa Ynez Peak

▼ 0.9   SO Cattle guard.
5.8 ▲   SO Cattle guard.
▼ 2.2   SO Cattle guard.
4.5 ▲   SO Cattle guard.
▼ 3.3   SO Track on left is private.
3.4 ▲   SO Track on right is private.
         GPS: N34°30.75′ W120°04.08′

▼ 3.6   SO Cross over creek on bridge.
3.1 ▲   SO Cross over creek on bridge.

GIVE MUDDY TRAILS A BREAK

TRAVELING ON SOGGY TRAILS CAUSES RUTS AND EROSION AND CAN LEAD TO MAJOR TRAIL DAMAGE

PLEASE RESPECT THE RIGHTS OF ALL TRAIL USERS TO ENJOY THE SANTA BARBARA BACKCOUNTY

Avoid muddy trails

▼ 3.7   SO Cross over creek on bridge.
3.0 ▲   SO Cross over creek on bridge.
▼ 3.8   SO Cross over creek on bridge.
2.9 ▲   SO Cross over creek on bridge.
▼ 3.9   SO Cross over creek on bridge.
2.8 ▲   SO Cross over creek on bridge.
▼ 5.0   SO Cross over creek on bridge.
1.7 ▲   SO Cross over creek on bridge.
         GPS: N34°29.47′ W120°03.87′

▼ 6.4   SO Cross over creek on bridge.
0.3 ▲   SO Cross over creek on bridge.
▼ 6.5   SO Cross over creek on bridge.
0.2 ▲   SO Cross over creek on bridge.
▼ 6.7   Trail ends at intersection with US 101 at the Refugio State Beach exit. Refugio Beach is straight ahead. Enter freeway south for Santa Barbara or north for Santa Maria.
0.0 ▲   Trail commences on US 101 at Refugio State Beach exit. Exit freeway and proceed to the north side. Zero trip meter and then proceed north on paved, two-lane Refugio Road.
         GPS: N34°28.01′ W120°04.07′

Miranda Pine Road

STARTING POINT Central Mountains #37: Sierra Madre Road, 8.6 miles from California 166

FINISHING POINT Tepusquet Road, 5.6 miles north of Foxen Canyon Road

TOTAL MILEAGE 25 miles

UNPAVED MILEAGE: 25 miles

DRIVING TIME 2 hours

ELEVATION RANGE 1,000–3,800 feet

USUALLY OPEN April to November

BEST TIME TO TRAVEL Dry weather

DIFFICULTY RATING 2

SCENIC RATING 9

REMOTENESS RATING +0

Special Attractions

- Alternative exit from Central Mountains #37: Sierra Madre Road.
- Long winding trail that includes both ridge top and canyon scenery.
- Many crossings of North Fork La Brea Creek.

Description

This trail can be combined with Central Mountains #37: Sierra Madre Road to make an easy loop that travels through a wide variety of beautiful scenery within Los Padres National Forest. The trail leaves Sierra Madre Road, 8.6 miles from California 166. The turn is unmarked but it is opposite the turn to Miranda Pine USFS Campground. This campground is small and very pretty, offering great views from its ridge top location.

From the outset, the trail descends a wide shelf road that runs down from the main backbone of the Sierra Madres. It travels through open vegetation of low shrubs, manzanitas, and the tall spikes of century plants (a type of yucca). The route wraps around Kerry Canyon and passes the Kerry Canyon Trail, a black-rated trail for motorbikes and non-motorized use. There is a good campsite at the intersection that is roomy with plenty of shade.

The trail snakes above Kerry Canyon

Short trail to Johnson Surprise Spring

The trail continues to descend as it runs below Treplett Mountain, giving good views out to the west. A second trail, this one suitable for 4WD vehicles, is Central Mountains #36: Buckhorn Ridge Trail—a more difficult, loose sandy trail that travels along the narrow Buckhorn Ridge. The main trail enters Smith Canyon before traveling alongside the pretty, rocky North Fork La Brea Creek, crossing it often.

Leaving North Fork La Brea Creek, the route climbs up Rattlesnake Canyon, crossing a saddle and descending the western side of the tighter Colson Canyon. The Colson USFS Campground is located just over the western side of the saddle at the head of the canyon. The trail ends at the intersection with Tepusquet Road, 5.6 miles north of Foxen Canyon Road.

A Forest Adventure Pass is required to be displayed on all parked vehicles or if you are undertaking any recreational activities. The campgrounds do not require any additional fees.

Current Road Information

Los Padres National Forest
Santa Lucia Ranger District
1616 North Carlotti Drive
Santa Maria, CA 93454
(805) 925-9538

Map References

BLM San Luis Obispo, Santa Maria
USFS Los Padres National Forest:
      Monterey and Santa Lucia Ranger
      Districts
USGS 1:24,000 Miranda Pine Mtn.,
      Manzanita Mt., Tepusquet Canyon
      1:100,000 San Luis Obispo, Santa
      Maria
Maptech CD-ROM: San Luis Obispo/Los
      Padres National Forest
*Southern & Central California Atlas &
      Gazetteer,* pp. 60, 74
California Road & Recreation Atlas, p. 100

Route Directions

▼ 0.0   From Central Mountains #37: Sierra
           Madre Road, 8.6 miles from California

166, zero trip meter and turn south on graded dirt road. Turn is unmarked but is opposite the turn to Miranda Pine Campground. Immediately track on right to Miranda Pine Spring; then closure gate. Trail starts to descend along shelf road.

3.2 ▲   Trail passes through closure gate; then track on left to Miranda Pine Spring. Trail ends at intersection with Central Mountains #37: Sierra Madre Road, opposite the turn to Miranda Pine Campground. Turn left to exit to California 166; turn right to continue along Sierra Madre Road to exit via Central Mountains #38: Bates Canyon Trail.
           GPS: N35°01.95' W120°02.00'

▼ 1.4   SO Cross through wash.
1.8 ▲   SO Cross through wash.
▼ 3.2   SO Campsite on left. Track on right is Kerry Canyon Trail to Pine Canyon Road #31 (30W02) for motorbikes only—rated black. Zero trip meter at sign.
0.0 ▲   Continue to the southeast.
               GPS: N35°01.36' W120°03.45'

▼ 0.0   Continue to the south.
5.8 ▲   SO Campsite on right. Track on left is Kerry Canyon Trail to Pine Canyon Road #31 (30W02) for motorbikes only—rated black. Zero trip meter at sign.
▼ 0.1   SO Kerry Canyon Trail on left goes to Lazy Camp.
5.7 ▲   SO Kerry Canyon Trail on right goes to Lazy Camp.
               GPS: N35°01.28' W120°03.40'

▼ 0.3   SO Cross through wash.
5.5 ▲   SO Cross through wash.
▼ 4.4   SO Track on right goes 0.4 miles to Johnson Surprise Spring.
1.4 ▲   BR Track on left goes 0.4 miles to Johnson Surprise Spring.
               GPS: N35°00.78' W120°05.22'

▼ 5.1   SO Tank on right.
0.7 ▲   SO Tank on left.

▼ 5.8   TL   Turn sharp left; graded road 11N04
                continues ahead to Horseshoe Spring
                Campground. Intersection is unmarked.
                Zero trip meter.
0.0 ▲   Continue to the southeast.

GPS: N35°00.01' W120°05.83'

▼ 0.0   Continue to the southwest.
1.0 ▲   TR   Turn sharp right; graded road 11N04
                continues ahead to Horseshoe Spring
                Campground. Intersection is unmarked.
                Zero trip meter.
▼ 1.0   SO   Small track on right; then Central
                Mountains #36: Buckhorn Ridge Trail
                on right at sign. Zero trip meter.
0.0 ▲   Continue to the north past small track
                on left.

GPS: N34°59.22' W120°05.68'

▼ 0.0   Continue to the south.
7.2 ▲   SO   Central Mountains #36: Buckhorn Ridge
                Trail on left at sign. Zero trip meter.
▼ 0.8   SO   Cross through creek in Smith Canyon.
6.4 ▲   SO   Cross through creek in Smith Canyon.
▼ 0.9   SO   Tank on left.
6.3 ▲   SO   Tank on right.

GPS: N34°58.84' W120°05.58'

▼ 1.0   SO   Cross through wash; then track on left.
6.2 ▲   SO   Track on right; then cross through wash.
▼ 1.7   SO   Closure gate.
5.5 ▲   SO   Closure gate.
▼ 2.3   SO   Gate; then cattle guard.
4.9 ▲   SO   Cattle guard; then gate.

GPS: N34°57.71' W120°05.79'

▼ 2.5   SO   Cross through two washes.
4.7 ▲   SO   Cross through two washes.
▼ 2.6   SO   Kerry Canyon Trail on left; then cross
                through wash.
4.6 ▲   BL   Cross through wash; then Kerry
                Canyon Trail on right.

GPS: N34°57.51' W120°05.81'

▼ 2.7   SO   Wagon Flat USFS Campground on left
                alongside North Fork La Brea Creek.
4.5 ▲   SO   Wagon Flat USFS Campground on right
                alongside North Fork La Brea Creek.

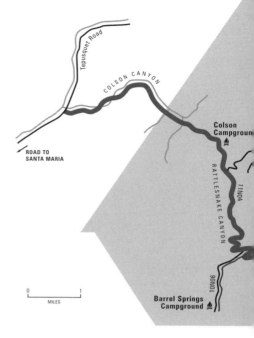

GPS: N34°57.42' W120°05.82'

▼ 3.0   SO   Cross through North Fork La Brea
                Creek wash. There are many creek
                crossings in the next 4.2 miles.
4.2 ▲   SO   Cross through North Fork La Brea
                Creek wash for the last time.
▼ 4.7   SO   Faint track on right.
2.5 ▲   SO   Faint track on left.
▼ 6.0   SO   Faint track on right.
1.2 ▲   SO   Faint track on left.

GPS: N34°55.68' W120°07.64'

▼ 7.0   SO   Cross through North Fork La Brea
                Creek wash.
0.2 ▲   SO   Cross through North Fork La Brea
                Creek wash.
▼ 7.1   SO   Cattle guard.
0.1 ▲   SO   Cattle guard.

GPS: N34°55.14' W120°08.42'

▼ 7.2   TR   Turn right onto 11N04, following sign
                to Tepusquet Road. Track ahead is
                10N06, which goes to Barrel Springs
                Campground and stops 0.5 miles after-
                wards. Zero trip meter.
0.0 ▲   Continue to the north.

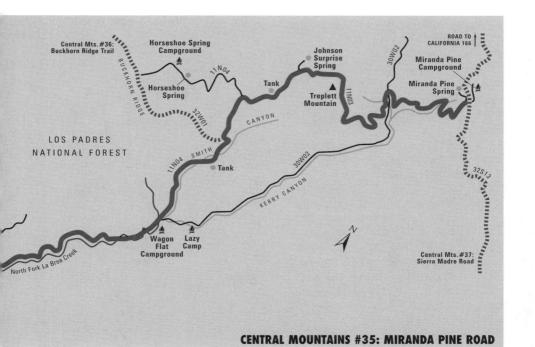

CENTRAL MOUNTAINS #35: MIRANDA PINE ROAD

GPS: N34°55.05' W120°08.53'

▼ 0.0   Continue to the east and cross through North Fork La Brea Creek wash for the last time.

3.7 ▲   TL   Cross through North Fork La Brea Creek wash. There are many creek crossings in the next 4.2 miles. T-intersection. Track on right is 10N06, which goes to Barrel Springs Campground and stops 0.5 miles afterwards. Turn left onto 11N04, following sign to Miranda Pine Road. Zero trip meter.

▼ 0.2   SO   Track on right.
3.5 ▲   SO   Track on left.
GPS: N34°55.16' W120°08.52'

▼ 3.1   SO   Gate; then cattle guard; then gated track on right.
0.6 ▲   SO   Gated track on left; then cattle guard; then gate.
GPS: N34°56.03' W120°09.75'

▼ 3.5   SO   Track on left.
0.2 ▲   SO   Track on right.
GPS: N34°56.26' W120°10.02'

▼ 3.7   SO   Track on right goes to Colson USFS Campground. Small sign at intersection. Zero trip meter.
0.0 ▲   Continue to the northeast.
GPS: N34°56.31' W120°10.11'

▼ 0.0   Continue to the west.
4.1 ▲   SO   Track on left goes to Colson USFS Campground. Small sign at intersection. Zero trip meter.

▼ 1.3   SO   Cross over wash.
2.8 ▲   SO   Cross over wash.

▼ 1.5   SO   Cross through creek; then exit Los Padres National Forest at sign; then cross through creek again.

2.6 ▲   SO   Cross through creek; then enter Los Padres National Forest at sign; then cross through creek again.
GPS: N34°56.34' W120°11.37'

▼ 1.7   SO   Cross through creek twice.
2.4 ▲   SO   Cross through creek twice.
▼ 2.0   SO   Cross through creek.
2.1 ▲   SO   Cross through creek.
▼ 2.2   SO   Cattle guard.
1.9 ▲   SO   Cattle guard.

▼ 2.9	SO	Cross through creek.
1.2 ▲	SO	Cross through creek.
▼ 3.1	SO	Cross through wash.
1.0 ▲	SO	Cross through wash.
▼ 3.2	SO	Cross through wash.
0.9 ▲	SO	Cross through wash.
▼ 3.3	SO	Track on left through gate.
0.8 ▲	BL	Track on right through gate.
▼ 3.8	SO	Cattle guard.
0.3 ▲	SO	Cattle guard.
▼ 4.0	SO	Cattle guard.
0.1 ▲	SO	Cattle guard.
▼ 4.1		Trail ends at T-intersection with Tepusquet Road. Turn left for Santa Maria.
0.0 ▲		Trail commences on Tepusquet Road, 5.6 miles north of Foxen Canyon Road. Zero trip meter and turn east over cattle guard onto Colson Canyon Road. Road crosses private property for first 3 miles.

GPS: N34°55.43' W120°13.14'

CENTRAL MOUNTAINS #36: BUCKHORN RIDGE TRAIL

CENTRAL MOUNTAINS #36

Buckhorn Ridge Trail

STARTING POINT Central Mountains #35: Miranda Pine Road, 10 miles south of Central Mountains #37: Sierra Madre Road

FINISHING POINT Buckhorn Ridge

TOTAL MILEAGE 3.6 miles (one-way)

UNPAVED MILEAGE: 3.6 miles

DRIVING TIME 1 hour (one-way)

ELEVATION RANGE 1,800–2,400 feet

USUALLY OPEN Year-round

BEST TIME TO TRAVEL Dry weather

DIFFICULTY RATING 3

SCENIC RATING 9

REMOTENESS RATING +0

Special Attractions

■ Moderately challenging spur trail.

■ Excellent wide ranging views over the Sierra Madre Range.

■ Access to trails suitable for motorbikes and non-motorized use.

Description

Buckhorn Ridge Trail is a spur trail that runs in a northwest direction from the main Central Mountains #35: Miranda Pine Road. The trail is designated for 4WDs, ATVs, and motorbikes and undulates for 3.6 miles along the narrow Buckhorn Ridge. Views from the ridge are fantastic. To the north is Pine Canyon, with the Sierra Madre rising in the distance. To the south is Bear Canyon. Three trails for motorbikes and non-motorized recreation lead off from the main trail. These side trails are not designated for vehicles.

In recent times, brush threatened to obscure this beautiful ridge trail, but the track was widened in mid-2000 and is now suitable for wide vehicles for most of its length. The final 2 miles to the Los Padres National Forest boundary can be very brushy at times, and most people will probably prefer to turn back shortly after the intersection with the Bear Canyon Trail, which is the final point described in the directions.

Yucca growing beneath Greasewood on a dry ridge above Smith Canyon

The trail is seldom used and brushy, but it gives some good views

The trail's main difficulty comes from steep climbs and descents, which, combined with the loose, low traction surface and occasional side slope, make this a moderately challenging trail. It should be avoided in wet weather.

Current Road Information
Los Padres National Forest
Santa Lucia Ranger District
1616 North Carlotti Drive
Santa Maria, CA 93454
(805) 925-9538

Map References
BLM   Santa Maria
USFS Los Padres National Forest: Monterey
      and Santa Lucia Ranger Districts
USGS 1:24,000 Manzanita Mtn.,
      Tepusquet Canyon
      1:100,000 Santa Maria
Maptech CD-ROM: San Luis Obispo/Los
      Padres National Forest
*Southern & Central California Atlas &
      Gazetteer,* pp. 60, 74
California Road & Recreation Atlas, p. 100

Route Directions

▼ 0.0   From Central Mountains #35: Miranda
               Pine Road, 10 miles south of Central
               Mountains #37: Sierra Madre Road,
               zero trip meter and turn southeast on
               small formed trail at sign for Buckhorn
               Ridge ORV Trail.
               GPS: N34°59.22' W120°05.68'

▼ 2.1   SO   Tank on left; then Bear Canyon Spur
               Trail #34 (31W14) on left for motor-
               bikes only—rated black.
               GPS: N34°59.08' W120°07.44'

▼ 2.7   SO   Track on right is Horseshoe Spring
               Spur #33 (31W12) for motorbikes and
               non-motorized use—rated blue. Zero
               trip meter.
               GPS: N34°59.39' W120°07.89'

▼ 0.0   Continue to the northwest.
▼ 0.4   SO   Tank on left.
               GPS: N34°59.58' W120°08.24'

▼ 0.9   Track on left is Bear Canyon #34A

Sections of Buckhorn Ridge Trail can be loose and slightly off-camber

(31W13) for motorbikes and non-motorized use—rated black. Trail continues past this point to national forest boundary, but it quickly becomes overgrown.

GPS: N34°59.67′ W120°08.74′

CENTRAL MOUNTAINS #37

Sierra Madre Road

STARTING POINT California 166, 26.3 miles east of US 101

FINISHING POINT McPherson Peak

TOTAL MILEAGE 29.7 miles (one-way)

UNPAVED MILEAGE: 29.7 miles

DRIVING TIME 3 hours (one-way)

ELEVATION RANGE 1,400–5,900 feet

USUALLY OPEN Year–round

BEST TIME TO TRAVEL Dry weather

DIFFICULTY RATING 2

SCENIC RATING 8

REMOTENESS RATING +0

Special Attractions

- Wildlife viewing—chance to see Tule elk and the California condors.
- Long, winding ridge trail with great views.
- Can be combined with Central Mountains #38: Bates Canyon Trail to make a loop back to California 166.

History

The name Sierra Madre (Spanish for "Mother Range") reflects the fact that this mountain range serves as a backbone from which other ranges branch off. The range was officially designated as the Sierra Madre in 1965.

The trail leaves from the Cuyama Valley, which is best known for the oil strikes of the 1940s and 1950s. The town of Cuyama was a company town established by the Richfield Oil Company to house its employees. In its heyday, Richfield's oil fields were the fifth most productive in California. The oil and gas industry still figures quite prominently in the valley and is a major local employer.

The name Cuyama is pronounced "Kwee-ah-ma," though mispronunciations abound. The name is thought to have originated from

the Chumash word for Valley of the Clams. This theory is supported by a deep layer of fossilized marine sediment that has been found throughout the valley. Dating back about 25 million years, this sediment includes remains of the *Ostrea titan,* or huge oyster. The name Cuyama is documented as far back as 1843, as part of the name Arroyo Llamado de Cuyam.

Some of the earliest inhabitants of the valley were Chumash Indians, whose population reached about 20,000 before the arrival of the Spanish. The Chumash were hunter-gatherers who harvested pinyon nuts on the ridges and hunted pronghorn, rabbits, and quails in the valley. They did not practice agriculture. The valley is home to cave and rock paintings that are approximately 500 to 800 years old.

It is not known what became of the Chumash Indians who made their homes in the valley. One persistent legend relates the tale of an unscrupulous trader, Alexis Godey. Godey

Central Mountains #35: Miranda Pine Road meanders down Kerry Canyon from Miranda Pine Campground

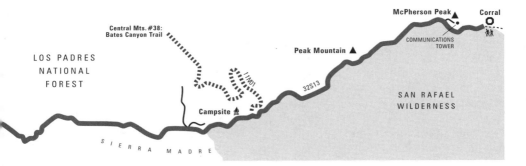

took over land in the valley in the 1850s and appropriated government cattle intended for the Chumash. He sold the cattle to local miners and kept the profits for himself. Despite his mistreatment of the Chumash, he was still annoyed by their presence in the valley. Seeking to end his "problem," he invited all the local Chumash to a meal and fed them poisoned beans, sparing only one young girl whom he wanted for himself. This story is largely unsubstantiated and has been vigorously denied on several occasions, but it still persists in the oral tradition of present-day locals.

The first Europeans in the Cuyama Valley were the Spanish, who traveled north from Mexico. There were two large Mexican land grants in the Cuyama Valley. On the whole, Spanish ranches did not flourish in the region; no provision was made for the long periods of drought. The land soon became overgrazed and a number of the imported longhorn cattle were left to die.

The beginning of this trail provides spectacular views of Cuyama Valley

Description

This long graded road runs along the ridge tops of the Sierra Madre for more than 30 miles to McPherson Peak. Along the way it passes many other peaks, including Timber Peak, Spoor Peak, Center Peak, and Peak Mountain.

There are only a few side trails that leave from this road. The San Rafael Wilderness is on the western side, which precludes vehicular access. The Cuyama River Valley is to the east, with a steep drop down from the range that limits potential exit points.

Ten miles from the start of the road is the small Miranda Pine Campground, located on top of the ridge. The open campground has a couple of tables, fire rings, and a pit toilet. A Forest Adventure Pass is required, but there is no other fee. Opposite the turn to the campground is a short spur to Miranda Pine Spring and one of the major exits from this area, Central Mountains #35: Miranda Pine Road.

The main trail continues along the ridge for another 22 miles, running underneath the row of peaks that make up the range. It passes the top of Central Mountains #38: Bates Canyon Trail, which can be used as an exit to California 166. There is a shady campsite just prior to this intersection, one of the few along the trail.

The final section of the trail forks, with one branch climbing up to the communications towers on McPherson Peak, and the other continuing to a locked gate on the edge of the San Rafael Wilderness. The trail beyond the gate is an administrative road; there is no public use. There is hiking access into the wilderness beyond this point, and the region contains a few examples of prehistoric rock art.

The area is used as part of the California condor recovery program. These massive birds can often be seen soaring above and are recognizable from underneath by numbered identification tags and a white triangle spreading over both wings. Do not approach or feed the condors; this will jeopardize their chances of remaining wild. Condors have also been known to approach humans and should be discouraged by yelling or clapping your hands loudly. The end of the trail is an excellent place for seeing these birds.

Current Road Information

Los Padres National Forest
Santa Lucia Ranger District
1616 North Carlotti Drive
Santa Maria, CA 93454
(805) 925-9538

Map References

BLM   San Luis Obispo, Cuyama
USFS   Los Padres National Forest: Monterey and Santa Lucia Ranger Districts
USGS   1:24,000   Miranda Pine Mt., Manzanita Mt., Bates Canyon, Peak Mt.
           1:100,000   San Luis Obispo, Cuyama
Maptech CD-ROM: San Luis Obispo/Los Padres National Forest
Southern & Central California Atlas & Gazetteer, pp. 60, 61, 75
California Road & Recreation Atlas, pp. 91, 100, 101

Route Directions

▼ 0.0   From California 166, 26.3 miles east of US 101, zero trip meter and turn southeast on graded dirt road at sign for Sierra Madre Road. Turn is signposted to McPherson Peak. Road is marked 32S13 and is 0.3 miles east of Central Mountains #39: Big Rocks Trail. Immediately cross cattle guard.

4.9 ▲   Trail ends at intersection with California 166. Turn left for Santa Maria; turn right for Maricopa. Central Mountains #39: Big Rocks Trail is 0.3 miles to the west.
           GPS: N35°06.69′ W120°05.41′

▼ 0.1   SO Information board on right.
4.8 ▲   SO Information board on left.
▼ 0.5   SO Cattle guard. Entering Los Padres National Forest.
4.4 ▲   SO Cattle guard. Leaving Los Padres National Forest.
▼ 2.0   SO Cross over petroleum pipeline.
2.9 ▲   SO Cross over petroleum pipeline.
▼ 2.9   SO Track on left.
2.0 ▲   SO Track on right.
▼ 3.2   SO Track on right.
1.7 ▲   SO Track on left.
           GPS: N35°05.26′ W120°04.17′

▼ 3.8　SO　Cattle guard.

1.1 ▲　SO　Cattle guard.

▼ 4.9　SO　Track on right over rise is Old Sierra Madre Road, which goes 2.5 miles to a locked gate. Zero trip meter.

0.0 ▲　　　Continue to the north.

GPS: N35°04.29′ W120°03.40′

▼ 0.0　　　Continue to the southeast.

3.7 ▲　SO　Track on left over rise is Old Sierra Madre Road, which goes 2.5 miles to a locked gate. Zero trip meter.

▼ 0.2　SO　Track on left to tank.

3.5 ▲　SO　Track on right to tank.

GPS: N35°04.19′ W120°03.21′

▼ 0.8　SO　Track on right.

2.9 ▲　SO　Track on left.

▼ 2.4　SO　Track on left goes 0.3 miles to communications towers on Plowshare Peak.

1.3 ▲　BL　Track on right goes 0.3 miles to communications towers on Plowshare Peak.

GPS: N35°02.86′ W120°02.23′

▼ 3.7　SO　Track on left goes 0.4 miles to Miranda Pine Campground. Two tracks on right—first goes 0.4 miles to Miranda Pine Spring, second goes through closure gate and is Central Mountains #35: Miranda Pine Road. Zero trip meter.

0.0 ▲　　　Continue to the northwest.

GPS: N35°01.95′ W120°02.00′

▼ 0.0　　　Continue to the southeast.

12.8 ▲　SO　Track on right goes 0.4 miles to Miranda Pine Campground. Two tracks on left—first goes through closure gate and is Central Mountains #35: Miranda Pine Road, second goes 0.4 miles to Miranda Pine Spring. Zero trip meter.

▼ 7.3　SO　Cattle guard.

5.5 ▲　SO　Cattle guard.

GPS: N34°58.04′ W119°58.12′

▼ 10.8　SO　Two tracks on left up hill.

2.0 ▲　SO　Two tracks on right up hill.

▼ 12.5　SO　Campsite on left.

0.3 ▲　SO　Campsite on right.

GPS: N34°55.14′ W119°54.71′

▼ 12.8　SO　Graded road on left is Central Mountains #38: Bates Canyon Trail (11N01) to California 166. Zero trip meter.

0.0 ▲　　　Continue to the west.

GPS: N34°54.99′ W119°54.47′

▼ 0.0　　　Continue to the southeast, remaining on 32S13 and following sign to McPherson Peak.

▼ 6.8　BR　Trail forks. Track to the left goes 0.8 miles to towers on McPherson Peak. Zero trip meter.

GPS: N34°53.57′ W119°49.04′

▼ 0.0　　　Continue to the east.

▼ 1.5　　　Vehicle trail ends at a corral and locked gate on the edge of the San Rafael Wilderness. Hikers and horses only past this point.

GPS: N34°52.73′ W119°48.33′

Please respect Native American historical artifacts

Bates Canyon Trail

STARTING POINT Central Mountains #37: Sierra Madre Road, 21.4 miles from California 166

FINISHING POINT California 166, 12.5 miles west of New Cuyama

TOTAL MILEAGE 11.9 miles

UNPAVED MILEAGE: 7.2 miles

DRIVING TIME 1 hour

ELEVATION RANGE 1,800–5,200 feet

USUALLY OPEN Year-round

BEST TIME TO TRAVEL Dry weather

DIFFICULTY RATING 2

SCENIC RATING 8

REMOTENESS RATING +0

Special Attractions

■ Alternative exit from the long Central Mountains #37: Sierra Madre Road.

■ Winding descent into Bates Canyon.

History

The lower end of this trail travels along Cottonwood Canyon, which is the final resting place of one of the most famous pioneers in the region. In 1841, the Bartleson-Bidwell Party was heading west to settle in California. Sixty-nine men, women, and children left Missouri, but six months later only twenty-four of them had reached the San Joaquin Valley. Many were turned back by fierce weather and harsh conditions. Two of the survivors were Nancy Kelsey and her husband, Benjamin. Nancy became the first white woman to cross the Sierra Nevada into California.

Nancy's main claim to fame was that she was chosen to create the flag for the California Republic during the Bear Flag Revolt of 1846. Using a design created by William Todd, a nephew of Abraham Lincoln's, Nancy created the new flag from unbleached muslin and a strip torn from her red petticoat. Her creation is still the state flag of California, though the grizzly bear represented on it is now extinct in the state.

The trail begins to wind slowly into Bates Canyon—a meandering descent of nearly 3,500 feet

The old, steel-banded wooden tank of Cole Spring is well camoflagued beneath the canopy of oaks

MEXICAN WAR (1846–48) AND THE BEAR FLAG REVOLT

The American annexation of Texas in 1845 set the stage for war between Mexico and the United States. Continued border disputes fueled anger between the two nations. Mexico severed relations in March 1845. President James Polk would not be refused. He sent John Slidell on a secret mission to Mexico City. His orders were to settle U.S. claims and to purchase California and the New Mexico territory for $30 million. Slidell's mission wasn't a complete secret. Mexican officials knew he was coming and would not talk to him about an issue they considered irrelevant to the more immediate boundary question. Polk ordered Zachary Taylor to occupy the disputed territory between the Nueces and Rio Grande Rivers in Texas. Mexican troops crossed the Rio Grande and fired on American soldiers, killing 16. Polk proclaimed that Mexico "invaded our territory and shed American blood on American soil." On May 11, 1846, Congress overwhelmingly supported a declaration of war.

As Taylor began his march into the heart of Mexico, Colonel Stephen Kearny (later brevetted brigadier general) was to march through Mexican territory and take New Mexico and California. Kearny's march through the Southwest went without a hitch. Mexican citizens generally welcomed his occupation and only a few resented it. Hearing reports that the American flag was flying throughout California, Kearny left the bulk of his force in Santa Fe and proceeded toward Los Angeles with only 100 men.

Fighting had been going on in California for several months when Kearny arrived. Even before the United States declared war on Mexico, volunteers had organized into a "California Battalion" under the guidance of explorer John Charles Frémont, son-in-law of Thomas Benton, the chairman of the Senate Committee on Territories. The unpaid battalion captured Mexican General Mariano Vallejo and began to raise their distinctive flag over California towns, declaring a California Republic. The banner depicted a grizzly bear and the uprising became known as the Bear Flag Revolt.

Even as the Bear Flaggers were conquering Sonoma, Commodore John Drake Sloat was sailing with 250 troops to California. On July 7, 1846, he landed in Monterey and raised the Stars and Stripes above the provincial capital. By the time Commodore Robert F. Stockon arrived to replace Sloat a week later, the American flag was flying over Yerba Buena (San Francisco), Sutter's Fort, Sonoma, and Bodega Bay.

Commodore Stockton organized the Bear Flaggers under the United States banner and entered Los Angeles, conquering the town and leaving a force of 50 to guard it. However,

---

Nancy and Benjamin were keen travelers and were some of the first to stake mining claims in the Sierra Nevada foothills. Kelsey's Dry Diggings in El Dorado County is named after them, as is Kelsey Canyon in the Sierra Nevada. After Benjamin's death in 1888, Nancy received a government homestead plot of 160 acres in what is now Cottonwood Canyon in the Cuyama Valley. She earned her living raising hens and traveling into Santa Maria by buckboard to sell them. Nancy died August 9, 1896, at age 73, and was buried on private property in Cottonwood Canyon.

Description

This trail leaves the long Central Mountains #37: Sierra Madre Road nearly two-thirds of the way along its route. The graded road immediately starts winding down some gentle switchbacks, passing Bates Peak, to drop into Bates Canyon. The deep gullies within the canyon hide a couple of springs that are visible beside the trail. Older topographical maps show campgrounds at these springs, but they no longer exist.

Close to the exit of Bates Canyon is the Bates Canyon USFS Campground. The open area has some shade and a couple of picnic tables and fire rings. A Forest Adventure Pass is required.

the occupying force soon angered local Californios (Hispanic Californians) and on September 23 they surrounded the American garrison and forced the troops to flee. Reinforcements arrived two weeks later, but these too were rebuffed by the Angelenos. The engagement became known as "The Battle of the Old Woman's Gun," after the unique tactics with which it was won. During the earlier occupation of Los Angeles, a superannuated lady had buried an antique cannon in her yard. Unearthed for the uprising, the Mexicans tied the weapon to a mud wagon. They rushed it along their defenses, disorienting the U.S. forces and convincing them that their adversaries were well armed.

Meanwhile, General Kearny was having problems of his own. South of Los Angeles, near present-day Escondido, Kearny's forces were surrounded by Mexican troops. The Americans were already short of supplies and their gunpowder was damp. In the hand-to-hand combat that ensued, Kearny lost a quarter of his small force. The besieged Americans ate mule meat for four days before Commodore Stockton sent relief from San Diego. Together, Stockton, Kearny, and Frémont planned to retake Los Angeles with a combined force of 1,000 men. On January 13, 1847, Mexican commander Andrés Pico surrendered to Frémont. His brother, Pío Pico, the last Mexican governor, had already fled. The war in California was won.

The main conflict, however, was still raging. General Taylor was confronted several times in his march through Mexico. His troops emerged victorious, but their march south was slow. President Polk decided to send General Winfield Scott with an army by sea to capture the seaport of Veracruz. After a three-week siege, the city fell. Scott now had a clear path to Mexico City, which he took on September 14, 1847.

On February 2, 1848, just a few days after the discovery of gold near Sutter's Fort, Mexico signed the Treaty of Guadalupe Hidalgo, thereby relinquishing control over the huge parcel of land that now composes New Mexico, Utah, Nevada, Arizona, western Colorado, Texas, and California. For this vast territory the United States paid just $15 million. Although the United States gained a large stretch of land, the acquisition nearly vaulted the nation into civil war. Discussions raged over which states should be slave states. The country slipped further into feelings of separation between North and South, but the Compromise of 1850 settled the immediate argument. This agreement also allowed California to enter the union as a free state.

The trail exits the forest past the disused White Oaks Forest Station. The road past here was paved once, but has fallen into disrepair and is rougher than the graded dirt road above it. At Cottonwood Canyon, the road becomes paved and crosses private land, looking north to the Caliente Range, before it finishes on California 166.

Current Road Information

Los Padres National Forest
Santa Lucia Ranger District
1616 North Carlotti Drive
Santa Maria, CA 93454
(805) 925-9538

Map References

BLM   Cuyama, Taft
USFS   Los Padres National Forest:
       Monterey and Santa Lucia Ranger
       Districts
USGS   1:24,000   Bates Canyon, Taylor
       Canyon
       1:100,000 Cuyama, Taft
Maptech CD-ROM: San Luis Obispo/Los
       Padres National Forest
*Southern & Central California Atlas &
       Gazetteer,* pp. 75, 61
California Road & Recreation Atlas, p. 101

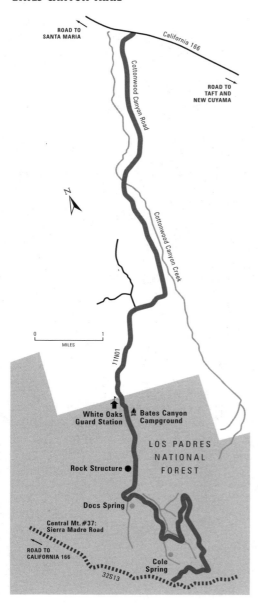

Route Directions

▼ 0.0   Trail commences on Central Mountains #37: Sierra Madre Road, 21.4 miles from California 166. Zero trip meter at sign for Bates Canyon Road and proceed southeast on roughly graded dirt

road, following sign to California 166 through closure gate.

5.6 ▲   Trail finishes on Central Mountains #37: Sierra Madre Road. Turn right to exit to California 166; turn left to continue to the end of the trail.
         GPS: N34°54.99' W119°54.47'

▼ 2.8   SO Cross through wash.
2.8 ▲   SO Cross through wash.
         GPS: N34°55.44' W119°54.17'

▼ 3.1   SO Cross through wash; then Cole Spring on left.
2.5 ▲   SO Cole Spring on right; then cross through wash.
         GPS: N34°55.55' W119°54.47'

▼ 4.1   SO Cross through wash. Tank on left is Doc Spring.
1.5 ▲   SO Tank on right is Doc Spring. Cross through wash.
         GPS: N34°56.17' W119°54.81'

▼ 4.8   SO Stone structure on left.
0.8 ▲   SO Stone structure on right.
         GPS: N34°56.55' W119°54.56'

▼ 5.4   SO Closure gate.
0.2 ▲   SO Closure gate.
▼ 5.6   SO Bates Canyon USFS Campground on right. Zero trip meter.
0.0 ▲   Continue to the southeast.
         GPS: N34°57.28' W119°54.43'

▼ 0.0   Continue to the northwest.
6.3 ▲   BR Bates Canyon USFS Campground on left. Zero trip meter.
▼ 0.1   SO Track on left.
6.2 ▲   SO Track on right.
▼ 0.2   SO White Oaks Forest Service Station (now closed) on right and left. Leaving Los Padres National Forest.
6.1 ▲   SO White Oaks Forest Service Station (now closed) on right and left. Entering Los Padres National Forest.
         GPS: N34°57.42' W119°54.45'

▼ 0.7   SO Two cattle guards. Road was once paved but is breaking up and is mainly dirt.

The trail snakes down Bates Canyon from Sierra Madre Ridge

5.6 ▲　SO　Two cattle guards. Road is now graded dirt.

▼ 1.7　BR　Bear right onto small paved road.
Paved road on left.

4.6 ▲　BL　Bear left at sign for Bates Canyon
Road. Paved road on right.
GPS: N34°58.55′ W119°53.83′

▼ 2.1　TL　Turn left onto Cottonwood Canyon
Road. Private entrance ahead.

4.2 ▲　TR　Turn right onto Foothill Road. Private
entrance on left. Follow sign for Los
Padres National Forest.
GPS: N34°58.62′ W119°53.34′

▼ 2.8　SO　Cattle guard.

3.5 ▲　SO　Cattle guard.

▼ 3.9　SO　Cross through Cottonwood Canyon
Creek on concrete ford.

2.4 ▲　SO　Cross through Cottonwood Canyon
Creek on concrete ford.
GPS: N35°00.22′ W119°53.41′

▼ 6.3　　　Cattle guard; then trail ends at T-intersection with California 166. Turn right
for Maricopa; turn left for Santa Maria.

0.0 ▲　　　Trail starts on California 166, 12.5 miles

west of New Cuyama and immediately
west of mile marker 52. Zero trip meter
and turn southwest on paved road
sign-posted Cottonwood Canyon Road.
Immediately cross cattle guard.
GPS: N35°02.07′ W119°52.56′

CENTRAL MOUNTAINS #39

Big Rocks Trail

STARTING POINT California 166, 26 miles
east of US 101
FINISHING POINT Central Mountains #42:
Paradise Road at the western end
TOTAL MILEAGE 4.4 miles
UNPAVED MILEAGE: 4.4 miles
DRIVING TIME 30 minutes
ELEVATION RANGE 1,400–2,000 feet
USUALLY OPEN Year-round
BEST TIME TO TRAVEL Dry weather
DIFFICULTY RATING 2
SCENIC RATING 8
REMOTENESS RATING +0

Big Rocks are a striking feature along this easy trail

Special Attractions

- Wildlife viewing for Tule elk.
- Access to many challenging trails for 4WDs, ATVs, and motorbikes.

History

The area around Branch Creek is a habitat of the Tule elk. Although once plentiful in the central coast woodlands, these elk were driven to near extinction by 1850 because of loss of habitat. One herd in Kern County, the Tupman herd, was protected and has managed to survive. The herd thrived so well that farmers found them to be a nuisance, and some were relocated to other areas in California.

Tule elk were re-introduced into this area in 1983 with the transplant of 17 animals from the Tupman herd. The Tule elk, the smallest subspecies of elk in North America, are now thriving, with approximately 3,000 animals spread throughout 19 regions of the state.

Description

This short, roughly graded road forms the backbone for a network of trails within this region. However, the trail is attractive in its own right, running along a roughly graded dirt road from California 166. It crosses the Cuyama River and runs alongside Branch Creek into Los Padres National Forest. There is a network of side 4WD trails of varying standards that offer access to the more open ridge tops on either side of the valley.

The road is roughly graded and suitable for high-clearance 2WD vehicles in dry weather; in wet weather it is likely to be impassable for any vehicle. A couple of the steeper sections of the trail are paved in order to control erosion.

The trail passes alongside the Big Rocks, large outcroppings of conglomerate rocks that line the small valley. The trail continues on, passing a couple of very pleasant camping areas to finish at the boundary of private property.

A Forest Adventure Pass is required for all national forest recreation activities.

Current Road Information

Los Padres National Forest
Santa Lucia Ranger District
1616 North Carlotti Drive
Santa Maria, CA 93454
(805) 925-9538

Map References

BLM San Luis Obispo
USFS Los Padres National Forest:
      Monterey and Santa
      Lucia Ranger Districts
USGS 1:24,000 Miranda Pine Mtn.,
      Branch Mtn., Los Machos Hills
      1:100,000 San Luis Obispo
Maptech CD-ROM: San Luis Obispo/Los
      Padres National Forest
Southern & Central California Atlas &
      Gazetteer, p. 60
California Road & Recreation Atlas, p. 91

Route Directions

▼ 0.0   From California 166, 26 miles east of
            US 101, zero trip meter and turn north-
            west on graded dirt road. Pass under
            the entrance of Rock Front Ranch and
            immediately bear left. There is no for-
            est road marker on the highway.
1.9 ▲   Trail bears right and finishes on
            California 166. Turn left for Taft; turn
            right for US 101 and Santa Maria.

GPS: N35°06.65' W120°05.68'

▼ 0.1 SO Cross through Cuyama River on
          concrete ford.
1.8 ▲ SO Cross through Cuyama River on
          concrete ford.
▼ 0.2 SO Cattle guard.
1.7 ▲ SO Cattle guard.
▼ 0.3 SO Parking area and information board
          on left.
1.6 ▲ SO Parking area and information board
          on right.
▼ 0.4 SO Closure gate; then cross through wash.
1.5 ▲ SO Cross through wash; then closure gate.
▼ 0.5 SO Cattle guard.
1.4 ▲ SO Cattle guard.
▼ 0.6 SO Cross through wash.
1.3 ▲ SO Cross through wash.
▼ 0.7 SO Cross through two washes. Road is
          paved as it climbs the hill.
1.2 ▲ SO Road is paved as it descends the hill.
          Cross through two washes.
▼ 1.5 BL Track on right is Big Rocks Road #28
          (32S25) for 4WDs, ATVs, and motor-
          bikes—rated black.

This pleasant trail hugs the wash, weaving through oaks beneath Big Rocks

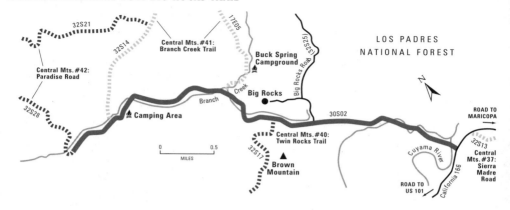

0.4 ▲   BR   Track on left is Big Rocks Road #28 (32S25) for 4WDs, ATVs, and motorbikes—rated black.
GPS: N35°07.46' W120°06.65'

▼ 1.9   BR   Track on left is Central Mountains #40: Twin Rocks Trail, marked Twin Rocks Road #30 (32S17) for 4WDs, ATVs, and motorbikes—rated black. Zero trip meter.

0.0 ▲   Continue to the east.
GPS: N35°07.68' W120°06.99'

▼ 0.0   Continue to the northwest.

0.7 ▲   BL   Track on right is Central Mountains #40: Twin Rocks Trail, marked Twin Rocks Road #30 (32S17) for 4WDs, ATVs, and motorbikes-rated black. Zero trip meter.

▼ 0.4   SO   Cross through wash.

0.3 ▲   SO   Cross through wash.

▼ 0.6   SO   Cross through wash.

0.1 ▲   SO   Cross through wash.

▼ 0.7   SO   Track on right is Central Mountains #41: Branch Creek Trail #27 (17E05) for 4WDs, ATVs, and motorbikes-rated blue. Zero trip meter.

0.0 ▲   Continue to the southwest.
GPS: N35°08.08' W120°07.26'

▼ 0.0   Continue to the west and cross through wash.

1.4 ▲   SO   Cross through wash; then track on left is other end of Central Mountains #41: Branch Creek Trail #27 (17E05) for 4WDs, ATVs, and motorbikes—rated blue. Zero trip meter.

▼ 0.1   SO   Cross through wash.

1.3 ▲   SO   Cross through wash.

▼ 0.2   SO   Cross through wash.

1.2 ▲   SO   Cross through wash.

▼ 0.3   SO   Cattle guard.

1.1 ▲   SO   Cattle guard.

▼ 0.6   SO   Cross through wash. Trail crosses wash many times in next 0.8 miles.

0.8 ▲   SO   Cross through wash.

▼ 1.2   SO   Camping area on left.

0.2 ▲   SO   Camping area on right.
GPS: N35°08.38' W120°08.24'

▼ 1.4   SO   Cattle guard; then track on right is other end of Central Mountains #41: Branch Creek Trail. Initially marked as 35 Canyon (32S14) for 4WDs, ATVs, and motorbikes—rated green. Zero trip meter.

0.0 ▲   Continue east and cross second cattle guard.
GPS: N35°08.35' W120°08.42'

▼ 0.0   Continue to the southwest and cross second cattle guard.

0.4 ▲   SO   Cattle guard; then track on left is Central Mountains #41: Branch Creek Trail. Initially marked as 35 Canyon (32S14) for 4WDs, ATVs, and motorbikes—rated green. Zero trip meter. Trail crosses wash many times in next 0.8 miles.

▼ 0.3 SO Cross through wash.

0.1 ▲ SO Cross through wash.

▼ 0.4 Cross through wash; then track on right is Central Mountains #42: Paradise Road, marked as Los Machos #25 (32S28) for 4WDs, ATVs, and motorbikes—rated green. Trail ends immediately past this intersection at a locked gate before private property.

0.0 ▲ Trail commences at the western end of Central Mountains #42: Paradise Road. Zero trip meter and turn northeast on graded dirt road. Trail to the west is blocked by a locked gate before private property.
  GPS: N35°08.30′ W120°08.85′

CENTRAL MOUNTAINS #40

Twin Rocks Trail

STARTING POINT Central Mountains #39: Big Rocks Trail, 1.9 miles north of California 166

FINISHING POINT Shaw Ridge

TOTAL MILEAGE 5.6 miles (one-way)

UNPAVED MILEAGE: 5.6 miles

DRIVING TIME 45 minutes (one-way)

ELEVATION RANGE 1,400–2,500 feet

USUALLY OPEN Year-round

BEST TIME TO TRAVEL Dry weather

DIFFICULTY RATING 6, 7 for last 0.7 miles

SCENIC RATING 9

REMOTENESS RATING +0

Special Attractions

■ Winding trail with a very steep grade.
■ Views into the Cuyama River Valley.

History

There are some small pieces of private property in this section of Los Padres National Forest. One of them was settled in 1893 by John Logan, after whom Logan Ridge is named. It is likely that John worked on a nearby ranch and gained his property through continuous occupation of the land, a common practice in those days.

Description

The trail leaves Central Mountains #39: Big Rocks Trail, the main backbone through this region of forest, and immediately starts to climb steeply, switchbacking its way out of the valley to the ridge tops. The trail is rated a 6 for difficulty because of the steepness of the grade and occasional low traction sections. The surface is generally smooth; it is not a rock crawling trail.

At the top of the first steep climb on Brown Mountain, a short spur trail leads off to a viewpoint over the Cuyama Valley. The mile-long spur leads down to a steeply sloping overlook that offers great views. The best view of the Twin Rocks is to the south from the spur trail.

The trail descends steeply to cross a creek before climbing again to run along Shaw Ridge. There are some steep sections, particularly after the trail passes the Shaw Ridge Trail sign. The final 0.6 miles of the trail jumps in difficulty to a 7 because of the extreme steepness and looseness of the trail. Traction is very poor. The trail ends at a Road Closed sign, so be prepared to return the way you came. Unless you are driving a suitably equipped vehicle to tackle the steepest section—lockers are advised—it is best to turn around at the point indicated in the route description. This will keep the difficulty level at a 6.

Current Road Information

Los Padres National Forest
Santa Lucia Ranger District
1616 Carlotti Drive
Santa Maria, CA 93454
(805) 925-9538

Map References

BLM   San Luis Obispo
USFS Los Padres National Forest: Monterey and Santa Lucia Ranger Districts
USGS 1:24,000 Branch Mtn., Miranda Pine Mtn., Chimney Canyon, Los Machos Hills
      1:100,000 San Luis Obispo
Maptech CD-ROM: San Luis Obispo/Los Padres National Forest
Southern & Central California Atlas & Gazetteer, p. 60
California Road & Recreation Atlas, p. 91

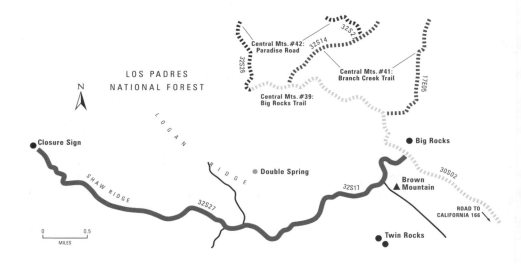

Route Directions

▼ 0.0   From Central Mountains #39: Big Rocks Trail, 1.9 miles north of California 166, zero trip meter and turn southeast on formed trail. Road is marked Twin Rocks Road #30 (32S17) for 4WDs, ATVs, and motorbikes-rated black.

GPS: N35°07.68' W120°06.99'

▼ 0.2   SO   Turnout on right.

▼ 0.6   BR   Well-used, unmarked track on left goes

Big Rocks area seen from the steep climb up Twin Rocks Road

Descending the final part of this ridge trail

The descent toward Big Rocks

1 mile to a viewpoint with superb views over the Cuyama River Valley and Twin Rocks. Zero trip meter.
GPS: N35°07.45' W120°07.25'

▼ 0.0   Continue to the southwest.
▼ 0.3   SO   Cattle guard.
▼ 0.6   SO   Track on right.
▼ 2.0   SO   Track on right leads into private property.
         GPS: N35°06.92' W120°09.00'

▼ 2.2   BR   Track on left; bear right onto trail marked Shaw Ridge #22 (32S27) for 4WDs, ATVs, and motorbikes-rated black. Zero trip meter.
         GPS: N35°06.91' W120°09.12'

▼ 0.0   Continue to the northwest.
▼ 2.1   SO   Trail increases in difficulty in 0.1 miles. Turn here if not equipped to tackle the steeper, looser 7-rated trail. This is the final turning point before the 7-rated section. It is a very tight turn.
         GPS: N35°07.34' W120°10.80'

▼ 2.3   SO   Trail becomes extremely steep as it descends from Shaw Ridge.
         GPS: N35°07.36' W120°11.10'

▼ 2.8   Trail ends at road closure sign.
         GPS: N35°07.70' W120°11.40'

CENTRAL MOUNTAINS #41

Branch Creek Trail

STARTING POINT Central Mountains #39: Big Rocks Trail, 2.6 miles north of California 166

FINISHING POINT Central Mountains #39: Big Rocks Trail, 4 miles north of California 166

TOTAL MILEAGE 7.3 miles

UNPAVED MILEAGE: 7.3 miles

DRIVING TIME 1.5 hours

ELEVATION RANGE 1,400–2,400 feet

USUALLY OPEN Year-round

BEST TIME TO TRAVEL Dry weather

DIFFICULTY RATING 5

SCENIC RATING 8

REMOTENESS RATING +0

Bear prints are easy to spot in the deep dust below Branch Mountain

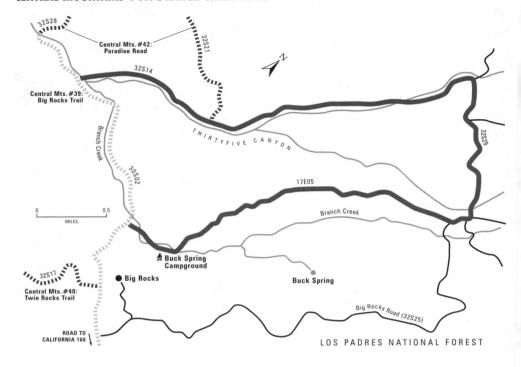

Special Attractions

- Moderately challenging ridge top and canyon trail.
- Intersects with a number of other 4WD trails.

Description

This trail offers a moderately difficult loop from Central Mountains #39: Big Rocks Trail. Initially the trail is formed, passing through the forest service camping area at Buck Spring. This large open area has no marked sites, just a couple of tables and a fire ring. A Forest Adventure Pass is required, but there is no other fee.

The trail continues along Branch Creek for a short distance, before leaving the creek to climb steeply onto the ridge top. The grade is moderately steep, and the surface is even but loose. Branch Creek is seen down to the east through the low, scrubby vegetation. The moderately steep grade continues along the ridge tops. Panoramic views encompass the surrounding hills, and you will be able to see many of the other 4WD trails in the area.

The trail forks 2.4 miles from the start; both forks become black-rated trails because of steep grades and deep, talcum powderlike surface that makes traction difficult. Travel is easier if following the forward route directions. Following the reverse directions forces you to climb up the loosest section. The final section joins the better-surfaced trail that runs along Thirty-five Canyon to rejoin Big Rocks Road.

The soft surface makes it easy to see the tracks of animals that have walked along the trail. Look out for Tule elk tracks and the distinctive tracks of black bears.

Current Road Information

Los Padres National Forest
Santa Lucia Ranger District
1616 North Carlotti Drive
Santa Maria, CA 93454
(805) 925-9538

Map References

BLM   San Luis Obispo
USFS   Los Padres National Forest:

BLACK BEAR

Black bears can actually be black, brown, or cinnamon. Their bodies are powerful and densely furred, with slight shoulder humps, small rounded ears, small close-set eyes, and five dark, strongly curved claws on each paw. Females range in weight from 120 to 200 pounds, and males range from 200 to 400 pounds. Nocturnal and solitary, black bears prefer forested habitats throughout the year, although they can sometimes be seen on open slopes searching for fresh greens. They usually make their dens in tree cavities, under logs, in brush piles, or under buildings; the dens are lined with leaves or grass. Black bears are omnivorous. They feast on grasses, sedges, berries, fruits, tree bark, insects, honey, eggs, fish, rodents, and even garbage. In the fall they go into a feeding frenzy to gain as much weight as possible to get them through their winter hibernation, often adding a 4-inch layer of fat to keep them warm and nourished. During hibernation, black bears crawl into their dens, and their bodies go dormant for the winter; they do not eat, drink, urinate, or

Black Bear

defecate during their long sleep. Their kidneys continue to make urine, but it is reabsorbed into their bloodstream. They awaken by an internal clock in the spring and wander out in search of food. The black bear has a lumbering walk but can actually travel up to 30 miles per hour in a bounding trot. Black bears are powerful swimmers, able fishers, and agile tree climbers. They breed in the summer; the females undergo a phenomenon in which the fertilized egg passes into the uterus but changes very little until late fall, when it implants and then begins to grow quickly. Females commonly give birth to a litter of one to five cubs in January or February.

Despite its appearance on the state flag, the grizzly bear is extinct in California, and the black bear is the only bear that is encountered here today.

Branch Creek Trail snakes its way along the ridge above Buck Spring

Monterey and Santa Lucia Ranger
Districts
USGS 1:24,000 Branch Mtn., Los
    Machos Hills
    1:100,000 San Luis Obispo
Maptech CD-ROM: San Luis Obispo/Los
    Padres National Forest
*Southern & Central California Atlas &
    Gazetteer*, p. 60
California Road & Recreation Atlas, p. 91

Route Directions

▼ 0.0   From Central Mountains #39: Big
           Rocks Trail, 2.6 miles north of California
           166, zero trip meter and turn northeast
           on formed trail and cross cattle guard.
           Trail is marked as Branch Creek #27
           (17E05) for 4WDs, ATVs, and motor-
           bikes—rated blue. Trail crosses Branch
           Creek many times for next 0.5 miles.
2.6 ▲   Trail ends on Central Mountains #39:
           Big Rocks Trail. Turn left to exit to
           California 166.
           GPS: N35°08.08′ W120°07.26′

▼ 0.3 BL Buck Spring Campground on right.
2.3 ▲ BR Buck Spring Campground on left.

GPS: N35°08.09′ W120°06.99′

▼ 0.5 BL Bear left, crossing Branch Creek. Trail
           climbs steeply up ridge. Track on right
           to Buck Spring.
2.1 ▲ BR End of descent. Bear right, crossing
           Branch Creek. Track on left to Buck
           Spring. Trail crosses Branch Creek
           many times for next 0.5 miles.
           GPS: N35°08.23′ W120°06.89′

▼ 2.6 BL Trail forks. Track on right is Big Rocks
           Road #28 (32S25) for 4WDs, ATVs,
           and motorbikes—rated black. Bear left
           onto Jack Spring Road #29 (32S29)
           and zero trip meter.
0.0 ▲   Continue to the southwest.
           GPS: N35°09.63′ W120°05.94′

▼ 0.0   Continue to the north.
3.5 ▲ SO Track on left is Big Rocks Road #28
           (32S25) for 4WDs, ATVs, and motor-
           bikes—rated black. Continue straight
           ahead on Branch Creek Road #27
           (30S92, which is a different number
           than far end). Zero trip meter.

▼ 0.3 TL 4-way intersection. Track straight
           ahead goes to parking area and track

on right goes to locked gate. Follow
most-used trail.

3.2 ▲ TR 4-way intersection. Track straight
ahead goes to locked gate and track
on left goes to parking area. Follow
most-used trail.

GPS: N35°09.79' W120°05.74'

▼ 1.2 SO Closed track on right.

2.3 ▲ SO Closed track on left. Route is now
marked Jack Spring Road #29
(32S29)—rated black.

GPS: N35°10.13' W120°06.45'

▼ 1.6 TL Well-used, unmarked track on right.
Turn left and join roughly graded road.

1.9 ▲ TR Well-used, unmarked track ahead. Turn
right onto smaller formed trail.

GPS: N35°10.35' W120°06.67'

▼ 1.9 SO Cross over creek. Trail crosses creek
many times for next 2.8 miles.

1.6 ▲ SO Cross over creek.

▼ 3.5 BL Track on right is Central Mountains
#42: Paradise Road (32S21) for
4WDs, ATVs, and motorbikes—rated
green. Zero trip meter.

0.0 ▲   Continue to the northeast.

GPS: N35°08.85' W120°07.53'

▼ 0.0   Continue to the south.

1.2 ▲ BR Track on left is Central Mountains
#42: Paradise Road (32S21) for
4WDs, ATVs, and motorbikes—rated
green. Zero trip meter.

▼ 1.2   Trail ends at T-intersection with Central
Mountains #39: Big Rocks Trail. Turn
right to continue along the trail; turn
left to exit to California 166.

0.0 ▲   Trail commences on Central Mountains
#39: Big Rocks Trail, 4 miles from
intersection with California 166. Zero
trip meter and turn west on small graded road at sign for Thirtyfive Canyon
(32S14) for 4WDs, ATVs, and motorbikes—rated green. Trail follows along
creek in Thirtyfive Canyon, crossing it
often for next 1.5 miles.

GPS: N35°08.35' W120°08.42'

Paradise Road

STARTING POINT End of Central Mountains
#39: Big Rocks Trail, 4.4 miles from
California 166

FINISHING POINT Central Mountains #41:
Branch Creek Trail, 1.2 miles from
northern intersection of Central
Mountains #39: Big Rocks Trail

TOTAL MILEAGE 3.4 miles, plus 1.1-mile spur

UNPAVED MILEAGE: 3.4 miles, plus 1.1-mile spur

DRIVING TIME 1 hour (including spur)

ELEVATION RANGE 1,300–2,200 feet

USUALLY OPEN Year-round

BEST TIME TO TRAVEL Dry weather

DIFFICULTY RATING 3, optional 4-rated spur

SCENIC RATING 8

REMOTENESS RATING +0

Special Attractions

- Loop trail from the main Central Moun-
tains #39: Big Rocks Trail.
- Connects to a number of other 4WD
trails in this region of Los Padres National
Forest.
- Optional 4-rated spur trail.

Description

This short trail follows one of the green-rated
(easiest) trails through Los Padres National
Forest. The trail describes a loop from the end
of Central Mountains #39: Big Rocks Trail. It
climbs to a saddle through open grasslands
studded with mature oak trees. From the saddle, there is an optional 4-rated spur trail that
climbs up the ridge away from the saddle and
travels for just over a mile before finishing at
the boundary of private property. This spur is
more difficult because of the loose trail surface
and steep grade. The main trail is 3-rated because of the rutted surface and some moderately steep climbs and descents.

The main trail descends to Paradise Camp,
a national forest campground with two small
sites along the creek. A Forest Adventure Pass
is required to camp there, but no other fee is
charged. From the camp, the trail follows

CENTRAL MOUNTAINS #42: PARADISE ROAD

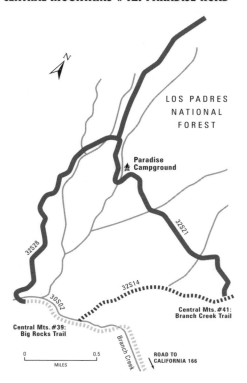

Current Road Information

Los Padres National Forest
Santa Lucia Ranger District
1616 Carlotti Drive
Santa Maria, CA 93454
(805) 925-9538

Map References

BLM San Luis Obispo
USFS Los Padres National Forest: Monterey
and Santa Lucia Ranger Districts
USGS 1:24,000 Los Machos Hills
1:100,000 San Luis Obispo
Maptech CD-ROM: San Luis Obispo/Los
Padres National Forest
Southern & Central California Atlas &
Gazetteer, p. 60
California Road & Recreation Atlas, p. 91

through denser vegetation to finish on Central Mountains #41: Branch Creek Trail, 1.2 miles from the main Big Rocks Trail.

Route Directions

▼ 0.0   From the end of Central Mountains
           #39: Big Rocks Trail, 4.4 miles from
           California 166, zero trip meter and
           turn northwest over cattle guard on
           to formed trail. Trail is marked Los
           Machos #25 (32S28) for 4WDs, ATVs,
           and motorbikes—rated green.
1.6 ▲   Trail ends at end of Central Mountains
           #39: Big Rocks Trail. Turn left for
           California 166.
           GPS: N35°08.30′ W120°08.85′

▼ 1.2   SO Cross through wash.
0.4 ▲   SO Cross through wash.
▼ 1.5   SO Cross through wash.
0.1 ▲   SO Cross through wash.
           GPS: N35°09.40′ W120°08.82′

▼ 1.6   BR Well-used unmarked track on left is
            start of spur trail that climbs ridge.
            Zero trip meter and join Paradise Road
            #26 (32S21) for 4WDs, ATVs, and
            motorbikes—rated green.
0.0 ▲   Continue to the west.
           GPS: N35°09.39′ W120°08.76′

Ridge Top Spur

▼ 0.0   Proceed to the north. Immediately trail
           climbs ridge.
▼ 0.9   SO Cattle guard.
▼ 1.1   UT Spur ends at a locked gate into private
            property.
           GPS: N35°10.26′ W120°08.59′

Continuation of Main Trail

▼ 0.0   Continue to the southeast.
1.8 ▲   BL Well-used unmarked track on right is
            start of spur trail that climbs ridge.
            Zero trip meter and continue straight
            ahead.
           GPS: N35°09.39′ W120°08.76′

▼ 0.3   BL Paradise Campground on right and left;
            then cross over creek.
1.5 ▲   BR Cross over creek; then Paradise
            Campground on right and left.

A spur trail off Paradise Road climbs the ridge into Los Machos Hills

Mature oaks dot the hillsides along Paradise Road

Sand Highway

GPS: N35°09.15′ W120°08.62′

▼ 0.8   SO Cross through wash.
1.0 ▲   SO Cross through wash.
▼ 1.2   SO Cross over wash.
0.6 ▲   SO Cross over wash.
GPS: N35°08.98′ W120°07.89′

▼ 1.8   Trail ends on Central Mountains #41: Branch Creek Trail, 1.2 miles from the end. Turn right to exit via Central Mountains #39: Big Rocks Trail to California 166; turn left to continue along Branch Creek Trail.

0.0 ▲   Trail starts on Central Mountains #39: Branch Creek Trail, 1.2 miles from the northern end. Zero trip meter and turn southwest on formed trail marked Paradise Road #26 (32S21).
GPS: N35°08.85′ W120°07.53′

STARTING POINT End of Pier Avenue, at the fee station

FINISHING POINT Gate to wilderness area

TOTAL MILEAGE 5.3 miles

UNPAVED MILEAGE: 5.3 miles

DRIVING TIME 45 minutes

ELEVATION RANGE 0–30 feet

USUALLY OPEN Year-round

BEST TIME TO TRAVEL Year-round

DIFFICULTY RATING 3

SCENIC RATING 9

REMOTENESS RATING +0

Special Attractions

- Beautiful views over the dunes to the Pacific Ocean.
- Dunes offer a scenic challenge to all levels of off-highway enthusiasts.

Description

The Oceano Dunes State Vehicular Recreation Area is located at the end of Pier Avenue in Oceano. From California 1, turn west onto Pier Avenue. After a couple of blocks the road will dead-end at the fee station for the recreation area. After paying a small fee, you are free to explore the beach and dunes to your heart's content. Although you can go anywhere your vehicle will take you in the recreation area, one route, called Sand Highway, has been marked with orange marker posts. This route follows along the shoreline at the start, before branching off into the dunes. Once in the dunes, orange signs mark the route about every tenth of a mile. The rolling course of Sand Highway is usually consistent, avoiding the major drops and ridgelines. However, the dunes are constantly changing shape, and drivers should approach drop-offs with caution.

A few campsites are scattered along the route. They are typically tucked beneath the dunes to provide some shelter from the ocean wind. There are a few roped areas for long-term RV camping along the shoreline. The trail ends at a gate and information board before the start of a hiking trail to Oso Flaco Lake. This wide-open area is a great place to park and take in the scenery. The natural area around freshwater Oso Flaco Lake was set up by the state and federal governments to protect plants and animals deemed threatened. The lake is also an annual refuge for migrating waterfowl.

As you drive along the sand, remember that it can be soft in some areas and quite hard in others. It is a good idea to avoid building up your speed on descents because there are often hard bottoms that will have your vehicle rocking like a seesaw. If you are having problems getting adequate traction, lower your tire pressure. There is a gas station nearby to refill them after you are finished on the dunes.

Current Road Information

Oceano Dunes SVRA District Office
576 Camino Mercado
Arroyo Grande, CA 93420
(805) 473-7230

Barbeque Flats Camping Area

Sunset over the Pacific Ocean

Misty view over Oso Flaco Lake

Map References

BLM   San Luis Obispo
USGS   1:24,000   Oceano
   1:100,000 San Luis Obispo
Maptech CD-ROM: San Luis Obispo/Los
   Padres National Forest
Southern & Central California Atlas &
   Gazetteer, p. 59
California Road & Recreation Atlas, p. 91
Other: Oceano Dunes State Vehicular
   Recreation Area map

Route Directions

▼ 0.0 Trail begins at fee station at the end of
    Pier Avenue (fee required). Zero trip
    meter at fee station and bear left onto
    the beach. Ocean will be on your right
    as you head south.
    GPS: N35°00.33′ W120°37.79′

▼ 0.5 SO Marker post 1.
▼ 0.6 SO Cross through wash.
▼ 0.9 SO Marker post 2.
▼ 1.4 SO Marker post 3.
▼ 1.9 SO Marker post 4.
▼ 2.1 BL Sign at beginning of Sand Highway.
    Zero trip meter and bear left just past
    restrooms and camping area.
    GPS: N35°04.48′ W120°37.15′

▼ 0.0 SO Continue southeast on Sand Highway.
▼ 0.1 SO Marker post 10.
▼ 0.3 SO Marker post 11 and Worm Valley
    Camp and restrooms.
▼ 0.4 SO Marker post 12; then Barbeque Flats
    Camping Area on right.
▼ 0.6 SO Marker post 13.
▼ 0.8 SO Marker post 14.
▼ 1.0 SO Marker post 15.
▼ 1.3 SO Marker post 16; Cottonwood Camping
    Area on right.
    GPS: N36°03.63′ W120°37.14′

▼ 1.4 SO Marker post 17.
▼ 1.6 SO Marker post 18.
▼ 1.8 SO Marker post 19.
▼ 1.9 SO Marker post 20.
▼ 2.0 SO Marker post 21. Competition Hill
    on right.

CENTRAL MOUNTAINS #43: SAND HIGHWAY

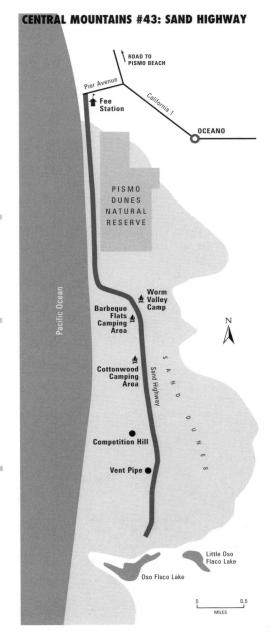

▼ 2.2 SO Marker post 22.
▼ 2.5 SO Marker post 24. There is a large vent
    pipe on the right.
▼ 2.6 SO Marker post 25.
▼ 3.2 Trail ends at gate and hiking trailhead
    in wide, open area.
    GPS: N35°02.10′ W120°37.15′

Pozo Road

STARTING POINT California 58 (Carrisa Highway), 0.4 miles west of mile marker 35
FINISHING POINT Pozo Road at the Pozo Station
TOTAL MILEAGE 18.2 miles
UNPAVED MILEAGE: 10.7 miles
DRIVING TIME 1 hour
ELEVATION RANGE 1,400–2,800 feet
USUALLY OPEN Year-round
BEST TIME TO TRAVEL Dry weather
DIFFICULTY RATING 1
SCENIC RATING 8
REMOTENESS RATING +0

Special Attractions
- Old Pozo stage stop, now the Pozo Saloon.
- Main route through the Pozo–La Panza OHV Area.

History

La Panza takes its name from early Spanish bear hunters and their baiting technique. These hunters used the paunch, or *la panza,* of a cow to attract bears. To the north of La Panza, Carnaza Creek refers to these same hunters; *carnaza* is animal meat with the skin still attached.

Grizzly bears, although now extinct in California, were noticed in great numbers by early expeditions through the region. Although they posed a significant danger, they were an essential part of the food supply for these expeditions.

In 1772, Spanish settlers experienced near famine conditions just two years after establishing the Presidio of Monterey. This period was made worse when supply ships, an essential part of the supply chain in Southern California, failed to arrive with provisions. The troops remembered that the men on Portolá's coastal expedition of 1769 had encountered many lean bears to the south, which were found to be very savory. In an attempt to alleviate the food shortage, the commander of the presidio, Pedro Fages, led a dozen troops

Pozo Road running down toward La Panza Campground

Pozo Saloon

south into the region surrounding today's San Luis Obispo in search of grizzlies. This venture has been referred to as one of the largest grizzly bear hunts of Southern California. Pack load after pack load of salted bear meat was shipped north to the starving Spaniards at Mission San Antonio de Padua and farther still to settlers at the Presidio of Monterey. Jerked grizzly meat became the order of the day for months, thus saving the Spanish from starvation. Father Junipero Serra, the head of the Presidio in Monterey, had one regret following this successful venture. Many of the soldiers had taken a liking to the region because of its plentiful food supply and friendly Indian maidens. Needless to say, many chose not to return to the mission.

In the 1860s, the settlement of Pozo had both a Wells Fargo stage stop and a pony express delivery stop. Built in 1858, the existing Pozo Saloon was once the stage stop. In 1878, there was a short-lived gold rush in the nearby canyons and a post office was opened shortly thereafter. Pozo, though taken to mean "well" in Spanish, also refers to a saucer-shaped depression. Pozo was chosen as

the name for the post office because early settlers found the saucer-shaped valley to have water. Thus they were able to grow corn, beans, and other crops without needing to develop an irrigation system.

The Pozo Saloon was closed during Prohibition. However, it reopened its doors in 1967 and was run by a former sheriff of San Luis Obispo named Paul Merrick. The 12-foot-long mahogany bar in the main room was transported around Cape Horn in 1860 and was originally the bar in the Cosmopolitan Hotel in San Luis Obispo. The saloon is definitely worth a visit for one of its great burgers and a Pozo Martini—a draught beer with two green olives dropped into the glass.

San Miguel Mission records mention an Indian village to the north of this trail. The village bordered the Obispeño Chumash and Migueleño Salinan tribes and was called Camata. This village name has lingered on in the name of Camatta Creek, which flows away from this trail to the north.

Another descriptive name is witnessed as the trail passes over Pozo Summit. Here, an OHV trail called Las Chiches leads off to the

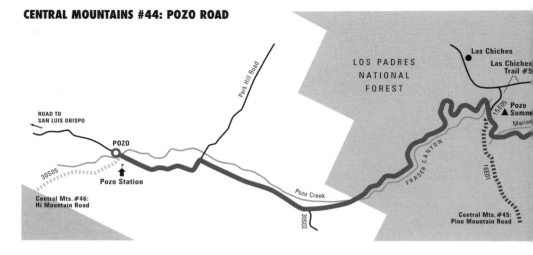

north to climb up to a flat of the same name. *Las chiches* is Spanish for "the nipples."

Description

Together, Pozo and Redhill Roads form the main backbone through the Pozo–La Panza OHV Area, with many trails branching off from them. Pozo Road itself is suitable for passenger vehicles in dry weather and, like all the trails in this area, should be avoided when wet. Within Los Padres National Forest, a Forest Adventure Pass is required for all parked vehicles, as well as for any recreational activity.

Pozo Road leaves California 58 along a paved road as it enters Los Padres National Forest. The vegetation is open, consisting mainly of low shrubs. The area was burned severely by wildfire a few years ago. Central Mountains #45: Pine Mountain Road, a lovely blue-rated trail, leaves from La Panza Summit, before Pozo Road descends to the shaded La Panza Campground.

From here, the trail climbs along a wide shelf road, running around the Mariana Creek valley to Pozo Summit. Two difficult trails lead off from the summit—Pine Mountain Road and Las Chiches Trail. Both are black-rated trails that are suitable for 4WDs, ATVs, and motorbikes. The second section of the trail descends along Fraser Canyon to the trail's end at the old settlement of Pozo.

Current Road Information

Los Padres National Forest
Santa Lucia Ranger District
1616 North Carlotti Drive
Santa Maria, CA 93454
(805) 925-9538

Map References

BLM   San Luis Obispo
USFS   Los Padres National Forest:
        Monterey and Santa Lucia Ranger
        Districts
USGS   1:24,000   Pozo Summit, La Panza
        Ranch, La Panza, Santa Margarita
        Lake
        1:100,000 San Luis Obispo
Maptech CD-ROM: San Luis Obispo/Los
        Padres National Forest
*Southern & Central California Atlas &
        Gazetteer,* p. 60
California Road & Recreation Atlas, p. 91

Route Directions

▼ 0.0   From California 58 (Carrisa Highway),
           0.4 miles west of mile marker 35, zero
           trip meter and turn southwest onto
           Pozo Road, sign-posted to Pozo. The
           road is initially paved.
5.7 ▲   Trail ends at T-intersection with
           California 58 (Carrisa Highway). Turn
           left for Santa Margarita; turn right for
           Taft and I-5.

           GPS: N35°23.20′ W120°09.89′

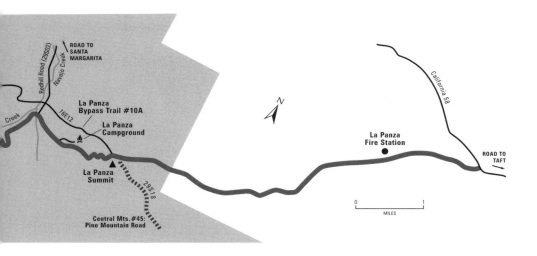

▼ 1.4 SO La Panza Fire Station on right.
4.3 ▲ SO La Panza Fire Station on left.
GPS: N35°22.77' W120°11.27'

▼ 3.5 SO Road turns to graded dirt.
2.2 ▲ SO Road is now paved.
▼ 5.1 SO Entering Los Padres National Forest.
0.6 ▲ SO Leaving Los Padres National Forest.
GPS: N35°21.47' W120°14.50'

▼ 5.7 SO Central Mountains #45: Pine Mountain Road on left at information board at La Panza Summit. Zero trip meter.
0.0 ▲ Continue to the northeast.
GPS: N35°21.31' W120°15.06'

▼ 0.0 Continue to the west. Track on right is La Panza Bypass Trail #10A (16E12) for ATVs and motorbikes—rated blue.
1.9 ▲ SO Track on left is La Panza Bypass Trail #10A (16E12) for ATVs and motorbikes—rated blue. Then Central Mountains #45: Pine Mountain Road on right at information board at La Panza Summit. Zero trip meter.
▼ 1.3 SO La Panza USFS Campground on right. Forest Adventure Pass required, no other fee.
0.6 ▲ SO La Panza USFS Campground on left. Forest Adventure Pass required, no other fee.
GPS: N35°21.16' W120°15.93'

▼ 1.7 SO Track on left.
0.2 ▲ SO Track on right.
▼ 1.9 BL Track on right is Redhill Road (29S02), sign-posted to California 58. Zero trip meter.
0.0 ▲ Continue to the southeast.
GPS: N35°21.42' W120°16.48'

▼ 0.0 Continue to the southwest.
2.6 ▲ BR Track on left is Redhill Road (29S02), sign-posted to California 58. Zero trip meter.
▼ 0.1 SO Turnout on right.
2.5 ▲ SO Turnout on left.
▼ 2.6 SO Pozo Summit. Track on left is Central Mountains #45:Pine Mountain Road (16E01)—rated black. Route is recommended for travel in opposite direction. Track on right is Las Chiches Trail #5 (15E05) for 4WDs, ATVs, and motorbikes—rated black. Zero trip meter.
0.0 ▲ Continue to the west.
GPS: N35°20.85' W120°17.67'

▼ 0.0 Continue to the east.
4.9 ▲ SO Pozo Summit. Track on right is Centtral Mountains #45: Pine Mountain Trail Road (16E01)—rated black. Route is recommended for travel in opposite direction. Track on left is Las Chiches Trail #5 (15E05) for 4WDs, ATVs, and motorbikes-rated black. Zero trip meter.

▼ 4.0   SO   Cross over Fraser Creek on bridge; then two tracks on left. Information board on left. Leaving Los Padres National Forest. Road is now paved.

0.9 ▲   SO   Entering Los Padres National Forest. Road turns to graded dirt. Information board on right and two tracks on right; then cross over Fraser Creek on bridge.
         GPS: N35°19.12′ W120°18.83′

▼ 4.9   TR   Paved road on left is San Jose Avenales Road (30S02) to American Canyon Campground. Zero trip meter.

0.0 ▲   Continue to the northeast, following sign to La Panza Campground.
         GPS: N35°18.64′ W120°19.59′

▼ 0.0   Continue to the southwest.

3.1 ▲   BL   Paved road on right is San Jose Avenales Road (30S02) to American Canyon Campground. Zero trip meter.

▼ 1.7   TL   T-intersection. Park Hill Road on right.

1.4 ▲   TR   Turn right, remaining on Pozo Road. Park Hill Road continues straight ahead.
         GPS: N35°18.65′ W120°21.40′

▼ 3.1   Trail ends in Pozo at the Pozo USFS Station on Pozo Road. Continue straight for San Luis Obispo. Turn left to commence Central Mountains #46: Hi Mountains Road.

0.0 ▲   Trail commences in Pozo at the Pozo USFS Station on Pozo Road. Zero trip meter at Pozo Station and continue east on Pozo Road, following sign to La Panza Campground. Paved road on right is Central Mountains #46: Hi Mountains Trail.
         GPS: N35°18.23′ W120°22.55′

Pine Mountain Road

STARTING POINT Central Mountains #44: Pozo Road at La Panza Summit

FINISHING POINT Central Mountains #44: Pozo Road at Pozo Summit

TOTAL MILEAGE 8.8 miles

UNPAVED MILEAGE: 8.8 miles

DRIVING TIME 1.5 hours (one-way) for 4-rated section.

ELEVATION RANGE 2,000–3,600 feet

USUALLY OPEN Year-round

BEST TIME TO TRAVEL Dry weather only

DIFFICULTY RATING 4, with one short 9-rated descent; 6 for final 1.4 miles

SCENIC RATING 9

REMOTENESS RATING +0

Special Attractions

■ Chance to see the California condor in its native habitat.

■ Very scenic ridge trail, with the option for an extremely difficult finale for modified vehicles.

Description

Pine Mountain Road (30S14, shown on some maps as 30S17) is one of the 4WD trails suitable for vehicles as well as ATVs and motorbikes within the Pozo–La Panza OHV Area. The route travels around the northern edge of the Machesna Mountain Wilderness, running for the most part along ridge tops, with spectacular views in all directions.

The trail starts by leaving the main backbone route through the region, Central Mountains #44: Pozo Road, 5.7 miles west of California 58. It heads southeast, following alongside the small Queen Bee Creek and passing two flowing springs and a couple of shady campsites along the creek. This section of the trail is suitable for high-clearance vehicles.

Once the route turns onto the steep Pine Mountain Road, a high-clearance 4WD is required. From this intersection, the trail climbs steadily, becoming steeper and rougher the higher it goes. The trail should not be attempted in wet weather because the surface becomes extremely greasy, which, combined with the narrow trail, makes for dangerous driving. The forest service will often close the trail in wet weather to avoid road damage. In dry weather the surface is uneven, with reasonable traction and a number of embedded rocks.

An observation point on the left of the trail over Castle Crag is located 0.6 miles from the turnoff onto Pine Mountain Road. From this point, you may see California condors if you are lucky. It is the largest land bird of North America, with a wingspan of 9 feet. Although once common from Baja California to the Pacific Northwest, the California condor population declined so dramatically through habitat loss and illegal shooting that it was put on the endangered species list in 1967. The Los Angeles and San Diego Zoos began a program in 1981 that successfully raised the threatened birds in captivity. The first birds were released back into the wild in 1992. There is now a secure population within Los Padres National Forest.

As the trail climbs higher, there are views over the La Panza Range to the north and the Machesna Mountain Wilderness to the south. Hikers can access the wilderness along an old vehicle trail.

The trail starts to descend at the top of Pine Mountain. The top of the mountain makes a good place to turn around if you are driving a stock 4WD vehicle or if you do not wish to tackle the more difficult trail ahead. It is possible to continue for 0.8 miles before the trail requires a heavily modified vehicle. The first portion of the descent is rated a 5 for difficulty and follows along a narrow, rough shelf road before reaching a national forest sign warning of the difficult road ahead. Only heavily modified, short-wheelbase vehicles should continue past here. A short, approximately 60-yard section of rock steps, each approximately 2 feet high and very rugged, follows the sign and is rated 9 for difficulty when approached in its entirety. Even modified vehicles with experienced drivers risk significant vehicle damage along this short section. If

Modified vehicles only! These steps are good at damaging vehicles

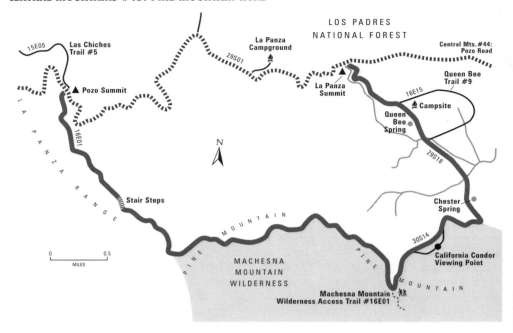

you continued to this point, you can turn around at the sign and view the steps from above.

From the bottom of the steps, the trail continues to undulate steeply, with some steep loose sections to negotiate before it finishes on Pozo Summit. The final descent to Pozo Summit is steep and loose. From the bottom of the steps to Pozo Summit, the trail is rated a 6 for difficulty. The forest service recommends travel only from Queen Bee to Pozo Summit, so that vehicles descend the most difficult sections. The trail can be treated in the reverse direction as a 6-rated spur trail to the bottom of the steps.

Current Road Information
Los Padres National Forest
Santa Lucia Ranger District
1616 North Carlotti Drive
Santa Maria, CA 93454
(805) 925-9538

Map References
BLM   San Luis Obispo
USFS Los Padres National Forest:
Monterey and Santa Lucia Ranger Districts
USGS 1:24,000   La Panza, Pozo Summit
1:100,000 San Luis Obispo
Maptech CD-ROM: San Luis Obispo/Los Padres National Forest
Southern & Central California Atlas & Gazetteer, p. 60
California Road & Recreation Atlas, p. 91

Route Directions

▼ 0.0   Trail begins on Central Mountains #44: Pozo Road at La Panza Summit, 5.7 miles west of California 58. Zero trip meter at information board and turn east onto graded dirt road. There is no route name or number at the intersection.

2.2 ▲   Trail ends on Central Mountains #44: Pozo Road at information board at La Panza Summit. Turn right for California 58.
           GPS: N35°21.31′ W120°15.06′

▼ 0.1   SO Closure gate.
2.1 ▲   SO Closure gate.

▼ 0.4   SO Cattle guard; then track on left is

Top of the steps on Pine Mountain

CALIFORNIA CONDOR

The California condor is a large, majestic bird. It can be 4 feet in length and its wingspan is the largest in North America, often approaching 9 feet. Adult condors are black with a naked orange head. Immature birds have a gray head. From below, observers will notice white wing linings. California condors eat a variety of small animals, mostly rodents. They should not be fed as this increases their reliance on humans and decreases their chances of independent survival.

California Condor

In prehistoric times, the range of the California condor extended from British Columbia to Florida, but by the twentieth century it was confined to the mountains north of Los Angeles. By the 1980s a combination of factors had reduced its numbers to just five. Lead poisoning from eating pellets imbedded in game was a major killer. The surviving birds were placed in captivity, where attempts are being made to breed the species. Condors have been reintroduced into the wild in limited areas, but for now the main battle is merely to prevent extinction. In 2006, the total population of California condors was 275, only 125 of which were flying free. Several trails in this book provide opportunities for viewing these rare and beautiful raptors.

		Queen Bee Trail #9 (16E15) for ATVs and motorbikes—rated blue.	▼ 0.5	SO Track on right.
1.8 ▲	SO	Track on right is Queen Bee Trail #9 (16E15) for ATVs and motorbikes—rated blue; then cattle guard.	1.7 ▲	SO Track on left.
			▼ 0.8	SO Track on left.
			1.4 ▲	SO Track on right.
		GPS: N35°21.17′ W120°14.83′	▼ 0.9	SO Queen Bee Spring on right.

Easy shelf road at the start of Pine Mountain Road

1.3 ▲   SO   Queen Bee Spring on left.
         GPS: N35°21.06' W120°14.41'

▼ 1.3   SO   Cross through wash.
0.9 ▲   SO   Cross through wash.
▼ 1.5   SO   Track on left is Queen Bee Trail #9
             (16E15) for ATVs and motorbikes—
             rated blue.
0.7 ▲   SO   Track on right is Queen Bee Trail #9
             (16E15) for ATVs and motorbikes—
             rated blue.
         GPS: N35°20.70' W120°13.91'

▼ 1.6   SO   Track on left.
0.6 ▲   SO   Track on right.
▼ 1.7   SO   Cross through wash.
0.5 ▲   SO   Cross through wash.
▼ 1.8   SO   Track on left; then Chester Spring
             on right.
0.4 ▲   SO   Chester Spring on left; then track
             on right.
         GPS: N35°20.47' W120°13.73'

▼ 2.2   BR   Bear right onto Pine Mountain Road
             #8 (30S14, called 30S17 on forest
             service map), and zero trip meter. Trail

is suitable for 4WDs, ATVs, and motorbikes—rated green.
0.0 ▲   Continue to the northwest.
         GPS: N35°20.20' W120°13.54'

▼ 0.0   Continue to the south.
4.4 ▲   BL   Bear left onto larger graded dirt road
             and zero trip meter.
▼ 0.6   SO   Track on left to viewpoint over Castle
             Crag and Machesna Mountain
             Wilderness (California condor viewing
             point).
3.8 ▲   BL   Track on right to viewpoint over Castle
             Crag and Machesna Mountain
             Wilderness (California condor viewing
             point).
         GPS: N35°20.11' W120°13.91'

▼ 0.9   SO   Track on left.
3.5 ▲   SO   Track on right.
▼ 1.6   SO   Machesna Mountain Wilderness
             access trail 16E01 on left for hikers
             only. No trailhead parking.
2.8 ▲   SO   Machesna Mountain Wilderness
             access trail 16E01 on right for hikers
             only. No trailhead parking.

▼ 4.1 SO Track on right goes short distance to viewpoint.
0.3 ▲ SO Track on left goes short distance to viewpoint.
  GPS: N35°19.81' W120°16.16'

▼ 4.4 SO Gated road on left goes into wilderness. Remain on Pine Mountain Trail #7—now rated black. Zero trip meter.
0.0 ▲ Continue to the northeast.
  GPS: N35°19.63' W120°16.36'

▼ 0.0 Continue to the southwest.
2.2 ▲ Gated road on right goes into wilderness. Remain on Pine Mountain Trail #7—now rated green. Zero trip meter.

▼ 0.7 SO Warning sign. Trail past this point has a difficulty rating of 9. The most difficult section of the trail, the stair steps, is immediately past the sign. The most difficult section is near the bottom and is not immediately visible.
1.5 ▲ SO Warning sign and end of 9-rated section. Trail is now 4-rated.
  GPS: N35°19.93' W120°16.91'

▼ 0.8 Bottom of the steps. Trail is now 6-rated.
1.4 ▲ SO Trail past this point has a difficulty rating of 9. The most difficult section of the trail, the stair steps, is visible straight ahead.
  GPS: N35°20.00' W120°16.99'

▼ 2.2 Trail ends on Central Mountains #44: Pozo Road at Pozo Summit. Turn left for Pozo; turn right for California 58. Ahead is Las Chiches Trail #5 (15E05) for 4WDs, ATVs, and motorbikes—rated black.
0.0 ▲ Trail commences on Central Mountains #44: Pozo Road at Pozo Summit. Zero trip meter and turn south on formed trail suitable for 4WDs, ATVs, and motorbikes—rated black.
  GPS: N35°20.85' W120°17.67'

Hi Mountain Road

STARTING POINT Pozo Road at Pozo Station
FINISHING POINT Big Falls Hiking Trailhead
TOTAL MILEAGE 12.1 miles
UNPAVED MILEAGE: 12 miles
DRIVING TIME 1 hour
ELEVATION RANGE 1,400–3,000 feet
USUALLY OPEN Year-round
BEST TIME TO TRAVEL Dry weather
DIFFICULTY RATING 1
SCENIC RATING 8
REMOTENESS RATING +0

Special Attractions

■ Ridge top trail with views over the La Panza Range and Santa Lucia Wilderness.
■ Hiking access into wilderness.

History

As the trail runs northwest down the Santa Lucia Range, it overlooks the headwaters of the Salinas River, which feeds Santa Margarita Lake (also visible to the north). The Salinas River gained its name from the salt marshes near the mouth of the river, where it enters the Pacific Ocean in Monterey Bay. On the south face of Hi Mountain, the name of Salt Creek reflects the taste of the water.

Garcia Mountain, south of Pozo, is named after Don Ynocento Garcia, who owned the property within the San Jose Valley. Though it was believed by many that he owned a Mexican land grant in the area, it was not until Americans took over the land that it was discovered he had filed incorrect claims.

The small Salsipuedes Creek begins on the north face of Hi Mountain and flows into Santa Margarita Lake. *Sal si puedes* (meaning, "get out if you can") was a name often given to canyons that were difficult to get out of. Though the upper and lower stretches of this creek can be tight, its middle section opens out into the broader valley downstream from Pozo.

Santa Margarita Lake was formerly known as Salinas Reservoir. Prior to the 1790s, the

Hi Mountain Road travels below the ridge

settlement of Santa Margarita (located northwest of the lake) was a hog-breeding location for the San Luis Obispo Mission. The mission named the location after St. Margaret of Cortona. This name was also given to a land grant in September of 1841 of nearly 18,000 acres on the western side of the Santa Lucia Range to Joaquin Estrada. It was patented 20 years later to Joaquin and is still evident on regional maps today.

After Mexico became independent from Spain in 1822, the padres began to lose control of their missions. Indian neophytes were released from the missions, and missionary lands became available as land grants. What was originally planned as a land-holding policy for an eventual return of mission lands to Indians turned into a large-scale sale of land to ranchers. The Santa Margarita Mission lands became known as El Rancho de Santa Margarita and were granted to Don Joaquin Estrada. Estrada was renowned for his lavish behavior, including throwing expensive celebrations for his guests. He was soon bought out by Martin Murphy, an Irish emigrant

who was expanding his land holdings after he moved west in the mid-1840s. By the 1870s, the town was showing up on maps of the day, and it gained a post office by 1880. A small land boom hit the settlement in the late 1880s and early 1890s, with the arrival of the railroad from the north. Today, the Assistencia de Santa Margarita is merely ruins located on private land just northwest of Santa Margarita.

Another saint remembered in these mountains is Saint Lucy of Syracuse (whose feast day is celebrated by the Roman Catholic church on December 13). The Sierra de Santa Lucia, or Santa Lucia Range, is named in her honor. The Hi Mountain Trail is situated near the southern end of the range, which runs all the way north to Carmel Bay. During the nineteenth century, the range was considered to run continuously as far south as the Santa Clara River at Ventura.

Description

Hi Mountain Road begins in Pozo and travels through the Los Padres National Forest to finish at the Big Falls Hiking Trailhead. Much of the easy graded road

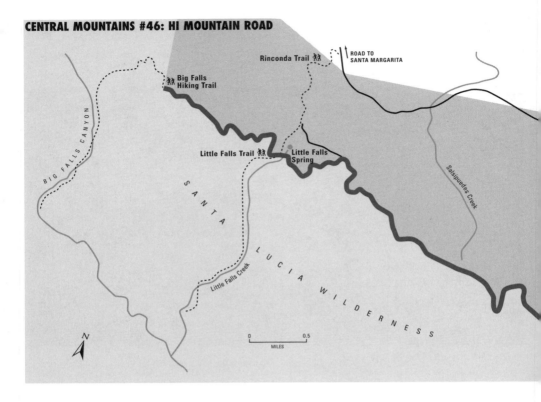

runs along a ridge top, offering stunning views in all directions.

Initially the trail passes through a short section of private property. A mile from the start, the trail crosses the Salinas River. The river crossing typically has water year-round, but it is normally shallow and should pose no difficulty to high-clearance vehicles under normal conditions.

From the intersection with Garcia Ridge Road, Hi Mountain Trail swings west and begins a long run along the ridge tops of the Santa Lucia Range. The La Panza Range is to the north of the ridge and the Santa Lucia Wilderness and Lopez Lake are to the south. The trail along Garcia Ridge is steep and rocky in places and is of a moderate to difficult standard.

The main trail passes the developed Hi Mountain Campground, which has pit toilets and a few shady camping spots. A mile and a half farther, you will come to a T-intersection with great views over Lopez Lake and the Santa Lucia Wilderness. A short spur trail to the left at this point leads to the abandoned fire lookout on Hi Mountain. You can climb up the tower for a glimpse of the breathtaking 360-degree views. A small outhouse near the tower tells of the meager and lonely life of a fire lookout.

Hi Mountain Road then follows along a wide shelf road with views to the left into wilderness area. The surface is roughly graded all the way. The Rinconada Trail leaves this route to the north and drops steeply from the ridge to join Pozo Road. The trail finally comes to an end at a turning loop and hiking trailhead to Big Falls.

Current Road Information

Los Padres National Forest
Santa Lucia Ranger District
1616 North Carlotti Drive
Santa Maria, CA 93454
(805) 925-9538

Map References

BLM   San Luis Obispo
USFS   Los Padres National Forest:

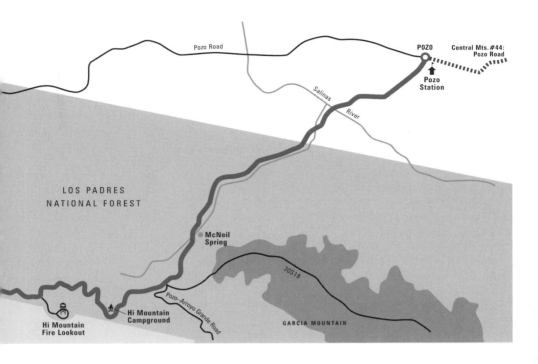

LOS PADRES
NATIONAL FOREST

Pozo Road

POZO

Central Mts. #44:
Pozo Road

Pozo
Station

Salinas

River

McNeil
Spring

30S18

Pozo–Arroyo Grande Road

Hi Mountain
Campground

GARCIA MOUNTAIN

Hi Mountain
Fire Lookout

Year-round crossing of the Salinas River

ERA OF THE SPANISH AND MEXICAN MISSIONS AND PRESIDIOS

By 1769, Spain had claimed California as part of New Spain for more than 200 years. Despite this, no Spaniards had visited the land they knew as Alta California since Vizcaíno's voyage in 1602. But when Russian trappers began to visit North America's Pacific shores in search of furs, Spanish officials decided the to place the area under firmer imperial control. For this and other reasons, Father Junípero Serra and his civilian counterpart, Governor Gaspar de Portolá, were sent from Mexico to establish a series of Franciscan missions and related presidios, or forts.

Two land parties and two sea parties left La Paz, on the Gulf of California, after arranging to meet in San Diego Bay. In July 1769, after months of hard traveling, the four parties met on the shore of California. Of the 219 men who had departed, only about a hundred had survived, and many of those were exhausted and sick. Father Serra was undeterred. On July 16, 1769, he erected a tall wooden cross on a hill overlooking the bay. In doing so, he established San Diego de Alcalá, the first of 21 missions in California. By the time Serra built his first brushwood church, Portolá was already marching north in search of Monterey Bay.

When Portolá returned to San Diego six months later after failing to find the elusive bay, the mission

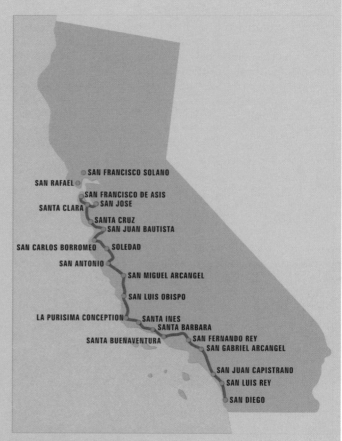

Spanish and Mexican Missions

was in dire straits. Serra's attempts to befriend the local Indians had failed. He had tried handing out food and beads, but this only encouraged the Indians to raid the vulnerable settlement. Food and supplies were running dangerously low, and 19 graves had already been filled. Not a single Indian had been persuaded to convert to Christianity. Portolá's men were also suffering after their long, unsuccessful journey. The governor wanted to return to Mexico; Serra persuaded him to wait for a supply ship. On the very last night before they were due to depart, the San Antonio's sail appeared on the horizon; the Franciscan presence in Alta California was saved.

Leaving Father Jayme in charge of the Mission San Diego, which was moved 6 miles upstream to more fertile soil, Serra sailed north in another attempt to find Monterey Bay. Portolá reached the bay first, by land, and this time he recognized it. He began construction of a presidio where soldiers could be stationed to protect a nearby mission and secure the Spanish claim to the land. Three more military presidios were eventually built in California. Father Serra decided to build the second California mission a few miles from the bay, in the Carmel Valley. San Carlos Borromeo was officially established on June 3, 1770. It was here that Serra would spend the majority of his time as the leader of the California missions, until his death in 1784.

Serra went on to establish another seven missions and traveled thousands of miles along El Camino Real. (Spanish for "the King's Highway," El Camino Real was the name given to the trail that connected the various missions.) By the time of his death, many of the settlements had begun to flourish. The Spanish were becoming accustomed to California's climate and growth cycles. Indians started to enter the missions, encouraged by the ready supply of food. Sturdy adobe buildings replaced crude brushwood structures. Three civilian pueblos had also been established, at San Luis Obispo (1772), San Juan Capistrano (1776), and Los Angeles (1781). Four more were added after Serra's death.

Life at the missions was often hard. Supply ships came infrequently, and the settlements were forced to be self-sufficient. Workdays were long and hard, especially for Native Americans unused to agricultural labor. Discipline was strictly enforced by whipping and daily life was rigorously regimented. Any neophyte (as the Indian converts were called) who attempted to escape was tracked down and returned to the mission. Sanitation was also a problem and many Indians, with no immunity to European ailments, died of imported diseases. Treatment of neophytes by nearby soldiers was harsh, to the dismay of most priests. Rape of Indian women was not uncommon.

Recent historians have strongly criticized the Franciscan mission system in California for squashing native culture and oppressing Indian converts. Although it is true that the neophytes were viewed with condescension by their Spanish guardians, it should be remembered that most of the priests were genuinely concerned about their subjects' welfare. Treatment of the California Indians is abhorrent when viewed through modern eyes, but the flagellation, poor sanitation, and cultural elitism were standard practice in the eighteenth century. Also, most Indians entered the mission system voluntarily and some settlements, notably San Gabriel Arcángel near Los Angeles, developed quite large populations. Nevertheless, the missions indisputably had a devastating effect on the culture of coastal Indian tribes, much as the gold rush would destroy the inland tribes decades later. Traditional practices were forgotten, populations were destroyed, and at least one cultural group, the Esselen, was lost forever.

The breakup of the mission system, which came after Mexican independence from Spain in 1821, only exacerbated the Indians' problems. The government ceded large tracts of mission land to civilian settlers, who stole much more. Some Indians worked on the new Mexican ranches, often as virtual slaves; others returned to the wilderness whence they had come.

For years, the buildings of the missions lay in a state of decay. Some, such as the Mission Santa Barbara, were continuously inhabited by Franciscan priests, but most were abandoned. Many are now just ruins, but a few have been restored and can be viewed today. The Mission Delores in San Francisco remains a tourist attraction; in Southern California, San Diego County's Mission San Luis Rey is particularly picturesque and the mission at San Juan Capistrano is famous for its annual festival celebrating the return of the swallows.

Monterey and Santa Lucia Ranger
Districts
USGS 1:24,000 Santa Margarita Lake
  1:100,000 San Luis Obispo
Maptech CD-ROM: San Luis Obispo/Los
  Padres National Forest
*Southern & Central California Atlas &
  Gazetteer,* pp. 60, 59
California Road & Recreation Atlas, p. 91

Route Directions

▼ 0.0　　From the western end of Central
　　　　Mountains #44: Pozo Road at the Pozo
　　　　USFS Station, turn south on paved Hi
　　　　Mountain Road and zero trip meter.
3.5 ▲　　Trail finishes in Pozo at the Pozo USFS
　　　　Station. Turn left for Santa Margarita;
　　　　turn right to continue along Central
　　　　Mountains #44: Pozo Road.
　　　　GPS: N35°18.23′ W120°22.54′

▼ 0.1　SO　Closure gate.
3.4 ▲　SO　Closure gate.
▼ 0.7　SO　Closure gate.
2.8 ▲　SO　Closure gate.
▼ 1.0　SO　Cross through Salinas River.
2.5 ▲　SO　Cross through Salinas River.
　　　　GPS: N35°17.66′ W120°23.30′

▼ 1.2　SO　Cross through wash.
2.3 ▲　SO　Cross through wash.
▼ 1.5　SO　Entering Los Padres National Forest
　　　　over cattle guard.
2.0 ▲　SO　Leaving Los Padres National Forest
　　　　over cattle guard.
　　　　GPS: N35°17.24′ W120°23.55′

▼ 2.8　SO　McNeil Spring on left.
0.7 ▲　SO　McNeil Spring on right.
　　　　GPS: N35°16.47′ W120°24.25′

▼ 3.4　SO　Cattle guard.
0.1 ▲　SO　Cattle guard.
▼ 3.5　TR　Track on left is Garcia Ridge Road #18
　　　　(30S18)—rated blue. Track ahead and
　　　　to the left is Pozo–Arroyo Grande
　　　　Road, which goes to Arroyo Grande
　　　　Station and Lopez Lake. Zero trip meter
　　　　and turn right, following sign to Hi

Mountain Campground.
0.0 ▲　Continue to the north.
　　　　GPS: N35°15.98′ W120°24.41′

▼ 0.0　　Continue to the west.
▼ 0.5　SO　Water trough on left.
▼ 0.7　SO　Hi Mountain USFS Campground on
　　　　right. Forest Adventure Pass required;
　　　　no other fee.
　　　　GPS: N35°15.66′ W120°24.75′

▼ 2.2　BR　Track on left through gate goes to Hi
　　　　Mountain Fire Lookout.
　　　　GPS: N35°15.66′ W120°25.76′

▼ 2.3　SO　Cattle guard.
▼ 2.5　SO　Viewpoint on left with views over
　　　　Lopez Lake.
▼ 4.1　SO　Track on left to viewpoint.
　　　　GPS: N35°15.96′ W120°27.10′

▼ 4.9　SO　Track on right up hill. Viewpoint and
　　　　campsite on left.
　　　　GPS: N35°16.26′ W120°27.60′

▼ 5.2　SO　Track on right in wide area.
　　　　GPS: N35°16.38′ W120°27.85′

▼ 5.7　SO　Faint track on left.
▼ 5.8　SO　Well-used track on right and faint track
　　　　on left rejoins.
　　　　GPS: N35°16.58′ W120°28.11′

▼ 6.6　SO　Tank on right. Little Falls Spring
　　　　on right.
▼ 6.7　SO　Rinconada Trail on right for hiking and
　　　　horses only. Zero trip meter.
　　　　GPS: N35°16.50′ W120°28.68′

▼ 0.0　　Continue to the southwest.
▼ 0.1　SO　Little Falls Trail on left into the Santa
　　　　Lucia Wilderness and track on right.
　　　　GPS: N35°16.47′ W120°28.75′

▼ 0.4　SO　Two tracks on right.
▼ 1.9　　Trail ends at Big Falls Hiking Trailhead.
　　　　Hiking trail continues to the west
　　　　down Big Falls Canyon.
　　　　GPS: N35°16.82′ W120°29.89′

Parkfield Grade Trail

STARTING POINT California 198, 9.5 miles southwest of Coalinga

FINISHING POINT Intersection of Cholame Road and Vineyard Canyon Road in Parkfield

TOTAL MILEAGE 18.4 miles

UNPAVED MILEAGE: 10 miles

DRIVING TIME 1.25 hours

ELEVATION RANGE 1,200–3,600 feet

USUALLY OPEN Year-round

BEST TIME TO TRAVEL Dry weather

DIFFICULTY RATING 1

SCENIC RATING 8

REMOTENESS RATING +0

Special Attractions

■ Meandering road that follows the Parkfield Grade.

■ Views of Middle Mountain and Joaquin Canyon.

History

Parkfield was originally called Russelsville, but the post office denied the request for that name in 1883, forcing the occupants to choose a new one. Parkfield was chosen to reflect the parklike setting of the locality dotted with majestic oaks. The town is located in Cholame Valley, a name reputed to mean "evil people."

Parkfield, one of the few settlements in this remote region along the San Andreas Fault, was a center of seismic research between 1984 and 1992. Criteria were developed for predicting earthquakes and a system was designed to alert the public. In 1991, that system warned Parkfield of a possible earthquake predicted to reach a 6 on the Richter scale. Fortunately, nothing happened. The calculation was based on the fact that such earthquakes had been recorded in 1857, 1881, 1901, 1922, 1934, and lastly in 1966. Instrumentation remains to assist in the ongoing study of earthquakes in Parkfield.

This trail crosses Jacalitos (Mexican Spanish for "Little Hut") Creek. It seems to have been named by surveyors who noticed a small hut during their work in the Jacalitos Hills to the east.

The vista over Jacalitos Creek Valley typifies the landscape along the Parkfield Grade Trail

CENTRAL MOUNTAINS #47: PARKFIELD GRADE TRAIL

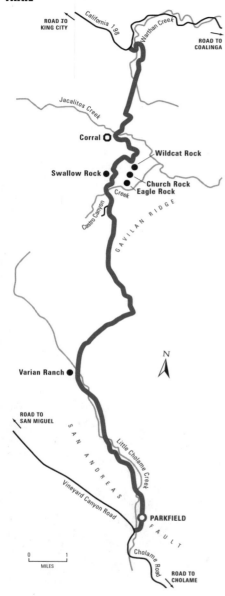

Description

This route passes through ranchland in the Cholame Hills south of Coalinga. The graded road is suitable for passenger vehicles in dry weather, but it is often impassable when wet. There are no public lands along the trail. Please respect the private property on either side of the road and remain on the designated county road.

The road turns to graded dirt after crossing Jacalitos Creek and climbs toward Gavilan Ridge. Traveling around the head of Castro Canyon, there are spectacular views over the oak-studded hills and rocky outcrops, back down into the Jacalitos Creek Valley. A prominent ridge of rocks can be seen that includes Church Rock, Eagle Rock, Wildcat Rock, and Swallow Rock. After crossing a saddle, the trail gradually descends toward Parkfield. The views are now to the west over the Cholame Creek Valley to the Cholame Hills on the far side.

The trail ends in the small settlement of Parkfield. According to a sign, the town is bustling with a population of 37 and is the self-proclaimed earthquake capital of the world.

Current Road Information

BLM Hollister Field Office
20 Hamilton Court
Hollister, CA 95023
(831) 630-5000

Map References

BLM   Coalinga, Paso Robles
USGS 1:24,000   Curry Mtn., Parkfield
         1:100,000 Coalinga, Paso Robles
Maptech CD-ROM: San Luis Obispo/Los
         Padres National Forest; Central
         Coast/Fresno
*Southern & Central California Atlas &
         Gazetteer,* pp. 34, 46
California Road & Recreation Atlas, p. 83

Route Directions

▼ 0.0	From California 198, 9.5 miles southwest of Coalinga, zero trip meter and turn east on paved road marked Parkfield Grade.
3.4 ▲	Trail ends on California 198. Turn right for Coalinga.
	GPS: N36°04.92′ W120°28.79′

▼ 1.5	SO	Cross through Warthan Creek.
1.9 ▲	SO	Cross through Warthan Creek.
▼ 3.4	SO	Cross over Jacalitos Creek. Corral on right. Road becomes graded dirt. Zero trip meter.
0.0 ▲		Continue to the south.

Pozo Road runs down toward La Panza campground

Parkfield—earthquakes have been regularly reported here since 1857

▼ 0.0   Continue to the northeast.
10.0 ▲ SO Cross over Jacalitos Creek. Corral on left. Road is now paved. Zero trip meter.
▼ 1.1   SO Wildcat Rock on left.
8.9 ▲ SO Wildcat Rock on right.

GPS: N36°02.44' W120°28.11'

▼ 2.4   SO Swallow Rock on right.
7.6 ▲ SO Swallow Rock on left.

GPS: N36°01.91' W120°28.57'

▼ 2.5   SO Cattle guard.
7.5 ▲ SO Cattle guard.
▼ 3.0   SO Cross over Castro Canyon Creek.
7.0 ▲ SO Cross over Castro Canyon Creek.

GPS: N36°01.53' W120°28.69'

▼ 3.1   SO Track on right into private property.
6.9 ▲ SO Track on left into private property.
▼ 4.5   SO Cattle guard.
5.5 ▲ SO Cattle guard.

GPS: N36°00.59' W120°28.27'

▼ 6.0   SO Cattle guard.
4.0 ▲ SO Cattle guard.
▼ 9.2   SO Track on right is marked Lake Track; then cattle guard.
0.8 ▲ SO Cattle guard; then track on left is marked Lake Track.

GPS: N35°57.87' W120°28.40'

▼ 10.0 SO Cross over Little Cholame Creek on bridge; then Varian Ranch on right. Road is now paved. Zero trip meter.
0.0 ▲   Continue to the northwest.

GPS: N35°57.18' W120°28.49'

▼ 0.0   Continue to the southeast.
5.0 ▲ SO Road turns to graded dirt. Varian Ranch on left; then cross over Little Cholame Creek on bridge. Zero trip meter.
▼ 0.6   SO Cross over Little Cholame Creek on bridge.
4.4 ▲ SO Cross over Little Cholame Creek on bridge.
▼ 1.9   SO Cross over Little Cholame Creek on bridge.

3.1 ▲   SO Cross over Little Cholame Creek on bridge.
▼ 3.8   SO Cross over Little Cholame Creek on bridge.
1.2 ▲ SO Cross over Little Cholame Creek on bridge.

GPS: N35°54.60' W120°26.18'

▼ 4.5   SO Entering Parkfield. Graded road on right and left is Park Street. Continue on paved road through town.
0.5 ▲ SO Leaving Parkfield. Graded road on right and left is Park Street. Continue on paved Parkfield-Coalinga Road.
▼ 5.0   Cross over Little Cholame Creek on bridge; then trail ends at intersection of Cholame Road and Vineyard Canyon Road. Turn left for Cholame; turn right for San Miguel.
0.0 ▲   Trail commences at intersection of Cholame Road and Vineyard Canyon Road in Parkfield. Zero trip meter at intersection and turn east on paved Parkfield-Coalinga Road. Immediately cross over Little Cholame Creek on bridge.

GPS: N35°53.72' W120°26.05'

CENTRAL MOUNTAINS #48

Willow Creek Road

STARTING POINT California 1, just south of Willow Creek Campground
FINISHING POINT Central Mountains #49: South Coast Ridge Road, 14.3 miles from the northern end
TOTAL MILEAGE 7.4 miles, plus 1.9-mile spur to San Martin Top
UNPAVED MILEAGE: 7.4 miles, plus 1.9-mile-spur
DRIVING TIME 45 minutes
ELEVATION RANGE 100–3,200 feet
USUALLY OPEN Year-round
BEST TIME TO TRAVEL Year-round
DIFFICULTY RATING 1, 3 for spur trail
SCENIC RATING 9
REMOTENESS RATING +0

Willow Creek Road climbs high above the Pacific Ocean

Special Attractions
- Spur trail to San Martin Top.
- Spectacular views from high above the Pacific Ocean.

Description
Willow Creek Road starts off of California 1 and heads east into Los Padres National Forest. Just north of the trailhead is the Willow Creek USFS Campground. The campground, only a short walk from the ocean, has a number of sites with fire pits and bathroom facilities. You must have a Forest Adventure Pass and pay a fee to stay at the campground.

As you head out on Willow Creek Road, the trail climbs high above the Pacific Ocean. Within the first mile are a couple of great spots from which to take in a breathtaking sunset. The trail enters the trees at 1.4 miles and continues to meander in and out of forested areas on a graded dirt road. The trail is relatively easygoing and passes a number of closed trails as well as some private property.

At the 3-way intersection, you can proceed southwest on a spur trail to San Martin Top. This trail rates more difficult than the main

trail, and a high-clearance 4WD is required to negotiate some of the rutted sections. At the end of the spur is a primitive campsite with excellent views. Back at the 3-way intersection, the second trail leads 1.4 miles along a 2-rated track to Alder Creek Camp. This campground, set alongside Alder Creek, provides a beautiful, sheltered spot to pitch a tent. It is somewhat isolated, and you will most likely be the only one camping there. A narrow track leads out from the back of the campground, but it is very overgrown and not suitable for driving.

From the intersection, the main trail continues for 1.6 miles before coming to an end halfway along Central Mountains #49: South Coast Ridge Road.

On some maps, this trail is called Los Burros Road.

Current Road Information
Los Padres National Forest
Monterey Ranger District
406 South Mildred
King City, CA 93930
(831) 385-5434

CENTRAL MOUNTAINS #48: WILLOW CREEK ROAD

Map References

BLM   Cambria
USFS   Los Padres National Forest:
          Monterey and Santa Lucia Ranger
          Districts
USGS   1:24,000   Cape San Martin
          1:100,000 Cambria
Maptech CD-ROM: San Luis Obispo/Los
          Padres National Forest
*Southern & Central California Atlas &
          Gazetteer,* pp. 43, 44
California Road & Recreation Atlas, p. 82

Route Directions

▼ 0.0   Trail starts on California 1, just south
              of Willow Creek Campground, 1 mile
              north of gas station at Gorda. Turn
              northeast onto graded dirt road and
              immediately cross cattle guard. Zero
              trip meter and turn left onto Willow
              Creek Road (23S01). Track on right is
              private.

2.3 ▲   Turn right and cross cattle guard onto
              California 1. Track continues ahead. Turn

Clouds roll over the Santa Lucia Mountains along Willow Creek Road

Spur to San Martin Top

left for Gorda; turn right for Big Sur.
GPS: N35°53.15′ W121°27.46′

▼ 0.4 SO Parking area for hiking trail on left.
1.9 ▲ SO Parking area for hiking trail on right.
▼ 1.7 SO Cross over South Fork Willow Creek.
0.6 ▲ SO Cross over South Fork Willow Creek.
▼ 2.0 SO Viewpoint on left.
0.3 ▲ SO Viewpoint on right.
▼ 2.3 SO Willow Creek Hiking Trail on left.
            Zero trip meter.
0.0 ▲   Continue to northwest.
            GPS: N35°53.38′ W121°26.25′

▼ 0.0   Continue to the southeast.
3.5 ▲ SO Willow Creek Hiking Trail on right.
            Zero trip meter.
▼ 0.3 SO Track on right goes short distance
            to campsite.
3.2 ▲ SO Track on left goes short distance
            to campsite.
▼ 1.2 SO Gated road on left.
2.3 ▲ SO Gated road on right.

▼ 1.4 SO Gated road on right.
2.1 ▲ SO Gated road on left.
▼ 1.7 SO Gated road on right.
1.8 ▲ SO Gated road on left.
▼ 1.9 BR Gated road on left.
1.6 ▲ SO Gated road on right.
▼ 2.9 SO Gated road on left.
0.6 ▲ SO Gated road on right.
▼ 3.0 BL Gated road on right.
0.5 ▲ SO Gated road on left.
▼ 3.5 SO Two tracks on right at sign for California
            1, San Martin Top, and Alder Creek
            Camp. First track is spur to San Martin
            Top. Second track goes 1.4 miles to
            Alder Creek Camp. Zero trip meter and
            turn first right for San Martin Top.
0.0 ▲   Continue to the north on main trail.
            GPS: N35°53.12′ W121°23.77′

Spur Trail to San Martin Top

▼ 0.0   Continue to the southwest toward
            San Martin Top.

▼ 0.6   SO   Track on left.
          GPS: N35°52.72′ W121°24.17′

▼ 0.8   SO   Track on right.
▼ 1.0   SO   Gated road joins on left.
▼ 1.1   SO   Track on left rejoins almost immediately.
▼ 1.6   BR/ Trail forks on left; then track
         SO   on left.
▼ 1.7   TL   Track straight ahead goes to campsite.
▼ 1.8   SO   Trail forks and rejoins at viewpoint.
▼ 1.9   UT   Viewpoint at San Martin Top. Turn
              around and retrace your route back
              to the main trail.
          GPS: N35°52.31′ W121°25.20′

Continuation of Main Trail

▼ 0.0   Continue to the southeast.
1.6 ▲   Two tracks on left at sign for California
              1, San Martin Top, and Alder Creek
              Camp. First track goes 1.4 miles to
              Alder Creek Camp. Second track is spur
              to San Martin Top. Zero trip meter and
              turn second left for San Martin Top.
          GPS: 35°53.12′ W121°23.77′

▼ 0.1   SO   Gated road on right.
1.5 ▲   SO   Gated road on left.
▼ 0.2   SO   Gated road on right; then gated road
              on left.
1.4 ▲   BL   Gated road splits off on right;
         SO   then gated road on left.
▼ 0.7   SO   Gated road on left.
0.9 ▲   SO   Gated road on right.
▼ 0.8   SO   Track on left.
0.8 ▲   SO   Track on right.
▼ 1.6   Trail ends at Central Mountains #49:
              South Coast Ridge Road. Turn right to
              continue southeast along South Coast
              Ridge Road; turn left to follow South
              Coast Ridge Road to Nacimiento—
              Ferguson Road.

0.0 ▲   Trail starts on Central Mountains #49:
              South Coast Ridge Road, 14.3 miles
              from the northern end. Zero trip meter
              and head west on Willow Creek Road
              (23S01).
          GPS: N35°53.51′ W121°22.42′

South Coast Ridge Road

STARTING POINT   Nacimiento—Ferguson Road, 6.8 miles east of California 1
FINISHING POINT Gate before Fort Hunter Liggett
TOTAL MILEAGE 26.5 miles (one-way)
UNPAVED MILEAGE: 26.1 miles
DRIVING TIME 2.5 hours (one-way)
ELEVATION RANGE 2,200–3,400 feet
USUALLY OPEN Year-round
BEST TIME TO TRAVEL Year-round
DIFFICULTY RATING 2
SCENIC RATING 8
REMOTENESS RATING +1

Special Attractions

■ Long, scenic trail that follows a ridgeline on the Santa Lucia Range.
■ Many backcountry hiking and camping opportunities along the trail.

Description

South Coast Ridge Road begins on Nacimiento—Ferguson Road and heads south along the boundary between Los Padres National Forest and Fort Hunter Liggett. As its name indicates, the road follows a ridgeline along the Santa Lucia Range for much of its length. It is one of the few roads in this part of the national forest that allows vehicle access. The early part of the trail follows along a shelf road with outstanding views to the west over the Pacific Ocean. The route then turns inland as you travel beneath Chalk Peak.

The road is typically graded dirt; however it does wash out in places. At the time of research, there were still a number of bulldozed tracks that branch off the main trail and end shortly thereafter. Most of these were cut to fight a forest fire in 1999. The vegetation is in a state of regrowth and there are a number of barren, scarred areas with signs of new life springing up.

After you pass Central Mountains #48: Willow Creek Road, set beneath the shadows of Alder Peak, the trail standard drops slightly, mainly because it is less used. The trail from Willow Creek Road is no longer a through-road; rather, it ends at a gate before Fort Hunter Liggett. This last portion of the trail is typically used to access hiking trailheads into the Silver Peak Wilderness. A number of hiking opportunities and a particularly scenic backcountry camping spot can be found near the end of the trail.

Current Road Information

Los Padres National Forest
Monterey Ranger District
406 South Mildred
King City, CA 93930
(831) 385-5434

Map References

BLM   Point Sur, Cambria
USFS Los Padres National Forest:
      Monterey and Santa Lucia Ranger
      Districts
USGS 1:24,000   Cone Peak, Cape San
      Martin, Alder Peak, Burro Mtn.,
      Burnett Peak
      1:100,000 Point Sur, Cambria
Maptech CD-ROM: Central Coast/Fresno;
      San Luis Obispo/Los Padres
      National Forest
*Southern & Central California Atlas &
      Gazetteer,* pp. 31, 43, 44
California Road & Recreation Atlas,
      pp. 82, 90

Route Directions

▼ 0.0   Trail starts on Nacimiento—Ferguson Road at sign for South Coast Ridge Road (20S05). Turn is opposite the start of Central Mountains #50: Cone Peak Trail, 6.8 miles from California 1. Zero trip meter and turn southwest on graded dirt road.

6.5 ▲   Trail ends on Nacimiento—Ferguson Road, opposite the start of Central Mountains #50: Cone Peak Trail. Turn right for Fort Hunter Liggett; turn left for California 1.
            GPS: N36°00.60′ W121°27.07′

▼ 0.5		SO	Restricted track on right.
6.0 ▲		SO	Restricted track on left.
▼ 2.9		SO	Viewpoint on right over Pacific Ocean.
3.6 ▲		SO	Viewpoint on left over Pacific Ocean.
▼ 3.5		SO	Apple Camp on left.
3.0 ▲		SO	Apple Camp on right.

GPS: N35°58.83′ W121°26.04′

▼ 3.9		SO	Private road on right.
2.6 ▲		SO	Private road on left.
▼ 4.3		SO	Road to Prewitt Ridge Camp on right at sign.
2.2 ▲		SO	Road to Prewitt Ridge Camp on left at sign.

GPS: N35°58.30′ W121°26.40′

▼ 4.8		SO	Track on left.
1.7 ▲		SO	Track on right.
▼ 5.4		SO	Track on right.
1.1 ▲		SO	Track on left.
▼ 5.5		SO	Track on left.
1.0 ▲		SO	Track on right.
▼ 6.5		SO	Track on right at wide intersection goes 0.2 miles to campsite before ending at a gate in 1.2 miles. Zero trip meter and continue along South Coast Ridge Road.
0.0 ▲			Continue to the northwest.

GPS: 35°57.04′ W121°25.23′

▼ 0.0			Continue to the southeast.
7.8 ▲		SO	Track on left at wide intersection goes 0.2 miles to campsite before ending at a gate in 1.2 miles. Zero trip meter and continue along South Coast Ridge Road.
▼ 2.1		SO	Track on right and campsite on right.
5.7 ▲		SO	Track on left and campsite on left.
▼ 2.8		SO	Track on right.
5.0 ▲		SO	Track on left.
▼ 3.2		SO	Track splits off on left.
4.6 ▲		SO	Track rejoins on right.
▼ 3.4		SO	Steep, loose track rejoins on left.
4.4 ▲		SO	Steep, loose track splits off on right.

GPS: N35°55.96′ W121°23.12′

▼ 5.0		SO	Trail forks and rejoins immediately.
2.8 ▲		SO	Trail forks and rejoins immediately.
▼ 5.1		SO	Viewpoint on left.
2.7 ▲		SO	Viewpoint on right.
▼ 5.4		SO	Trail forks and rejoins immediately.
2.4 ▲		SO	Trail forks and rejoins immediately.

Trail follows along the ridge as a storm moves in

CENTRAL MOUNTAINS #49: SOUTH COAST RIDGE ROAD

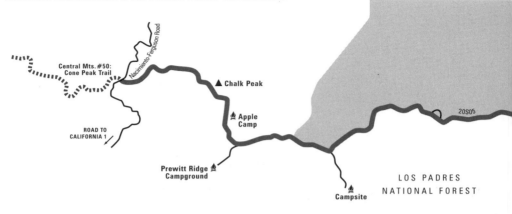

▼ 5.7   SO Track on left at faded No Trespassing sign.
2.1 ▲   SO Track on right at faded No Trespassing sign.
▼ 7.8   SO Central Mountains #48: Willow Creek
            Road on right. Zero trip meter.
0.0 ▲   Continue to northeast on South Coast
            Ridge Road.
            GPS: N35°53.51' W121°22.42'

▼ 0.0   Continue to the southeast toward
            Three Peaks and Lion Camps.
▼ 1.2   SO Overlook on right and gated road
            on left.
            GPS: N35°52.80' W121°22.18'

Trail meanders along the top of the Santa Lucia Range

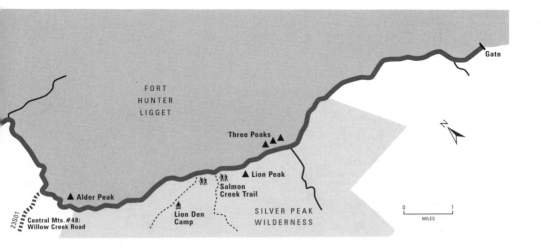

▼ 4.1   SO   Two tracks on right at sign. The first is gated and is the start of hiking trail to Lion Den Camp; the second goes a short distance to a viewpoint.
GPS: N35°51.63′ W121°19.85′

▼ 4.3   SO   Salmon Creek Trailhead on right at sign.
GPS: N35°51.44′ W121°19.61′

▼ 4.5   SO   Track on left.
▼ 6.3   BL   Sign for Three Peaks Camp (1.5 miles) and track on right. Zero trip meter.
GPS: N35°50.75′ W121°18.16′

▼ 0.0   Continue to the southeast.
▼ 0.4   SO   Cross through wash.
▼ 0.8   SO   Hiking trailhead on right at tight switchback.
▼ 2.5   SO   Track on right leads to primitive campsite (0.1 miles); track on left.
▼ 2.6   SO   Track on left.
▼ 2.7   SO   Track on left.
▼ 2.8   SO   Track on left; then sign for Fort Hunter Liggett (3 miles).
▼ 5.6   BL   Track on right goes to locked gate in 0.4 miles.
GPS: N35°49.42′ W121°13.79′

▼ 5.9   Trail ends at gate before Fort Hunter Liggett.
GPS: N35°49.44′ W121°13.54′

CENTRAL MOUNTAINS #50

Cone Peak Trail

STARTING POINT Nacimiento—Ferguson Road, 6.8 miles east of California 1
FINISHING POINT Gate at the boundary of Ventana Wilderness
TOTAL MILEAGE 6.4 miles (one-way)
UNPAVED MILEAGE: 6.4 miles
DRIVING TIME 30 minutes (one-way)
ELEVATION RANGE 2,600–4,200 feet
USUALLY OPEN Spring to fall
BEST TIME TO TRAVEL Dry weather
DIFFICULTY RATING 1
SCENIC RATING 8
REMOTENESS RATING +0

Special Attractions
■ Hiking access into the Ventana Wilderness.
■ Great views along a mild shelf road.

Description
Cone Peak Trail starts on paved Nacimiento—Ferguson Road—a very scenic road in its own right—and heads north into a corridor through the Ventana Wilderness. The trail immediately begins to climb along an easygoing, graded dirt road. Although it is an easy trail in dry weather, the road can become very slick when wet and can wash out

Spectacular view of the Santa Lucia Mountains from the end of the trail

in places. The bulk of the trail follows along a wide shelf road with ample passing places.

As you drive through the wilderness corridor, the trail passes a number of scenic overlooks that face across the valley to the Santa Lucia Range. Cone Peak comes in and out of view as you approach the closure gate at the trail's end.

Hikers often use this trail to reach the trailheads at the end of the road. Past the gate, the old vehicle trail continues to the northwest into the Ventana Wilderness. From there you can hike up to the top of Cone Peak or continue along North Coast Ridge Trail to connect with other trails and campsites in the more northerly parts of the wilderness area.

Current Road Information

Los Padres National Forest
Monterey Ranger District
406 South Mildred
King City, CA 93930
(831) 385-5434

Map References

BLM Point Sur
USFS Los Padres National Forest:
      Monterey and Santa Lucia Ranger
      Districts
USGS 1:24,000 Cone Peak
      1:100,000 Point Sur
Maptech CD-ROM: Central Coast/Fresno
*Southern & Central California Atlas &
      Gazetteer*, p. 31
California Road & Recreation Atlas, p. 82

Route Directions

▼ 0.0 TL Trail starts on Nacimiento—Ferguson
           Road. Turn west at intersection.
           Central Mountains #49: South Coast
           Ridge Road starts opposite. Follow
           sign for Central Coast Ridge Road and
           immediately pass through seasonal
           closure gate. Zero trip meter.
           GPS: N36°00.61′ W121°27.07′

▼ 0.5 SO Track on right goes to overlook.
▼ 0.7 SO Cross over creek.

Climbing the shelf road toward Cone Peak

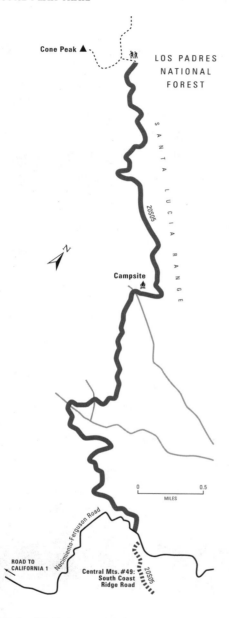

to campsite.
GPS: N36°02.46' W121°28.64'

▼ 5.2   SO   Hiking and horseback riding trail
on left.
▼ 6.4   Viewpoint on right. Trail ends at signs
for hiking trails and campsites—North
Coast Ridge Trail, Gamboa Trail, Arroyo
Seco Trail, Lost Valley Connect, and
Bee Camp Connect.
GPS: N36°03.27' W121°29.34'

Coast Road

STARTING POINT California 1, 2.5 miles
north of Big Sur
FINISHING POINT California 1, just north
of Bixby Bridge
TOTAL MILEAGE 10.1 miles
UNPAVED MILEAGE: 10.1 miles
DRIVING TIME 45 minutes
ELEVATION RANGE 100–1,200 feet
USUALLY OPEN Year-round
BEST TIME TO TRAVEL Year-round
DIFFICULTY RATING 1
SCENIC RATING 9
REMOTENESS RATING +0

Special Attractions

- Spectacular views over the Pacific Ocean.
- Pleasant, easygoing trail that travels
through some of California's southern-
most redwoods.

History

The Esselen were the first people to live in the
mountainous coastal region south of Monterey.
However, as Spanish missionaries made their
way into the area, the Esselen culture began to
disappear as many were baptized at the missions
in Carmel and Monterey. Many scholars believe
this period of assimilation to have occured
around the 1840s.

As Spanish and Mexican development of
the Monterey Peninsula spread, the rugged
Santa Lucia Mountains were a physical

▼ 1.9   SO   Cross over wash.
▼ 2.0   SO   Cross over wash.
▼ 2.4   SO   Cross over wash.
▼ 3.0   SO   Cross over wash.
▼ 3.6   SO   Saddle and campsite on left.
▼ 4.0   SO   Turnout on left at viewpoint.
▼ 4.7   SO   Track on right at viewpoint leads

Coast Road alternates between a shelf road and forest trail

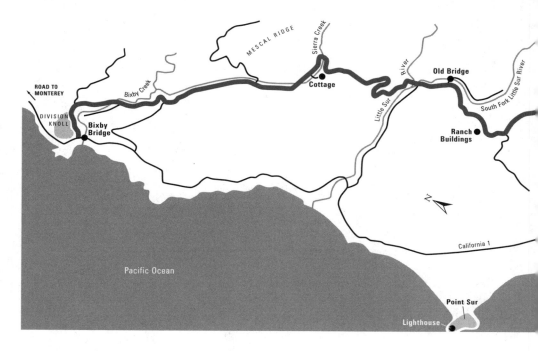

boundary that defied settlement. Early settlers generally referred to the unknown terrain along the Santa Lucias as *el pais grande del sur* (Spanish for "the big country to the south"). It wasn't until the early 1850s that a few intrepid men decided to move in and attempt to survive in the Big Sur wilderness. George Davis is thought to have been the first American to homestead in the region. He built a cabin along the banks of the Big Sur River in what is now Pfeiffer Big Sur State Park (located south of this trail). Mexican governor Figueroa had given the Rancho El Sur land grant to Juan Bautista Alvarado in 1834. This grant, which extended from the Little Sur River south to Cooper Point, remained mostly unsettled until the 1850s, when Roger Cooper started to run cattle in the area. Slowly but surely, the next 20 years saw the arrival of a small number of settlers. William Brainard Post, Michael Pfeiffer, Charles Bixby, John Partington, and Eusebio Molera are a few of the settlers whose names linger on in many of the area's landforms and parks.

The coastline along the Big Sur region was just as treacherous as the terrain it bordered. In the early years of Spanish exploration, the ocean provided the only access to this area and it remained an important link to other parts of California throughout the nineteenth century. A number of shipwrecks along the coast demonstrated the need for a lighthouse. However, it still took sailors 11 years of lobbying to get money for the construction of the Point Sur Light Station. Between 1887 and 1889, a lighthouse was constructed on the huge rock of Point Sur, which juts more than 300 feet above the ocean. The lighthouse has changed hands a few times over the years. It was abandoned in 1974 and lay dormant for 10 years until it was taken over by the state parks department. Volunteers currently tend to the aging lighthouse and give guided tours of the facility.

Near the end of this trail, the magnificent Bixby Bridge comes into view. Built in 1933, this bridge remains one of the world's highest single-span, concrete arch bridges. It stands

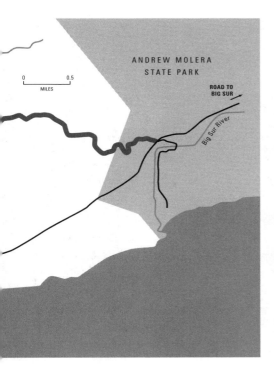

ANDREW MOLERA
STATE PARK

0   0.5
MILES

ROAD TO
BIG SUR

Big Sur River

of the trail, you can look west to see the highway, coast, and ocean. The views along this section are excellent and show just what you miss by staying on the main road.

The trail then goes through private property, passing a number of ranch access roads and private buildings. As it heads into the forested regions, the trail crosses Little Sur River before traveling along Sierra Creek. These wooded areas are on private property. Please respect landowners' rights and stay on the main trail.

As the trail winds along Mescal Ridge and heads back to the coast, it leaves the redwoods behind and travels on a shelf road through low shrubs. As the Bixby Bridge comes into view, the trail nears its end; it then descends to join California 1 at Division Knoll.

Current Road Information

BLM Hollister Field Office
20 Hamilton Court
Hollister, CA 95023
(831) 630-5000

Map References

BLM   Point Sur
USGS   1:24,000   Big Sur, Point Sur
        1:100,000 Point Sur
Maptech CD-ROM: Central Coast/Fresno
Southern & Central California Atlas & Gazetteer, pp. 31, 30
California Road & Recreation Atlas, p. 82

Route Directions

▼ 0.0		Trail starts off of California 1, 2.5 miles north of Big Sur. Turn northwest onto Coast Road. Entrance to Andrew Molera State Park is opposite. Zero trip meter.
6.9 ▲		Trail ends on California 1, opposite entrance to Andrew Molera State Park. Turn right for Monterey; turn left for Big Sur.

GPS: N36°17.32' W121°50.60'

▼ 0.2	SO	Two hiking trails on right.
6.7 ▲	SO	Two hiking trails on left.

about 285 above Bixby Creek and extends more than 700 feet in length. Its construction was a difficult and dangerous process. Access to the site entailed a number of hairpin turns and steep shelf roads. High winds against the arch's frames and high waves against its foundations posed additional problems. The bridge was named after early settler Charles Bixby. Bixby, a cousin of President James K. Polk's, ran a sawmill in the area and is credited with greatly improving the land. If you've ever seen the movie, *The Graduate,* you've seen a young, existential Dustin Hoffman speeding across the bridge in his famous red sports car.

Description

Coast Road begins and ends on California 1 and offers a great alternative to speeding down the Coast Highway. The trail begins 2.5 miles north of Big Sur, opposite the entrance to Andrew Molera State Park. It immediately begins to climb up a graded dirt road, passing through patches of thick trees and open ranchland. Along the early stretch

Overlooking the meandering course of Coast Road

▼ 0.7   SO   Cattle guard and private property sign.
Next 6 miles is property of El Sur Ranch.

6.2 ▲   SO   Cattle guard.

▼ 2.3   SO   Gate on right.

4.6 ▲   SO   Gate on left.

▼ 2.8   SO   Cattle guard.

4.1 ▲   SO   Cattle guard.

▼ 3.1   SO   Gated ranch road on left.

3.8 ▲   SO   Gated ranch road on right.

▼ 3.4   SO   House and ranch buildings on left.

3.5 ▲   SO   House and ranch buildings on right.

▼ 4.1   SO   Old bridge on right on private property.

2.8 ▲   SO   Old bridge on left on private property.

▼ 4.5   SO   Gated road on left; then bridge over
South Fork Little Sur River; then shed
on left.

2.4 ▲   SO   Shed on right; then bridge over South
Fork Little Sur River; then gated road
on right.

▼ 4.6   SO   Gated road on right; then cross over
Little Sur River on bridge.

2.3 ▲   SO   Cross over Little Sur River on bridge;
then gated road on left.

▼ 5.7   SO   Cattle guard.

1.2 ▲   SO   Cattle guard.

▼ 6.3   SO   Gates on left and right.

0.6 ▲   SO   Gates on left and right.

▼ 6.6   SO   Cross over Sierra Creek.

0.3 ▲   SO   Cross over Sierra Creek.

        GPS: N36°20.71′ W121°51.89′

▼ 6.8   SO   Cottage on left below trail.

0.1 ▲   SO   Cottage on right below trail.

▼ 6.9   SO   Cottage entrance on left. Zero
trip meter.

0.0 ▲   Continue to the northeast.

        GPS: N36°20.73′ W121°52.17′

▼ 0.0   SO   Continue to the west.

3.2 ▲   SO   Cottage entrance on right. Zero
trip meter.

▼ 0.7   SO   Gated road on right.

2.5 ▲   SO   Gated road on left.

▼ 1.7   SO   Gated road on left.

1.5 ▲   SO   Gated road on right.

▼ 2.3   SO   Gated road on left; then cross over
Bixby Creek on bridge; then private
road on right.

0.9 ▲   SO   Private road on left; then cross over
Bixby Creek on bridge; then gated road
on right.

▼ 2.4   SO   Gated road on left.

0.8 ▲	SO	Gated road on right.
▼ 2.9	SO	Gated road on right. Views ahead to Bixby Bridge.
0.3 ▲	SO	Gated road on left.
▼ 3.2	SO	Trail ends on California 1. Turn right for Monterey; turn left for Big Sur.
0.0 ▲		Trail begins on California 1, just north of the Bixby Bridge. Zero trip meter and head west on Coast Road.

GPS: N36°22.36' W121°54.09'

CENTRAL MOUNTAINS #52

Tassajara Road

STARTING POINT Tassajara Road, at Jamesburg
FINISHING POINT Tassajara Zen Mountain Center Monastery
TOTAL MILEAGE 13.6 miles (one-way)
UNPAVED MILEAGE: 13.6 miles
DRIVING TIME 1 hour (one-way)
ELEVATION RANGE 2,000–4,700 feet
USUALLY OPEN Year-round

BEST TIME TO TRAVEL May 1 to September 1
DIFFICULTY RATING 2
SCENIC RATING 8
REMOTENESS RATING +0

Special Attractions

■ Tassajara Hot Springs at the Tassajara Zen Mountain Center Monastery.
■ Scenic route traveling through a vehicle corridor in the Ventana Wilderness.
■ Numerous backcountry hiking trails.

History

The earliest inhabitants of the Carmel Valley near Tassajara Hot Springs are thought to have been members of the Esselen tribe. A pictograph depicting a series of hands has been found in a cave above the springs. The poet Robinson Jeffers used the pictograph as material for his poem "Hands."

Although some sources report the hot springs as being a tourist destination as early as the 1860s, a hotel was not established at the springs until 1904. Equipped with bathhouses, the hotel operated until 1949, when it was destroyed

Cement catchment basins above Tassajara Hot Springs

by a fire. The area remained relatively quiet for about 20 years until the San Francisco Zen Center purchased the land and developed the Tassajara Zen Mountain Center.

Attracted by the serene mountain setting and the soothing waters of the hot springs, students of Buddhism can come and practice monastic traditions at the center all year. The monastery is open to visitors from May 1 to September 7 every year. During this time, you can reserve rooms and take part in the daily monastic life. Please call ahead; do not show up unannounced expecting to use the hot springs. Please respect the monastery's time of closure and do not approach the gates during the off-season.

Description

To reach the starting point for Tassajara Road from Carmel Valley Road (G16), turn south onto the eastern entrance of Cachagua Road (signed for Tassajara Road). Follow signs for 2.9 miles to Jamesburg, staying right at the T about 1 mile along the road. When you see the Jamesburg snack bar, head south on the wide, graded dirt road along James Creek. For the first 3 miles, the road passes a number of private and/or gated roads. Only the major ones have been listed below.

The trail enters Los Padres National Forest after 3.3 miles, at the Ventana Wilderness Ranch. The ranch offers hiking and horseback expeditions of varying lengths into the Ventana Wilderness. The trail continues to climb onto Chews Ridge as it meanders along forested sections of shelf road. Once in the national forest, the trail passes a number of side roads that are either gated or peter out after a short distance. Up on the ridge, the trail passes two developed national forest campgrounds—White Oaks and China Camps. The Pine Ridge Hiking Trail heads off to the west from China Camp. Remember, if you plan to camp or park your vehicle and hike, you must have a Forest Adventure Pass from the forest service.

After traveling along Chews Ridge, the trail begins to descend along the west side of

Black Butte, offering excellent views over the valley to the west. The trail descends sharply at this point; watch out for overheating brakes in the summer. Toward the end, the trail passes a couple hiking trailheads before coming to an end at the Tassajara Zen Mountain Center Monastery, located on the north side of Tassajara Creek.

Current Road Information

Los Padres National Forest
Monterey Ranger District
406 South Mildred
King City, CA 93930
(831) 385-5434

Map References

BLM   Point Sur
USFS   Los Padres National Forest:
       Monterey and Santa Lucia Ranger
       Districts
USGS   1:24,000   Chews Ridge, Tassajara
       Hot Springs
       1:100,000 Point Sur
Maptech CD-ROM: Central Coast/Fresno
*Southern & Central California Atlas &
       Gazetteer,* p. 31
California Road & Recreation Atlas, p. 82

Route Directions

▼ 0.0   Trail starts in Jamesburg at sign for Tassajara Zen Mountain Center Monastery. Road turns from paved to graded dirt at this point. Head southeast past the Jamesburg snack bar. Zero trip meter.
         GPS: N36°22.13' W121°35.35'

▼ 0.3 SO Private road on left.
▼ 1.6 SO Private roads on left and right.
▼ 2.1 SO Private road on left.
▼ 3.0 SO Gated drive on right.
▼ 3.3 SO Ventana Wilderness ranch on right; then cattle guard; then sign for Los Padres National Forest.
         GPS: N36°20.55' W121°34.79'

▼ 3.5 SO Hiking trailhead on right (before second national forest sign).

Side trail fromTassajara Road dead-ends shortly

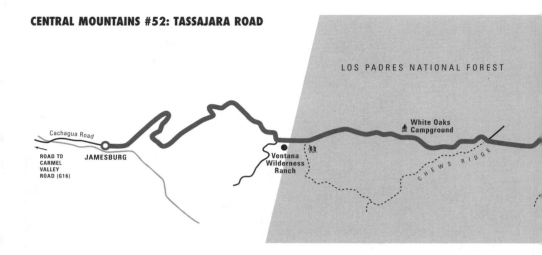

▼ 4.7 SO White Oaks Campground on left.
          Zero trip meter.
          GPS: N36°19.59' W121°34.44'

▼ 0.0 SO Continue to the southwest.
▼ 0.7 SO Cross through wash.
▼ 1.2 SO Gated roads on left and right.
▼ 1.6 SO Picnic area on right.

▼ 1.7 SO Hiking trailhead on left.
▼ 2.7 SO China Camp on right; then hiking
          trailhead on right.
          GPS: N36°17.72' W121°34.44'

▼ 3.5 SO Tracks on left and right.
▼ 3.7 SO Track on right.
▼ 4.3 SO Track splits off on left.

Trail descends along shelf road below Black Butte

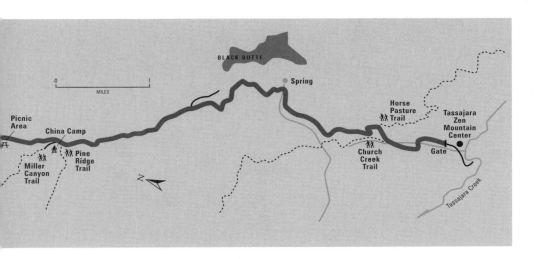

▼ 5.9　SO　Spring and rusted-out tub on left.
　　　　　GPS: N36°15.78′ W121°32.70′

▼ 6.7　SO　Viewpoint on right.
▼ 7.6　SO　Horse Pasture Trail for hiking and
　　　　　horseback riding on left.
▼ 7.9　SO　Church Creek Trail for hiking and horse-
　　　　　back riding on right.
▼ 8.4　SO　Cross over wash.
▼ 8.8　SO　Cement buildings on left.
▼ 8.9　SO　Trail ends at sign for Tassajara Zen
　　　　　Mountain Center.
　　　　　GPS: N36°14.19′ W121°32.92′

Selected Further Reading

Bauer, Helen. *California Mission Days.* New York: Doubleday & Company, Inc., 1951.

Beck, Warren A., and Ynez D. Haase. *Historical Atlas of California.* Norman, Okla.: University of Oklahoma Press, 1974.

Belden, L. Burr, and Mary DeDecker. *Death Valley to Yosemite: Frontier Mining Camps and Ghost Towns.* Bishop, Calif.: Spotted Dog Press, Inc., 1998.

Boessenecker, John. *Gold Dust and Gunsmoke.* New York: John Wiley & Sons, Inc., 1999.

Braasch, Barbara. *California's Gold Rush Country.* Medina, Wash.: Johnston Associates International, 1996.

Bright, William. *1500 California Place Names.* Berkeley and Los Angeles: University of California Press, 1998.

Broman, Mickey, and Russ Leadabrand. *California Ghost Town Trails.* Baldwin Park, Calif.: Gem Guides Book Co., 1985.

Brown, Vinson. *The Californian Wildlife Region.* Happy Camp, Calif.: Naturegraph Publishers, Inc., 1999.

Clarke, Herbert. *An Introduction To Southern California Birds.* Missoula, Mont.: Mountain Press Publishing Company, 1997.

Dunn, Jerry Camarillo, Jr. *National Geographic's Driving Guides to America: California and Nevada and Hawaii.* Washington, D.C.: The Book Division National Geographic Society, 1996.

Durham, David L. *Durham's Place-Names of California's Central Coast.* Clovis, Calif.: Word Dancer Press, 2000.

—. *Durham's Place-Names of Central California.* Clovis, Calif.: Word Dancer Press, 2001.

Fink, Augusta. *Monterey County: The Dramatic Story of Its Past.* Santa Cruz, Calif.: Western Tanager Press, 1972.

Florin, Lambert. *Ghost Towns of The West.* New York: Promontory Press, 1993.

Gersch-Young, Marjorie. *Hot Springs and Hot Pools of the Southwest.* Santa Cruz, Calif.: Aqua Thermal Access, 2001.

Gudde, Erwin G. *1000 California Place Names.* Berkeley and Los Angeles: University of California Press, 1959.

—. *California Place Names.* Berkeley and Los Angeles: University of California Press, 1998.

Hart, James D. *A Companion to California.* New York: Oxford University Press, 1978.

Heizer, Robert F. *The Destruction of California Indians.* Lincoln, Nebr.: University of Nebraska Press, 1993.

Hirschfelder, Arlene. *Native Americans.* New York: Dorling Kindersley Publishing, Inc., 2000.

Holmes, Robert. *California's Best-Loved Driving Tours.* New York: Macmillan Travel, 1999.

Hoxie, Frederick E., ed. *Encyclopedia of North American Indians.* Boston: Houghton Mifflin Company, 1996.

Indians of California, The. Alexandria, Va.: Time-Life Books, 1994.

Jameson, E. W., Jr., and Hans J. Peeters. *California Mammals.* Berkeley and Los Angeles: University of California Press, 1988.

Johnson, William Weber. *The Old West: The Forty-niners.* New York: Time-Life Books, 1974.

Kavanagh, James, ed. *The Nature of California.* Helena, Mont.: Waterford Press Ltd., 1997.

Keyworth, C. L. *California Indians.* New York: Checkmark Books, 1991.

Kroeber, A. L. *Handbook of the Indians of California.* New York: Dover Publications, Inc., 1976.

Kyle, Douglas E. *Historic Spots in California.* Stanford, Calif.: Stanford University Press, 1990.

Lamar, Howard R., ed. *The New Encyclopedia of the American West.* New Haven, Conn.: Yale University Press, 1998.

Lewis, Donovan. *Pioneers of California.* San Francisco: Scottwall Associates, 1993.

Lewellyn, Harry. *Backroad Trips and Tips.* Costa Mesa, Calif.: Glovebox Publications, 1993.

Martin, Don W., and Betty Woo Martin. *California-Nevada Roads Less Traveled.* Henderson, Nev.: Pine Cone Press, Inc., 1999.

Milner, Clyde A., II, Carol A. O'Conner, and Martha A. Sandweiss, eds. *The Oxford History of the American West.* Oxford: Oxford University Press, 1996.

Mitchell, James R. *Gem Trails of Southern California.* Baldwin Park, Calif.: Gem Guides Book Co., 1998.

Nadeau, Remi. *Ghost Towns and Mining Camps of California.* Santa Barbara, Calif.: Crest Publishing, 1999.

Nash, Jay Robert. *Encyclopedia of Western Lawmen and Outlaws.* New York: Da Capo Press, 1994.

National Audubon Society Field Guide to California. New York: Alfred A. Knopf, Inc., 1998.

National Audubon Society Field Guide to North American Birds: Western Region. New York: Alfred A. Knopf, Inc., 1998.

National Audubon Society Field Guide to North American Mammals. New York: Alfred A. Knopf, Inc., 1996.

O'Neal, Bill. *Encyclopedia of Western Gunfighters.* Norman, Okla.: University of Oklahoma Press, 1979.

Pierce, L. Kingston. *America's Historic Trails with Tom Bodett.* San Francisco: KQED Books, 1997.

Poshek, Lucy, and Roger Naylor, comps. *California Trivia.* Nashville, Tenn.: Rutledge Hill Press, 1998.

Powers, Stephen. *Tribes of California.* Berkeley and Los Angeles: University of California Press, 1976.

Rolle, Andrew. *California: A History.* Wheeling, Ill.: Harlan Davidson, Inc., 1998.

Sagstetter, Beth, and Bill Sagstetter. *The Mining Camps Speak.* Denver: Benchmark Publishing, 1998.

Schmoe, Floyd. *The Big Sur: Land of Rare Treasures.* San Francisco: Chronicle Books, 1975.

Sharp, Robert P., and Allen F. Glazner. *Geology Underfoot in Southern California.* Missoula, Mont.: Mountain Press Publishing Company, 1993.

Stob, Ron. *Exploring San Luis Obispo County and Nearby Coastal Areas.* San Luis Obispo, Calif.: Central Coast Press, 2000.

Sullivan, Noelle. *It Happened in Southern California.* Helena, Mont.: Falcon Publishing, Inc., 1996.

Taylor, Colin F. *The Native Americans: The Indigenous People of North America.* London: Salamander Books Ltd., 2000.

Thrap, Dan L. *Encyclopedia of Frontier Biography.* 3 vols. Lincoln, Nebr.: University of Nebraska Press, 1988.

Varney, Philip. *Southern California's Best Ghost Towns.* Norman, Okla.: University of Oklahoma Press, 1990.

Waldman, Carl. *Encyclopedia of Native American Tribes.* New York: Facts on File, 1988.

Wright, Ralph B., ed. *California's Missions.* Los Angeles: The Stirling Press, 1967.

Wurman, Richard Saul. *Access Los Angeles.* Dunmore, Pa.: Harper Collins Publishers, 1999.

Selected Web sources

California Mission, http://www.californiamissions.com

Desert USA, http://www.desertusa.com

Ghost Town Explorers,
http://www.geocities.com/ghosttownexplorers

GORP.com, http://www.gorp.com

Highway 395, http://395.com

Lone Pine, California,
http://www.lone-pine.com

National Center for Disease Control:
Hantavirus Pulmonary Syndrome,
http://www.cdc.gov/ncidod/diseases/
hanta/hps

Painted Cave Art of the Chumash Indians,
http://www.sbnature.org/research/anthro/
chumash/pcart.htm

Parkfield, California,
http://www.parkfield.com

Railway History, http://www.sdrm.org/
history

Route 66: The Mother Road,
http://www.hhjm.com/66/history.htm

San Luis Obispo, California,
http://www.ci.san-luis-obispo.ca.us

San Luis Obispo County History,
http://www.historyinslocounty.com

U.S. Bureau of Land Management,
California, http://www.ca.blm.gov

Visalia, California, http://www.ci.visalia.ca.us

Photo Credits

Unless otherwise indicated in the following list of acknowledgments (which is organized by page number), all photographs were taken by Bushducks—Maggie Pinder and Donald McGann.

29 California Historical Society, San Francisco; **127** Utah State Historical Society; **167** Corel; **212** San Diego Museum of Man; **249** Corel.

Cover photography: Bushducks—Maggie Pinder and Donald McGann

About the Authors

Peter Massey grew up in the outback of Australia, where he acquired a life long love of the backcountry. After retiring from a career in investment banking in 1986 at the age of thirty-five, he served as a director for a number of companies in the United States, the United Kingdom, and Australia. He moved to Colorado in 1993.

Jeanne Wilson was born and grew up in Maryland. After moving to New York City in 1980, she worked in advertising and public relations before moving to Colorado in 1993.

After traveling extensively in Australia, Europe, Asia, and Africa, the authors covered more than 80,000 miles touring the United States and the Australian outback between 1993 and 1997. This experience became the basis for creating the Backcountry Adventures and Trails guidebook series.

As the research team grew, a newcomer became a dedicated member of the Swagman team.

Angela Titus was born in Missouri and grew up in Virginia, where she attended the University of Virginia. She moved to Alabama and worked for *Southern Living Magazine* traveling, photographing, and writing about the southeastern U.S. She moved to Colorado in 2002.

Since research for the Backcountry Adventures and Trails guidebooks began, Peter, Jeanne, and Angela have traveled more than 75,000 miles throughout the western states.

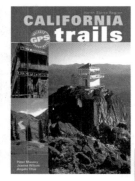

more
california trails
backroad guides

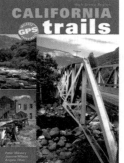

California Trails—Northern Sierra

This book outlines detailed trail information for 55 off-road routes located near the towns of Sacramento (east), Red Bluff (east), Truckee, South Lake Tahoe, Sonora, Susanville, Chico, Oroville, Yuba City, Placerville, Stockton (east), Jackson, and Sonora. **ISBN-10, 1-930193-23-8; ISBN-13, 978-1-930193-23-9; Price $19.95**

California Trails—High Sierra

This guidebook navigates and describes 50 trails located near the towns of Fresno (north), Oakhurst, Lone Pine, Bishop, Bridgeport, Coulterville, Mariposa, and Mammoth Lakes. **ISBN-10, 1-930193-21-1; ISBN-13, 978-1-930193-21-5; Price $19.95**

California Trails—North Coast

This guide meticulously describes and rates 47 off-road routes located near the towns of Sacramento, Redding (west), Red Bluff, Clear Lake, McCloud, Mount Shasta, Yreka, Crescent City, and Fort Bidwell. **ISBN-10, 1-930193-22-X; ISBN-13, 978-1-930193-22-2; Price $19.95**

California Trails—South Coast

This field guide includes meticulous trail details for 50 trails located near the towns of Los Angeles, San Bernardino, San Diego, Salton Sea, Indio, Borrego Springs, Ocotillo and Palo Verde. **ISBN-10, 1-930193-24-6; ISBN-13, 978-1-930193-24-6; Price $19.95**

California Trails—Desert

This edition of our Trails series contains detailed trail information for 51 off-road routes located near the towns of Lone Pine (east), Panamint Springs, Death Valley area, Ridgecrest, Barstow, Baker and Blythe. **ISBN-10, 1-930193-20-3; ISBN-13, 978-1-930193-20-8; Price $19.95**

to order
call 800-660-5107 or
visit 4WDbooks.com

arizona trails
backroad guides

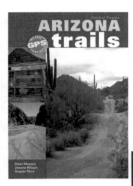

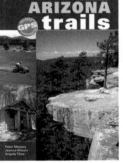

Arizona Trails—Northeast
This guidebook consists of meticulous details and directions for 47 trails located near the towns of Flagstaff, Williams, Prescott (northeast), Winslow, Fort Defiance and Window Rock. **ISBN-10, 1-930193-02-5; ISBN-13, 978-1-930193-02-4; Price $19.95**

Arizona Trails—West
This volume consists of comprehensive statistics and descriptions for 33 trails located near the towns of Bullhead City, Lake Havasu City, Parker, Kingman, Prescott (west), and Quartzsite (north). **ISBN-10, 1-930193-00-9; ISBN-13, 978-1-930193-00-0; Price $19.95**

Arizona Trails—Central
This field guide includes meticulous trail details for 44 off-road routes located near the towns of Phoenix, Wickenburg, Quartzsite (south), Payson, Superior, Globe and Yuma (north). **ISBN-10, 1-930193-01-7; ISBN-13, 978-1-930193-01-7; Price $19.95**

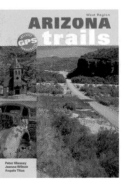

Arizona Trails—South
This handbook is composed of comprehensive statistics and descriptions for 33 trails located near the towns of Tucson, Douglas, Mammoth, Reddington, Stafford, Yuma (southeast), Ajo and Nogales. **ISBN-10, 1-930193-03-3; ISBN-13, 978-1-930193-03-1; Price $19.95**

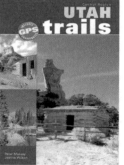

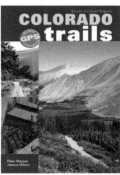
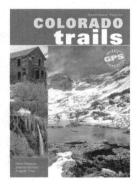

backcountry adventures
guides

Each book in the award-winning *Adventures* series listed below is a beautifully crafted, high-quality, sewn, 4-color guidebook. In addition to meticulously detailed backcountry trail directions and maps of every trail and region, extensive information on the history of towns, ghost towns, and regional history is included. The guides provide wildlife information and photographs to help readers identify the great variety of native birds, plants, and animals they are likely to see. This series appeals to everyone who enjoys the backcountry: campers, anglers, four-wheelers, hikers, mountain bikers, snowmobilers, amateur prospectors, sightseers, and more…

Backcountry Adventures Northern California

Backcountry Adventures Northern California takes readers along 2,653 miles of back roads from the rugged peaks of the Sierra Nevada, through volcanic regions of the Modoc Plateau, to majestic coastal redwood forests. Trail history comes to life through accounts of outlaws like Black Bart; explorers like Ewing Young and James Beckwourth; and the biggest mass migration in America's history—the Gold Rush. Contains 152 trails, 640 pages, and 679 photos.
ISBN-10, 1-930193-25-4; ISBN-13, 978-1-930193-25-3
Price, $39.95.

Backcountry Adventures Southern California

Backcountry Adventures Southern California provides 2,970 miles of routes that travel through the beautiful mountain regions of Big Sur, across the arid Mojave Desert, and straight into the heart of the aptly named Death Valley. Trail history comes alive through the accounts of Spanish missionaries; eager prospectors looking to cash in during California's gold rush; and legends of lost mines. Contains 153 trails, 640 pages, and 645 photos.
ISBN-10, 1-930193-26-2; ISBN-13, 978-1-930193-26-0
Price, $39.95.

to order
call 800-660-5107 or
visit 4WDbooks.com